- **NTDETECT.COM** PC hardware detection: reads device and config info before Windows NT boots. It resides in root directory of system partition. (Required for Windows NT boot floppy.)
- **NTLDR** OS loader program, loads Windows NT or other designated OS; relinquishes control once loading completes. Resides in the root directory of a system partition. (Required for Windows NT boot floppy.)
- **NTOSKRNL.EXE** Includes all basic capabilities and items necessary to establish runtime environment. Resides in \Winnt_root\system32 on boot partition.
- **OSLOADER.EXE** Provides services and info equal to NTDETECT.COM, BOOTSECT.DOS, and NTLDR on PCs. Resides in RISC boot PROM area.
- **NTBOOTDD.SYS** Used when system or boot SCSI drive has BIOS disabled. Replaces BIOS functions with software driver. Resides in root directory of system partition.

29. ARC name information:
- **scsi(*) or multi(*)** Most ARC names begin with **multi(*)**; **scsi(*)** appears only when SCSI has BIOS disabled. **multi(*)** applies to IDE, EIDE, ESDI, and SCSI (where BIOS enabled). **(*)** indicates address of hardware adapter. Numbers start at zero, with controller seated closest to slot 0 in PC.
- **disk(*)** Applies only when **scsi(*)** keyword appears. Value of **(*)** indicates SCSI bus ID, starting with zero, for drive where files reside. If **multi(*)** appears, **disk(*)** is always **disk(0)**.
- **rdisk(*)** Applies only when **multi(*)** keyword appears, indicates SCSI logical unit number (LUN) for the drive. Numbering begins with zero, so first drive in chain named **rdisk(0)**, second is **rdisk(1)**, and so on.
- **partition(*)** Indicates disk partition that contains designated files. Unlike other ARC numbering, partition numbers start at one, so first partition is **partition(1)**, second is **partition(2)**, and so on.

- \path [indicates directory on partition for O files W

30. ERD lems NTO

CONNECTIVITY

31. Establishing network connectivity—local and remote—RAS.

32. RAS connections have the same features and functions as local network connections, only difference is speed and increased security.

33. RAS maintains list of WAN resources: when referenced, attempts AutoDial to regain connection.

34. RAS only supports PPP dialup clients (not SLIP).

35. Multilink must be enabled on both ends.

36. RAS encryption: clear text, encrypted (CHAP, DES, PAP, SPAP), or MS-encrypted (MS-CHAP).

37. Methods to access network resources: UNC, Network Neighborhood, Map Share.

38. Using NT Workstation as a client for a NetWare server: CSNW, NWLink.

39. NT Workstation and TCP/IP—configuration, tools, and management—IP address, DHCP server, subnet mask, default gateway.

40. Install, configure, and use Dial-Up Networking—Start|Programs|Accessories|Dial-Up Networking.

41. Install, configure, and use Peer Web Services.

42. Peer Web Services offers Web, FTP, and Gopher information services.

RUNNING APPLICATIONS

43. Using applications on Windows NT Workstation: DOS, Win16, Win32, OS/2 1.0, POSIX.1.

44. Application subsystem abilities, limitations, dependencies, and configuration options:
- VDM is a Win32 process to host DOS applications.

8. For group permissions, the least restrictive right takes precedence, except No Access always wins! When combining NTFS or share permissions, the least restrictive wins for each kind (except No Access), when combining resulting NTFS and share permissions, the most restrictive wins.

9. You can perform the following in User Manager:

- Produce, change, duplicate, and remove user and local group accounts.
- Enable account policies (assign defaults for passwords, account lockouts, disconnect status, and so on).
- Create user rights and audit policies.

10. Profiles are local only by default. Made roaming through System applet.

11. Mandatory profiles: change NTUSER. DAT to NTUSER.MAN.

12. Create directory or printer share: set sharing, define share name, set permissions.

13. All new directory shares have default rights of Full Control to Everyone.

14. All new printer shares have Print access to Everyone, Full Control to Administrator and PowerUsers, and Manage Documents to the owner.

15. Attach to printer share: New Printer, Network Printer Server.

16. Attach to directory share: Map Drive or Network Neighborhood.

17. Each shared logical printer can be set to different priorities and access times.

18. Review Disk Administrator menus and options (see pages 101-102).

19. NT Workstation does not have any fault tolerant partition configurations.

20. Only primary partitions can be active: Select Mark Active from the Partition menu in Disk Administrator.

21. NTFS file and directory permission settings and issues: Read, Change, Full Control, No Access; set by group or user.

22. Vital statistics for FAT (Windows NT's version of FAT) and NTFS:

	FAT	NTFS
Maximum volume size	4 GB	16 EB
Maximum file size	4 GB	16 EB
File-level security	No	Yes
Long file name support	Yes	Yes
Self-repairing	No	Yes
Transaction logging capabilities	No	Yes
File-level compression	No	Yes
File-level security	No	Yes

23. Use FAT for 50 MB partitions or smaller, NTFS for partitions 400 MB or larger.

24. Rules for Permissions on NTFS Move and Copy operations:

- If you move a file within the same NTFS partition, it *retains* original permissions.
- If you copy a file anywhere in NTFS, it *inherits* parent folder permissions.
- If you create, copy, or move files from one NTFS partition to another, they *inherit* parent folder permissions.
- All NTFS permissions disappear when files moved or copied from NTFS to FAT.

25. Convert FAT partitions into NTFS using CONVERT.EXE; HPFS is not supported in Windows NT 4.

26. Two Registry editors: REGEDIT.EXE (search features) and REGEDT32.EXE (security features).

BOOT FACTS

27. Several Boot files—NTLDR, BOOT.INI, NTDETECT.COM, and so on—reside on the system partition, Windows NT OS files—including NTOSKRNL.EXE—reside on the boot partition. BACKWARDS!

28. Most important Windows NT boot process components:

- **BOOT.INI** Describes Windows NT boot defaults, plus OS location, settings, menu selections. It resides in the root directory of the system partition. (Required for Windows NT boot floppy.)
- **BOOTSECT.DOS** Used if NTLDR permits boot to some other Microsoft OS like DOS or Windows 95. It resides in the root directory of system partition. (Not required.)

- WOW is a Win32 process hosted by a VDM process to host Win16 applications.
- Each DOS application is hosted by its own VDM.
- All Win16 applications are launched within the same WOW instance, unless specified otherwise.
- All Win32 applications are launched separately.
- OS/2 v1 and POSIX.1 support is text or character based only.

45. Application and process priorities—Task Manager—alter priorities of applications and processes.

46. Applications can be launched with various priority levels: **START [/lowl/normall/highl/ realtime]** *<application>*. Note: **/realtime** is only accessible by administrators.

MONITORING AND OPTIMIZATION

47. Using Performance Monitor, Network Monitor, and other native Windows NT tools.

48. Isolate, identify, and solve a performance related problem.

49. Too little RAM results in disk thrashing—high rate of memory paging.

50. Processor: %Processor Time should remain below a constant level of 80%.

51. PhysicalDisk: %DiskTime should be less than 10 percent of Processor: %ProcessorTime.

52. LogicalDisk and PhysicalDisk counters will read zero until enabled by **diskperf -y**.

53. WINMSD or Windows NT Diagnostics can be used to view computer details, not alter them.

TROUBLESHOOTING

54. The Emergency Repair Disk is created using **rdisk /s**.

55. The ERD and the three setup floppies can be used to repair boot problems, reboot with setup floppies, select R from menu.

56. Dr. Watson saves memory dumps for failed or crashed applications, to access run DRWTSN32 from Start|Run.

57. Printer spool problems are often eliminated by stopping and starting the spooler service.

58. Event Viewer lists Application, Security, and System events.

59. Last Known Good Configuration returns system to state of last successful logon, accessed during bootup by pressing the spacebar when prompted.

NT Workstation 4

The Cram Sheet

This Cram Sheet contains the distilled, key facts about Windows NT Workstation 4. Review this information last thing before you enter the test room, paying special attention to those areas where you feel you need the most review. You can transfer any of these facts from your head onto a blank sheet of paper before you begin the exam.

INSTALLATION AND CONFIGURATION

1. Know these WINNT and WINNT32 switches:
   - **/OX** Creates boot floppies, does not start installation.
   - **/B** Installs Windows NT without making or using Setup boot floppies.
   - **/UDF, /U, and /I** Used for unattended and automated installs.

2. How to plan for, create, and use unattended installation files—UNATTEND.TXT and UDFs.

3. The SYSDIFF utility:
   - /snap [/log:<log_file>] <snapshot_file> creates an image of the base installation
   - /diff [/log:<log_file>] <snapshot_file> <difference_file> creates an image of the changes
   - /apply [/log:<log_file>] <difference_file> applies the difference file to a base installation
   - /inf [/log:<log_file>] <sysdiff_file> <oem_root> creates an .INF file for automating application install along with NT
   - /dump [/log:<log_file>] <difference_file> <dump_file> creates a document detailing the activity of the difference file

4. Setting up a dual-boot system: install DOS or Windows 95/98, then install Windows NT Workstation.

5. Install, configure, and remove hardware components using Control Panel applets: Network, SCSI Adapters, Tape Devices, UPS, Multimedia, Display, Keyboard, and Mouse.

6. When upgrading an existing version of NT, the following information stays intact:
   - Any edits made to Registry using Registry Editor
   - Custom program groups, desktop layout, setting, and Control Panel preferences
   - Local security accounts (users and groups)
   - Network adapter, protocol, service configurations, and addresses (including RAS)
   - Preferences for Accessories and Administrative Tools

MANAGING RESOURCES

7. There are two types of groups: local and global. Local groups are only available on the local machine; global groups are available throughout the domain. Local groups can contain users and global groups, global groups contain users only. You can't place groups within global groups, nor can you place local groups within other local groups.

MCSE
NT Workstation 4
Third Edition

Ed Tittel
Kurt Hudson
James Michael Stewart

 CORIOLIS

MCSE NT Workstation 4 Exam Cram, Third Edition
© 2000 The Coriolis Group. All Rights Reserved.

Limits of Liability and Disclaimer of Warranty
The author and publisher of this book have used their best efforts in preparing the book and the programs contained in it. These efforts include the development, research, and testing of the theories and programs to determine their effectiveness. The author and publisher make no warranty of any kind, expressed or implied, with regard to these programs or the documentation contained in this book.

The author and publisher shall not be liable in the event of incidental or consequential damages in connection with, or arising out of, the furnishing, performance, or use of the programs, associated instructions, and/or claims of productivity gains.

Trademarks
Trademarked names appear throughout this book. Rather than list the names and entities that own the trademarks or insert a trademark symbol with each mention of the trademarked name, the publisher states that it is using the names for editorial purposes only and to the benefit of the trademark owner, with no intention of infringing upon that trademark.

The Coriolis Group, LLC
14455 N. Hayden Road, Suite 220
Scottsdale, Arizona 85260

480/483-0192
FAX 480/483-0193
http://www.coriolis.com

Library of Congress Cataloging-in-Publication Data
Tittel, Ed
    MCSE NT Workstation 4 exam cram/by Ed Tittel, Kurt Hudson, and James Michael Stewart.-- 3rd ed.
        p.   cm.
    Includes index.
    ISBN 1-57610-620-9
    1. Electronic data processing personnel--Certification.   2. Microsoft software--Examinations--Study guides.   3. Microsoft Windows NT Server.   I. Hudson, Kurt.   II. Stewart, James Michael.   III. Title.
QA76.3.T573693   2000
005.4'4769--dc21   99-058379
                                                CIP

Printed in the United States of America
10 9 8 7 6 5 4 3 2 1

President, CEO
Keith Weiskamp

Publisher
Steve Sayre

Acquisitions Editor
Shari Jo Hehr

Marketing Specialist
Cynthia Caldwell

Project Editor
Sharon Sanchez
McCarson

Technical Reviewer
Bob Flynn

**Production
Coordinator**
Kim Eoff

Cover Design
Jesse Dunn

Layout Design
April Nielsen

⑥ CORIOLIS

14455 North Hayden Road • Suite 220 • Scottsdale, Arizona 85260

Coriolis: The Training And Certification Destination™

Thank you for purchasing one of our innovative certification study guides, just one of the many members of the Coriolis family of certification products.

Certification Insider Press™ has long believed that achieving your IT certification is more of a road trip than anything else. This is why most of our readers consider us their *Training And Certification Destination*. By providing a one-stop shop for the most innovative and unique training materials, our readers know we are the first place to look when it comes to achieving their certification. As one reader put it, "I plan on using your books for all of the exams I take."

To help you reach your goals, we've listened to others like you, and we've designed our entire product line around you and the way you like to study, learn, and master challenging subjects. Our approach is *The Smartest Way To Get Certified* ™.

In addition to our highly popular *Exam Cram* and *Exam Prep* guides, we have a number of new products. We recently launched *Exam Cram Audio Reviews*, which are audiotapes based on *Exam Cram* material. We've also developed *Practice Tests Exam Crams* and *Exam Cram Flash Cards*, which are designed to make your studying fun as well as productive.

Our commitment to being the *Training And Certification Destination* does not stop there. We just introduced *Exam Cram Insider*, a biweekly newsletter containing the latest in certification news, study tips, and announcements from Certification Insider Press. (To subscribe, send an email to **eci@coriolis.com** and type "subscribe insider" in the body of the email.) We also recently announced the launch of the Certified Crammer Society and the Coriolis Help Center—two new additions to the Certification Insider Press family.

We'd like to hear from you. Help us continue to provide the very best certification study materials possible. Write us or email us at **cipq@coriolis.com** and let us know how our books have helped you study, or tell us about new features that you'd like us to add. If you send us a story about how we've helped you, and we use it in one of our books, we'll send you an official Coriolis shirt for your efforts.

Good luck with your certification exam and your career. Thank you for allowing us to help you achieve your goals.

Keith Weiskamp
President and CEO

Look For These Other Books From The Coriolis Group:

MCSE Networking Essentials Exam Cram, Third Edition
Ed Tittel, Kurt Hudson, James Michael Stewart

MCSE NT Server 4 in the Enterprise Exam Cram, Third Edition
Ed Tittel, Kurt Hudson, James Michael Stewart

MCSE NT Server 4 Exam Cram, Third Edition
Ed Tittel, Kurt Hudson, James Michael Stewart

About The Authors

Ed Tittel is a 20-year veteran in the computing business who owes his high-tech career to an ongoing affection for beautiful Austin, Texas. Ed covers numerous Windows subjects, with over 30 Windows-related titles to his credit. He also teaches for NetWorld+Interop and The Internet Security Conference (TISC) on Windows security and performance tuning. Prior to starting a company in 1994, Ed worked at Novell for six years, where he started out as a field engineer and left as Director of Technical Marketing.

Ed has contributed to over 105 computer books, including many Exam Preps and Exam Crams, for which he is series editor. Ed has also written articles for *Certification Magazine*, *InfoWorld*, *Windows NT Magazine*, and *PC Magazine*.

In his spare time, Ed likes cooking homemade stock and the many good things that it makes possible. He also walks the company Lab, Blackie, at least five times a day. Reach Ed via email at **etittel@lanw.com**.

Kurt Hudson, president of HudLogic, Inc, has earned MCSE, MCSE+Internet, MCT, CCNA, and COMPTIA Network+ and A+ Certified Technician ratings. He began his technical career with the U.S. Air Force, earning medals for systems efficiency, training excellence, and national security. He has worked for Unisys, where he helped launch two Windows 95 support operations for Microsoft and Compaq, and for Productivity Point International, where he trained hundreds of computer support engineers and system administrators. Today, he writes commercial technical publications, trains computer professionals, and troubleshoots networking problems. He has authored or co-authored several publications, which are listed at **www.hudlogic.com**. You can reach Kurt via email at **kurt@hudlogic.com**.

James Michael Stewart is a full-time writer focusing on Windows NT and Internet topics. Most recently, he has worked on several titles in the *Exam Cram* and *Exam Prep* series. Michael has been developing Windows NT 4 MCSE-level courseware and training materials for several years, including both print and online publications, as well as classroom presentation of NT training materials. He has been an MCSE since 1997, with a focus on Windows NT 4. You can reach Michael by email at **michael@lanw.com**, or through his Web page at **www.lanw.com/jmsbio.htm**.

Acknowledgments

Thanks to the team at Haights-Cross, particularly Kevin McAlily, and to the whole crew at Coriolis, particularly Keith Weiskamp, Shari Jo Hehr, and Paula Kmetz, for making Exam Cram build upon its successes. Once again, we are glad for the opportunity to refresh and replenish these titles, and to add more information and value for our readers.

Many thanks are due to the people who make these books happen. On the LANWrights side, I want to thank Dawn Rader, project manager, and Mary Burmeister, project editor, for superhuman efforts to meet an insane sequence of entirely necessary deadlines. I'd also like to thank James Michael Stewart for his herculean efforts to update the content on this book and to create a battery of scenario questions and online resources. And finally, oodles of thanks to Chelsea Valentine, who has helped us to organize and manage our reading feedback and online updates to these books better than ever before.

On the Coriolis side, special thanks to all the people involved in this project, especially Sharon McCarson, who shepherded this third edition through the process, plus Kim Eoff, our production coordinator for this title. We'd also like to thank Cynthia Caldwell, Neil Gudovitz, and Gary Hull, among many others, for their efforts to make these books show up in as many places around the world as possible.

Finally, thanks to my friends and family for their support. To Robert Wiggins: Thanks for showing me that no matter how bad things get, they could always be worse! To Quge and the gang: Hang in there, relief is nigh! To Mom and Dad: Thanks for listening to me kvetch when nobody else would. And finally, to Blackie: Thanks for making me get up and walk around occasionally. It's helped me stay (relatively) sane.

—*Ed Tittel*

I would like to thank the following people for their professional contributions to this book: Julie A. Hudson, Doug Dexter, and Lori Marcinkiewicz.

—*Kurt Hudson*

Acknowledgments

Thanks to my boss and co-author, Ed Tittel, for including me in this book series. Thanks to Dawn Rader; without you, this book would never have been complete. A warm howdy to Mary Burmeister (our other work slave). To my parents, Dave and Sue: Thanks for always being there and making it clear how much you care. To Dave and Laura: Buy the $20,000 home theater and I'll camp on your couch and cook your meals! To Mark: The cult of the Pocketgods will come back to haunt you—it is already noted in your permanent record. To HERbert: Please stop digging your claws into the back of my neck while I'm asleep. And finally, as always, to Elvis—I've been looking high and low for a glittery white jumpsuit of my own, but it seems that Wal-Mart is always sold out!

—*James Michael Stewart*

Contents At A Glance

Table Of Contents

Introduction

Welcome to *MCSE NT Workstation 4 Exam Cram, Third Edition*! This book aims to help you get ready to take—and pass—the Microsoft certification Exam 70-073, titled "Implementing and Supporting Microsoft Windows NT Workstation 4.0." This Introduction explains Microsoft's certification programs in general and talks about how the *Exam Cram* series can help you prepare for Microsoft's certification exams.

Exam Cram books help you understand and appreciate the subjects and materials you need to pass Microsoft certification exams. *Exam Cram* books are aimed strictly at test preparation and review. They do not teach you everything you need to know about a topic (such as the ins and outs of managing automated Windows NT installations, or all the nitty-gritty details involved in using Windows NT Workstation 4.0). Instead, we (the authors) present and dissect the questions and problems we've found that you're likely to encounter on a test. We've worked from Microsoft's own training materials, preparation guides, and tests, and from a battery of third-party test preparation tools and practice exams. Our aim is to bring together as much information as possible about Microsoft certification exams.

Nevertheless, to completely prepare yourself for any Microsoft test, we recommend that you begin by taking the Self-Assessment included in this book immediately following this Introduction. This tool will help you evaluate your knowledge base against the requirements for an MCSE under both ideal and real circumstances.

Based on what you learn from that exercise, you might decide to begin your studies with some classroom training or some background reading. On the other hand, you might decide to pick up and read one of the many study guides available from Microsoft or third-party vendors on certain topics, including The Coriolis Group's *Exam Prep* series (for which a title on Windows NT Workstation 4.0 is also available).

We also strongly recommend that you install, configure, and fool around with the software that you'll be tested on, because nothing beats hands-on experience and familiarity when it comes to understanding the questions you're likely to encounter on a certification test. Book learning is essential, but hands-on experience is the best teacher of all!

The Microsoft Certified Professional (MCP) Program

The MCP Program currently includes six separate tracks, each of which boasts its own special acronym (as a would-be certificant, you need to have a high tolerance for alphabet soup of all kinds):

➤ **MCP (Microsoft Certified Professional)** This is the least prestigious of all the certification tracks from Microsoft. Passing any of the major Microsoft exams (except the Networking Essentials exam) qualifies an individual for MCP credentials. Individuals can demonstrate proficiency with additional Microsoft products by passing additional certification exams.

➤ **MCP+SB (Microsoft Certified Professional + Site Building)** This certification program is designed for individuals who are planning, building, managing, and maintaining Web sites. Individuals with the MCP+SB credential will have demonstrated the ability to develop Web sites that include multimedia and searchable content and Web sites that connect to and communicate with a back-end database. It requires one MCP exam, plus two of these three exams: "Designing and Implementing Commerce Solutions with Microsoft Site Server, 3.0, Commerce Edition," "Designing and Implementing Web Sites with Microsoft FrontPage 98," and "Designing and Implementing Web Solutions with Microsoft Visual InterDev 6.0."

➤ **MCSE (Microsoft Certified Systems Engineer)** Anyone who has a current MCSE is warranted to possess a high level of expertise with Windows NT (version 3.51 or 4.0) and other Microsoft operating systems and products. This credential is designed to prepare individuals to plan, implement, maintain, and support information systems and networks built around Microsoft Windows NT and its BackOffice family of products.

To obtain an MCSE, an individual must pass four core operating system exams, plus two elective exams. The operating system exams require individuals to prove their competence with desktop and server operating systems and networking components.

You must pass at least two Windows NT-related exams to obtain an MCSE: "Implementing and Supporting Microsoft Windows NT Server" (version 3.51 or 4.0) and "Implementing and Supporting Microsoft Windows NT Server in the Enterprise" (version 3.51 or 4.0). These tests demonstrate an individual's knowledge of Windows NT in smaller, simpler networks and in larger, more complex, and heterogeneous networks, respectively.

Note: The Windows NT 3.51 version will be retired by Microsoft on June 30, 2000.

You must pass two additional tests as well. These tests are related to networking and desktop operating systems. At present, the networking requirement can be satisfied only by passing the Networking Essentials test. The desktop operating system test can be satisfied by passing a Windows 95, Windows NT Workstation (the version must match the NT version for the core tests), or Windows 98 test.

The two remaining exams are electives. An elective exam may fall in any number of subject or product areas, primarily BackOffice components. However, it is also possible to test out on electives by taking advanced networking topics like "Internetworking with Microsoft TCP/IP on Microsoft Windows NT 4.0" (but the version of Windows NT must match that for the core requirements). If you're on your way to becoming an MCSE and have already taken some exams, visit **www.microsoft. com/mcp/certstep/mcse.htm** for information about how to complete your MCSE certification.

In September 1999, Microsoft announced its Windows 2000 track for MCSE, and also announced retirement of Windows NT 4.0 MCSE core exams on 12/31/2000. Individuals who wish to remain certified MCSEs after 12/31/2001 must "upgrade" their certifications on or before 12/31/2001. The details are too complex to discuss here; to obtain those details, please visit **www.microsoft.com/mcp/certstep/mcse.htm**.

Whatever mix of tests is completed toward MCSE certification, individuals must pass six tests to meet the MCSE requirements. It's not uncommon for the entire process to take a year or so, and many individuals find that they must take a test more than once to pass. Our primary goal with the *Exam Cram* series is to make it possible, given proper study and preparation, to pass all Microsoft certification tests on the first try. Table 1 shows the required and elective exams for the MCSE certification.

➤ **MCSD (Microsoft Certified Solution Developer)** The MCSD credential reflects the skills required to create multitier, distributed, and COM-based solutions, in addition to desktop and Internet applications, using new technologies. To obtain an MCSD, an individual must demonstrate the ability to analyze and interpret user requirements; select and integrate products, platforms, tools, and technologies; design and implement code and customize applications; and perform necessary software tests and quality assurance operations.

Table 1   MCSE Requirements*

Core

All 3 of these are required	
Exam 70-067	Implementing and Supporting Microsoft Windows NT Server 4.0
Exam 70-068	Implementing and Supporting Microsoft Windows NT Server 4.0 in the Enterprise
Exam 70-058	Networking Essentials
Choose 1 from this group	
Exam 70-064	Implementing and Supporting Microsoft Windows 95
Exam 70-073	Implementing and Supporting Microsoft Windows NT Workstation 4.0
Exam 70-098	Implementing and Supporting Microsoft Windows 98

Elective

Choose 2 from this group	
Exam 70-088	Implementing and Supporting Microsoft Proxy Server 2.0
Exam 70-079	Implementing and Supporting Microsoft Internet Explorer 4.0 by Using the Internet Explorer Administration Kit
Exam 70-087	Implementing and Supporting Microsoft Internet Information Server 4.0
Exam 70-081	Implementing and Supporting Microsoft Exchange Server 5.5
Exam 70-059	Internetworking with Microsoft TCP/IP on Microsoft Windows NT 4.0
Exam 70-028	Administering Microsoft SQL Server 7.0
Exam 70-029	Designing and Implementing Databases on Microsoft SQL Server 7.0
Exam 70-056	Implementing and Supporting Web Sites Using Microsoft Site Server 3.0
Exam 70-086	Implementing and Supporting Microsoft Systems Management Server 2.0
Exam 70-085	Implementing and Supporting Microsoft SNA Server 4.0

* This is not a complete listing—you can still be tested on some earlier versions of these products. However, we have included mainly the most recent versions so that you may test on these versions and thus be certified longer. We have not included any tests that are scheduled to be retired.

To become an MCSD, you must pass a total of four exams: three core exams and one elective exam. Each candidate must also choose one of these three desktop application exams—"70-016: Designing and Implementing Desktop Applications with Microsoft Visual C++ 6.0," "70-156: Designing and Implementing Visual FoxPro 6.0," or "70-176: Designing and Implementing Visual Basic 6.0"—*plus* one of these three distributed application exams—"70-015: Designing and Implementing Distributed Applications with Microsoft Visual C++ 6.0," "70-155: Designing and Implementing Visual FoxPro 6.0," or "70-175: Designing and Implementing Visual Basic 6.0." The third core exam is "70-100: Analyzing Requirements and Defining Solution Architectures."

Elective exams cover specific Microsoft applications and languages, including Visual Basic, C++, the Microsoft Foundation Classes, Access, SQL Server, Excel, and more.

➤ **MCDBA (Microsoft Certified Database Administrator)** The MCDBA credential reflects the skills required to implement and administer Microsoft SQL Server databases. To obtain an MCDBA, an individual must demonstrate the ability to derive physical database designs, develop logical data models, create physical databases, create data services by using Transact-SQL, manage and maintain databases, configure and manage security, monitor and optimize databases, and install and configure Microsoft SQL Server.

To become an MCDBA, you must pass a total of five exams: four core exams and one elective exam. The required core exams are "Administering Microsoft SQL Server 7.0," "Designing and Implementing Databases with Microsoft SQL Server 7.0," "Implementing and Supporting Microsoft Windows NT Server 4.0," and "Implementing and Supporting Microsoft Windows NT Server 4.0 in the Enterprise."

The elective exams that you can choose from cover specific uses of SQL Server and include "Designing and Implementing Distributed Applications with Visual Basic 6.0," "Designing and Implementing Distributed Applications with Visual C++ 6.0," "Designing and Implementing Data Warehouses with Microsoft SQL Server 7.0 and Microsoft Decision Support Services 1.0," and two exams that relate to NT: "Internetworking with Microsoft TCP/IP on Microsoft Windows NT 4.0" and "Implementing and Supporting Microsoft Internet Information Server 4.0."

➤ **MCT (Microsoft Certified Trainer)** Microsoft Certified Trainers are deemed able to deliver elements of the official Microsoft curriculum, based on technical knowledge and instructional ability. Thus, it is necessary for an individual seeking MCT credentials (which are granted on a course-by-course basis) to pass the related certification exam for a course and complete the official Microsoft training in the subject area, and to demonstrate an ability to teach. MCT candidates must also possess a current MCSE.

This teaching skills criterion may be satisfied by proving that one has already attained training certification from Novell, Banyan, Lotus, the Santa Cruz Operation, or Cisco, or by taking a Microsoft-sanctioned workshop on instruction. Microsoft makes it clear that MCTs are important cogs in the Microsoft training channels. Instructors must be MCTs before Microsoft will allow them to teach in any of its official training channels, including Microsoft's affiliated Certified Technical Education Centers (CTECs) and its online training partner network.

Microsoft has announced that the MCP+I and MCSE+I credentials will not be continued when the MCSE exams for Windows 2000 are in full swing because the skill set for the Internet portion of the program has been included in the new MCSE program. Therefore, details on these tracks are not provided here; go to **www.microsoft.com/train_cert/** if you need more information.

Once a Microsoft product becomes obsolete, MCPs typically have 12 to 18 months in which to recertify on current versions. (If individuals do not recertify within the specified time period, their certifications become invalid.) Because technology keeps changing and new products continually supplant old ones, this should come as no surprise. This explains why Microsoft has announced that MCSEs have 12 months past the scheduled retirement date for the Windows NT 4.0 exams to recertify on Windows 2000 topics. (Note that this means taking at least two exams, if not more.)

The best place to keep tabs on the MCP Program and related certifications is on the Web. The URL for the MCP program is **www.microsoft.com/mcp/ certstep/mcps**. But Microsoft's Web site changes frequently, so if this URL doesn't work, try using the Search tool on Microsoft's site with either "MCP" or the quoted phrase "Microsoft Certified Professional Program" as the search string. This will help you find the latest and most accurate information about the company's certification programs.

Taking A Certification Exam

Alas, testing is not free. Each computer-based MCP exam costs $100, and if you don't pass, you may retest for an additional $100 for each additional try. In the United States and Canada, tests are administered by Sylvan Prometric and by Virtual University Enterprises (VUE). Here's how you can contact them:

➤ **Sylvan Prometric** You can sign up for a test through the company's Web site at **www.slspro.com**. Or, you can register by phone at 800-755-3926 (within the United States or Canada) or at 410-843-8000 (outside the United States and Canada).

➤ **Virtual University Enterprises** You can sign up for a test or get the phone numbers for local testing centers through the Web page at **www.microsoft.com/train_cert/mcp/vue_info.htm**.

To sign up for a test, you must possess a valid credit card, or contact either company for mailing instructions to send them a check (in the U.S.). Only when payment is verified, or a check has cleared, can you actually register for a test.

To schedule an exam, call the number or visit either of the Web pages at least one day in advance. To cancel or reschedule an exam, you must call before 7 P.M. Pacific standard time the day before the scheduled test time (or you may be charged, even if you don't appear to take the test). When you want to schedule a test, have the following information ready:

➤ Your name, organization, and mailing address.

➤ Your Microsoft Test ID. (Inside the United States, this means your Social Security number; citizens of other nations should call ahead to find out what type of identification number is required to register for a test.)

➤ The name and number of the exam you wish to take.

➤ A method of payment. (As we've already mentioned, a credit card is the most convenient method, but alternate means can be arranged in advance, if necessary.)

Once you sign up for a test, you'll be informed as to when and where the test is scheduled. Try to arrive at least 15 minutes early. You must supply two forms of identification—one of which must be a photo ID—to be admitted into the testing room.

All exams are completely closed-book. In fact, you will not be permitted to take anything with you into the testing area, but you will be furnished with a blank sheet of paper and a pen or, in some cases, an erasable plastic sheet and an erasable pen. We suggest that you immediately write down on that sheet of paper all the information you've memorized for the test. In *Exam Cram* books, this information appears on a tear-out sheet inside the front cover of each book. You will have some time to compose yourself, to record this information, and take a sample orientation exam before you begin the real thing. We suggest you take the orientation test before taking your first exam, but because they're all more or less identical in layout, behavior, and controls, you probably won't need to do this more than once.

When you complete a Microsoft certification exam, the software will tell you whether you've passed or failed. Results are broken into several topic areas. Even if you fail, we suggest you ask for—and keep—the detailed report that the test administrator should print for you. You can use this report to help you prepare for another go-round, if needed.

If you need to retake an exam, you'll have to schedule a new test with Sylvan Prometric or VUE and pay another $100.

 The first time you fail a test, you can retake the test the next day. However, if you fail a second time, you must wait 14 days before retaking that test. The 14-day waiting period remains in effect for all retakes after the first failure.

Tracking MCP Status

As soon as you pass any Microsoft exam other than Networking Essentials, you'll attain Microsoft Certified Professional (MCP) status. Microsoft also generates transcripts that indicate which exams you have passed and your corresponding test scores. You can order a transcript by email at any time by sending an email to **mcp@msprograms.com**. You can also obtain a copy of your transcript by downloading the latest version of the MCT Guide from the Web site and consulting the section titled "Key Contacts" for a list of telephone numbers and related contacts.

Once you pass the necessary set of exams (one for MCP or six for MCSE), you'll be certified. Official certification normally takes anywhere from four to six weeks, so don't expect to get your credentials overnight. When the package for a qualified certification arrives, it includes a Welcome Kit that contains a number of elements:

➤ An MCP or MCSE certificate, suitable for framing, along with a Professional Program Membership card and lapel pin.

➤ A license to use the MCP logo, thereby allowing you to use the logo in advertisements, promotions, and documents, and on letterhead, business cards, and so on. Along with the license comes an MCP logo sheet, which includes camera-ready artwork. (Note: Before using any of the artwork, individuals must sign and return a licensing agreement that indicates they'll abide by its terms and conditions.)

➤ A subscription to *Microsoft Certified Professional Magazine*, which provides ongoing data about testing and certification activities, requirements, and changes to the program.

➤ A one-year subscription to the Microsoft Beta Evaluation program. This subscription will get you all beta products from Microsoft for the next year. (This does not include developer products. You must join the MSDN program or become an MCSD to qualify for developer beta products.)

Many people believe that the benefits of MCP certification go well beyond the perks that Microsoft provides to newly anointed members of this elite group. We're starting to see more job listings that request or require applicants to have an MCP, MCSE, and so on, and many individuals who complete the program can qualify for increases in pay and/or responsibility. As an official recognition of hard work and broad knowledge, one of the MCP credentials is a badge of honor in many IT organizations.

How To Prepare For An Exam

Preparing for any Windows NT Server-related test (including Windows NT Workstation 4.0) requires that you obtain and study materials designed to provide comprehensive information about the product and its capabilities that will appear on the specific exam for which you are preparing. The following list of materials will help you study and prepare:

➤ The Windows NT Workstation 4.0 product CD includes comprehensive online documentation and related materials; it should be a primary resource when you are preparing for the test.

➤ The exam prep materials, practice tests, and self-assessment exams on the Microsoft Training And Certification Download page (**www.microsoft.com/train_cert/download/downld.htm**). Find the materials, download them, and use them! (A practice test for Windows NT Workstation 4.0 is currently available.)

In addition, you'll probably find any or all of the following materials useful in your quest for Windows NT Workstation 4.0 expertise:

➤ **Microsoft Training Kits** Microsoft Press includes coverage of Windows NT Server 4.0 in a set of training kits. For more information, visit: **http://mspress.microsoft.com/prod/books/1294.htm**. These training kits focus on Windows NT 3.51, with an update section for Windows NT 4.0, and may not be as useful as other Microsoft training kits for that reason.

➤ **Resource Kit** Microsoft Press offers a comprehensive resource kit (and supplements) for Windows NT Workstation. An online description appears at **http://mspress.microsoft.com/prod/books/1318.htm**. This same resource kit also appears in electronic form on the TechNet CD (see next bullet).

➤ **Microsoft TechNet CD** This monthly CD-based publication delivers numerous electronic titles on Windows NT Workstation 4.0 on the Technical Information (TechNet) CD. Its offerings include a resource kit, product facts, technical notes, tools and utilities, and information on how to access the Seminars Online training materials for Windows NT Workstation 4.0. A subscription to TechNet costs $299 per year, but it is well worth the price. Visit **www.microsoft.com/technet/** and check out the information under the "TechNet Subscription" menu entry for more details.

➤ **Study Guides** Several publishers—including Certification Insider Press—offer Windows NT Workstation 4.0 titles. The Certification Insider Press series includes:

➤ The *Exam Cram* series These books give you information about the material you need to know to pass the tests.

➤ The *Exam Prep* series These books provide a greater level of detail than the *Exam Cram* books and are designed to teach you everything you need to know from an exam perspective. *MCSE NT Workstation 4 Exam Prep* is the perfect learning companion to prepare you for Exam 70-073, "Implementing and Supporting Microsoft Windows NT Workstation 4.0." Look for this book in your favorite bookstores.

Together, the two series make a perfect pair.

➤ **Multimedia** These Coriolis Group materials are designed to support learners of all types—whether you learn best by listening, reading, or doing:

➤ *Practice Tests Exam Cram* series Provides the most valuable test preparation material: practice exams. Each exam is followed by a complete set of answers, as well as explanations of why the right answers are right and the wrong answers are wrong. Each book comes with a CD that contains one ore more interactive practice exams.

➤ *Exam Cram Flash Card* series Offers practice questions on handy cards you can use anywhere. The question and its possible answers appear on the front of the card, and the answer, explanation, and a valuable reference appear on the back of the card. The set also includes a CD with an electronic practice exam to give you the feel of the actual test—and more practice!

➤ *Exam Cram Audio Review* series Offers a concise review of key topics covered on the exam, as well as practice questions.

➤ **Classroom Training** CTECs, online partners, and unlicensed training companies (like Wave Technologies, American Research Group, Learning Tree, Data-Tech, and others) all offer classroom training on Windows NT Workstation 4.0. These companies aim to help you prepare to pass the NT Workstation test. Although such training runs upwards of $350 per day in class, most of the individuals lucky enough to partake (including your humble authors, who've even taught such courses) find them to be quite worthwhile.

➤ **Other Publications** You'll find direct references to other publications and resources in this book, but there's no shortage of materials available about Windows NT Workstation 4.0. To help you sift through some of the publications out there, we end each chapter with a "Need To Know

More?" section that provides pointers to more complete and exhaustive resources covering the chapter's information. This should give you an idea of where we think you should look for further discussion.

By far, this set of required and recommended materials represents a nonpareil collection of sources and resources for Windows NT Workstation 4.0 and related topics. We anticipate that you'll find that this book belongs in this company. In the section that follows, we explain how this book works, and we give you some good reasons why this book counts as a member of the required and recommended materials list.

About This Book

Each topical *Exam Cram* chapter follows a regular structure, along with graphical cues about important or useful information. Here's the structure of a typical chapter:

➤ **Opening Hotlists** Each chapter begins with a list of the terms, tools, and techniques that you must learn and understand before you can be fully conversant with that chapter's subject matter. We follow the hotlists with one or two introductory paragraphs to set the stage for the rest of the chapter.

➤ **Topical Coverage** After the opening hotlists, each chapter covers a series of topics related to the chapter's subject title. Throughout this section, we highlight topics or concepts likely to appear on a test using a special Exam Alert layout, like this:

 This is what an Exam Alert looks like. Normally, an Exam Alert stresses concepts, terms, software, or activities that are likely to relate to one or more certification test questions. For that reason, we think any information found offset in Exam Alert format is worthy of unusual attentiveness on your part. Indeed, most of the information that appears on The Cram Sheet appears as Exam Alerts within the text.

Pay close attention to material flagged as an Exam Alert; although all the information in this book pertains to what you need to know to pass the exam, we flag certain items that are really important. You'll find what appears in the meat of each chapter to be worth knowing, too, when preparing for the test. Because this book's material is very condensed, we recommend that you use this book along with other resources to achieve the maximum benefit.

In addition to the Exam Alerts, we have provided tips that will help you build a better foundation for NT Workstation knowledge. Although the information may not be on the exam, it is certainly related and will help you become a better test-taker.

 This is how tips are formatted. Keep your eyes open for these, and you'll become a Windows NT Workstation 4.0 guru in no time!

➤ **Practice Questions** Although we talk about test questions and topics throughout each chapter, this section presents a series of mock test questions and explanations of both correct and incorrect answers. We also try to point out especially tricky questions by using a special icon, like this:

Ordinarily, this icon flags the presence of a particularly devious inquiry, if not an outright trick question. Trick questions are calculated to be answered incorrectly if not read more than once, and carefully, at that. Although they're not ubiquitous, such questions make regular appearances on the Microsoft exams. That's why we say exam questions are as much about reading comprehension as they are about knowing your material inside out and backwards.

➤ **Details And Resources** Every chapter ends with a section titled "Need To Know More?". This section provides direct pointers to Microsoft and third-party resources offering more details on the chapter's subject. In addition, this section tries to rank or at least rate the quality and thoroughness of the topic's coverage by each resource. If you find a resource you like in this collection, use it, but don't feel compelled to use all the resources. On the other hand, we recommend only resources we use on a regular basis, so none of our recommendations will be a waste of your time or money (but purchasing them all at once probably represents an expense that many network administrators and would-be MCPs and MCSEs might find hard to justify).

➤ Your authors have also prepared three adaptive exams for NT Workstation 4.0 that are available online. To take these practice exams, which should help you prepare even better for the real thing, visit **www. coriolis.com/cip/core4rev/**, follow the instructions from there, and pick the NT Workstation 4 book

The bulk of the book follows this chapter structure slavishly, but there are a few other elements that we'd like to point out. Chapters 19 and 21 each include a sample test that provides a good review of the material presented throughout the book to ensure you're ready for the exam. You can use Chapter 19 to assess your readiness to take the exam, and may only need to take the exam in Chapter 21, if you don't score at least 70 percent on the first try. Chapters 20 and 22 provide answer keys to the sample tests that appear in Chapters 19 and 21, respectively. Also, don't forget that you can take an adaptive version of the Workstation exam online through the Coriolis Web site, as explained in the preceding list item. Finally, you'll find the Glossary, which explains terms, and an index that you can use to track down terms as they appear in the text.

Finally, the tear-out Cram Sheet attached next to the inside front cover of this *Exam Cram* book represents a condensed and compiled collection of facts and tips that we think you should memorize before taking the test. Because you can dump this information out of your head onto a piece of paper before taking the exam, you can master this information by brute force—you need to remember it only long enough to write it down when you walk into the test room. You might even want to look at it in the car or in the lobby of the testing center just before you walk in to take the test.

How To Use This Book

If you're prepping for a first-time test, we've structured the topics in this book to build on one another. Therefore, some topics in later chapters make more sense after you've read earlier chapters. That's why we suggest you read this book from front to back for your initial test preparation. If you need to brush up on a topic or you have to bone up for a second try, use the index or table of contents to go straight to the topics and questions that you need to study. Beyond helping you prepare for the test, we think you'll find this book useful as a tightly focused reference to some of the most important aspects of Windows NT Workstation 4.0.

Given all the book's elements and its specialized focus, we've tried to create a tool that will help you prepare for—and pass—Microsoft Exam 70-073, "Implementing and Supporting Microsoft Windows NT Workstation 4.0." Please share your feedback on the book with us, especially if you have ideas about how we can improve it for future test-takers. We'll consider everything you say carefully, and we'll respond to all suggestions.

Send your questions or comments to us at **cipq@coriolis.com**. Our series editor, Ed Tittel, coordinates our efforts and ensures that all questions get answered. Please remember to include the title of the book in your message; otherwise, we'll be forced to guess which book you're writing about. And we don't like to guess—we want to *know*! Also, be sure to check out **www.certificationinsider.com** where you'll find information updates, commentary, and certification information.

Thanks, and enjoy the book!

Self-Assessment

Based on recent statistics from Microsoft, as many as 400,000 individuals are at some stage of the certification process but haven't yet received an MCP or other Microsoft certification. We also know that three or four times that number may be considering whether or not to obtain a Microsoft certification of some kind. That's a huge audience!

The reason we included a Self-Assessment in this *Exam Cram* book is to help you evaluate your readiness to tackle MCSE certification. It should also help you understand what you need to know to master the topic of this book—namely, Exam 70-067, "Implementing and Supporting Microsoft Windows NT Server 4.0." But before you tackle this Self-Assessment, let's talk about concerns you may face when pursuing an MCSE, and what an ideal MCSE candidate might look like.

MCSEs In The Real World

In the next section, we describe an ideal MCSE candidate, knowing full well that only a few real candidates will meet this ideal. In fact, our description of that ideal candidate might seem downright scary. But take heart: Although the requirements to obtain an MCSE may seem formidable, they are by no means impossible to meet. However, be keenly aware that it does take time, involves some expense, and requires real effort to get through the process.

More than 200,000 MCSEs are already certified, so it's obviously an attainable goal. You can get all the real-world motivation you need from knowing that many others have gone before, so you will be able to follow in their footsteps. If you're willing to tackle the process seriously and do what it takes to obtain the necessary experience and knowledge, you can take—and pass—all the certification tests involved in obtaining an MCSE. In fact, we've designed these *Exam Crams*, and the companion *Exam Preps*, to make it as easy on you as possible to prepare for these exams. But prepare you must!

The same, of course, is true for other Microsoft certifications, including:

➤ MCSD, which is aimed at software developers and requires one specific exam, two more exams on client and distributed topics, plus a fourth elective exam drawn from a different, but limited, pool of options.

➤ Other Microsoft certifications, whose requirements range from one test (MCP or MCT) to several tests (MCP+SB, MCDBA).

The Ideal MCSE Candidate

Just to give you some idea of what an ideal MCSE candidate is like, here are some relevant statistics about the background and experience such an individual might have. Don't worry if you don't meet these qualifications, or don't come that close—this is a far from ideal world, and where you fall short is simply where you'll have more work to do.

➤ Academic or professional training in network theory, concepts, and operations. This includes everything from networking media and transmission techniques through network operating systems, services, and applications.

➤ Three-plus years of professional networking experience, including experience with Ethernet, token ring, modems, and other networking media. This must include installation, configuration, upgrade, and troubleshooting experience.

➤ Two-plus years in a networked environment that includes hands-on experience with Windows NT Server, Windows NT Workstation, and Windows 95 or Windows 98. A solid understanding of each system's architecture, installation, configuration, maintenance, and troubleshooting is also essential.

➤ A thorough understanding of key networking protocols, addressing, and name resolution, including TCP/IP, IPX/SPX, and NetBEUI.

➤ A thorough understanding of NetBIOS naming, browsing, and file and print services.

➤ Familiarity with key Windows NT-based TCP/IP-based services, including HTTP (Web servers), DHCP, WINS, DNS, plus familiarity with one or more of the following: Internet Information Server (IIS), Index Server, and Proxy Server.

➤ Working knowledge of NetWare 3.x and 4.x, including IPX/SPX frame formats, NetWare file, print, and directory services, and both Novell and Microsoft client software. Working knowledge of Microsoft's Client Service For NetWare (CSNW), Gateway Service For NetWare (GSNW), the NetWare Migration Tool (NWCONV), and the NetWare Client For Windows (NT, 95, and 98) is essential.

Fundamentally, this boils down to a bachelor's degree in computer science, plus three years' experience working in a position involving network design, installation, configuration, and maintenance. We believe that well under half of all certification candidates meet these requirements, and that, in fact, most aspiring candidates meet less than half of these requirements—at least, when they begin the certification process. But because all 200,000 people who already have been certified have survived this ordeal, you can survive it too—especially if you heed what our Self-Assessment can tell you about what you already know and what you need to learn.

Put Yourself To The Test

The following series of questions and observations is designed to help you figure out how much work you must do to pursue Microsoft certification and what kinds of resources you may consult on your quest. Be absolutely honest in your answers, or you'll end up wasting money on exams you're not yet ready to take. There are no right or wrong answers, only steps along the path to certification. Only you can decide where you really belong in the broad spectrum of aspiring candidates.

Two things should be clear from the outset, however:

➤ Even a modest background in computer science will be helpful.

➤ Hands-on experience with Microsoft products and technologies is an essential ingredient to certification success.

Educational Background

1. Have you ever taken any computer-related classes? [Yes or No]

   If Yes, proceed to question 2; if No, proceed to question 4.

2. Have you taken any classes on computer operating systems? [Yes or No]

   If Yes, you will probably be able to handle Microsoft's architecture and system component discussions. If you're rusty, brush up on basic operating system concepts, especially virtual memory, multitasking regimes, user mode versus kernel mode operation, and general computer security topics.

   If No, consider some basic reading in this area. We strongly recommend a good general operating systems book, such as *Operating System Concepts*, by Abraham Silberschatz and Peter Baer Galvin (Addison-Wesley, 1997, ISBN 0-201-59113-8). If this title doesn't appeal to you, check out reviews for other, similar titles at your favorite online bookstore.

3. Have you taken any networking concepts or technologies classes? [Yes or No]

If Yes, you will probably be able to handle Microsoft's networking terminology, concepts, and technologies (brace yourself for frequent departures from normal usage). If you're rusty, brush up on basic networking concepts and terminology, especially networking media, transmission types, the OSI Reference Model, and networking technologies such as Ethernet, token ring, FDDI, and WAN links.

If No, you might want to read one or two books in this topic area. The two best books that we know of are *Computer Networks, 3rd Edition*, by Andrew S. Tanenbaum (Prentice-Hall, 1996, ISBN 0-13-349945-6) and *Computer Networks and Internets*, by Douglas E. Comer (Prentice-Hall, 1997, ISBN 0-13-239070-1).

Skip to the next section, "Hands-On Experience."

4. Have you done any reading on operating systems or networks? [Yes or No]

If Yes, review the requirements stated in the first paragraphs after questions 2 and 3. If you meet those requirements, move on to the next section. If No, consult the recommended reading for both topics. A strong background will help you prepare for the Microsoft exams better than just about anything else.

Hands-On Experience

The most important key to success on all of the Microsoft tests is hands-on experience, especially with Windows NT Server and Workstation, plus the many add-on services and BackOffice components around which so many of the Microsoft certification exams revolve. If we leave you with only one realization after taking this Self-Assessment, it should be that there's no substitute for time spent installing, configuring, and using the various Microsoft products upon which you'll be tested repeatedly and in-depth.

5. Have you installed, configured, and worked with:

➤ Windows NT Server? [Yes or No]

If Yes, make sure you understand basic concepts as covered in Exam 70067 and advanced concepts as covered in Exam 70-068. You should also study the TCP/IP interfaces, utilities, and services for this test, Exam 70-059, plus Internet Information Server capabilities for Exam 70-087.

 You can download objectives, practice exams, and other data about Microsoft exams from the Training and Certification Web page at **www.microsoft.com/train_cert/**. Use the "Find an Exam" link to obtain specific exam info.

If you haven't worked with Windows NT Server, TCP/IP, and IIS (or whatever product you choose for your final elective), you must obtain one or two machines and a copy of Windows NT Server. Then, learn the operating system, and do the same for TCP/IP and whatever other software components on which you'll also be tested.

In fact, we recommend that you obtain two computers, each with a network interface, and set up a two-node network on which to practice. With decent Windows NT-capable computers selling for about $500 to $600 apiece these days, this shouldn't be too much of a financial hardship. You may have to scrounge to come up with the necessary software, but if you scour the Microsoft Web site you can usually find low-cost options to obtain evaluation copies of most of the software that you'll need.

➤ Windows NT Workstation? [Yes or No]

If Yes, make sure you understand the concepts covered in Exam 70-073.

If No, you will want to obtain a copy of Windows NT Workstation and learn how to install, configure, and maintain it. You can use *MCSE NT Workstation 4 Exam Cram* to guide your activities and studies, or work straight from Microsoft's test objectives if you prefer.

 For any and all of these Microsoft exams, the Resource Kits for the topics involved are a good study resource. You can purchase softcover Resource Kits from Microsoft Press (search for them at **http://mspress.microsoft.com/**), but they also appear on the TechNet CDs (**www.microsoft.com/technet**). We believe that Resource Kits are among the best preparation tools available, along with the *Exam Crams* and *Exam Preps*, that you can use to get ready for Microsoft exams.

You have the option of taking the Window 95 (70-064) exam or the Windows 98 (70-098) exam, instead of Exam 70-073, to fulfill your desktop operating system requirement for the MCSE. Although we don't recommend these others (because studying for Workstation helps you prepare for the Server exams), we do recommend that you obtain Resource Kits and other tools to help you prepare for those exams if you decide to take one or both of them for your own reasons.

6. For any specific Microsoft product that is not itself an operating system (for example, FrontPage 98, SQL Server, and so on), have you installed, configured, used, and upgraded this software? [Yes or No]

If the answer is Yes, skip to the next section. If it's No, you must get some experience. Read on for suggestions on how to do this.

Experience is a must with any Microsoft product exam, be it something as simple as FrontPage 98 or as challenging as Exchange Server 5.5 or SQL Server 7.0. For trial copies of other software, search Microsoft's Web site using the name of the product as your search term. Also search for bundles like "BackOffice" or "Small Business Server."

> **TIP** If you have the funds, or your employer will pay your way, consider taking a class at a Certified Training and Education Center (CTEC) or at an Authorized Academic Training Partner (AATP). In addition to classroom exposure to the topic of your choice, you get a copy of the software that is the focus of your course, along with a trial version of whatever operating system it needs (usually, NT Server), with the training materials for that class.

Before you even think about taking any Microsoft exam, make sure you've spent enough time with the related software to understand how it may be installed and configured, how to maintain such an installation, and how to troubleshoot that software when things go wrong. This will help you in the exam, and in real life!

Testing Your Exam-Readiness

Whether you attend a formal class on a specific topic to get ready for an exam or use written materials to study on your own, some preparation for the Microsoft certification exams is essential. At $100 a try, pass or fail, you want to do everything you can to pass on your first try. That's where studying comes in.

We have included two practice exams in this book, so if you don't score that well on the first test, you can study more and then tackle the second test. We also have built adaptive exams that you can take online through the Coriolis Web site at **www.coriolis.com/cip/core4rev/**. If you still don't hit a score of at least 70 percent after these tests, you'll want to investigate the other practice test resources we mention in this section.

For any given subject, consider taking a class if you've tackled self-study materials, taken the test, and failed anyway. The opportunity to interact with an instructor and fellow students can make all the difference in the world, if you can afford that privilege. For information about Microsoft classes, visit the Training and Certification page at **www.microsoft.com/train_cert/** (use the "Find a Course" link).

If you can't afford to take a class, visit the Training and Certification page anyway, because it also includes pointers to free practice exams and to Microsoft Certified Professional Approved Study Guides and other self-study tools. And even if you can't afford to spend much at all, you should still invest in some low-cost practice exams from commercial vendors, because they can help you assess your readiness to pass a test better than any other tool. All of the following Web sites offer practice exams online for less than $100 apiece (some for significantly less than that):

➤ Beachfront Quizzer at **www.bfq.com/**

➤ Hardcore MCSE at **www.hardcoremcse.com/**

➤ LANWrights at **www.lanw.com/books/examcram/order.htm**

➤ MeasureUp at **www.measureup.com/**

7. Have you taken a practice exam on your chosen test subject? [Yes or No]

If Yes, and you scored 70 percent or better, you're probably ready to tackle the real thing. If your score isn't above that threshold, keep at it until you break that barrier.

If No, obtain all the free and low-budget practice tests you can find (see the list above) and get to work. Keep at it until you can break the passing threshold comfortably.

> When it comes to assessing your test readiness, there is no better way than to take a good-quality practice exam and pass with a score of 70 percent or better. When we're preparing ourselves, we shoot for 80-plus percent, just to leave room for the "weirdness factor" that sometimes shows up on Microsoft exams.

Assessing Readiness
For Exam 70-067

In addition to the general exam-readiness information in the previous section, there are several things you can do to prepare for the "Implementing and Supporting Microsoft Windows NT 4.0" exam. As you're getting ready for Exam 70-067, visit the MCSE mailing list. Sign up at **www.sunbelt-software.com** (look for the "Subscribe to…" button). You will find a great source of questions and related information at the CramSession site at **www.cramsession.com**. These are great places to ask questions and get good answers, or simply to watch the questions that others ask (along with the answers, of course).

You should also cruise the Web looking for "braindumps" (recollections of test topics and experiences recorded by others) to help you anticipate topics you're likely to encounter on the test. The MCSE mailing list is a good place to ask where the useful braindumps are, or you can check Shawn Gamble's list at **www.commandcentral.com** (he's also got some peachy—and free— practice tests on this subject) or Herb Martin's Braindump Heaven at **http:// 209.207.167.177/**.

 You can't be sure that a braindump's author can provide correct answers. Thus, use the questions to guide your studies, but don't rely on the answers in a braindump to lead you to the truth. Double-check everything you find in any braindump.

Microsoft exam mavens also recommend checking the Microsoft Knowledge Base (available on its own CD as part of the TechNet collection, or on the Microsoft Web site at **http://support.microsoft.com/support/**) for "meaningful technical support issues" that relate to Windows NT Server. Although we're not sure exactly what the quoted phrase means, we have also noticed some overlap between technical support questions on particular products and troubleshooting questions on the exams for those products.

As you review the material for Exam 70-067, you'll realize that hands-on experience with Windows NT Server 4.0 is not only invaluable, it's absolutely essential. You must be familiar with installing this operating system, configuring protocols, using Performance Monitor and Network Monitor, working with users, groups, and trust relationships, and so forth. In short, the more time you spend with the product, the better you'll do when you take the test!

Onward, Through The Fog!

Once you've assessed your readiness, undertaken the right background studies, obtained the hands-on experience that will help you understand the products and technologies at work, and reviewed the many sources of information to help you prepare for a test, you'll be ready to take a round of practice tests. When your scores come back positive enough to get you through the exam, you're ready to go after the real thing. If you follow our assessment regime, you'll not only know what you need to study, but when you're ready to make a test date at Sylvan or VUE. Good luck!

Microsoft Certification Exams

Terms you'll need to understand:

√ Radio button

√ Checkbox

√ Exhibit

√ Multiple-choice question formats

√ Careful reading

√ Process of elimination

√ Fixed-length tests

√ Adaptive tests

√ Short-form tests

√ Combination tests

√ Simulations

Techniques you'll need to master:

√ Assessing your exam-readiness

√ Preparing to take a certification exam

√ Practicing (to make perfect)

√ Making the best use of the testing software

√ Budgeting your time

√ Guessing (as a last resort)

Exam taking is not something that most people anticipate eagerly, no matter how well prepared they may be. In most cases, familiarity helps offset test anxiety. In plain English, this means you probably won't be as nervous when you take your fourth or fifth Microsoft certification exam as you'll be when you take your first one.

Whether it's your first exam or your tenth, understanding the details of exam taking (how much time to spend on questions, the environment you'll be in, and so on) and the exam software will help you concentrate on the material rather than on the setting. Likewise, mastering a few basic exam-taking skills should help you recognize—and perhaps even outfox—some of the tricks and snares you're bound to find in some exam questions.

This chapter, besides explaining the exam environment and software, describes some proven exam-taking strategies that you should be able to use to your advantage.

Assessing Exam-Readiness

Before you take any more Microsoft exams, we strongly recommend that you read through and take the Self-Assessment included with this book (it appears just before this chapter, in fact). This will help you compare your knowledge base to the requirements for obtaining an MCSE, and it will also help you identify parts of your background or experience that may be in need of improvement, enhancement, or further learning. If you get the right set of basics under your belt, obtaining Microsoft certification will be that much easier.

Once you've gone through the Self-Assessment, you can remedy those topical areas where your background or experience may not measure up to an ideal certification candidate. But you can also tackle subject matter for individual tests at the same time, so you can continue making progress while you're catching up in some areas.

Once you've worked through an *Exam Cram*, have read the supplementary materials, and have taken the practice tests, you'll have a pretty clear idea of when you should be ready to take the real exam. Although we strongly recommend that you keep practicing until your scores top the 70 percent mark, 75 percent would be a good goal to give yourself some margin for error in a real exam situation (where stress will play more of a role than when you practice). Once you hit that point, you should be ready to go. But if you get through both practice exams in this book and the sample adaptive online exam (discussed in the Self-Assessment, the Introduction, and later in this chapter) without attaining that score, you should keep taking practice tests and studying the materials until you get there. You'll find more information about other practice test vendors in the Self-Assessment, along with even more pointers on how to study and prepare. But now, on to the exam itself!

The Exam Situation

When you arrive at the testing center where you scheduled your exam, you'll need to sign in with an exam coordinator. He or she will ask you to show two forms of identification, one of which must be a photo ID. After you've signed in and your time slot arrives, you'll be asked to deposit any books, bags, or other items you brought with you. Then, you'll be escorted into a closed room. Typically, the room will be furnished with anywhere from one to half a dozen computers, and each workstation will be separated from the others by dividers designed to keep you from seeing what's happening on someone else's computer.

You'll be furnished with a pen or pencil and a blank sheet of paper, or, in some cases, an erasable plastic sheet and an erasable pen. You're allowed to write down anything you want on both sides of this sheet. Before the exam, you should memorize as much of the material that appears on The Cram Sheet (in the front of this book) as you can, so you can write that information on the blank sheet as soon as you are seated in front of the computer. You can refer to your rendition of The Cram Sheet anytime you like during the test, but you'll have to surrender the sheet when you leave the room.

Most test rooms feature a wall with a large picture window. This permits the exam coordinator to monitor the room, to prevent exam-takers from talking to one another, and to observe anything out of the ordinary that might go on. The exam coordinator will have preloaded the appropriate Microsoft certification exam—for this book, that's Exam 70-073—and you'll be permitted to start as soon as you're seated in front of the computer.

All Microsoft certification exams allow a certain maximum amount of time in which to complete your work (this time is indicated on the exam by an on-screen counter/clock, so you can check the time remaining whenever you like). All Microsoft certification exams are computer generated and most use a multiple-choice format. Although this may sound quite simple, the questions are constructed not only to check your mastery of basic facts and figures about Windows NT Workstation, but they also require you to evaluate one or more sets of circumstances or requirements. Often, you'll be asked to give more than one answer to a question. Likewise, you might be asked to select the best or most effective solution to a problem from a range of choices, all of which technically are correct. Taking the exam is quite an adventure, and it involves real thinking. This book shows you what to expect and how to deal with the potential problems, puzzles, and predicaments.

In the next section, you'll learn more about how Microsoft test questions look and how they must be answered.

Exam Layout And Design

Some exam questions require you to select a single answer, whereas others ask you to select one or more correct answers. The following multiple-choice question requires you to select a single correct answer. Following the question is a brief summary of each potential answer and why it is either right or wrong.

Question 1

> Windows NT fails to boot after you have modified the Registry. What is the quickest and easiest way to get the machine to boot?
>
> ○ a. Start the computer from the Windows NT boot disks and restore the Registry from a backup.
>
> ○ b. Start the computer from the Windows NT boot disks and select the Emergency Repair option.
>
> ○ c. Start the computer from the Emergency Repair Disk and follow the prompts.
>
> ○ d. Choose the Last Known Good Configuration Option when it appears during bootup.

Answer d is correct. The quickest and easiest approach to solving this kind of problem—be it caused by untoward Registry edits or installation of bogus drivers or system components—is to choose the Last Known Good Configuration option during bootup. Answers a and b may produce the desired results eventually (or they may not), but they're nowhere near as easy, nor are they likely to produce a Registry that's as up-to-date as the LKGC unless the Registry has been backed up quite recently, or a new ERD has been created. You cannot boot from the ERD, however, which is why answer c is incorrect.

This sample question format corresponds closely to the Microsoft certification exam format—the only difference on the exam is that questions are not followed by answer keys. To select an answer, you would position the cursor over the radio button next to the answer. Then, click the mouse button to select the answer.

Let's examine a question where one or more answers are possible. This type of question provides checkboxes rather than radio buttons for marking all appropriate selections.

Question 2

> Using Task Manager, which of the following priority settings can you apply to an active process? [Check all correct answers]
>
> ❑ a. Low
>
> ❑ b. Realtime
>
> ❑ c. System
>
> ❑ d. Normal
>
> ❑ e. Pause
>
> ❑ f. High

Answers a, b, d, and f are correct. To prove this for yourself, launch the Task Manager by right-clicking on an empty portion of the task bar at the bottom of a Windows NT screen. Select the processes tab, then right-click on any process except for system processes (like the System Idle Process, which won't work). If you position the cursor over the Set Priority entry on the resulting pop-up menu, the only entries it contains are Realtime, High, Normal, and Low. Thus, answers c and e are incorrect because neither System nor Pause appears on this menu.

For this particular question, four answers are required. As far as the authors can tell (and Microsoft won't comment), such questions are scored as wrong unless all the required selections are chosen. In other words, a partially correct answer does not result in partial credit when the test is scored. For Question 2, you have to check the boxes next to items a, b, d, and f to obtain credit for a correct answer. Notice that picking the right answers also means knowing why the other answers are wrong!

Although these two basic types of questions can appear in many forms, they constitute the foundation on which all the Microsoft certification exam questions rest. More complex questions include exhibits, which are usually screenshots of some kind of network diagram or topology.

For some of these questions, you'll be asked to make a selection by clicking on a checkbox or radio button on the screenshot itself. For others, you'll be expected to use the information displayed therein to guide your answer to the question. Familiarity with the underlying utility is your key to choosing the correct answer(s).

Other questions involving exhibits use charts or network diagrams to help document a workplace scenario that you'll be asked to troubleshoot or configure. Careful attention to such exhibits is the key to success. Be prepared to toggle frequently between the exhibit and the question as you work.

Microsoft's Testing Formats

Currently, Microsoft uses four different testing formats:

➤ Fixed-length

➤ Adaptive

➤ Short-form

➤ Combination

Some Microsoft exams employ more advanced testing capabilities than might immediately meet the eye. Although the questions that appear are still multiple choice, the logic that drives them is more complex than older Microsoft tests, which use a fixed sequence of questions, called a *fixed-length test*. Other exams employ a sophisticated user interface, which Microsoft calls a *simulation*, to test your knowledge of the software and systems under consideration in a more or less "live" environment that behaves just like the original.

For some exams, Microsoft has turned to a well-known technique, called *adaptive testing*, to establish a test-taker's level of knowledge and product competence. Adaptive exams look the same as fixed-length exams, but they discover the level of difficulty at which an individual test-taker can correctly answer questions. At the same time, Microsoft is in the process of converting some of its fixed-length exams into adaptive exams as well. Test-takers with differing levels of knowledge or ability therefore see different sets of questions; individuals with high levels of knowledge or ability are presented with a smaller set of more difficult questions, whereas individuals with lower levels of knowledge are presented with a larger set of easier questions. Two individuals may answer the same percentage of questions correctly, but the test-taker with a higher knowledge or ability level will score higher because his or her questions are worth more.

Also, the lower-level test-taker will probably answer more questions than his or her more-knowledgeable colleague. This explains why adaptive tests use ranges of values to define the number of questions and the amount of time it takes to complete the test.

Adaptive tests work by evaluating the test-taker's most recent answer. A correct answer leads to a more difficult question (and the test software's estimate of the test-taker's knowledge and ability level is raised). An incorrect answer leads to a less difficult question (and the test software's estimate of the test-taker's knowledge and ability level is lowered). This process continues until the test targets the test-taker's true ability level. The exam ends when the test-taker's level of accuracy meets a statistically acceptable value (in other words, when his or her performance demonstrates an acceptable level of knowledge and ability) or when the maximum number of items has been presented (in which case, the test-taker is almost certain to fail).

Microsoft has also introduced a short-form test for its most popular tests (as of this writing, all of the Core Four exams, plus TCP/IP, can appear in this format). This test delivers 30 questions to its takers, giving them exactly 60 minutes to complete the exam. This type of exam is similar to a fixed-length test, in that it allows readers to jump ahead or return to earlier questions, and to cycle through the questions until the test is done. Microsoft does not use adaptive logic in this test, but claims that statistical analysis of the question pool is such that the 30 questions delivered during a short-form exam conclusively measure a test-taker's knowledge of the subject matter in much the same way as an adaptive test. You can think of the short-form test as a kind of "greatest hits exam" (that is, the most important questions are covered) version of an adaptive exam on the same topic.

A fourth kind of test you might encounter is what we've dubbed the combination exam. Several test-takers have reported that some of the Microsoft exams, including Windows NT Server (70-067), Windows NT Server in the Enterprise (70-068), and Windows NT Workstation (70-073), can appear as combination exams. Such exams begin with a set of 15 to 25 adaptive questions, followed by 10 fixed-length questions. In fact, many test-takers have reported that although some combination tests claim that they will present both adaptive and fixed-length portions, when the test-taker finishes the adaptive portion (usually in exactly 15 questions), the test ends there. Because such users have all attained passing scores, it may be that a high enough passing score on the adaptive portion of a combination test obviates the fixed-length portion, but we're not completely sure about this, and Microsoft won't comment. Most combination exams allow a maximum of 60 minutes for the testing period.

Microsoft tests can come in any one of these forms. Whatever you encounter, you must take the test in whichever form it appears; you can't choose one form over another. Currently, the Windows NT Workstation exam may be adaptive (especially if you're taking it in some language other than English), in which case you'll have 90 minutes to answer between 15 and 30 questions (on average), or short-form, in which case you'll get 60 minutes to answer exactly 30 questions. If anything, it pays more to prepare thoroughly for an adaptive or combination exam than for a fixed-length or a short-form exam: The penalties for answering incorrectly are built into the test itself on an adaptive exam or the first part of a combination exam, whereas the layout remains the same for a fixed-length or short-form test, no matter how many questions you answer incorrectly.

> **TIP** The biggest difference between an adaptive test and a fixed-length or short-form test is that on a fixed-length or short-form test, you can revisit questions after you've read them over one or more times. On an adaptive test, you must answer the question when it's presented and will have no opportunities to revisit that question thereafter.

Strategies For Different Testing Formats

Before you choose a test-taking strategy, you must know if your test is fixed-length, short-form, adaptive, or combination. When you begin your exam, the software will tell you that the test is adaptive, if in fact the version you're taking is an adaptive test. If your introductory materials fail to mention this, you're probably taking a fixed-length test. If the total number of questions involved is exactly 30, you're taking a short-form test. Combination tests announce themselves by indicating that they will start with a set of adaptive questions, followed by fixed-length questions, but don't actually call themselves "combination tests" or "combination exams"—we've adopted this term purely for descriptive purposes.

You'll be able to tell for sure if you are taking an adaptive, fixed-length, short-form, or combination test by the first question. If it includes a checkbox that lets you mark the question for later review, you're taking a fixed-length or short-form test. If the total number of questions is 30, it's a short-form test; if more than 30, it's a fixed-length test. Adaptive test questions (and the first set of questions on a combination test) can be visited (and answered) only once, and they include no such checkbox.

The Fixed-Length And Short-Form Exam Strategy

A well-known principle when taking fixed-length or short-form exams is to first read over the entire exam from start to finish while answering only those questions you feel absolutely sure of. On subsequent passes, you can dive into more complex questions more deeply, knowing how many such questions you have left.

Fortunately, the Microsoft exam software for fixed-length and short-form tests makes the multiple-visit approach easy to implement. At the top-left corner of each question is a checkbox that permits you to mark that question for a later visit.

> *Note: Marking questions makes review easier, but you can return to any question by clicking the Forward or Back button repeatedly.*

As you read each question, if you answer only those you're sure of and mark for review those that you're not sure of, you can keep working through a decreasing list of questions as you answer the trickier ones in order.

> **TIP** There's at least one potential benefit to reading the exam over completely before answering the trickier questions: Sometimes, information supplied in later questions sheds more light on earlier questions. At other times, information you read in later questions might jog your memory about Windows NT Workstation facts, figures, or behavior that helps you answer earlier questions. Either way, you'll come out ahead if you defer those questions about which you're not absolutely sure.

Here are some question-handling strategies that apply to fixed-length and short-form tests. Use them if you have the chance:

➤ When returning to a question after your initial read-through, read every word again—otherwise, your mind can fall quickly into a rut. Sometimes, revisiting a question after turning your attention elsewhere lets you see something you missed, but the strong tendency is to see what you've seen before. Try to avoid that tendency at all costs.

➤ If you return to a question more than twice, try to articulate to yourself what you don't understand about the question, why answers don't appear to make sense, or what appears to be missing. If you chew on the subject awhile, your subconscious might provide the details you lack, or you might notice a "trick" that points to the right answer.

As you work your way through the exam, another counter that Microsoft provides will come in handy—the number of questions completed and questions outstanding. For fixed-length and short-form tests, it's wise to budget your time by making sure that you've completed one-quarter of the questions one-quarter of the way through the exam period. For a short-form test, as you may experience with the Windows NT Workstation exam, this means you must complete one-quarter of the questions one-quarter of the way through (the first 8 questions in the first 15 minutes) and three-quarters of the questions three-quarters of the way through (24 questions in 45 minutes).

If you're not finished when only five minutes remain, use that time to guess your way through any remaining questions. Remember, guessing is potentially more valuable than not answering, because blank answers are always wrong, but a guess may turn out to be right. If you don't have a clue about any of the remaining questions, pick answers at random, or choose all a's, b's, and so on. The important thing is to submit an exam for scoring that has an answer for every question.

 At the very end of your exam period, you're better off guessing than leaving questions unanswered.

The Adaptive Exam Strategy

If there's one principle that applies to taking an adaptive test, it could be summed up as "Get it right the first time." You cannot elect to skip a question and move on to the next one when taking an adaptive test, because the testing software uses your answer to the current question to select whatever question it plans to present next. Nor can you return to a question once you've moved on, because the software gives you only one chance to answer the question. You can, however, take notes, because sometimes information supplied in earlier questions will shed more light on later questions.

Also, when you answer a question correctly, you are presented with a more difficult question next to help the software gauge your level of skill and ability. When you answer a question incorrectly, you are presented with a less difficult question, and the software lowers its current estimate of your skill and ability. This continues until the program settles into a reasonably accurate estimate of what you know and can do, and takes you on average through somewhere between 15 and 30 questions as you complete the test.

The good news is that if you know your stuff, you'll probably finish most adaptive tests in 30 minutes or so. The bad news is that you must really, really know your stuff to do your best on an adaptive test. That's because some questions are so convoluted, complex, or hard to follow that you're bound to miss one or two, at a minimum, even if you do know your stuff. So the more you know, the better you'll do on an adaptive test, even accounting for the occasionally weird or unfathomable questions that appear on these exams.

TIP Because you can't tell in advance if a test is fixed-length, short-form, adaptive, or combination, you will be best served by preparing for the exam as if it were adaptive. That way, you should be prepared to pass no matter what kind of test you take. But if you do take a fixed-length or short-form test, remember our tips from the preceding section. They should help you improve on what you could do on an adaptive test.

If you encounter a question on an adaptive test that you can't answer, you must guess an answer immediately. Because of how the software works, you may suffer for your guess on the next question if you guess right, because you'll get a more difficult question next!

The Combination Exam Strategy

When it comes to studying for a combination test, your best bet is to approach it as a slightly longer adaptive exam, and to study as if the exam were adaptive only. Because the adaptive approach doesn't rely on rereading questions, and suggests that you take notes while reading useful information on test questions, it's hard to go wrong with this strategy when taking any kind of Microsoft certification test.

Mastering The Inner Game

In the final analysis, knowledge breeds confidence, and confidence breeds success. If you study the materials in this book carefully and review all the practice questions at the end of each chapter, you should become aware of those areas where additional learning and study are required.

Next, follow up by reading some or all of the materials recommended in the "Need To Know More?" section at the end of each chapter. The idea is to become familiar enough with the concepts and situations you find in the sample questions that you can reason your way through similar situations on a real exam. If you know the material, you have every right to be confident that you can pass the exam.

After you've worked your way through the book, take the practice exams in Chapters 19 and 21. You'll also want to check the Scenarios part of this book (immediately following the two sample tests), which includes our newly added scenario questions. The sample tests and scenarios provide a reality check and help you identify areas to study further. Make sure you follow up and review materials related to the questions you miss while practicing before scheduling a real exam. Only when you've covered that ground and feel comfortable with the whole scope of the practice questions should you take the online exam. Only if you score 75 percent or better should you proceed to the real thing (otherwise, obtain some additional practice tests and keep trying until you hit this magic number).

 If you take a practice exam and don't score at least 75 percent correct, you'll want to practice further. Microsoft provides free Personal Exam Prep (PEP) exams and also offers self-assessment exams from the Microsoft Certified Professional Web site's download page (**www.microsoft.com/train_cert/download/downld.htm**). If you're more ambitious or better funded, you might want to purchase a practice exam from a third-party vendor. Check the Online Resources part of this book (right before the Glossary) for pointers.

As a special bonus to readers of this book, your authors have created an adaptive practice exam on Windows NT Workstation. Coriolis offers this practice exam on its Web site at **www.coriolis.com/cip/core4rev**.

Additional Resources

A good source of information about Microsoft certification exams comes from Microsoft itself. Because its products and technologies—and the exams that go with them—change frequently, the best place to go for exam-related information is online.

If you haven't already visited the Microsoft Certified Professional site, do so right now. The MCP home page resides at **www.microsoft.com/mcp/certstep/mcps.htm**.

Note: This page might not be there by the time you read this, or may be replaced by something new and different, because things change regularly on the Microsoft site.

As you browse through this page, and other pages that it points to—and we strongly recommend that you do—you'll probably find other informational tidbits mentioned that are every bit as interesting and compelling.

Windows NT Architecture

Terms you'll need to understand:

√   Multitasking

√   Multithreaded

√   Multiprocessor

√   User mode

√   Kernel mode

√   Executive Services

√   Virtual Memory Manager (VMM)

√   Demand paging

√   Hardware Abstraction Layer (HAL)

√   File Allocation Table (FAT)

√   New Technology File System (NTFS)

√   CD-ROM File System (CDFS)

Techniques you'll need to master:

√   Understanding the Windows NT architecture

√   Knowing the differences between Windows NT Workstation, Windows NT Server, and Windows 95 and 98

Windows NT Workstation is the client product of the Microsoft Windows NT family of network operating systems. In this chapter, we introduce you to the major architectural underpinnings of Windows NT. This is a preparatory chapter that builds a framework for later discussions. This is not a chapter (or a book, for that matter) to introduce you to Windows NT. If you are not already familiar with the basics of Windows NT and the Microsoft product line, then much of the material covered in this and subsequent chapters will be fairly difficult to grasp. This book is designed to help you study for the certification exams; it is not a primer or an administrative guide to the network operating system (NOS).

Basic Features

Windows NT Workstation is a graphical, secure, 32-bit network operating system. The most notable difference between this version and previous versions is the adoption of the Windows 95 look and feel. The real differences between Windows NT Workstation and Windows 95 and 98 are detailed later in this chapter.

Each of these features is discussed in detail in subsequent chapters:

➤ **Portable** Windows NT can be installed on Intel 486, Pentium; IBM/Motorola PowerPC; MIPS R4x00; and DEC Alpha AXP CPUs. (Microsoft support has terminated support for MIPS and PowerPC.) The CPU-specific source files are all found on the distribution CD.

➤ **Multitasking** Windows NT is a preemptive, multitasking OS that also supports cooperative multitasking for Win16 applications within a single Windows on Windows (WOW) instance.

➤ **Multithreaded** More than one thread from a single application can be executed simultaneously.

➤ **Multiprocessor** Windows NT Workstation runs on a one- or two-CPU system.

➤ **File Systems** Windows NT supports FAT, NTFS, and CDFS (read-only CD-ROM support).

➤ **Security** Windows NT offers numerous security features, such as user authentication, access tokens, ACLs, auditing, memory protection, and so on. Windows NT can be configured to meet the U.S. DOD Class C2 and the EEC E3 security specifications.

➤ **Clients** Windows NT can directly support all the Microsoft OSs as clients; in addition, it has limited support for OS/2, Macintosh, and Unix. Via Peer Web Service (PWS), Windows NT Workstation can service any client that supports TCP/IP.

➤ **Applications** Windows NT supports Win32, Win16, DOS, POSIX-1, and OS/2 1.x applications.

➤ **Storage** Windows NT supports 4 GB of physical memory and 16 EB (Exabytes) of storage space. (1 EB = 1,024 PB [petabytes] = 1,048,596 TB. 1 PB = 1,024 TB = 1,048,596 GB.)

➤ **Networks** Windows NT supports TCP/IP, NWLink (IPX/SPX), NetBEUI, AppleTalk, and DLC network protocols.

For these topics to make sense, we need to establish the base architecture of Windows NT. The next sections are devoted to this. We cover such architecture components as Windows NT's different modes, its memory organization, as well as the differences between the Windows NT Workstation, Windows NT Server, and Windows 95 and 98 operating systems.

User And Kernel Mode

Windows NT is a modular NOS. This means that Windows NT is not a single, contiguous collection of programming code, but rather, it is a multi-faceted entity built by combining individual components. Each significant system function is packed within a single module or component. No two modules share any code—they are completely "code isolated" from each other. This enables the Microsoft engineers to improve, exchange, or correct a single feature of Windows NT without affecting the entire system or requiring lengthy system-wide reprogramming.

Figure 2.1 illustrates a high-level view of the larger components of Windows NT. Within each of these sections are even smaller modules. However, this level of division adequately separates different activities and conglomerated related functions. The most significant division presented in this image is that of User mode and Kernel mode.

A mode is a programming and operational separation of components, functions, and services. Each mode contains only those features required to perform any and all operations delegated to that mode.

Figure 2.1 The major architectural divisions of Windows NT.

User Mode

User applications and the environmental subsystems live or execute in the User mode. The User mode is the only mode within which a user can interact with the OS. This mode is nonprivileged—all processes operating within User mode must use the Executive Services (a component of the Kernel mode) to gain access to memory or hardware devices. The User mode contains two important subsystem types: environment and security.

Environment

The environmental subsystems host the virtual machines within which user applications are executed. The following are the three main native environmental subsystems:

➤ **Win32** Supports Windows 32-bit, Windows 16-bit, and DOS applications. Win32 also controls the Windows NT user interface.

➤ **POSIX** Limited support for POSIX-1 applications.

➤ **OS/2** Limited support for OS/2 1.x applications.

These subsystems are discussed in Chapter 16.

Security

The security subsystem is responsible for the logon process. It works with the Executive Services' Security Reference Monitor to validate users. Each time a logon attempt occurs, an authentication package is created and sent into the Kernel mode. The Security Reference Monitor compares its contents with its security accounts database (known as the SAM database). The Security Reference Monitor then builds and returns an access token if a valid username and password are contained in the authentication package.

Logon-related security issues are discussed in Chapters 4, 7, and 8.

Kernel Mode

The Kernel mode is the inner core of the operating system. It is a privileged processor mode, meaning the components in this mode have execution priority over all User mode processes. A significant portion of the Kernel is maintained in memory and cannot be (or is not) swapped out to disk by the Virtual Memory Manager (VMM).

Through the Kernel mode, Windows NT protects the hardware and all system-level components from user applications. Therefore, user applications cannot make hardware-direct calls; instead, the application must make a request to the Kernel mode. This surrogate-like activity maintains a reliable computing environment and protects the system from poorly written applications.

The Kernel mode contains three important subsystems:

➤ Executive Services

➤ Kernel

➤ Hardware Abstraction Layer (HAL)

Executive Services

Executive Services (also known as the Windows NT Executive) is the interface between the Kernel and the environmental subsystems of the User mode.

The Windows NT Executive provides services through the following six modules:

➤ **Object Manager** Controls activities related to objects. These activities include use, naming, removing, tracking, and security of objects.

➤ **Security Reference Monitor** Handles logon procedures, user authentication, access validation, and the security subsystem in the User mode.

➤ **Process Manager** Manages process activities, such as creation, deletion, and tracking.

➤ **Local Procedure Call Facility** Maintains communications, user applications, and environmental subsystems.

➤ **Virtual Memory Manager** Maintains and controls physical and virtual memory.

➤ **I/O Manager** Oversees all input and output. The I/O Manager acts like a proxy by intercepting an application's requests and directing commands to the appropriate hardware drivers.

Kernel

The central core of the Windows NT operating system is called the Kernel. Its primary task is to manage all system activities (threads) while attempting to maintain optimal system performance through scheduling CPU allocation time for applications.

Hardware Abstraction Layer (HAL)

The Hardware Abstraction Layer (HAL) is the Windows NT module where all hardware-specific components and configurations are stored. The collection of hardware-specific information in this module enables Windows NT to be easily ported to different platforms. The HAL is the only module of Windows NT that must be customized for new hardware.

Windows NT Memory Organization

Windows NT's memory architecture is one of the central design elements that has established this NOS as robust, reliable, and scaleable. Windows NT's memory organization is a single, contiguous block without any divisions. This type of memory is called "flat linear 32-bit addressing memory."

Windows NT does not divide memory into conventional, upper, and extended sections; however, these settings can be defined for a subsystem virtual machine if required by a DOS or Win16 application.

Windows NT's memory is managed by the Virtual Memory Manager (VMM) of the Executive Services. Each time an application is launched (more specifically, each time a new subsystem virtual machine is created), the VMM assigns it a 4 GB memory address space. Through a process of memory address mapping, the VMM maintains the relationship between the 4 GB assigned address space of each application and the actual memory present on the machine.

The total amount of memory used by Windows NT is a combination of physical RAM and the size of the paging file. A paging file is a temporary storage file on a hard drive used by the VMM to hold seldom-used memory pages. The extra memory availed by this process is called "virtual memory." VMM manages physical RAM, virtual memory, and the address space of each application. The management process completely fools the application into perceiving that 4 GB of real, usable memory exists.

The process used by the VMM to manage virtual memory is called "demand paging." The address space of applications and the usable memory of a system are segmented into 4 K chunks. Unused or little-used (memory blocks that are accessed infrequently) blocks of memory are moved from physical RAM to the hard drive's paging file. When an application requests a segment of memory not in physical RAM, the VMM swaps a section of physical RAM with the requested section of paging file stored data. This page swapping occurs on demand.

Because virtual memory relies on a hard drive to extend the physical RAM, the performance of the machine can be affected if too much paging takes place. Hard drive speeds are extremely slow when compared to that of RAM.

Details on setting paging file parameters and detecting high levels of page swapping are highlighted in Chapter 15.

Server And Workstation Differences

Windows NT Server and Windows NT Workstation are at the core of the same operating system because they have so many modules and code segments

Table 2.1 Differences between Windows NT Server and Windows NT Workstation.

Area	Windows NT Workstation	Windows NT Server
Simultaneous connections	10	Unlimited
Multiprocessor	2	4 (32 with OEM)
RAS sessions	1	256
Replication	Import	Import and export
Network services	None	DHCP server, DNS server, and WINS server
Internet services	Peer Web Services	Internet Information Server
Network server	No	Yes
Macintosh services	No	Yes
Disk fault tolerance	No	Yes (RAID 1, 5)
Domain logon validation	No	Yes

in common. However, there are still significant differences of which you need to be aware. These are listed in Table 2.1.

As you can see in this table, most of the differences relate to issues around supporting network functionality and features.

Windows NT Workstation And Windows 95 and 98 Comparison

Even though Windows NT Workstation shares the same look and feel with Windows 95 and 98, there are many significant differences between them. These differences are detailed in Table 2.2.

Table 2.2   The differences between Windows NT Workstation and Windows 95 and 98.

Area	Windows NT Workstation	Windows 95 and 98
Uses DOS and Win16 device drivers	No	Yes
Multiplatform	Yes	No
Multiprocessors	Yes	No
Win16 applications	Yes	Yes
DOS applications	Yes	Yes
POSIX and OS/2 applications	Yes	No
File systems	NTFS, FAT	VFAT, FAT32
Plug and Play	No	Yes
Application/memory protection	Yes	No
Internet services	Peer Web Services	Yes (add-on product)
RAS	Inbound and outbound	Outbound only

* The versions of FAT implemented in Windows NT are virtually identical to one version of FAT, sometimes called VFAT, introduced with Windows 95 OSR1.

From this table, you can see the wide variance in OS capabilities between Windows NT Workstation and Windows 95 and 98.

Practice Questions

Question 1

> Which of the following are features of Windows NT Workstation?
> [Check all correct answers]
>
> ❑ a. Multiplatform support
>
> ❑ b. Wide range of security features
>
> ❑ c. Supports POSIX and OS/2 1.x character mode
>   applications
>
> ❑ d. Supports DNS and WINS servers
>
> ❑ e. Supports DLC and IPX/SPX protocols

Answers a, b, c, and e are correct. Windows NT Workstation supports many platforms, has numerous security features, supports POSIX and OS/2 1.x character mode applications, and supports DLC and IPX/SPX protocols. Windows NT Workstation does not support or host DNS or WINS servers—these are found only on Windows NT Server. Therefore, answer d is incorrect.

Question 2

> In which mode do the application subsystems exist?
>
> ○ a. User
>
> ○ b. Kernel

Answer a is correct. The application subsystems exist in the User mode.

Question 3

> Windows NT can host 5 GB of storage space.
>
> ○ a. True
>
> ○ b. False

Answer a is correct. Windows NT can support up to 16 EB of storage space, and 5 GB is less than that. However, the trick to this question is that 4 GB is the limitation of memory, and the use of that number may throw you off.

Question 4

> Which of the following is not true about Windows NT Workstation?
>
> ○ a. Supports up to two processors
>
> ○ b. Supports the AppleTalk protocol
>
> ○ c. Supports the FAT file system
>
> ○ d. Supports the Sun Solaris platform
>
> ○ e. Supports multithreading

Answer d is correct. Windows NT Workstation does not support the Sun Solaris platform. Windows NT Workstation supports two processors, AppleTalk, FAT, and multithreading. Therefore, answers a, b, c, and e are incorrect.

Question 5

> What components are found in the Kernel mode? [Check all correct answers]
>
> ❑ a. HAL
>
> ❑ b. Executive Services
>
> ❑ c. Security Reference Monitor
>
> ❑ d. Logon process
>
> ❑ e. I/O Manager
>
> ❑ f. User applications

Answers a, b, c, and e are correct. The Kernel mode is host to the HAL, the Executive Services, the Security Reference Monitor, and the I/O Manager. The logon process and user applications exist in the User mode. Therefore, answers d and f are incorrect.

Question 6

> Which of the following statements are true for virtual memory?
> [Check all correct answers]
>
> ❑ a. Managed by a component of the Executive Services
> ❑ b. Created by using hard drive space
> ❑ c. Accessed directly by applications
> ❑ d. Combined with physical RAM to increase usable memory
> ❑ e. Faster than physical RAM

Answers a, b, and d are correct. Virtual memory is managed by a component of the Executive Services, is created by using hard drive space, and is combined with physical RAM to increase usable memory. Virtual memory is not accessed directly by applications and is slower than physical RAM. Therefore, answers c and e are incorrect.

Question 7

> Which of the following two items do Windows NT Workstation
> and Windows NT Server have in common? [Check all correct
> answers]
>
> ❑ a. Some replication support
> ❑ b. Unlimited simultaneous connections
> ❑ c. 256 RAS sessions
> ❑ d. Fault tolerance
> ❑ e. Multiprocessor support

Answers a and e are correct. Windows NT Server and Windows NT Workstation only share replication support (Windows NT Workstation is import-only) and multiprocessor support (Windows NT Workstation is 2, Windows NT Server is 4 or up to 32 with OEM). Windows NT Workstation is limited to 10 simultaneous connections, 1 RAS session, and has no fault tolerance. Therefore, answers b, c, and d are incorrect.

Question 8

What do Windows NT Workstation and Windows 95 have in common? [Check all correct answers]

❑   a. Plug and Play

❑   b. Win16 and DOS application support

❑   c. VFAT

❑   d. Outbound RAS

Answers b, c, and d are correct. Windows NT Workstation and Windows 95 both support Win16 and DOS, VFAT, and outbound RAS. Windows NT Workstation does not support Plug and Play. Therefore, answer a is incorrect.

Question 9

How large is a VMM managed page?

○   a. 2 K

○   b. 4 K

○   c. 64 K

○   d. 4 GB

Answer b is correct. A VMM page is 4 K in size.

Question 10

The HAL is the only significant component of Windows NT that varies between the supported hardware platforms.

○   a. True

○   b. False

Answer a is correct. The HAL is where all the platform-specific configuration is stored, and it is easily replaced with an alternative version for other platforms.

Need To Know More?

Perkins, Charles, Matthew Strebe, and James Chellis: *MCSE: NT Workstation Study Guide, 2nd Edition.* Sybex Network Press, San Francisco, CA, 1998. ISBN 0-7821-2223-X. Chapter 1 discusses the overall architecture of Windows NT Workstation as well as a few more introductory details we did not mention (because they are not on the test).

Solomon, David A.: *Inside Windows NT, 2nd Edition.* Microsoft Press, Redmond, WA, 1998. ISBN 1-57231-677-2. Provides the best overview of Windows NT architecture and internals available in print today.

Search the TechNet CD (or its online version through **www.microsoft.com**) and the *Windows NT Workstation Resource Kit* CD using the keywords "mode," "Executive Services," "VMM," "HAL," "Windows 95 comparison," and "Windows NT Server comparison."

Installing And Configuring Workstation

3

- -

Terms you'll need to understand:

- √ Hardware Compatibility List (HCL)
- √ Windows NT Hardware Qualifier (NTHQ)
- √ Dual boot
- √ BOOT.INI
- √ WINNT.EXE
- √ WINNT32.EXE
- √ FDISK
- √ UNATTEND.TXT
- √ Uniqueness Database File (UDF)
- √ SYSDIFF

Techniques you'll need to master:

- √ Understanding the different ways you can install Windows NT
- √ Knowing how to perform an unattended installation
- √ Performing a Windows NT installation
- √ Uninstalling Windows NT

The procedures involved in installing Windows NT Workstation are key elements for understanding the OS. In this chapter, we present the details you must know for installation, but we highly recommend you take the time to install Windows NT Workstation once or twice on your own. Doing so will help you establish a solid understanding of the processes encountered during setup.

Preinstallation Requirements

The Windows NT operating system will only function properly if it is installed onto a computer comprised of compatible components. The list of these components is called the Hardware Compatibility List (HCL). In addition to listing supported devices, it also informs you if the driver for each device is:

➤ Included in the standard collection of distribution files

➤ Stored on the CD-ROM, but in an alternate specialized directory

➤ Only available directly from the vendor

A version of the HCL, dated August 9, 1996, is stored on the Windows NT Workstation 4 distribution CD-ROM in \SUPPORT\HCL.HLP. The latest version of the HCL is available on the Microsoft Web site (**www.microsoft.com**) for direct viewing or downloading. To find the newest HCL, search Microsoft's search engine for "HCL."

Fortunately, you don't need to memorize the HCL, but there are some important prerequisites you do need to know:

Intel-based:

➤ 486 DX33 (or faster) or Pentium-based system

➤ 12 MB of memory (RAM); 16 MB recommended

➤ 120 MB of available hard disk space

➤ CD-ROM drive or access the installation files over a computer network

➤ VGA or higher-resolution display adapter

RISC-based:

➤ Alpha AXP, MIPS R4x00 or PowerPC processor

➤ 16 MB of memory; 24 MB recommended

➤ 150 MB of available hard disk space

➤ CD-ROM drive

➤ VGA or higher-resolution display adapter

Optional hardware:

➤ Network adapter card

➤ Audio board/sound card

➤ Microsoft Mouse or compatible pointing device

Microsoft has provided a useful tool called the NTHQ that helps determine if your computer meets the minimum requirements and if your components are on the HCL.

Windows NT Hardware Qualifier Disk

The Windows NT Hardware Qualifier (NTHQ) disk is a simple utility that inspects your computer and provides you with a detailed report of any suspected or definite incompatibility problems. NTHQ is found in the \SUPPORT\HQTOOL directory on the CD-ROM. It is installed onto a floppy and used to boot the computer.

 The NTHQ is only as good as the HCL it references, which is dated Aug. 9, 1996. Therefore, the CD-ROM version no longer has many useful applications.

Installing Vs. Upgrading

There are two possible methods for Windows NT Workstation installation: complete and upgrade. In the following sections, we explain each of these methods in detail.

Complete Installation Of Windows NT 4 Workstation

A complete installation of Windows NT assumes that the computer is without a current OS or that any existing OS can be completely overwritten. Performing a complete install overwrites any existing version of Windows NT, and a new Security ID (SID) will be assigned to that computer. This method is used for the initial installation, installing multiple OSs on different partitions, or starting over from scratch.

Upgrade Installation Of Windows NT 4 Workstation

An upgrade installation replaces all Windows NT files, but it retains most of the Registry settings, application installation changes, and the SID. An upgrade can be performed on many OSs, including DOS, Windows 3.x, Windows 95 and 98, and Windows NT Workstation 3.51 and 4. However, little to nothing from DOS, Windows 3.x, and Windows 95 and 98 is migrated into Windows NT 4 due to wide variance in architecture. Therefore, upgrading is only a realistic possibility for the Windows NT level of Microsoft OSs. The upgrade installation is a common troubleshooting tool when less drastic measures have already been exhausted.

Booting Multiple OSs

Although it's a security risk on production machines, Windows NT Workstation can be installed with other OSs on the same computer. Windows NT Workstation can exist without problems on a computer with Windows 95 or 98, Windows For Workgroups, Windows 3.x, or DOS. For such a dual-boot to exist, it is recommended that you install the Microsoft non-Windows NT OS first and then install Windows NT onto a different partition. The resultant BOOT.INI file will contain the two standard lines for Windows NT's normal and safe boot modes as well as a third entry for the alternate operating system—which is usually labeled MS-DOS, by default. You do have to keep in mind that non-Windows NT OSs will not be able to read any data stored on NTFS volumes.

 It is important to install each OS onto a different partition because Microsoft's Windows OSs use similar naming conventions for directories. By installing each on a separate partition, the required files are not overwritten by the same-named files from another OS. Two examples of this are the \Windows default directory name and the \Program Files common application installation folder.

Windows NT can also be installed in a multiboot configuration with other OSs, but the ease of installation and operation will vary. OS/2 is shipped with its own version of a boot manager. When Windows NT is installed onto an OS/2 machine, the OS/2 boot manager is disabled in favor of the Windows NT boot manager. You can revert to the OS/2 boot manager by setting the small OS/2 boot manager partition to active through Disk Administrator. If this change is made, the OS/2 boot manager will be displayed. If DOS or Windows is selected, the Windows NT boot manager is then displayed.

To remove an alternate OS from the boot manager, simply edit the BOOT.INI file and delete the ARC name\path entry. These procedures are discussed in Chapters 17 and 18.

Planning Windows NT Workstation Installation

The actual installation of Windows NT is not difficult. However, to ensure that the operation goes smoothly, several issues must be resolved beforehand.

The WINNT Installation File And Distribution Directories

The installation of Windows NT Workstation is initiated through the execution of the WINNT.EXE utility, which is a 16-bit application that will function under DOS, Windows 3.x, Windows 95 and 98, and Windows NT. There is also a 32-bit version, WINNT32.EXE, for exclusive use within Windows NT for better performance.

This utility has many switches and parameters for controlling or altering the installation procedure. These parameters, shown in Table 3.1, are important to know for installation.

Table 3.1 WINNT.EXE and WINNT32.EXE switches and parameters.	
Parameter	**Description**
/B	Installs Windows NT Workstation without using the boot floppies.
/C	Skips the check for available space on the installation boot floppies. WINNT.EXE only.
/F	Copies the files from the boot floppies without verifying the copies. WINNT.EXE only.
/I:*inf_file*	Specifies the file name for the setup information file. The default is DOSNET.INF.
/OX	Creates boot floppies but does not start the installation.
/R	Specifies optional directory to be installed.
/RX	Specifies optional directory to be copied.

(continued)

Table 3.1   WINNT.EXE and WINNT32.EXE switches and parameters (continued).

Parameter	Description
/S:*sourcepath*	Specifies the source of the Windows NT setup files. This must be a fully qualified path in the form drive_letter:\path or \\server_name\share\path. The current directory is the default source for the installation files.
/T:*drive*	Specifies the drive in which to place the temporary setup files.
/U:*answer_file*	Specifies an unattended installation and lists the optional script file.
/UDF:*id*, [*UDF_file*]	Specifies the identifier that is to be used to apply sections of the UDF_file in place of the same section in the answer_file. If no UDF is specified, the Setup program will prompt the user to insert a disk that contains a file called $UNIQUE$.UDF. If a UDF is specified, Setup will look for the identifier in that file.

There are four OS-specific directories on the Windows NT Workstation distribution CD-ROM. These directories correspond to the four CPU types supported by Windows NT. Be sure to launch the WINNT utility from the appropriate directory for your platform type.

➤ **\alpha** DEC Alpha AXP

➤ **\i386** Intel CPUs

➤ **\mips** MIPS R4x00

➤ **\ppc** IBM/Motorola PowerPC

If you do not have the three Windows NT boot and setup disks, you can create them by launching WINNT or WINNT32 with or without the /OX parameter. The floppies must be preformatted. The /OX parameter will not start the install once the floppies are created; without the /OX parameters, the install process will begin after the floppies are created. The floppies are built in reverse order, starting with 3, moving to 2, and then 1.

Selecting An Installation Method

Windows NT Workstation can be installed via several methods:

➤ From an HCL-compatible CD-ROM with boot floppy disks

➤ From a CD-ROM in an existing OS without boot floppies

➤ From a network share

Each of these methods is discussed in the following sections.

From An HCL-Compatible CD-ROM Drive With Boot Floppies

If the CD-ROM is HCL-compatible, the three Windows NT boot floppies can be used to install Windows NT. No OS is required to be present on the computer. Using the boot floppies is effectively launching WINNT.EXE without any parameters.

From A CD-ROM In An Existing OS Without Boot Floppies

If an OS is present on the computer, boot floppies can be avoided by launching WINNT.EXE with the /B option. This instructs the Setup utility to copy the files otherwise found on the boot floppies to a hard drive so they can be launched when the machine next reboots.

If an OS is present and the CD-ROM is not HCL compatible, the distribution directory for the appropriate platform can be copied to the hard drive. Then, the WINNT utility can be launched from the hard drive with the /B option.

From A Network Share

If an OS is present on the computer and it has network access, the Windows NT distribution files can be accessed from a network share. The Setup utility can be launched from the share, provided that the NIC and the network's protocols are supported by Windows NT. Once again, the /B option can be used to avoid the floppies. The share can be the CD-ROM itself or a copy of the distribution directory on a server's hard drive. We recommend the latter for its performance (speed) benefits.

If the NIC or protocols are not supported by Windows NT, the entire distribution directory can be copied to the local drive. Then, WINNT can be launched locally with the /B option.

If your computer does not have an OS, a client boot/install disk can be built from a Windows NT Server's Client Administrator utility. This disk will bootstrap the computer to the network with a DOS OS, giving the machine just enough network capabilities to copy the distribution files to a local drive.

Windows NT does *not* support a network installation for RISC platforms.

Partitioning The Hard Drive

If multiple OSs are to be used on the same machine, partitioning the hard drive is best performed using the DOS utility FDISK. Otherwise, the Setup utility will enable you to modify your partitions before selecting the destination partition for the NOS. When changing partitions, you should keep in mind that removing a partition destroys the data it contains.

Details To Collect

The installation process will prompt you for numerous pieces of information; it's a good idea to have the following information at hand before starting:

➤ **Computer name** The name of the computer. This should comply with a naming convention used by your organization.

➤ **Domain or Workgroup name** The name of the domain or workgroup in which this computer will participate.

➤ **Device configuration settings** The configuration settings for each device in your computer, especially NICs and devices that require third-party drivers.

➤ **Partitions** The number, order, and size of existing or desired partitions.

➤ **Name of the Windows NT directory** The name of the main Windows NT system directory; the default is \WINNT.

➤ **Protocols** Which protocol(s) you want to use, as well as any settings related to the selected protocols (see Chapters 9, 10, and 11).

➤ **Licensing** Who the product is licensed to. Enter the name and organization.

➤ **Administrator password** This is the initial password for the Administrator account.

Automated Windows NT Workstation Installation

Even though the installation of Windows NT is often fairly simple, it can take over an hour to complete, especially if the CD-ROM or network transfer speed is poor. Microsoft has provided two ways to speed and automate the install process.

Unattended Install

An unattended (or automated) install can be performed by using special script files that contain all of the details normally provided by a human operator. The first file, UNATTEND.TXT, can be used to install or upgrade to Windows NT Workstation 4 on multiple machines with similar configurations. An example of this file can be found in each of the platform-specific subdirectories. Here is the Intel sample file:

```
; Microsoft Windows NT Workstation Version 4.0 and
; Windows NT Server Version 4.0
; (c) 1994 - 1996 Microsoft Corporation. All rights reserved.
;
; Sample Unattended Setup Answer File
;
; This file contains information about how to automate the
; installation or upgrade of Windows NT Workstation and Windows
; NT Server so the Setup program runs without requiring user
; input.
;
; For information on how to use this file, read the appropriate
; sections of the Windows NT 4.0 Resource Kit.

[Unattended]
OemPreinstall = no
ConfirmHardware = no
NtUpgrade = no
Win31Upgrade = no
TargetPath = WINNT
OverwriteOemFilesOnUpgrade = no

[UserData]
FullName = Your User Name
OrgName = Your Organization Name
ComputerName = COMPUTER_NAME
```

```
[GuiUnattended]
TimeZone = (GMT-08:00) Pacific Time (US & Canada); Tijuana

[Display]
ConfigureAtLogon = 0
BitsPerPel = 16
XResolution = 640
YResolution = 480
VRefresh = 70
AutoConfirm = 1

[Network]
Attend = yes
DetectAdapters = ""
InstallProtocols = ProtocolsSection
JoinDomain = Domain_To_Join

[ProtocolsSection]
TC = TCParameters

[TCParameters]
DHCP = yes
```

You can modify this file manually to match your needs. Or, you can use the SETUPMGR.EXE utility (located in the \support\deptools*platform type* directory) to create this file. The Setup Manager uses a three-button (General, Networking, and Advanced) GUI interface to simplify the process of creating the UNATTEND.TXT file. You might want to use this utility once just to familiarize yourself with it.

To use the UNATTEND.TXT file to automate an installation, you need to use specific parameters on the WINNT Setup utility, as follows:

```
WINNT /S:d:\i386 /U:c:\unattend.txt
```

Note that /S is required to define the source of the distribution files when /U is used.

A second script file can be used in conjunction with the UNATTEND.TXT file to specify different computer-specific details without having to create a unique UNATTEND.TXT for each machine. This is called a Uniqueness Database File (UDF). A UDF is created by hand using a text editor. It begins with a section that defines IDs for each computer and what sections of UNATTEND.TXT need modification for this specific computer. The remainder of the UDF simply defines the changes for each machine, based on the ID of that machine and the section of the install to which the modification corresponds. The details used in the text portion of the install (see the section entitled "Text Portion" later in this chapter) are only specified in the UNATTEND.TXT file, not in the UDF. The sections can be the following:

➤ **[OEM_Ads]** Defines the banner, logo, and background bitmap to be displayed during GUI mode setup.

➤ **[DisplayDrivers]** Specifies display drivers.

➤ **[Display]** Specifies video display settings.

➤ **[GuiUnattended]** Defines the behavior of the Setup program during GUI mode setup.

➤ **[UserData]** Specifies information associated with each user or computer.

➤ **[Network]** Specifies network settings, such as protocols and adapters. If this section is not present, support for networking will not be installed.

➤ **[Modem]** Identifies whether a modem should be installed. It is used by RAS to install a modem if **DeviceType = Modem** is in the list of RAS parameters.

If the sample UNATTEND.TXT file was used, a possible UDF file could look like this:

```
[UniqueIds]
id1 = UserData,GuiUnattended
id2 = UserData
id3 = UserData,GuiUnattended,Display
[id1:userdata]
FullName = "Bob Smith"
OrgName = "LivePeople Inc."
ComputerName = Sales_02
[id1:GuiUnattended]
TimeZone = "(GMT-06:00) Central Time (US & Canada)"
[id2:userdata]
FullName = "Mary Jones"
OrgName = "LivePeople Inc."
ComputerName = Sales_05
[id3:userdata]
FullName = "Rebecca Doe"
OrgName = "LivePeople Inc."
```

```
ComputerName = Sales_01
[id3:GuiUnattended]
TimeZone = "(GMT-06:00) Central Time (US & Canada)"
[id3:Display]
XResolution = 1024
YResolution = 768
```

To use a UDF file to automate installation, apply the following syntax on each defined machine, but alter the ID value to match that of the computer:

```
WINNT /S:d:\i386 /U:c:\unattend.txt /UDF:ID1,udfsales.txt
```

SYSDIFF Utility

Another method for customizing Windows NT's installation process is to use the SYSDIFF utility. SYSDIFF is used to record the differences between a normal (or default) installation of Windows NT Workstation and an installation of Windows NT that has been customized and has had additional applications added. Thus, with this data, the setup of other machines with the same (or nearly the same) requirements of hardware and software is greatly simplified.

The SYSDIFF program can perform five functions:

➤ **Snap** A snapshot of Windows NT, including the Registry and file system, is taken and recorded to a file.

➤ **Diff** Records another snapshot of Windows NT that only stores the changes made since the original snapshot. This is the difference file.

➤ **Apply** Applies the difference file to another installation of Windows NT.

➤ **Inf** Creates an INF file and installation data files from a difference file. These items can be stored with a network share copy of the Windows NT distribution files to automate the process of initial setup of Windows NT and application of the difference file to the new install (used with **/I:*INF_FILE***).

➤ **Dump** Creates a directory or contents list of the changes to be found in the difference file.

The command-line parameters and syntax of SYSDIFF are

```
sysdiff /snap [/log:log_file] snapshot_file
sysdiff /diff [/c:title] [/log:log_file] snapshot_file
difference_file
```

```
sysdiff /apply /m [/log:log_file] difference_file
sysdiff /inf /m [/u] difference_file oem_root
sysdiff /dump difference_file dump_file
```

where:

- ➤ **/log:log_file** records the activity of the utility.

- ➤ **snapshot_file** is the recording of the initial state of the Windows NT installation.

- ➤ **/c:*title*** defines a title for the difference package.

- ➤ **difference_file** is the recording of the difference between the current state of the Windows NT installation and the snapshot_file.

- ➤ **/m** forces file changes in the per-user profile structure to be mapped to the Default User profile structure, rather than to the profile structure of the user logged on when the difference file was created.

- ➤ **/u** specifies that the INF file should be generated as a Unicode text file instead of the default system ANSI codepage.

- ➤ **oem_root** is the destination of the INF and data files for custom installation.

- ➤ **dump_file** defines the name for the dump file.

Actual Installation Step-By-Step

Once you have started the installation, whether by using the three boot floppies or by launching WINNT(32) /B, it proceeds in the following order.

Text Portion

The installation process begins in a blue background with a white text-based environment. When the text portion completes, your computer will reboot to the GUI portion of the installation.

Initial Selection Screen

The first menu presented by Setup includes the following choices:

- ➤ **F1** Learn more about Windows NT Workstation before continuing with Setup

- ➤ **ENTER** Set up Windows NT

> ➤ **R** Repair damage to an existing installation of Windows NT (as described in Chapter 18)

> ➤ **F3** Exit Setup

Hardware Detection

Windows NT attempts to identify the storage devices and controller cards present on your system. It will display a list of what it finds. If the list is incomplete or wrong, pressing **S** will enable you to select from a list of supported devices or to install a vendor-provided driver.

Next, Windows NT Workstation displays what it has found for other devices: computer type, display, keyboard, language, and pointing device. You are given the opportunity to change these settings or continue.

File Systems And Partitions

The next section displays a list of existing partitions and unused space on your hard drives. If the correct partition is present, it can be selected as the destination for Windows NT. If not, new partitions can be created and existing ones deleted. Once the destination partition is selected, Windows NT prompts you for a file system type to be used to format the partition. You have the choices of leaving it "as is" (for preexisting partitions only), or selecting FAT or NTFS. You also have the choice of converting preexisting FAT partitions to NTFS; all existing data will be maintained.

Windows Main Directory

Setup will detect if an existing version of Windows NT Workstation is present on the destination partition. If one is found, you'll be prompted to upgrade or overwrite it (the current main directory name will be used). If no other version exists, you are prompted for the main directory name for Windows NT. The default is \WINNT.

System Examination

Setup prompts for a cursory or an exhaustive hard disk examination. The former will take a few seconds, whereas the latter will take much longer (depending on the partition size). Once the examination is complete, Setup performs file copies and then reboots your computer.

GUI Portion

The remainder of the setup process occurs in a basic Windows graphical environment. You can use a mouse or keyboard commands to move around and respond to queries.

Option Selection

A menu appears with the following selections:

➤ **Typical** Installs those features Microsoft deems the most common.

➤ **Portable** Optimizes the installation for a mobile computer or one not always connected to the network.

➤ **Compact** Installs the minimum necessary features.

➤ **Custom** Installs only manually selected features.

Next, enter your name and the name of your organization.

Computer Name

You can define the computer name for this machine—it can be up to 15 characters long—as well as the Administrator account password.

Emergency Repair Disk

You can instruct the Setup utility to create or bypass an ERD once installation is complete.

Components

You can choose the noncritical components of Windows NT Workstation for installation by selecting the most common option or displaying a list that allows you to choose.

Network Configuration

You can select whether the computer is attached directly to a network, through remote access, or not at all. Next, the network interface card (NIC) is installed. By selecting Detect, you cause Windows NT Workstation to attempt to discover through hardware calls the nature of the NIC. If found, you need to verify the make and model. If not found, you can select from a list or install drivers from the vendor.

If you do not have an adapter already installed, select Microsoft, MS Loopback Adapter. This is a software device that fools Windows NT into thinking a real NIC exists. Once you physically install a NIC, you can install the correct drivers and remove this facade.

Protocols

You select the protocols to be used on the network. The default options are TCP/IP, NWLink, and NetBEUI. Additional protocols, such as DLC, can be installed at this point. Once the protocols are selected, you'll need to define and set the relevant parameters for each protocol.

Workgroup/Domain

Windows NT Workstation can be a member of a workgroup or a domain, but not both at the same time. At this point, choose the appropriate membership type and then define that group's name—WORKGROUP and DOMAIN are default values for these. If you select DOMAIN, you need to provide the name of a domain Administrator account and its password so that a computer account can be created for the Windows NT Workstation. This is not required if an account with the same computer name has already been created through the Server Manager on a domain controller.

Final Settings

The last two option screens allow you to define the time zone, set the time, and select the display settings. Once the computer reboots, the Windows NT installation is complete.

Uninstalling Windows NT Workstation

If you need to remove Windows NT Workstation from your computer, you'll have to do it manually. Workstation does not have a specific uninstall utility. However, the following steps can be used to remove it:

1. Back up all important files from any NTFS partitions.

2. Remove NTFS partitions.

3. Change the bootstrap routine.

4. Delete the following Windows NT Workstation directories and files: \winnt, \program files, NTLDR, BOOT.INI, NTDETECT.COM, PAGEFILE.SYS, and BOOTSECT.DOS

A primary NTFS partition can be deleted by DOS FDISK, but not logical drives in an extended partition. That requires using the three boot diskettes to return to the destination partition section, deleting all existing partitions, and then exiting setup.

Changing the bootstrap routine involves using the command **SYS C:** from a DOS disk to remove the Windows NT boot manager.

Practice Questions

Question 1

> Which of the following are provided by the HCL? [Check all correct answers]
>
> ❑ a. A list of Windows NT Workstation supported hardware
>
> ❑ b. A list of tested but nonfunctioning hardware
>
> ❑ c. Contact information for each vendor
>
> ❑ d. Where the driver is located on the CD-ROM

Answers a and d are correct. The HCL only provides a list of the supported hardware and where the driver for that device is located. The HCL does not list unsupported hardware or vendor contact information. Therefore, answers b and c are incorrect.

Question 2

> What does the /OX parameter do when it is used on WINNT32.EXE?
>
> ○ a. An alternative drive for the temp files is defined.
>
> ○ b. Three setup disks are created and the installation is started.
>
> ○ c. The three setup disks are created.
>
> ○ d. Starts the install without using the floppies.

Answer c is correct. The /OX parameter creates the setup disks without starting the installation. The /T command specifies an alternate temp drive; not using any parameters with WINNT32 creates the floppies and starts the installation; /B starts the install without floppies. Therefore, answers a, b, and d are incorrect.

Question 3

> Which of the following items can be part of an automated or custom installation of Windows NT Workstation? [Check all correct answers]
>
> ❑ a. Setup Manager
>
> ❑ b. UNATTEND.TXT
>
> ❑ c. Uniqueness Database File
>
> ❑ d. WINNT.EXE or WINNT32.EXE

Answers a, b, c, and d are correct. All of these items can or are involved in an automated or customized installation of Windows NT.

Question 4

> Which of the following are optional hardware requirements for Windows NT? [Check all correct answers]
>
> ❑ a. Mouse
>
> ❑ b. Audio card
>
> ❑ c. Network card
>
> ❑ d. SCSI storage devices

Answers a, b, and c are correct. Windows NT's optional hardware requirements are a mouse, audio card, and a network card. SCSI storage devices are preferred over IDE, but this is neither mandated nor listed as optional. Therefore, answer d is incorrect.

Question 5

> What methods or choices of installation are possible with Windows NT Workstation 4? [Check all correct answers]
>
> ❑ a. Network share
>
> ❑ b. Local, non-HCL CD-ROM
>
> ❑ c. All-floppy installation
>
> ❑ d. System image transfer
>
> ❑ e. CD-ROM and floppy combo

Answers a, b, and e are correct. Windows NT can be installed from a network share, from a non-HCL CD-ROM (if an OS is present), or with a CD-ROM and floppy combo. Windows NT is not available in an all-floppy install—that would take over 120 disks. Therefore, answer c is incorrect. A system image transfer is a process used in the OS/2 world; the closest Windows NT equivalent is the SYSDIFF utility, but it still requires the normal installation before its special difference file is applied to the computer. Therefore, answer d is incorrect.

Question 6

Windows NT Workstation can exist in a multiboot environment with what other OSs on a Pentium computer? [Check all correct answers]

❏ a. Windows 95 or 98

❏ b. DOS

❏ c. Macintosh System 7.51

❏ d. OS/2

❏ e. Windows NT 3.51

Answers a, b, d, and e are correct. Windows NT can exist with any other Intel-supporting OS, such as Windows 95 or 98, DOS, OS/2, and Windows NT 3.51. Windows NT cannot exist with Mac OS 7.51. Therefore, answer c is incorrect. The trick to this question is knowing that the Mac OS is not supported on the Intel platform.

Question 7

The Windows NT Hardware Qualifier disk is used to inspect your computer for compatible hardware before installation of Windows NT Workstation.

○ a. True

○ b. False

Answer a is correct. The NTHQ should be used prior to installing Windows NT.

Question 8

When an upgrade is performed, which of the following occurs? [Check all correct answers]

❏ a. The Registry is left mostly intact.

❏ b. The SID is changed.

❏ c. Installed applications are removed.

❏ d. Drivers are overwritten.

Answers a and d are correct. The upgrade method of installation leaves the Registry mostly intact and overwrites the original distributed files on the hard drive. The upgrade install does not change the SID or uninstall applications. Therefore, answers b and c are incorrect.

Question 9

Which of the following SYSDIFF command lines will enable you to automatically install Windows NT Workstation and a custom set of applications with a single execution of WINNT?

○ a. sysdiff /dump difference_file dump_file

○ b. sysdiff /apply /m [/log:log_file] difference_file

○ c. sysdiff /inf /m [/u] difference_file oem_root

○ d. sysdiff /snap [/log:log_file] snapshot_file

Answer c is correct. The command "sysdiff /inf /m [/u] difference_file oem_root" will enable Windows NT and custom applications to be automatically installed with a single command. Answer a creates a contents list of the difference file; answer b applies a difference file to an installation of Windows NT; and answer d creates the initial snapshot of Windows NT. Therefore, answers a, b, and d are incorrect.

Question 10

Which WINNT command-line parameters are required when using a Uniqueness Database File? [Check all correct answers]

❏ a. /B

❏ b. /T

❏ c. /U

❏ d. /C

❏ e. /S

Answers c and e are correct. The required command-line parameters are /S and /U. /U initiates an unattended installation that is modified by a UDF. /S defines the distribution file location and is required when /U is used. /B performs a "floppy-less" install; /T defines an alternate drive for temp files; and /C skips the boot floppy space check. Therefore, answers a, b, and d are incorrect.

Need To Know More?

 Chellis, James , Matthew Strebe, and Perkins, Charles: *MCSE: NT Workstation Study Guide, 2nd Edition.* Sybex Network Press, San Francisco, CA, 1998. ISBN 0-7821-2223-X. Chapter 3 discusses Windows NT Workstation installation.

Tittel, Ed, Christa Anderson, and David Johnson: *NT Workstation 4 Exam Prep.* Coriolis, Scottsdale, AZ, 1998. ISBN 1-57610-238-6. Chapter 1 covers Windows NT architecture; Chapter 2 covers installing Windows NT Workstation.

 Search the TechNet CD (or its online version through **www.microsoft.com**) and the *Windows NT Workstation Resource Kit* CD using the keywords "INSTALL," "WINNT," "NTHQ," "UNATTEND.TXT," "Uniqueness Database File," and "SYSDIFF."

Users, Groups, And Policies

4

. . . .

Terms you'll need to understand:

√ Domain Model

√ User accounts

√ User rights and permissions

√ Groups

√ Policies

√ Profiles

√ Auditing

Techniques you'll need to master:

√ Familiarization with Windows NT's User Manager

√ Understanding the group concept

√ Setting up and maintaining user accounts

√ Setting up user rights and permissions

√ Establishing system policies and user profiles

√ Auditing events on your Windows NT system

The main impetus behind setting up a network is to share resources among users. Windows NT makes managing such resources fairly intuitive. We begin this chapter with a discussion of how to manage user accounts, which is where you assign rights to individual users. From there, we move on to groups and security policies.

Users And User Accounts

For most networks, user management on a per-user basis is frustrating. To relieve this administrative burden, Windows NT Workstation 4 comes equipped with an administrative tool for managing users. This tool is the User Manager, which is accessed from Start|Programs|Administrative Tools (Common)|User Manager. This is essentially the same tool as the one found on Windows NT Server, with a few variances. You cannot manage domain user accounts or global groups from within User Manager; however, you can add and remove them from local groups. User Manager is not used to establish trust relationships or manage other domains—these functions are handled by a Server program called User Manager For Domains.

User Manager is where local administrators create and manage user and group accounts. After you have familiarized yourself with this tool, the User Manager will be your primary access control tool for users and groups.

To ease management, the group administration philosophy is the trick for managing users. Rather than managing users one by one, it's easier to place individual users into groups and assign rights to the groups rather than the users. Once a user is a member of a group, he or she inherits the access rights and restrictions assigned to that group.

To simplify matters further, Microsoft had the foresight to provide built-in local groups for user management. Please note that you cannot delete or rename the built-in groups. It is a good idea to make use of these groups for administering user rights and restrictions. In addition, these built-in groups have certain users assigned to them by default. You may add or remove users from these groups as needed. Group concepts, as well as Windows NT's built-in local groups, are discussed throughout this chapter.

Working With The User Manager

The User Manager is the primary tool for controlling users' rights. Here are the various functions and tasks of User Manager:

➤ Produce, change, duplicate, and remove local group accounts

➤ Produce, change, duplicate, and remove local user accounts

➤ Enable account policies (this function establishes defaults for password requirements, account lockouts, disconnect status, and so on)

➤ Create user rights and audit policies

Creating New Users And Groups

To create a new user (see Figure 4.1) or group account in User Manager, perform the following steps:

1. Open User Manager and then click the User menu.

2. Select New User or New Local Group, as desired.

3. Complete the New User dialog box by filling in the Username, Full Name (optional), Description (optional), Password, and Confirm Password fields.

4. Select the appropriate buttons from the four checkboxes at the bottom of the New User dialog box as needed. The options are:

   ➤ User Must Change Password At Next Logon

   ➤ User Cannot Change Password

   ➤ Password Never Expires

   ➤ Account Disabled

Figure 4.1   The New User dialog box.

In addition to these checkboxes, there are three option buttons at the bottom of the dialog box (as opposed to six on the Windows NT Server version). These buttons govern many of the user's capabilities, as described in the following list:

➤ **Groups** This button enables you to add users to and remove users from a certain group or groups.

➤ **Profile** This button enables you to define the path to the user profiles for individual users, to logon scripts, and to a user's home directory.

➤ **Dialin** This is where you establish the right for users to dial in to the network, as well as establish callback security if desired.

Default Accounts

There are two default user accounts: Administrator and Guest. The Administrator account:

➤ Needs a password that is impossible to guess.

➤ Has full, unrestricted system access.

➤ Cannot be disabled or locked out.

➤ Cannot be deleted.

➤ Can be renamed.

The Guest account:

➤ Does not save user preferences or configuration changes.

➤ Has a default blank password.

➤ Can be disabled and locked out.

➤ Cannot be deleted.

➤ Can be renamed.

It is important to rename and assign a password for these two accounts to maximize security.

Modifying Existing User Accounts

A common action for network administrators is setting up accounts for users. Often, new users take the place of existing users, and it is easier to rename an account for an employee who is taking the place of another than to create a new account. To do this, simply select User|Rename from the

User Manager. Be sure to instruct the new employee to change the account's password at first logon because the old employee's password will be retained along with all other settings.

Another method for creating new user accounts involves creating a copy of the old account for the new user instead of renaming it. Windows NT recognizes users by their Security Identifiers (SIDs), not their usernames. Everything the previous user did will now be associated with the new user. By making a copy of the old account, you duplicate everything except the Username, Full Name, and Password. Also, the checkbox for Account Disabled is deselected. If the User Cannot Change Password checkbox is selected on the original account, the copied account will also have this selection checked and the User Must Change Password At Next Logon checkbox is not selected. But if the User Cannot Change Password checkbox is not selected on the original account, the copied account will have the User Must Change Password At Next Logon checkbox selected. Fill these in and you've got a new account with a new SID, but with the same privileges. The old account can now be disabled instead of deleted—this makes it available for possible future security auditing.

It is (unfortunately) common to accidentally delete a user's account. The only way to remedy this is to start anew and create a user account with the same name, rights, and restrictions. This is not as bad as it sounds because you can create a template for departments or groups. Then, from the User menu, you can copy the template, type in the new user's information, and add additional rights or restrictions as needed. If an account is deleted, its SID is destroyed and any new account—even with the same name and settings—is considered a different account by Windows NT.

If you change the access rights for a user, that user must log off and then log back on for the new rights to take effect. This is because the access token for a user is created at logon and is not updated until the next time he or she logs on.

Managing Local Groups

Managing users would be difficult if it weren't for group administration. The group concept is to assign access rights only to groups and then control access by adding and deleting users from the various groups as needed. By taking this approach, you rarely have to adjust access rights for individual users to a resource. The user accounts by themselves have almost no rights assigned; all of these rights are inherited from the groups in which they are placed.

A good method for approaching user security in Windows NT is to create groups for each resource on the network so that each resource has a group that manages access for that particular resource. After establishing this setup of resource groups, you'll spend most of your time managing the groups and their members, not the resources.

Windows NT has two types of groups: local and global. Local groups are only available on the local machine; global groups are available throughout the domain. This distinction is very important to understand. Another important difference is that local groups can contain both users and global groups, whereas global groups can only contain users. No local or global groups can be members of another global group. Global groups must be created and managed on a Windows NT Server with the User Manager For Domains. Local groups are managed from the computer hosting the group, but global groups from the domain can be added as members.

As previously mentioned, Windows NT Workstation comes with some built-in local groups that have default users and access privileges assigned. Table 4.1 describes these groups and lists the default users assigned.

When a user belongs to multiple groups in a domain, rights accumulate across all of them, so that the least restrictive rights take precedence (except for No Access, which always takes precedence, no matter what other rights a user may be assigned). "File And Directory Security," goes into more detail about NTFS and share access, as well as how multiple access settings resolve.

Table 4.1   Windows NT Workstation's built-in local groups.

Group Name	Default Users	Description
Administrators	Administrator, Domain Admins	Members can administer the computer.
Backup Operators	None	Members can bypass file security to back up files.
Guests	Guest, Domain Guests	Users are granted minimal access to the computer.
Power Users	None	Members can manage directories and printers.
Replicator	None	Supports file replication in a domain.
Users	Domain Users	Ordinary users.

Security Policies

Windows NT has three security policies that are managed through the User Manager:

➤ Account

➤ User Rights

➤ Auditing

There are also system policies that control a user's environment, such as customization controls, Control Panel applets, network settings, logon access, and so on. System polices—whether they apply to a user, a computer, or a group—are managed with the System Policy Editor, which only ships with Windows NT Server.

Account Policy

The account policy governs passwords for user accounts and the lockout feature. Settings made to the account policy will apply to all users on the workstation. Users who are currently logged in will not be affected by the new settings until they log out and then log on again. Figure 4.2 shows the Account Policy dialog box.

The settings of the account policy are described in Table 4.2.

Figure 4.2   The Account Policy dialog box.

Table 4.2   Windows NT Workstation account policy settings.

Policy	Action	Settings	Default
Maximum Password Age	When password change is required	1 to 999 days or never	42 days
Minimum Password Age	When password change is prevented	1 to 999 days, or immediately	Immediately
Minimum Password Length	Minimum length	1 to 14, or blank	Permit blank
Password Uniqueness	Forces password uniqueness	1 to 24 history list, or none	No history
Account Lockout	Enables failed log-account lockout	Selected or not	No lockout
Lockout After	Number of attempts before lockout	1 to 999	Blank
Reset Count After	Time until auto-matic reset of counter	1 to 99,999 minutes	Blank
Lockout Duration	Length of lockout	1 to 99,999 minutes, or forever	Blank
Users Must Log On In Order To Change Password	Requires users to log on to change password	Selected or not	Not selected

These settings must be managed carefully to maximize security while mini-mizing the burden placed on users (for example, requiring frequent pass-word changing).

User Rights Policy

User rights restrict or grant specific computer-based abilities to a user or group. User rights are assigned through the Policies menu of the User Manager. There are 10 basic user rights and 17 additional advanced rights on Windows NT Workstation (as opposed to 11 and 16, respectively, on Windows NT Server). Through the User Rights Policy dialog box, you can view any of these rights, as well as the users and groups to which each right is currently granted. Note that to view the advanced rights, you must check Show Advanced User Rights at the bottom of the dialog box.

The basic user rights, their purposes, and their members (in parentheses) are shown in Table 4.3.

Table 4.3	Windows NT Workstation user rights.	
User Right	**Description**	**Default Groups**
Access This Computer From Network	Allows remote access to shared resources on this workstation	Administrators, Everyone, Power Users
Backup Files And Directories	Allows backups	Administrators, Backup Operators
Change System Time	Allows clock changing	Administrators, Power Users
Force Shutdown From Remote System	Allows remote system shutdown	Administrators, Power Users
Load And Unload Device Drivers	Allows drivers to be changed	Administrators
Log On Locally	Allows the workstation to be used locally	Administrators, Backup Operators, Everyone, Guests, Power Users, Users
Manage And Audit Security Log	Allows security policy changes	Administrators
Restore Files And Directories	Allows restoration	Administrators, Backup Operators
Shut Down The System	Allows system shutdown	Administrators, Backup Operators, Everyone, Power Users, Users
Take Ownership Of Files Or Other Objects	Allows users to gain authority over system object	Administrators only

The advanced rights are associated with software development and are not generally used for Windows NT Workstation administration. Do not use the advanced user rights unless you are certain about their functions and effect on the workstation.

Auditing Policy

On a computer running Windows NT, the administrator has the option to audit access to resources such as directories, printers, and shares. The audit informs the administrator if someone attempts to access secured resources or just how often a particular resource is accessed. The information gathered by Windows NT's auditing system can be brought to bear against performance problems, security risks, and expansion planning.

The auditing system is designed to watch every event occurrence on a system. To simplify the act of fine-tuning the areas you want to audit, there are three levels of switches with which you'll need to work. The master switch is the Audit These Events radio button located on the Audit Policy dialog box (see Figure 4.3). This dialog box is accessed through the User Manager's Policies pull-down menu.

This master switch turns on and off Windows NT's entire audit system. By default, this switch is set to Do Not Audit.

The second level of switches becomes available when you set the master switch. There are seven event types listed in the Audit Policy dialog box. Each event type can be audited by tracking its success or failure. Here are the seven event types and descriptions of the events they control:

➤ **Logon And Logoff** Tracks logons, logoffs, and network connections.

➤ **File And Object Access** Tracks access to files, directories, and other NTFS objects, including printers.

➤ **Use Of User Rights** Tracks when users make use of user rights.

➤ **User And Group Management** Tracks changes in the accounts of users and groups (password changes, account deletions, group memberships, renaming, and so forth).

➤ **Security Policy Changes** Tracks changes of user rights, audit policies, and trusts.

➤ **Restart, Shutdown, And System** Tracks server shutdown and restarts; also logs events affecting system security.

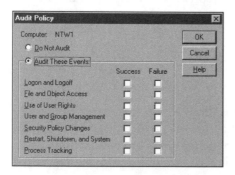

Figure 4.3   The Audit Policy dialog box.

➤ **Process Tracking** Tracks program activation, program termination, and other object/process access.

The third level of audit switches is on the object level. This level of control only applies to File And Object Access events. These switches reside within the properties of each NTFS object, such as file, directory, and printer. Figures 4.4 through 4.6 show the audit switch screens for file, directory, and print access. Note the differences in the tracking events among the object types. Both the file and directory objects have Read, Write, Execute, Delete, Change Permissions, and Take Ownership; but the printer object has Print, Full Control, Delete, Change Permissions, and Take Ownership.

A second, important difference to notice is on the directory object. The directory object allows you to change the files and/or subdirectories within the current directory to the same audit settings. Although this is convenient, you should use it with caution because any current audit settings on these objects will be cleared and replaced with the new settings.

To get to these dialog boxes, right-click over the object, select Properties from the pop-up menu, select the Security tab, and then click the Auditing button. Remember, object auditing is only available for NTFS objects, not FAT objects.

Figure 4.4   The File Auditing dialog box.

Figure 4.5 The Directory Auditing dialog box.

Note: By default, the object-level audit switches are all blank, with no users or groups present in the Name field. We added the Everyone group before capturing these images so the Events list at the bottom of the dialog boxes would become readable instead of almost invisible gray.

Figure 4.6 The Printer Auditing dialog box.

The object-level audit dialog boxes allow you to set the same success/failure event tracking for all users and groups listed in the Names field. You cannot track success for one group and failure for another.

Again, here are the steps required to audit:

1. Turn on the master Audit These Events switch.

2. Select one or more of the event types to track success or failure.

3. If you choose the File And Object Access option, you must also edit the auditing settings for each NTFS object.

Auditing system events demands large amounts of computing overhead, especially if the event monitored, such as file access, occurs often. It is not recommended to audit any event or object more than is absolutely necessary to track a problem or test equipment. Otherwise, your system will experience overall performance degradation.

The information gathered by Windows NT's auditing system is stored in the Security log. You can view this log using the Event Viewer. The Event Viewer lists detailed information about each tracked event. Some of the data recorded includes user logon identification, the computer used, time, date, and the action or event that instigated an audit.

When numerous objects or events are audited, the Security log can grow large quite quickly. You need to monitor the size of this log and possibly implement a size restriction and/or automated new file creation to prevent data loss and maximize the usefulness of the gathered data.

Practice Questions

Question 1

> You suspect that an Account group member is accessing a direc-
> tory that the user should be prevented from reaching. This might
> mean that you've set up the group memberships incorrectly. You
> aren't sure who it is, but you do know what directory is being
> accessed. What feature of Windows NT will let you track who gains
> access to this directory?
>
> ○ a. NTFS file activity logging
>
> ○ b. Event auditing
>
> ○ c. Event Viewer
>
> ○ d. Account lockout

Answer b is correct. Event auditing will track the activity around any object
within Windows NT. NTFS file activity logging is a fault tolerance feature
used to ensure the integrity of stored data. It cannot be used to track access.
Therefore, answer a is incorrect. The Event Viewer is used to review the
Security log created by the auditing system, but it is not the feature that
does the actual tracking. Therefore, answer c is incorrect. Account lockout
is the feature used to prevent compromised accounts from being used. Therefore, answer d is incorrect.

Question 2

> Which of the following are valid activities for User Manager on
> Windows NT Workstation? [Check all correct answers]
>
> ❏ a. Create global groups
>
> ❏ b. Manage local users
>
> ❏ c. Add global groups to local groups
>
> ❏ d. Create domain users
>
> ❏ e. Manage local groups

Answers b, c, and e are correct. You can use the User Manager to manage
local users, add global groups to local groups, and manage local groups.
Only the Windows NT Server version, not the NT Workstation version, is
able to create global groups and domain users. Therefore, answers a and d
are incorrect.

Question 3

> Mary is leaving the company and David is her replacement. What is the best way to give David the same access to all of the resources previously used by Mary?
>
> ○ a. Create an account in Server Manager for David using Mary's account as a template; then delete Mary's account.
>
> ○ b. Let David use Mary's account by giving him the password.
>
> ○ c. Rename Mary's account in User Manager and tell David to change the account password when he logs on for the first time.
>
> ○ d. Create an account for David in the User Manager using Mary's account as a template; then disable Mary's account.

Trick! question

Answer c is correct. Renaming Mary's account through User Manager and instructing David to change the password is the best way to give David the same access as Mary. Server Manager is not used to manage user accounts. Therefore, answer a is incorrect. Because answer b does not recommend changing the account's username or password, answer b is incorrect. Although creating a new account by copying the existing account is a possible method, it is not Microsoft's current position that this is the best course of action. Therefore, answer d is incorrect.

Question 4

> Which of the following built-in groups, other than Administrators, have the default right to log on locally to Windows NT Workstation?
>
> ○ a. Power Users, Users, and Guests only
>
> ○ b. Users only
>
> ○ c. Backup Operators, Power Users, and Users only
>
> ○ d. Backup Operators, Power Users, Users, Guests, and Everyone

Answer d is correct. The default groups that can log on locally to Windows NT Workstation are Backup Operators, Power Users, Users, Guests, and Everyone. All the other answers—a, b, and c—do not list all of the correct default groups and are therefore incorrect.

Question 5

> You want to track the activity around a new high-speed color laser printer so that you can use the tracking information to restrict and grant privileged and priority access. Which of the following are required steps for implementing printer auditing? [Check all correct answers]
>
> ❑ a. Set the auditing switches on the printer object to track the successful print events for the Everyone group.
>
> ❑ b. Grant the Everyone group the auditing right through the User Rights policy.
>
> ❑ c. Set the Audit policy to Audit These Events through the User Manager.
>
> ❑ d. Set the audit switch of File and Object Access to Success under Audit These Events.
>
> ❑ e. Set the priority of the printer to 99 (maximum) under the Scheduling tab on the printer's Properties dialog box.

The correct answers are a, c, and d. Setting the auditing switches on the object is required to enable printer tracking. Therefore, answer a is correct. Setting the master auditing switch to Audit These Events is required to track printer access. Therefore, answer c is correct. Setting the event type switch of File And Object Access to Success is required to track printer usage. Therefore, answer d is correct. There is not an auditing user right. Therefore, answer b is incorrect. Setting a printer's priority has nothing to do with tracking access. Therefore, answer e is incorrect.

Question 6

> An important new custom application is conflicting with an existing utility. The conflict seems to cause both programs to terminate prematurely. Which audit event type should be tracked to record some information about the conflict and which programs are affected?
>
> ○ a. File And Object Access
>
> ○ b. Security Policy Changes
>
> ○ c. Restart, Shutdown, And System
>
> ○ d. Process Tracking
>
> ○ e. Application Activity

Answer d is correct. Process Tracking tracks threads and processes (for example, applications). File And Object Access is for tracking NTFS objects such as files and printers. Therefore, answer a is incorrect. Security Policy Changes tracks modifications to security and policies. Therefore, answer b is incorrect. Restart, Shutdown, And System tracks system restarts. Therefore, answer c is incorrect. Application Activity is not a valid selection. Therefore, answer e is incorrect.

Question 7

Which of the following settings cannot be managed through the Account Policy dialog box? [Check all correct answers]

❏ a. Password length

❏ b. Password history

❏ c. User Must Change Password At Next Logon

❏ d. User Must Logon To Change Password

❏ e. Password age

❏ f. User Cannot Change Password

Answers c and f are correct. User Must Change Password At Next Logon and User Cannot Change Password are settings of the user account through the Properties dialog box of each account. Password length, history, and age, as well as User Must Logon To Change Password are all set by using the Account Policy dialog box. Therefore, answers a, b, d, and e are incorrect.

Question 8

Which of the following is the best application to use to create a new shared directory on a domain server from your Windows NT Workstation?

○ a. User Manager

○ b. Server Manager

○ c. Windows NT Explorer

○ d. Network Client Administrator

Answer b is correct. Server Manager allows users to create new shares on remote computers. The "trick" in this question is knowing that, although you can use Windows NT Explorer to manage share locally, you cannot manage shares remotely from it. You must use Server Manager to do this. You should remember that the Server Manager is a Windows NT Server utility and not a native Windows NT Workstation utility. You must install Server Manager from SRVTOOLS directory from the Windows NT Server distribution CD on Windows NT Workstation to gain access to this tool and the ability to remotely manage shares.

Question 9

When you create a copy of an existing user account, what pieces of information are reset or left blank? (Assume the User Cannot Change Password checkbox is selected on the original account.) [Check all correct answers]

❑ a. User Must Change Password At Next Logon

❑ b. Username

❑ c. Account Disabled

❑ d. Password Never Expires

❑ e. Profile settings

❑ f. Password

❑ g. Group memberships

Answers a, b, c, and f are correct. The fields that are reset or left blank when a user account is copied are User Must Change Password At Next Logon, Username, Account Disabled, and Password. The Password Never Expires, profile settings, and group membership options remain as they were set in the original account. Therefore, answers d, e, and g are incorrect.

Question 10

Which characteristic do the default Administrator and Guest accounts share?

○ a. Both give Full Access to the network

○ b. Both have unrestricted access to the system

○ c. Both cannot be deleted

○ d. Both can be locked out

Answer c is correct. Neither account can be deleted. Only the Administrator account has Full Access to the network. Therefore, answer a is incorrect. Only the Administrator account has unrestricted access to the system. Therefore, answer b is incorrect. Only the Guest account can be locked out. Therefore, answer d is incorrect.

Need To Know More?

 Perkins, Charles, Matthew Strebe, and James Chellis: *MCSE: NT Workstation Study Guide, 2nd Edition*. Sybex Network Press, San Francisco, CA, 1998. ISBN 0-7821-2223-X. Chapter 3 has a detailed account of users, groups, and policies.

 Tittel, Ed, Christa Anderson, and David Johnson: *NT Workstation 4 Exam Prep*. Coriolis, Scottsdale, AZ, 1998. ISBN 1-57610-238-6. Chapter 3 covers groups and policies in the same detail.

The *Windows NT Server Resource Kit* contains a lot of useful information about shares and share permissions. You can search the TechNet (either online or CD version) or *Resource Kit* CD versions using keywords such as "users," "groups," and "policies."

 Search the TechNet CD (or its online version through **www.microsoft.com**) using the keywords "user management," "security policy," and "groups."

Configuring Windows NT Workstation

5

Terms you'll need to understand:

✓ Control Panel applets

✓ User profiles

✓ Logon scripts

✓ Registry

✓ REGEDIT

✓ REGEDT32

✓ Windows NT Diagnostics (WINMSD)

Techniques you'll need to master:

✓ Understanding and using Control Panel applets

✓ Installing and configuring hardware

✓ Implementing and maintaining user profiles and logon scripts

✓ Working with the Windows NT Registry

✓ Understanding and using Windows NT Diagnostics (WINMSD)

Although users, groups, and policies are essential for a network to function, there are still many issues and elements regarding system configuration that must be addressed before optimum use of Windows NT Workstation can be achieved. A broad range of configuration issues exist. In this chapter, we cover nearly all the configuration interfaces so that you'll have a complete picture of what can and cannot be done within the Windows NT Workstation environment.

Control Panel Applets

Most system alterations are controlled through the numerous applets found in the Control Panel. Each of these applications has a specific purpose and modifies the Registry behind the scenes. We'll talk about the Registry later in this chapter, in the section titled "Working With The Windows NT Registry."

Some of the Control Panel applets are present only if their corresponding services or devices have been installed. In other cases, the applets are present even if you don't use them.

The two basic divisions or types of Control Panel applets are system and user. The system applets modify hardware or software settings for the entire computer. In other words, when a system applet is used, all users experience the change. The user applets only modify how the environment for a specific user operates, not the entire computer. System applets are only accessible by Administrators, whereas the user applets are available to standard users (unless a system profile prevents this). This dichotomy is usually fairly easy to recognize; however, there are some applets, such as the Display applet, that have both system- and user-level option tabs. In the following sections, we separate the system applets from the user applets and list all the important applets located in the Control Panel.

 We recommend you spend time on a Windows NT Workstation working through this text while viewing the applets online to get a full grasp of what's involved.

System Configuration Applets

The system-level applets are those applets that modify the operation of hardware or software for the entire computer.

The System Applet

The System applet is used to alter environmental variables, pagefile parameters, and startup options. This applet has six tabs:

➤ **General** Lists the OS version, registration detail, and basic computer configuration (see Figure 5.1).

➤ **Performance** Sets the performance boost for foreground apps (2 = max) and the virtual memory pagefile (see Figure 5.2). (Chapter 15 discusses the Performance tab in more detail.)

➤ **Environment** Displays and modifies the environmental variable settings (see Figure 5.3).

➤ **Startup/Shutdown** The top portion of this tab modifies the BOOT.INI file by setting the default startup selection and timeout; the bottom portion defines the action to take when a STOP error occurs, such as create a memory dump file and/or reboot the system (see Figure 5.4). (Chapter 18 discusses the Startup/Shutdown tab in detail.)

➤ **Hardware Profiles** Multiple hardware configurations can be configured through this tab, thus allowing a portable computer to interact with PC cards (also called PCMCIA) or a docking station. The top

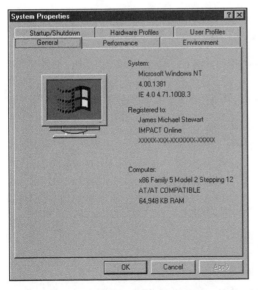

Figure 5.1   The General tab of the System applet.

Figure 5.1 The Performance tab of the System applet.

profile is the default, and a timeout can be set for the selection menu that appears during bootup. The most common use for hardware profiles is a notebook that is sometimes detached from a network.

Figure 5.1 The Environment tab of the System applet.

Figure 5.4   The Startup/Shutdown tab of the System applet.

➤ **User Profiles** User profiles can be copied and deleted from this tab (see Figure 5.5). Also, profiles can be modified to be roaming or local through the Change Type button.

Figure 5.5   The User Profiles tab of the System applet.

The Date/Time Applet

This simple, but useful applet sets the system time and date on the Date & Time tab, and it defines the time zone on the Time Zone tab.

The Services Applet

Through the Services applet, you can obtain the status of available services and alter when and if the services load. To modify the startup method of a service, double-click the item in the Services list, then choose from the following three choices for Startup Type:

➤ **Automatic** The service loads if possible when Windows NT boots.

➤ **Manual** The service is started only when it is needed by other processes.

➤ **Disabled** The service will not be started.

By default, services run under the System account. However, certain network services, such as the Directory Replication service, require a network logon. In such cases, you can define the user account to be used by the service.

Additionally, hardware profiles can be modified through the HW Profiles button for each service.

The Ports Applet

Through this applet, you can set the operational parameters of the communications ports. The settings include baud rate, data bits, stop bits, and flow control, as well as advanced settings of COM port number, base I/O address, IRQ, and FIFO serial buffer setting.

The Telephony Applet

The Telephony applet is the primary area where a dialing location can be defined and modified. A dialing location simply sets the area code, long-distance dialing requirements, credit card calls, whether to disable call waiting, and tone or pulse dialing. All these options are listed on the My Locations tab. The other tab, Telephony Drivers, lists the TAPI or communication drivers installed on the machine. This is usually not the place where new drivers for communication devices are installed.

UPS Applet

Uninterruptible Power Supplies, or UPSs, are invaluable devices for production computers. A UPS is a power supply that can be used by a computer for a short time after normal power is terminated. The UPS applet enables the integration of UPS features with Windows NT through a serial port using an RS-232 cable. Depending on the type of UPS, you need to configure the applet to properly interpret signals from the device. The most important item to get correct is the voltage type for each signal—it's either positive or negative. The wrong voltage definition can cause your system to turn itself off prematurely or to fail to shut down before electricity is terminated. Other details to define are battery life, recharge time, and warning timeouts.

Another issue in regard to UPSs occurs during bootup. By default, Windows NT polls the serial ports for mice. If a UPS is present, this signal can be interpreted by the UPS as a terminate power command; thus, the machine will lose power and fail to boot. However, the **/NOSERIALMICE=[COM***x* **|** **COM***x,y,z***...]** BOOT.INI parameter can be used to disable serial mouse detection of one or more specified COM ports.

Configuring And Installing Hardware

Unlike Windows 95, from which Windows NT received its current look and feel, the Control Panel lacks an Add New Hardware applet. This is mainly due to Windows NT's lack of support for the Plug and Play architecture. However, two methods are available for installing and configuring new hardware:

➤ Use one of the device type-specific applets (defined later in this section)

➤ Use the manufacturer-supplied installation/setup utility

If neither of these methods is available to you, the device cannot be installed into Windows NT. Generally, the install process involves powering down the system, installing the device, booting to install the driver, and then rebooting. Removing a device follows a reverse path: remove the driver, shut down, remove the device, and then reboot.

Configuring a hardware device under Windows NT is tricky. As we've stated already, Windows NT does not support Plug and Play. This means the hardware device does not have the capability to directly modify the configuration settings as stored in the device's BIOS. Usually, you must boot to DOS (even if it means booting with a floppy), use a DOS-based configuration tool to alter the settings on the card, boot to Windows NT and modify the settings of the driver to match that of the device, and then reboot.

There are numerous hardware-related Control Panel applets. We've already talked about UPSs earlier in this chapter, and the Modems applet is discussed in Chapter 13. The remaining applets are discussed in the following sections.

Network Applet

Network adapter drivers are installed, modified, and removed through the Network applet on the Adapters tab. The other features of the Network applet are discussed in Chapters 9, 10, and 11.

SCSI Adapters Applet

The SCSI Adapters applet is where the installation, modification, and removal of SCSI devices and controllers occur. However, many IDE controllers, especially those built into the motherboard, will appear in this applet. The Devices tab lists all the SCSI adapters installed on the system and the devices connected to each daisy chain. Details for any of these devices can be obtained through the Properties button. The Drivers tab allows the installation and removal of SCSI drivers. CD-ROMs, although often thought of as multimedia devices, are installed through the SCSI Adapters applet instead of the Multimedia applet.

Tape Devices Applet

The Tape Devices applet is where backup devices are installed. The Detect button will search for known devices and install drivers for any devices located. If your device is not detected, it can be manually installed on the Drivers tab.

Multimedia Applet

The Multimedia applet is used to configure audio, MIDI, and video settings for Windows NT. On its Devices tab, new drivers for audio and multimedia cards or features can be installed and removed.

Display Applet

The Display applet is where video display drivers are installed for VGA cards and the parameters for your display are set (this all occurs on the Settings tab). The other tabs of the Display applet are user controls.

Keyboard And Mouse Applets

Two applets, namely Keyboard and Mouse, are used to install drivers for these input devices, as well as configure their operational parameters.

PC Card (PCMCIA) Applet

This applet is only functional on those computers with a PC card (also referred to as PCMCIA) interface. Through this applet, drivers can be installed for these add-on cards.

> *Note: Windows NT does not respond favorably to the insertion and removal of PC cards; changing of PC cards should be done only when Windows NT is shut down to avoid problems.*

Devices Applet

The Devices applet is where all the drivers installed onto Windows NT are listed with their respective Status and Startup parameters. The Startup parameters can be set to boot, system, automatic, manual, or disabled. Additionally, hardware profiles can be modified through the HW Profiles button for each device driver.

Application Control

Most software applications are installed through their own setup utility. However, Windows NT offers an interface to launch applications with special Control Panel tie-ins. Also, on the Install/Uninstall tab of the Add/Remove Programs applet is a list of applications known by Windows NT that can be uninstalled. The Windows NT Setup tab offers the ability to install or remove Windows NT-specific components.

User Configuration Applets

The user applets are those portions of the Control Panel that any and all users (unless denied or restricted by a system policy) can access to fine-tune their computing environment. These user-applets include the following:

➤ Display

➤ Keyboard

➤ Mouse

➤ Regional Settings

➤ Sounds

Display

The Display applet in the Control Panel has four tabs for user-specific control. The Background tab controls desktop wallpaper and the default pattern. The Screen Saver tab controls screen savers and password protection. The Appearance tab controls the color and font scheme used by windows and dialog boxes. The Plus! tab controls default icon images and special visual effects.

Keyboard And Mouse

Users generally have access privileges to change the operational parameters of the keyboard and mouse using the Control Panel Keyboard and Mouse applets. These controls include typing speed, language support, multiple key mappings, pointer schemes, and motion speeds.

Regional Settings

The Regional Settings applet is where settings for language, time zone, number appearance, currency type, time and date display methods, and input locales (a language scheme) appear.

Sounds

The Sounds applet is where sounds are associated with events (for example, a warning buzzer that is played each time a system error occurs). All sound/event associations are unique to each individual and can be saved into a single scheme for transfer to another user or machine.

User Profiles

A user profile is a stored collection of elements that defines a user's desktop and computing environment. Through a profile, users can customize their desktops to meet their computing needs. Settings such as screen savers, network connections, customized desktops, mouse settings, and program groups are specified with a user profile. Profiles can be created for both users and groups. User profiles are located in the %systemroot%\ Profiles\<*username*>\Desktop directory.

A profile can be a local profile or a roaming profile. A local profile is only stored on a local client and cannot be used on any other client. A roaming profile is stored on a network share, typically a domain controller, and is used on any client with the same OS that the user logs in to.

You can force a user to use a certain profile by creating a mandatory user profile that cannot be changed or saved by the user. This is produced by establishing a profile (local or roaming) for a user, changing the name of the NTUSER.DAT file to NTUSER.MAN, and entering the profile UNC path into User Profile Path, located in the User Environment Profile screen for each user.

 So that a user's mandatory profile is not accessible in the event of a network failure, users will not be granted access to the network nor their local Windows NT Workstation. If this is the first time the user has logged on and the mandatory profile is unavailable, the logon attempt is denied. If a non-mandatory profile is used, a cached local copy of the profile will be used so the user can gain local and network access.

Use the following steps to create a roaming profile:

1. Copy the user's profile from the workstation to a shared network path. This means copy the %systemroot%\Profiles\<*username*> directory and all of its contents.

2. Open the Control Panel and double-click System.

3. Select the user's profile entry, select Copy To, and type in the full UNC path name to the server where the profile will reside.

4. In the User Profile dialog box (accessed through a user account's Properties via User Manager by clicking the Profile button), enter the full UNC path name for the profile in the User Profile path field.

You also can set the user's home directory settings in the user's profile. To define a home directory for an existing user account, you must perform the following steps:

1. Select the Connect option in the User Environment Profile dialog box in the User Manager.

2. Select a local drive letter to be used to map the full UNC path name for the user's new home directory.

   The full UNC path name contains the server name on which the home directory resides (the domain name is not required). The variable %HOMEPATH% contains the user's home directory UNC path name only after the new home directory has been established.

If you have users who change settings constantly and/or inappropriately, it's a good idea to establish profiles and force users to stick to these settings by using mandatory profiles.

Logon Scripts

When you consider all the user configuration utilities and capabilities that come with Windows NT Workstation, it seems strange to include logon scripts. However, to maintain backward compatibility, you must provide for the use of logon scripts—for several reasons. First, because user profiles only work with Windows NT-based computers, DOS-based clients require logon scripts to provide consistent network connections. Also, if you still have an old LAN Manager server on your network, logon scripts preserve backward compatibility to those servers for all clients.

In addition, you can specify a user's network connections or network printer connections without developing a sophisticated user profile plan. In the event that you only have defined personal profiles but you want to define persistent network connections, logon scripts can do that, too. Finally, if you don't want to spend an extensive amount of time developing a complex and coherent user profile strategy, logon scripts are a quick and easy alternative.

Using logon scripts is beneficial in custom-building a user's environment without managing all aspects of it. For backup purposes, you should replicate logon scripts from the PDC to all BDCs on the network. That way, should the PDC go down, the BDCs maintain a copy of the logon scripts and make them available to users at logon. Logon scripts do not need to be exported to every workstation. Always place files that are to be exported into subdirectories of the %systemroot%\System32\Repl\Export directory. Files that are located in the root %systemroot%\System32\Repl\ directory will not be replicated. The default export directory for logon scripts on the PDC is %systemroot%\System32\Repl\Export\Scripts.

Working With The Windows NT Registry

The Registry is a hierarchical database of information about the system hardware, installed software, system settings, and user settings. This database replaces INI, CONFIG.SYS, and AUTOEXEC.BAT files where this information was stored in previous versions of Windows. The Registry is made up of several files, but it isn't necessary to edit any of these files individually. To the end-user, the Registry appears as one seamless database. Fortunately, most information that is contained in the Registry is set through the user interface, primarily with the applets found in the Control Panel.

For items that are not controlled through the user interface, Windows NT provides two editing utilities: REGEDT32.EXE and REGEDIT.EXE. These utilities are not available on the Start menu—they must be launched from the Run command or a command prompt.

The Registry is organized in a hierarchical structure, much like the directory structure of a hard drive. This hierarchy consists of subtrees, hives, keys, values, and data. Table 5.1 lists the hives and presents a summary of the information located in them.

The Registry is not an exhaustive record of a Windows NT system configuration. Instead, it only contains those values that are different from the system defaults. In other words, the data in the Registry is the exception. When the Windows NT system makes a system call and no Registry setting says otherwise, it assumes the intuitive defaults. Unfortunately, this makes editing the Registry a real nightmare, because the default values are generally known only to the OS.

HKEY_LOCAL_MACHINE

From an administrative point of view, the HKEY_LOCAL_MACHINE key contains the most useful information about the local system. This subtree has five direct hives: Hardware, SAM, Security, Software, and System. Table 5.2 lists the general information contained in each of these hives.

Table 5.1 The five main hives of the Windows NT Registry.	
Hive	**Description**
HKEY_CLASSES_ROOT	Establishes OLE file associations (retained for backward compatibility).
HKEY_CURRENT_USER	Displays user profile information for the user currently logged in.
HKEY_LOCAL_MACHINE	Manages hardware and software configuration, installed drivers, and security.
HKEY_USERS	Provides user profile information for all users.
HKEY_CURRENT_CONFIG	Displays the currently used hardware profile (a subset of HKEY_LOCAL_MACHINE).

Table 5.2	The five subkeys of the HKEY_LOCAL_MACHINE hive of the Windows NT Registry.
Subkey	**Description**
Hardware	Shows devices attached to the system and their current state.
SAM	Displays the Security Account Manager, which includes local user, group account, and domain values. This information is not available for direct editing using the Registry Editor.
Security	Shows security information used locally by the security subsystem.
Software	Displays the software settings that apply to all local users.
System	Shows boot information and associated device drivers.

REGEDIT Vs. REGEDT32

The only real difference between these two Registry editing tools—besides the Explorer-type interface of REGEDIT and the File Manager-type interface of REGEDT32—is in their power to search or modify security settings. REGEDIT can be used to search for keys, values, and data throughout the entire Registry at once, whereas REGEDT32 can only search for keys. However, REGEDT32 can be used to alter any security settings.

Windows NT Diagnostics (WINMSD)

The Windows NT Diagnostics (or WINMSD) utility gives you a shallow insight into the current configuration of the Windows NT software and the hardware on which it is operating. This tool is similar to both the MSD utility for DOS and the Device Manager for Windows 95 and 98. WINMSD can only be used to view system information—it cannot make any modifications to installed software or devices. However, users can get a quick view of system information and configurations through WINMSD.

Practice Questions

Question 1

What Control Panel applet should be used to create a roaming profile for a user?

○ a. System

○ b. Network

○ c. Regional Settings

○ d. User Manager

Answer a is correct. The User Profile tab, located in the System applet, is where roaming profiles are established. The Network applet is not involved in the creation of user profiles. Therefore, answer b is incorrect. The Regional Settings applet makes changes that are stored in a user profile, but roaming profiles are not managed through this tool. Therefore, answer c is incorrect. The User Manager is not a Control Panel applet and is not used to create profiles. Therefore, answer d is incorrect.

Question 2

After the successful installation of Windows NT Workstation, you need to remove an old network interface card and install a new high-speed interface. Where should you attempt to remove the old drivers and install the new drivers?

○ a. Devices

○ b. SCSI

○ c. Network

○ d. System

Answer c is correct. The Adapters tab in the Network applet is used to install and remove NIC drivers. The Devices applet is where drivers can be started and stopped; however, they cannot be installed or removed through this interface. Therefore, answer a is incorrect. The SCSI applet is used to install and remove SCSI device drivers. Therefore, answer b is incorrect. The System applet is not involved in the operation or installation of NICs. Therefore, answer d is incorrect.

Question 3

> After you have installed a new application, the instructions state that you must manually modify the PATH statement so that the software will function properly. How can this be accomplished?
>
> ○ a. Edit the PATH.BAT file.
>
> ○ b. Modify the PATH variable on the Environment tab of the System applet.
>
> ○ c. Edit the CONFIG.NT file.
>
> ○ d. Edit the PATH value in the Registry located in the \HKEY_LOCAL_MACHINE\CurrentControlSet\System\ key.

Answer b is correct. The Environment tab of the System applet is the proper place to modify the PATH variable. There is no such thing as a PATH.BAT file. Therefore, answer a is incorrect. The CONFIG.NT file does not contain path information. Therefore, answer c is incorrect. The Registry key listed for this PATH value is fictitious. Therefore, answer d is incorrect.

Question 4

> How can you change the timeout value for the boot menu? [Check all correct answers]
>
> ❏ a. Edit the BOOT.INI file.
>
> ❏ b. Set the TimeOut variable on the Environment tab of the System applet.
>
> ❏ c. Set the timeout on the Startup/Shutdown tab of the System applet.
>
> ❏ d. Through the BootMenu key in the Registry.

The correct answers are a and c. Editing the BOOT.INI file is one method of changing the timeout value of the boot menu. Therefore, answer a is correct. The Startup/Shutdown tab of the System applet has a timeout control for the boot menu. Therefore, answer c is correct. There is no TimeOut variable that relates to the boot menu to be found on the Environment tab of the System applet. Therefore, answer b is incorrect. There is no BootMenu key in the Registry. Therefore, answer d is incorrect.

Question 5

> When installing a new SCSI-based tape device, which of the fol-
> lowing steps are required to complete the installation of the new
> device? [Check all correct answers]
>
> ❑   a. Reboot.
>
> ❑   b. Install SCSI controller drivers through the SCSI Adapters
>   applet.
>
> ❑   c. Use the Add New Hardware applet.
>
> ❑   d. Detect the tape device through the Tape Devices applet.

Answers a, b, and d are correct. Rebooting, installing SCSI controller drivers through the SCSI Adapters applet, and detecting the tape device through
the Tape Devices applet are all required steps for installing a new SCSI-
based tape device. There is no Add New Hardware applet in Windows NT.
Therefore, answer c is incorrect.

Question 6

> How can you use your Windows NT Workstation-based notebook
> computer at the office on a LAN as well as at home over a modem
> without launching the network services while not connected to
> the network?
>
> ○   a. Create two local user profiles.
>
> ○   b. Create two computer system policies.
>
> ○   c. Create two hardware profiles.
>
> ○   d. Create two user accounts.

Answer c is correct. Two hardware profiles will allow the non-network profile to be selected when not physically connected to the network. Two user
profiles will not prevent the network services from launching when not
physically connected to the network. Therefore, answer a is incorrect. Two
computer system polices will not prevent the network services from launching either. Therefore, answer b is incorrect. Two user accounts will not offer
the desired effect. Therefore, answer d is incorrect.

Question 7

You recently purchased a UPS to protect your computer from power failures and spikes. You have taken the precaution of adding the **/NOSERIALMICE** parameter to your BOOT.INI file. After charging the UPS and attaching it to the correct serial port, you boot your Windows NT Workstation computer. You test your configuration by unplugging the UPS from the wall. After five minutes, the UPS battery is drained, cutting off power to your computer. Windows NT did not shut down gracefully, even though you heard the repeated beeps from the UPS device. What is a possible explanation of this?

○ a. The UPS drivers were not installed through the Devices applet.

○ b. The voltages were reversed in the UPS applet.

○ c. Windows NT is not compatible with UPS devices.

○ d. The UPS variables were not defined in the System applet on the Environment tab.

Answer b is correct. If the voltages defining the communications from a UPS are reversed, the computer will fail to understand its signals. The Devices applet is not used to install drivers; also, a UPS requires no additional drivers for operation. Therefore, answer a is incorrect. Windows NT is UPS-compatible. Therefore, answer c is incorrect. There are no UPS variables to be defined through the System applet. Therefore, answer d is incorrect.

Question 8

Where would drivers for a MIDI device be installed under Windows NT?

○ a. Drivers applet

○ b. System applet

○ c. SCSI applet

○ d. Multimedia applet

Answer d is correct. The Multimedia applet is used to install MIDI device drivers. The Drivers and System applets cannot be used to install drivers. Therefore, answers a and b are incorrect. The SCSI applet is not used to install MIDI device drivers. Therefore, answer c is incorrect.

Question 9

> Which Registry editing tool can be used to change the security settings on individual Registry keys?
>
> ○ a. REGEDIT
>
> ○ b. REGEDT32

Answer b is correct. REGEDT32 is the Registry editing tool that can modify the security permissions on Registry keys.

Question 10

> Users whose profiles are defined by the NTUSER.MAN file can be changed to their personal preferences, and these changes will be stored for their next computing session.
>
> ○ a. True
>
> ○ b. False

Answer b is correct. Profiles defined by NTUSER.MAN are mandatory profiles. Any changes a user makes are not stored.

Need To Know More?

 Perkins, Charles, Matthew Strebe, and James Chellis: *MCSE: NT Workstation Study Guide, 2nd Edition*. Sybex Network Press, San Francisco, CA, 1998. ISBN 0-7821-2223-X. Chapter 4 discusses most of these Control Panel and configuration issues.

Tittel, Ed, Christa Anderson, and David Johnson: *NT Workstation 4 Exam Prep*. Coriolis, Scottsdale, AZ, 1998. ISBN 1-57610-238-6. Chapter 4 covers the Control Panel in the same detail.

 Search the TechNet CD (or its online version through **www.microsoft.com**) and the *Windows NT Workstation Resource Kit* CD using the keywords "Control Panel," "profile," and the name of each Control Panel applet discussed in this chapter.

Windows NT File Systems And Structures

6

Terms you'll need to understand:

- ✓ File Allocation Table (FAT)
- ✓ New Technology File System (NTFS)
- ✓ High Performance File System (HPFS)
- ✓ Compact Disk File System (CDFS)
- ✓ 8.3 file names
- ✓ Long file names (LFNs)
- ✓ Virtual FAT (VFAT)
- ✓ FAT32
- ✓ CONVERT.EXE

Techniques you'll need to master:

- ✓ Selecting a file system for Windows NT
- ✓ Using CONVERT.EXE to convert FAT to NTFS
- ✓ Using Disk Administrator to establish a disk structure

Windows NT supports two primary file systems to save and retrieve data from storage systems of all kinds (primarily hard disks): File Allocation Table (FAT) and New Technology File System (NTFS). In this chapter, we review these file systems and explore the key aspects of their features, functions, and behavior. We also examine a couple of other special-purpose file systems that work with Windows NT so that you're familiar with Microsoft Windows NT file systems' alphabet soup. Then, we conclude with some sample file-system-related practice questions and some good places to go looking for more information on this fascinating subject.

FAT Comes In Many Flavors

FAT stands for File Allocation Table and refers to a linear table structure used to represent information about files. The information represented includes file names, file attributes, and other directory entries that locate where files (or segments of files) are stored in the FAT environment.

Original FAT

FAT is the file system originally used with DOS. The file allocation table from which FAT draws its name stores directory information in a simple table structure that must be searched from beginning to end, one entry at a time, when users access directories or the files that reside within them.

 Although FAT is both primitive and simple, its implementations abound: A variety of versions for DOS, Windows 3.x, Windows NT, many flavors of Unix, and Macintosh are available. Numerous other, more exotic operating systems also support FAT file structures. For this reason, Microsoft recommends using FAT-formatted volumes with Windows NT Workstation (or Server) whenever many different types of clients (i.e., multi-boot systems) must exchange data through a single file system.

One of the most important characteristics of original FAT is its use of so-called 8.3 (pronounced "eight-dot-three") file names, where the name of a file can be up to eight characters long, all extensions must be preceded by a period, and file extensions can be no more than three characters long. The latter specification has led to the proliferation of many common three-character file extensions, such as .TXT for text files, .DOC for word processing files, .XLS for Excel spreadsheet files, and more. For many users, this is a defining characteristic for DOS, but it's really a requirement of the FAT file system.

Because the size of files and partitions that FAT can manage has grown with each new version of DOS, FAT uses two kinds of pointers in its allocation tables. Partitions smaller than 50 MB use 12-bit pointers, whereas larger partitions require the use of 16-bit pointers. That's why sometimes you'll see FAT volumes labeled as either "FAT12" (the volume's FAT uses 12-bit pointers) or "FAT16" (the volume's FAT uses 16-bit pointers). As shown in Figure 6.1, a FAT12 or FAT16 label appears in disk partition management utilities like the FDISK command that ships with most versions of DOS. Table 6.1 shows the features and capabilities of the FAT file system. For versions of DOS from 3.0 to 6.22, all FAT drives are 16-bit only (but this does not affect whether a volume is called FAT12 or FAT16—that's purely a function of the size of the FAT volume itself).

In addition to ordinary FAT, there are two other flavors of FAT in use in the most modern Microsoft operating systems (Windows 95 and 98 and Windows NT, to be precise): Virtual FAT (VFAT) and the FAT32 File System. We'll cover those in the sections that follow.

Virtual FAT (VFAT)

The Virtual FAT (VFAT) file system was first introduced with Windows For Workgroups 3.11 to process file I/O in protected mode. With the introduction of Windows 95, VFAT added support for long file names (LFNs). Nevertheless, VFAT remains backward compatible with original FAT, which means that it supports access using 8.3 file names as well as LFNs and, in fact, maintains an equivalence mechanism that maps 8.3 names into LFNs, and vice versa.

Figure 6.1   The DOS FDISK utility indicates whether a FAT volume is FAT12 or FAT16.

Table 6.1   Vital statistics for the FAT file system.

Feature	Capability/Maximum
Maximum volume size	2 GB
Maximum file size	2 GB
Maximum files in root directory	512
Maximum files in non-root directory	65,535
File-level security	No
Long file name support	No
Self-repairing	No
Transaction logging capabilities	No
File-level compression	No
Dual file fork support (Macintosh)	No
POSIX support	No

VFAT is the version of FAT that the original releases of Windows 95 and Windows NT 3.51 support. VFAT is also nearly identical to the FAT implementation that Windows NT supports. When using VFAT file systems, it's absolutely essential to use file management utilities that understand VFAT in general and LFNs in particular. Earlier DOS file management utilities will happily reorganize what appears to them as an original FAT structure and will often lose or damage any LFN information contained in the FAT table maintained by VFAT (or FAT32 for that matter). Therefore, when working with VFAT volumes, you must be certain to use file management utilities that can understand and preserve VFAT file structures.

Note: VFAT for Windows 95 differs from FAT for Windows NT 4. The primary difference appears in Table 6.2 for Windows 95, VFAT volumes and files are limited to a maximum of 2 GB!

In the initial release of Windows 95, the 32-bit VFAT file system is the primary file system. VFAT can use either 32-bit protected-mode drivers or 16-bit real-mode drivers. Actual allocation on disk is still 12 or 16 bit (depending on the size of the volume), so VFAT on the disk uses the same structure as earlier implementations of FAT. VFAT handles all hard drive requests and uses 32-bit code for all file access to hard drive volumes. Table 6.2 shows the features and capabilities of the VFAT file system.

Table 6.2   Vital statistics for the Windows NT FAT file system.

Feature	Capability/Maximum
Maximum volume size	4 GB
Maximum file size	4 GB
Maximum files in root directory	512
Maximum files in non-root directory	No limit
File-level security	No
Long file name support	Yes
Self-repairing	No
Transaction logging capabilities	No
File-level compression	No
Dual file fork support (Macintosh)	No
POSIX support	No

As Table 6.2 illustrates, the primary differences between VFAT and FAT are an increase in maximum volume and file sizes, an increase in non-root directory container size, and the addition of long file name support to 8.3 file names. VFAT also supports both 16- and 32-bit calls, whereas original FAT supports only 16-bit calls.

The FAT32 File System

FAT32 is the 32-bit successor to VFAT that was introduced with Microsoft Windows 95 OEM Service Release 2, in September 1996. You will sometimes see this release, called Windows 95 OSR2 in Microsoft publications. FAT32 is a completely native 32-bit file system (much like NTFS), and it supports numerous updates and enhancements compared to other FAT implementations.

Most importantly, FAT32 uses disk space more efficiently than other FAT implementations. FAT32 can use smaller disk clusters than earlier implementations, which were limited to a maximum of 65,635 clusters per volume (so as drives got bigger, cluster sizes had to increase as well). This means that even for drives up to 8 GB in size, FAT32 can use 4 K clusters. This results in a 10 to 15 percent savings in storage allocation and more efficient disk space usage compared to FAT16 drives.

This information is provided to offer you a contrasting view of FAT in comparison with NTFS. Windows 98 supports FAT 32.

FAT32 can also relocate the root directory and use a backup copy of FAT, rather than the default copy. FAT32 supports an expanded boot record to include copies of critical data structures, making FAT32 drives less susceptible to failures owing to FAT corruption than earlier implementations. FAT32 even represents the root directory as an ordinary cluster chain, which means that the directory can be located anywhere on a drive. Also, the prior limitation of 512 entries on a root directory no longer applies (as it does to earlier FAT implementations). Table 6.3 shows the features and capabilities of FAT32.

> *Note: The asterisk (*) under the self-repairing column denotes that the FAT32 self-repairing characteristics, although useful, fall short of NTFS's broader set of self-repair capabilities.*

Windows 95 OSR2 and Windows 98 are the only current Microsoft operating systems that support FAT32. This means that not even Windows NT 4, with the latest service pack applied supports this file system. If you create a multiboot configuration on a machine with Windows 95 OSR2 or Windows 98 and Windows NT installed, Windows NT will not be able to access any files that reside in a FAT32 partition. Windows 95 OSR2 and Windows 98 can, however, access the VFAT partitions that Windows NT creates.

The same proviso about using VFAT utilities on VFAT volumes applies to FAT32 volumes. Because earlier FAT utilities (including both FAT and VFAT, where FAT32 is concerned) can damage or lose critical disk information, *never* use anything but FAT32 file management utilities on FAT32 volumes.

In addition to increasing FAT's storage capacity (to a whopping 4 TB maximum for files and volumes), FAT32 makes some much-needed improvements to the root directory structure for FAT. Previous implementations required that all information in a FAT root directory fit into a single disk cluster. For all intents and purposes, this limited the number of files in the root to a maximum of 512 entries.

The introduction of LFNs further limited what the root directory could hold. Because the maximum length of an LFN is 255 characters, a single full-length LFN can consume 25 entries in a FAT (one for the 8.3 name, 24 more for the LFN itself). This reduces the number of entries possible in a VFAT root directory to 21. Microsoft recommends that LFNs be avoided in FAT root directories unless FAT32 is in use.

Table 6.3 Vital statistics for the FAT32 file system.	
Feature	**Capability/Maximum**
Maximum volume size	4 TB
Maximum file size	4 TB
Maximum files in root directory	No limit
Maximum files in non-root directory	No limit
File-level security	No
Long file name support	Yes
Self-repairing	Yes*
Transaction logging capabilities	No
File-level compression	No
Dual file fork support (Macintosh)	No
POSIX support	No

Then, too, full file specifications, which require both path names and file names (whether LFNs or 8.3 names), are limited to a total of 260 characters. FAT32 does away with the problems that LFNs in root directories can pose, but it does nothing to increase the 260-character limit on full file specifications. For that reason, Microsoft recommends that even LFNs not be allowed to exceed 75 to 80 characters in length in order to leave plenty of room for path designations (up to 180 to 185 characters).

Finally, FAT32 delivers several improvements to FAT's fault tolerance. For one thing, FAT32 boot records now capture important file system data (such as partition table information). For another, FAT mirroring can be enabled in FAT32 so another copy of the FAT can be used to drive file lookup and access. That's why Table 6.3 includes a "Yes" under the Self-repairing category.

New Technology File System (NTFS)

In keeping with the "New Technology" part of its name, NTFS incorporates significant improvements and changes to the file system native to Windows NT. From a user's point of view, files remain organized into directories (often called "folders" in the Windows environment). But unlike with FAT, there is no special treatment for root directories, nor limitations set by underlying hardware (such as the capability to access only a maximum number of disk sectors or clusters, as is the case with FAT). Likewise, there are no special indexing structures on an NTFS volume, like the file allocation table that gives FAT its name.

NTFS was designed to provide the following characteristics:

➤ **Reliability** Desirable on high-end or shared systems, such as file servers, reliability is a key element of NTFS design and behavior.

➤ **Added functionality** NTFS is designed to be extensible and incorporates advanced fault tolerance, emulates other file systems easily, supports a powerful security model, handles multiple data streams, and permits the addition of user-defined attributes to files.

➤ **POSIX support** Because the U.S. government requires minimal POSIX compliance in all systems it buys, NTFS provides them. Basic POSIX file system capabilities include optional use of case-sensitive file names, an additional timestamp for time of last file access, and an aliasing mechanism called "hard links" that lets two or more file names (potentially in different directories) point to the same file.

➤ **Flexibility** NTFS supports a highly flexible clustering model, with cluster sizes from 512 bytes to 64 K, based on a multiple of the hardware's built-in disk allocation factor. NTFS also supports LFNs and the Unicode character set, as well as maintains 8.3 file names for all files for backward compatibility with FAT.

Table 6.4   Vital statistics for the NTFS file system.

Feature	Capability/Maximum
Maximum volume size	16 EB
Maximum file size	16 EB
Maximum files in root directory	No limit
Maximum files in non-root directory	No limit
File-level security	Yes
Long file name support	Yes
Self-repairing	Yes
Transaction logging capabilities	Yes
File-level compression	Yes
Dual file fork support (Macintosh)	Yes
POSIX support	Yes

NTFS Advantages

NTFS is constructed to handle large collections of data particularly well (see Table 6.4 for the details), and it also works well for volumes of 400 MB or greater. Because the directory structure for NTFS is based on a highly efficient data structure called a "B-tree," search time for files under NTFS does not degrade as the number of files to be searched increases (as it does for FAT-based systems).

NTFS has also been designed with sufficient recoverability so users should never need to employ any kind of disk repair utility on an NTFS partition. Among other things, NTFS maintains a Recycle Bin so that users can ordinarily retrieve their own deleted files without having to run an Undelete utility of any kind. But NTFS also supports a variety of file system integrity mechanisms, including automatic transaction logging, which permits all file system writes to be replayed from a special System log. Should a Windows NT system fail for some reason, all data up to the last completed file system write can be re-created by restoring from a good system backup, and then replaying the transaction log captured since that backup was made.

NTFS also supports Windows NT's native object-level security and treats all volumes, directories, and files as individual objects. Every time users request a file system object, they will be subjected to a security check that matches their right to access the requested object against a list of permissions for that object. Requests from users with sufficient rights will be granted; requests from users with insufficient rights will be denied. This security applies whether users are logged in to a Windows NT machine locally or they make their requests across a network. Table 6.4 shows the features and capabilities of the NTFS file system.

The vital statistics for NTFS show it as the powerhouse it is. In addition to a staggering capacity of 16 EB for volumes or files (an Exabyte is 2^{64}, or approximately 16 GBs' worth of Gigabytes!), NTFS offers built-in compression that can be applied to individual files, entire directories, or complete volumes (and selectively removed or applied thereafter).

NTFS offers file-level security, which means that access to volumes, directories, and files can be controlled by an individual's account and the groups to which that account belongs. LFNs are customary with NTFS, but NTFS can map to 8.3 names to maintain support for FAT-based users. In addition to maintaining multiple copies of file system information, Windows NT offers multiple mechanisms to repair and restore an NTFS volume, should problems arise. Likewise, NTFS's transaction logging helps minimize the potential for data loss.

Finally, NTFS supports a much richer file structure, which means it's easy to graft support for other file systems onto an NTFS foundation. Microsoft exploits this capability to provide native support for the Macintosh Hierarchical Filing System (HFS) in NTFS, when Windows NT Server's Services For Macintosh are installed. Likewise, third parties have built native implementations of Sun's Network Filing System (NFS) that run on top of NTFS. (NFS is a popular distributed file system on Unix networks.)

Differences Between FAT And NTFS

Where file system overhead is concerned, FAT is more compact and less complex than NTFS. Most FAT volumes impose an overhead of less than 1 MB for the file allocation table structures that represent the directory entries for all files stored in the volume. Because of this low overhead, it is possible to format small hard disks and floppy disks with FAT. NTFS, on the other hand, has a larger overhead than FAT, partly because each directory entry requires 2 K (this has the advantage, however, of enabling NTFS to store files of 1,500 bytes or less entirely within their directory entries).

NTFS cannot be used to format floppy disks, and it shouldn't be used to format partitions smaller than 50 MB. Its relatively high overhead means that for small partitions, directory structures would consume as much as 25 percent of the available storage space.

 Microsoft recommends always using FAT for partitions of 50 MB or smaller, and NTFS for partitions of 400 MB or larger. In the "gray area" between 50 and 400 MB, other factors come into play. Chief among these is file-level security: If this is important, NTFS is the way to go. If security is not an issue, FAT may offer what you want (but performance degrades as the size increases).

In relation to file size, FAT and VFAT partitions can be up to 2 GB, Windows NT FAT up to 4 GB, and FAT32 up to 4 TB; however, FAT partitions work best when they are 200 MB or less, because of the way the FAT itself is organized. NTFS partitions can be as much as 16 EB; however, they currently are restricted to 2 TB by hardware and other system constraints.

FAT partitions may be used by Windows 95, Windows 98, Windows NT, MS-DOS, and Windows For Workgroups, not to mention other operating systems with added FAT support (for example, both Unix and Macintosh can accommodate such add-ons). With a few notable exceptions, only Windows NT can directly access NTFS partitions. NTFS information is readable across the network by many operating systems (including DOS, Windows 3.x, 95, and 98, as well as other operating systems), partly because of its backward compatibility with FAT and because of its capability to host other file systems. Also, a recently released utility called NTFSDOS makes it possible to read NTFS data on a PC booted into DOS.

Local security is not an option when you are using FAT partitions (see the next section for more details). NTFS partitions, on the other hand, allow both files and directories to be locally secured. Another difference is that FAT partitions are required for Windows NT to dual boot with other operating systems; likewise, one FAT partition of at least 2 MB is required to install and operate Windows NT on RISC-based systems.

A Matter Of Conversion

Windows NT includes a utility named CONVERT.EXE that converts FAT volumes to NTFS equivalents, but there is no utility to perform a conversion from an NTFS volume to a FAT version. To do this, you would have to create a FAT partition, copy the files from an NTFS partition to that FAT partition, and then delete the NTFS originals. Remember that when files are copied from NTFS to FAT, they lose all their NTFS security attributes (FAT lacks the ability to associate and store security attributes with the files under its care). When installing Windows NT across a network, files are copied to a FAT partition, and the install program automatically invokes the CONVERT.EXE utility just before the install switches from character mode to the GUI interface (which occurs about halfway through the Windows NT installation process).

What About HPFS?

HPFS stands for High Performance File System. Originally introduced with OS/2 1.2 and LAN Manager, HPFS was the first PC-compatible file system that supported LFNs. Like FAT, HPFS maintains a directory structure, but it adds automatic sorting of the directory and includes support for special attributes to better accommodate multiple naming conventions and file-level security.

With the introduction of Windows NT 4, Windows NT no longer supports HPFS directly. Also, HPFS file security is not directly compatible with NTFS security. However, a special conversion utility, ACLCONV.EXE, is available from Microsoft. This utility converts HPFS volumes (from LAN Manager, LAN Server, or Windows NT 3.51 or earlier Windows NT versions) to an NTFS equivalent. The utility's README file also explains how HPFS security is mapped into an NTFS near-equivalent.

> Remember, HPFS is no longer supported in Windows NT 4!

CDFS

Windows 95, 98, Windows NT 3.51, and higher number versions (including 4) support a special read-only file system called the Compact Disk File System (CDFS) to permit easy access to CDs in these operating systems. One interesting enhancement that CDFS confers is the capability to boot a PC directly from the CD that contains the Windows NT distribution media.

Windows NT Volume Structures

Windows NT Workstation does not have native support for fault tolerant volume structures—such as disk mirroring, disk duplexing, or disk striping with parity—which are supported by Windows NT Server. However, Windows NT Workstation does support volume and stripe sets. In the following sections, these structures and the Disk Administrator utility are examined.

Disk Administrator

The manipulation of disk volumes is primarily handled through the Disk Administrator utility (see Figure 6.2). Without the fault tolerance features found on Windows NT Server, the Workstation version of this utility is not as versatile.

Take time to familiarize yourself with the layout of Disk Administrator's menus, the locations of commands, and the resulting dialog boxes. If you are visually inclined, you may be able to work with the tool for a short time and then be able to "see" it in your mind's eye. Those of you unable to visualize the utility must memorize its menus. Table 6.5 is a chart that will help you with that task. (Note that we omitted the Help menu.)

> One important command is Commit Changes Now. This command instructs Windows NT to make your requested changes to the affected storage devices. In other words, partitions and drives will not be created or changed in Disk Administrator until this menu option is chosen.

Figure 6.2   The Disk Administrator utility.

Obviously, there are many commands in the five menus found in Disk Administrator. Some of these commands are discussed in further detail in this chapter. If a menu selection is not discussed further in this text, it's safe to assume you need know little (if anything) about it.

Table 6.5 Disk administrator's menus and options.			
Partition	**Tools**	**View**	**Options**
Create	Format	Volumes	Toolbar
Create Extended	Assign Drive Letter	Disk Configuration	Status Bar
Delete	Eject	Refresh	Legend
Create Volume Set	Properties		Colors and Patterns
Extend Volume Set			Disk Display
Create Stripe Set			Region Display
Mark Active			Customize Toolbar
Configuration			
Commit Changes Now			
Exit			

Disk Administrator can be used to create a floppy backup of the entire SYSTEM Registry key by using the Partition|Configuration| Save command from the menu bar.

Disk Structure 101

Hopefully, you are already familiar with storage devices and the terminology used to describe their configuration and operation. Be sure you're equipped with the bare minimum of such information—a short refresher follows.

Partitions

Hard drives are subdivided into partitions. A logical drive can contain one or more file systems, each of which enables a NOS or OS to store and retrieve files. Even though Windows NT only supports FAT and NTFS natively, partitions that support other file systems can reside on a machine that runs Windows NT (even if Windows NT cannot access them). Windows NT FAT is almost identical to VFAT, but Microsoft consistently refers to this file system as FAT instead of calling it VFAT. It is important to remember the VFAT details in regards to Windows NT's support for FAT. For instance, it's possible that a drive on a dual-boot machine running Windows 95 OEM release 2 (OSR2) and Windows NT 4 could contain a FAT32 partition; in that case, only Windows 95 or Windows 98 could access that partition.

In general, a hard drive can contain between 1 and 32 separate partitions. Therefore, a single physical hard drive can appear as multiple logical drives. Hard drives should be partitioned to maximize their usage by the underlying NOS and its applications. If you attempt to change a partition, any information stored in that space on disk will be destroyed. If there is free unpartitioned space on a drive, you may create new partitions without damaging existing partitions. Likewise, deleting any one partition does not affect other partitions on a drive.

The NTFS file system supports a variety of partition schemes. A single drive may contain up to four primary partitions, or one to three primary partitions and a single extended partition. An extended partition can be subdivided further into multiple logical drives. The total number of primary partitions plus logical drives, however, cannot exceed 32 on any one physical hard drive under Windows NT's control.

Volumes

A volume is an organizational structure imposed on one or more partitions that support file storage. If you select one or more partitions on a physical drive and format them with a specific file system, the resulting disk structure is a volume. Under Windows NT, volumes can span multiple partitions on one or more physical drives.

A volume set is a volume comprised of 2 to 32 partitions. An NTFS volume set may be extended at any time by adding another partition to the set without damaging existing stored data. However, a volume set and its data must be destroyed to reduce the size of a volume. All the partitions in a volume set must use the same file system, and the entire volume set is assigned a single drive letter. A volume set provides no fault tolerance for its data. If any one of the partitions or drives within a volume set fails, all of the data is lost.

The best way to remember the impact of losing a volume set element is the phrase "You lose one, you lose them all." This also means that the only way to recover the data in a damaged volume set is to restore the data from a backup.

Drive Letters

Nearly every volume on a Windows NT machine has an associated drive letter; in fact, Windows NT cannot access a volume unless it has an associated drive letter. Drive letters simplify the identification of an exact physical drive, partition, and volume for any referenced folder or file. Windows NT can assign drive letters to storage devices using the letters C through Z (A and B are reserved for floppy disk drives). Because this only covers 24 potential drives, and Windows NT supports as many as 32, the assumption is that some volumes will span multiple physical drives (which all share a single drive letter).

Windows NT automatically assigns the next available drive letter to each new volume created. You can reassign dynamically or shuffle drive letters using the Assign Drive Letter option on the Tools menu in Disk Administrator.

Another exception to association of volumes with drive letters applies to volumes formatted with file systems not supported by Windows NT. These volumes generally are not assigned drive letters because Windows NT cannot access them.

Master Boot Record

A special BIOS bootstrap routine (that is launched by hardware-based system code stored in Read-Only Memory, or ROM) reads a special record on the hard disk, called the Master Boot Record (MBR), which initiates the software boot sequence on a PC. By default, the MBR resides in the first sector (number 0) of the first cylinder (number 0) under the first head (number 0) on a disk drive. This, in turn, calls a bootstrap loader, which commences loading the machine's designated operating system. The MBR directs the hardware to a so-called "active partition" from where the designated operating system may be loaded.

Only a primary partition can be made active using the Mark Active command in the Disk Administrator's Partition menu. The MBR always resides at the beginning of the hard disk (sector 0, cylinder 0, head 0). The system partition is where the boot loader and other key boot files reside; for Windows NT, the boot partition is where the Windows NT system files reside.

Disk Striping

Disk striping stores data across multiple physical storage devices. In a stripe set, multiple partitions of equal size on separate devices are combined into a single logical device. When data is stored to a stripe set, it is written in 64K chunks—"stripes"—across the drives, starting at the drive on the left with data block 1, then on the middle drive with data block 2, and so on (see Figure 6.3 for an example of a stripe set).

Disk striping is fast, especially when the individual storage devices are attached to separate disk controllers. You only need two devices to create a stripe set, and such a stripe set can include as many as 32 devices. Disk striping can be implemented using either FAT or NTFS.

Figure 6.3 A stripe set.

> Note that disk striping without parity provides no fault tolerance. Should any drive in a stripe set without parity fail, all data on all disks is lost (once again, it's "Lose one, lose them all!"). If any of the drive controllers fails, none of the data is accessible until that drive controller is repaired.
>
> The boot and system partitions cannot be part of a disk stripe set or a volume set.

Special Boot Considerations

The BOOT.INI file, which lives on the system partition, uses Advanced RISC Computing (ARC) name syntax to map the path to the system files (stored on the boot partition). This path designation starts by identifying the hard disk controller and finishes with the name of the folder that contains the Windows NT system files.

Here are some examples of BOOT.INI entries:

```
multi(1)disk(0)rdisk(1)partition(2)\WINNT="Windows
NT Workstation Version 4.00"

scsi(0)disk(0)rdisk(0)partition(1)\WINNT="Windows
NT Workstation Version 4.00"
```

Should a boot or system partition fail, these entries might need to be changed, especially if the order, number, or configuration of your drives and partitions changes, or if the Windows NT system files must be accessed from an alternate location.

BOOT.INI lives in the system partition, usually on the C drive, on your Windows NT machine. BOOT.INI is a text file, which means you can edit it with any text editor. BOOT.INI attributes are set as a system, hidden, and read-only; therefore, you must turn off these attribute settings before you can edit the file and then reset them once your changes are complete. Here's an example of a BOOT.INI file:

```
[boot loader]
timeout=10
default=scsi(0)disk(0)rdisk(0)partition(1)\WINNT
[operating systems]
scsi(0)disk(0)rdisk(0)partition(1)\WINNT="Windows NT
Workstation Version 4.00"
scsi(0)disk(0)rdisk(0)partition(1)\WINNT="Windows NT
Workstation Version 4.00 [VGA mode]" /basevideo /sos
C:\="MS-DOS 6.22"
```

To edit the BOOT.INI file properly, you must know the following about ARC names:

➤ To change the BOOT.INI file to point to the proper location, you must edit both the **default=** line and the main NOS line (which is **scsi(0)disk(0)rdisk(0)partition(1) \WINNT="Windows NT Workstation Version 4.00"** in the preceding example). Both ARC names must match exactly.

➤ The first four elements of an ARC name are always lowercase in the BOOT.INI file. We use uppercase in this discussion to set them off from normal text.

➤ The first element in an ARC name, either SCSI or MULTI, is the controller type. SCSI indicates that a SCSI disk controller is being used that does not support BIOS translation. This means that the use of SCSI indicates that the controller has its BIOS disabled, whereas the use of MULTI indicates the controller has its BIOS enabled. If SCSI appears, it also means that a driver file named NTBOOTDD.SYS must appear in the system partition to handle BIOS translation for the controller. MULTI indicates the drive controller is of a type that supports BIOS translation, including IDE and SCSI (among others).

➤ The number immediately following SCSI or MULTI identifies the position of the controller within the system, numbered ordinally. Thus, the first controller is numbered (0), the second is (1), and the third is (2).

➤ The second element in an ARC name, DISK, designates the device number for a SCSI controller with no BIOS translation capabilities. DISK will appear in an ARC name. But, if SCSI is the first element in the name, the number that follows DISK identifies the storage device, numbered ordinally. Thus, the first device also is numbered (0), the second is (1), and so on. If MULTI appears first in an ARC name, DISK is ignored and will always be set to (0).

➤ The third element, RDISK, designates the device number for a BIOS translating SCSI controller or for any other controller. RDISK always appears in any ARC name. But, only if MULTI is its first element does the number following RDISK identify the storage device, numbered ordinally. Again, the first device is numbered (0), the second (1), and so on. If SCSI appears first in an ARC name, RDISK is ignored and is always set to (0).

➤ The fourth element in an ARC name identifies a disk partition. PARTITION indicates the partition where system files reside, numbered cardinally. Unlike the other terms, the first partition is (1), the second is (2), the third is (3), and so on.

➤ The fifth element in an ARC name is the name of the folder where the system files reside. "\WINNT" indicates that the folder (or directory) on the specified partition named WINNT is where system information may be found. Whatever the directory is named, this element must reflect that exact name.

➤ The data following the folder name provides the information that appears in the Windows NT Boot menu. The equals sign and the quotes that enclose the text string must follow the folder name without any additional spaces outside the quotes.

➤ After the Boot menu name, additional command-line parameter switches may be added to control how Windows NT boots. These switches include /SOS and /BASEVIDEO. /SOS causes Windows NT to display the named drivers on screen as they are loaded during system boot. /BASEVIDEO puts Windows NT into VGA mode, which is useful when troubleshooting video configuration problems.

One important item to remember is that Microsoft reversed what you might expect the terms "boot partition" and "system partition" to mean. As it happens, boot files are stored on the system partition—that is, the active partition where BOOT.INI and NTLDR reside. System files are stored on the boot partition, where the default WINNT directory resides. Remember that the boot files reside on the system partition, and vice versa. We can only guess at Microsoft's thinking—that system files are for low-level hardware initiation of the boot process, and therefore reside on the boot partition, and boot files supply bootup intelligence for Windows NT itself, and therefore, reside on the system partition. Just remember that it's the opposite of common sense, and you'll do just fine!

Practice Questions

Question 1

> Using free, unpartitioned space on a SCSI drive, you create a new partition. You highlight the free space, select Create from the Partition menu, and then specify the size of the partition and click OK. Now, the new drive appears in the Disk Administrator display. What should you do next in your endeavor to create a new place to store data?
>
> ○ a. Assign a drive letter
>
> ○ b. Select Configuration|Save
>
> ○ c. Format
>
> ○ d. Commit Changes Now

Answer d is correct. You must use the Commit Changes Now command to save the partition creation changes as the next step, then you can proceed to format the partition and assign it a drive letter. A drive letter is automatically assigned to a newly created primary partition or a logical drive within an extended partition. Thus, it is not necessary to assign a drive letter. Therefore, answer a is incorrect. The Configuration|Save command stores the current configuration status as stored in the Registry to an Emergency Repair Disk, and is not a step in creating a usable volume. Therefore, answer b is incorrect. Formatting a partition to create a volume is a required step, but this cannot be performed until the partition creation changes are committed. Therefore, answer c is also incorrect.

Question 2

> You have two IDE hard drives on a single drive controller in your Windows NT Workstation computer. There is only one partition on each of the two drives. The first drive's partition is formatted with FAT, and the second drive's partition is formatted with NTFS. The boot files are located on the second drive. What is the ARC name for the system partition?
>
> ○ a. multi(0)disk(1)rdisk(0)partition(1)
>
> ○ b. multi(0)disk(0)rdisk(1)partition(1)
>
> ○ c. multi(1)disk(0)rdisk(1)partition(1)
>
> ○ d. multi(0)disk(0)rdisk(1)partition(0)
>
> ○ e. multi(1)disk(0)rdisk(0)partition(1)

Answer b is correct. Answer b indicates the first partition of the second hard drive on the first MULTI type drive controller; this is the location of the system partition for this question. The trick is that BOOT.INI includes the ARC name for the boot partition, not the system partition. Answer a displays an improperly formatted ARC name—when MULTI is used the DISK(0) number must be zero. Therefore, answer a is incorrect. Answer c points to a second drive controller that doesn't exist for this example. Therefore, answer c is incorrect. Answer d uses an incorrect number for the partition element—this number can never be zero; the first partition is defined by using the number one. Therefore, answer d is incorrect. Answer e indicates a second drive controller that doesn't exist and the first drive on that controller. The system partition for this example is on the first and only existing controller and on the second hard drive. Therefore, answer e is incorrect.

Question 3

> You have a 50 MB partition you wish to use as a share for users to store document files. What is the best file system type to format this partition with?
>
> ○ a. FAT
>
> ○ b. CDFS
>
> ○ c. NTFS
>
> ○ d. HPFS

Answer a is correct. FAT is the best choice because it requires much less overhead than NTFS, and Microsoft does not recommend NTFS on partitions smaller than 400 MB. CDFS is not a file system type that can be used to format a hard drive—it is a CD-ROM. Therefore, answer b is incorrect. NTFS has too much overhead for a partition of this size. Therefore, answer c is incorrect. HPFS is not supported by Windows NT 4.0. Therefore, answer d is incorrect.

Question 4

You want to install Windows NT Workstation onto your system. You create two 500 MB partitions—one for the NOS and applications, and the other for personal data and confidential documents. How would you format these volumes? [Check all correct answers]

❑ a. Format both with FAT.

❑ b. Format both with NTFS.

❑ c. Format the NOS partition with FAT and the data partition with NTFS.

❑ d. Format the NOS partition with NTFS and the data partition with FAT.

Answers a, b, c, and d are correct. Because security is not mentioned as an issue in this scenario, all of these methods of formatting can be used.

Question 5

Which of the following ARC names indicates the third partition of the fourth SCSI drive on the second controller that has its BIOS disabled?

○ a. multi(1)disk(3)rdisk(0)partition(3)

○ b. multi(1)disk(0)rdisk(3)partition(3)

○ c. scsi(1)disk(3)rdisk(0)partition(3)

○ d. scsi(1)disk(3)rdisk(0)partition(4)

Answer c is correct. Answer c indicates the third partition on the fourth drive on a non-BIOS SCSI controller. Answer a indicates a BIOS-enabled controller. Therefore, answer a is incorrect. Answer b also indicates a BIOS-enabled controller. Therefore, answer b is incorrect. Answer d indicates the fourth partition. Therefore, answer d is incorrect.

Question 6

Your Windows NT Workstation has been designated as the file storage area for your small peer-to-peer workgroup. To accommodate the additional files, an 8 GB SCSI hard drive has been installed into your system. You must set up a FAT partition to maximize access for non-Windows NT clients. If most of the files your organization works with are large, what is the best configuration for this new drive?

O a. A single 8 GB FAT partition

O b. Two 4 GB FAT partitions

O c. Eight 1 GB FAT partitions

O d. Sixteen 500 MB FAT partitions

Answer b is correct. The best solution is to maximize the size of each partition, i.e., two 4 GB partitions that are valid under Windows NT. FAT does not support 8 GB partitions. Therefore, answer a is incorrect. Neither of the final selections is really practical because they would require users to search through too many partitions. Therefore, answers c and d are incorrect.

Question 7

You want to upgrade from Windows NT Workstation 3.51 to 4. Your main data directory, H, is an HPFS volume. After Windows NT Workstation 4 is installed, you can use the CONVERT.EXE utility to convert H from HPFS to NTFS.

O a. True

O b. False

Answer b is correct. Because Windows NT 4 no longer supports HPFS, you'll have to obtain the ACLCONV.EXE utility from Microsoft to convert the HPFS partition into NTFS. The Windows NT 4 utility CONVERT.EXE can only transform FAT partitions into NTFS partitions. However, because Windows NT 3.51's convert utility works with HPFS, it might be even better to convert HPFS to NTFS before installing the upgrade to Windows NT 4.

Question 8

Which of the following characteristics are true of Windows NT FAT but not true of FAT? [Check all correct answers]

❏ a. Maximum volume size of 4 GB

❏ b. Support for file sizes of 2 GB

❏ c. No file-level security

❏ d. Is self-repairing

❏ e. Support for LFNs

Answer a and e are correct. FAT can only support volumes up to 2 GB in size, whereas NT FAT can handle volumes up to 4 GB. Therefore, answer a is correct. Answer e is also correct because of the 8.3 limitation of FAT and the LFN support of NT FAT. Both VFAT and FAT can support 2 GB sized files. Therefore, answer b is incorrect. Neither Windows NT FAT nor FAT has file-level security, and neither is self-repairing. Therefore, answers c and d are incorrect.

Question 9

What files should be placed on a boot disk in order to boot to the duplicate drive of a disk duplex from a floppy in the event of a failure of the original drive? Assume the drive controller is SCSI that does not support BIOS translation. [Check all correct answers]

❏ a. NTDETECT.COM

❏ b. BOOT.INI

❏ c. NTLDR

❏ d. WINA20.386

❏ e. NTBOOTDD.SYS

Answers a, b, c, and e are correct. NTDETECT.COM is required on the boot floppy. Therefore, answer a is correct. BOOT.INI is required on the boot floppy. Therefore, answer b is also correct. NTLDR is required on the boot floppy. Therefore, answer c is also correct. NTBOOTDD.SYS is the driver for SCSI translation required for non-BIOS controllers. Therefore, answer e is also correct. WINA20.386 is a Windows device driver that is not needed on the boot floppy. Therefore, answer d is incorrect.

Question 10

On your Windows NT Workstation, you have partitions from six drives linked together in a stripe set. One of these drives fails due to a power spike. How can you restore your system to proper working order?

- ○ a. No restoration is necessary; Windows NT will automatically rebuild the lost data on the fly.
- ○ b. Replace the failed drive and use the Reconstruct command from Disk Administrator.
- ○ c. Rebuild the volume with a new drive and restore all data from a backup.
- ○ d. Use the three setup disks and the ERD to perform a system repair.

Answer c is correct. Rebuilding the volume and restoring from backup is the only method available to Windows NT Workstation to restore failed sets. Windows NT Workstation does not have any fault tolerant disk features; the solution described in answer a would occur only with disk striping with parity, which is not available on Windows NT Workstation. Therefore, answer a is incorrect. Answer b describes the activity involved in restoring a stripe set with parity, a feature not available on Windows NT Workstation. Therefore, answer b is incorrect. The ERD repair process will not restore the failed drive to operational status; this is a useless solution attempt for this particular problem. Therefore, answer d is incorrect.

Need To Know More?

 Perkins, Charles, Matthew Strebe, and James Chellis: *MCSE: NT Workstation Study Guide, 2nd Edition.* Sybex Network Press, San Francisco, CA, 1998. ISBN 0-7821-2223-X. Chapter 5 focuses on NT file systems, volume structures, and the use of Disk Administrator.

Tittel, Ed, Christa Anderson, and David Johnson: *NT Workstation 4 Exam Prep.* Coriolis, Scottsdale, AZ, 1998. ISBN 1-57610-238-6. Chapter 5 covers Windows NT's various file systems, and compares them with other Microsoft file systems.

Search the TechNet CD (or its online version through **www.microsoft.com**) and the *Windows NT Workstation Resource Kit* CD using the keywords "FAT," "VFAT," "FAT32," and "NTFS." KnowledgeBase article Q100108 "Overview of FAT, HPFS, and NTFS File Systems" is particularly informative.

File And Directory Security

7

. . . .

Terms you'll need to understand:

√ File Allocation Table (FAT)

√ New Technology File System (NTFS)

√ Security Accounts Manager (SAM)

√ Objects

√ Access control list (ACL)

√ Permissions

√ NTBACKUP

√ Share

√ No Access

√ Read

√ Change

√ Full Control

√ Add

√ Add and Read

√ List

√ Auditing

√ Transaction logging

Techniques you'll need to master:

√ Selecting a file system for Windows NT

√ Securing system resources

√ Establishing access permissions

√ Creating shares and implementing share permissions

√ Understanding the difference between copying and moving files

√ Setting up auditing to monitor network activity

The purpose of security is to regulate access to data and protect that data from destruction. This is accomplished through many activities—ranging from limiting physical access to computers to allowing certain users the ability to work with important files. Backup methods can be used to protect data from being destroyed due to hardware problems, viruses, or malicious file commands. However, protecting data from copyright violations, unauthorized disclosure, and malicious alteration requires complete control of files, applications, and users.

How much and what type of restrictions are placed on your network must be determined by your organization's security policy. To successfully manage a network, you must have a solid understanding of access rights, permissions, and user access. In this chapter, we discuss these topics thoroughly.

Basics Of Security

Before we launch into a detailed discussion of the security features of Windows NT that focus on the protection of data files, we need to establish the context where file security occurs.

Logon And User Identification

The first step in understanding Windows NT security must start where every user starts—at logon. By pressing Ctrl+Alt+Del at the initial Windows NT splash screen, you initiate the WINLOGON utility. This utility displays the Logon dialog box and sends the account name, password, and domain data (if applicable) to the security manager. The security manager (part of the Executive Services in the Kernel) verifies the name and password, creates an access token, and launches the user's shell (usually Windows NT Explorer). The verification process is the act of comparing the username and password with the data stored in the Security Accounts Manager (SAM). This database also contains the list of access privileges for each user. From this list, the access token is built. After this process is complete, the user is able to use the computer for productive work.

The access token created by the security manager is the collection of identifiers and permissions unique to each individual. The NOS uses this access token to verify authority to access and manipulate every object and resource. The access token is built by combining the individual settings of a user with those of each group to which he or she belongs.

The access token is created when a user logs in, and it is not changed until that user logs out and then logs in again. This means that any changes to a user account or a group to which that user belongs will not affect those users who are currently logged in— the changes will only affect them the next time they log in.

The access token not only defines what objects and resources a user can interact with, but it is also attached to every process launched by that user. WINLOGON uses the access token it creates to launch the shell for a user. The shell inherits the same access privileges as the user, based on the access token. Every process launched or initiated by the user can only have the level of access authority granted by the user's access token, or less. (In fact, every single process has an access token assigned to it.) Under Windows NT, it is nearly impossible for a user to launch a process or access an object that requires a higher level of access than that defined by his or her current access token.

Objects

The ultimate purpose of security is to control who has access to what. The WINLOGON process determines the "who," and objects are the "what." Within the world of Windows NT, everything is an object. An object has a type, a collection of services, and a set of attributes.

The type of an object defines what services and attributes are valid. Object types within Windows NT include files, directories, symbolic links, printers, processes, threads, ports, devices, and even windows (see Figure 7.1).

Directory
List
Read
Add
Change
Delete
File Name
Data
Access Control List

Figure 7.1 A Windows NT object.

The services of an object are the activities that can be performed on, with, or by the object. For example, a directory object has services of List, Read, Change, Delete, and so on; a printer object has services of Print, Manage, Delete, and so on.

The attributes of an object include the name of the object, the actual data, and the access control list (ACL).

Access Control List

An access control list (or ACL) is the attribute of each object that defines which users and groups have what level of services for that object (see Figure 7.2). An ACL is merely comprised of a list of services (Read, Write, Delete) and the associated users and groups who can perform each action (Mary, Bob, Sales group, Marketing group).

When a user attempts to use an object, that user's access token is compared to the objects ACL. You can think of the access token as a key ring with multiple keys, each related to a group membership or specific permission setting for that user. You can also think of the ACL as a linked group of padlocks for each object, and each lock will open only for a specific user or group key and then only allow the specified level of access.

Figure 7.2 A visualization of a user's access token and an object's access control list.

You can set the ACLs on an object in two ways. First, you can use the GUI dialog boxes and your mouse to point and click to make any and all ACL changes you desire. Go check it out for yourself—right-click over an object, select Properties, the Securities tab, and then click the Permissions button. The second method is to use the CACLS command. This command can display or modify the ACL of files. Here's the syntax:

```
cacls filename [/t] [/e] [/c] [/g user:r|c|f] [/r user [...]]
[/p user:n|r|c|f [...]] [/d user [...]]
```

The parameters are as follows:

➤ *filename* Displays ACLs of specified file(s)

➤ /t Changes ACLs of specified files in the current directory and all subdirectories

➤ /e Edits the ACLs instead of replacing them

➤ /c Continues changing ACLs, ignoring errors

➤ /g *user*:r|c|f Grants specified user access rights of Read, Change, or Full Control

➤ /r *user* Revokes specified user's access rights (only valid with /e)

➤ /p *user*:n|r|c|f Replaces specified user's access rights of None, Read, Change, or Full Control

➤ /d *user* Deny specified user access

Checking Permissions

When a user attempts to access an object, the security system performs a permissions check to determine if that user has proper authority to access the object and which services he or she can invoke. Using the key-and-lock analogy, the security system tries the keys on the user's key ring (access token) in each of the object's locks (ACL). If a match is found, the user can proceed with the intended activity.

This analogy doesn't quite explain every aspect of the permissions check, but it does give you a good mental image of what goes on. One important facet of the permissions check that the lock-and-key analogy fails to communicate is No Access. Any user or group can be assigned No Access for an object. If such an assignment is made, a user cannot gain any access whatsoever.

Putting the lock-and-key analogy aside, when a user requests access to an object's service, the security system performs the following authority check:

1. Checks for any specified No Access for the user or any groups the user is a member of. If No Access is found, the user is denied access.

2. Checks for any specific granting of access based on the service requested for the user and any groups. If access is found, the user is granted access.

3. If neither a specific No Access or service permission is found, the user is denied access.

As you can see, a specific No Access is like a trump card—it overrides any other settings, including specific granting of access. Plus, if no specific permission is given (that is, no key is present in the access token), the user cannot gain entry.

Note: No Access under Windows NT prevents a user from using any of the six file operations, but a user is still able to see the name of the object as stored in the Master Browser object list.

NTFS Security

The Windows NT File System (NTFS) has a standard set of access permissions for files and directories. Through these permissions, every single file and directory within the file system namespace can be controlled through the use of access tokens and ACLs. Six specific operations can occur on a file or directory:

➤ R Read. The object's data contents can be viewed.

➤ W Write. The object's data contents can be changed.

➤ X Execute. The object can be executed (in relation to directories, this means the directory can be opened).

➤ D Delete. The object can be deleted.

➤ P Change Permissions. The object's access permissions can be altered.

➤ O Take Ownership. The ownership of the object can be changed.

Note: Ownership can only be taken; it cannot be given. However, you must have the Take Ownership permission or the user right in order to do so. As the owner of an object, you have Full Control permission over that object.

These six operations are combined into the standard permissions sets for files and directories. The standard permissions for files are:

➤ **Read (RX)** The file can be read and/or executed.

➤ **Change (RWXD)** Includes Read (RX), plus Modify and Delete.

➤ **Full Control (RWXDPO)** Includes Change (RWXD), plus Change Permissions and Take Ownership.

➤ **No Access ()** Absolutely no access.

The standard permissions for directories are (the first pair of parentheses refers to the directory itself, and the second refers to the contents of the directory, but not the contents in any subdirectories):

➤ **List (RX)(not specified)** Users can view the names of the contents of this directory; no content-specific settings are specified.

➤ **Read (RX)(RX)** Users can read and traverse the directory as well as read and execute the contents.

➤ **Add (WX)(not specified)** Users can add files to the directory but cannot read or change the contents of the directory.

➤ **Add and Read (RWX)(RX)** Users can add files to and read files from the directory, but they cannot change them.

➤ **Change (RWXD)(RWXD)** Users can add, read, execute, modify, and delete the directory and its contents.

➤ **Full Control (RWXDPO)(RWXDPO)** Users have full control over the directory and its contents.

➤ **No Access ()()** Absolutely no access is granted to the directory and its contents.

In addition to these sets of standard file and directory permissions, special access can be defined on a directory or file basis. Special access consists of one or more of the six file/directory object operations (RWXDPO). Special access can be set for files and for directories—but directories have two levels of settings: one for the directory itself and another for the contents of that directory.

Other object types have their own unique set of operations and permissions. For example, print objects have a Print operator but do not have a Read operator. For each object type, the NTFS permissions might be slightly different to accommodate the functionality of that object. For the printer's permission discussion, please see Chapter 14.

Shares And Permissions

Windows NT uses two types of permission settings to control object access—local and remote. Local access includes the NTFS permissions just discussed, and remote access is controlled by shares.

A share is a network resource that allows remote users to gain access to an object. The share is an object in itself that points to the resource object. The share knows how to translate data from the user (or more specifically an application employed by the user) to interact with the resource over the network. Shares enable a local resource to be used anywhere on the network.

Shares have their own set of permission levels (notice these are the same as the standard file permissions):

➤ **No Access** Absolutely no access

➤ **Read (RX)** Read and execute

➤ **Change (RWXD)** Read, write, execute, delete

➤ **Full Control (RWXDPO)** Full control

For users who belong to more than one group with permission settings to the same share, these permissions are cumulative, except the No Access permission. When the No Access permission is assigned, all other permissions become obsolete. In other words, the broadest permission always will apply, unless No Access appears anywhere. When that happens, No Access always "wins."

These permissions grant or restrict a users interaction with the share itself. If a user has access, the NTFS permissions on the object itself determine what services the user can access. When a share is used to access a resource, the combination of the share restrictions and NTFS restrictions will result in granting only the most restrictive permissions common to both the share and the object itself. You can think of a share as a door and the services of an object as boxes. The share will only allow object services to pass through its gateway if they are the same or less restrictive than the permissions on the share itself. As you can see in Figure 7.3, the "boxes" of NTFS permissions will only fit through the "doors" of a share if they are smaller than the opening.

Permissions on a share only apply to users attempting to access a resource through that share (that is, over the network). Local users are not affected by the share restrictions because they have direct access to the resource. Therefore, local users are only restricted by the NTFS permissions on an object, whereas remote or network users are restricted by both the share permissions and the NTFS object permissions.

 An extremely important item to remember about shares is that the initial default settings of all newly created shares is Full Control to the Everyone group. This can cause some interesting problems if you don't reduce the access range for premium shares.

Mapping Shares

Mapping shares (or mapping a drive) is the process of defining a local drive letter that points to a network resource, such as a share. This can be accomplished many ways, but only two are worth noting here:

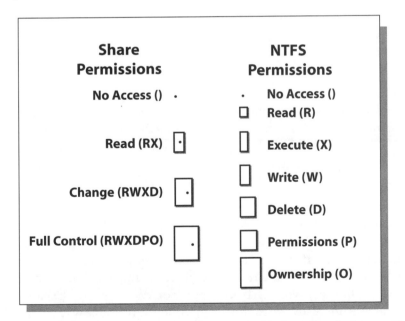

Figure 7.3 A visualization of share permissions in relation to NTFS object permissions.

➤ The Map Network Drive command of Windows NT Explorer or Network Neighborhood can be used to define the assigned drive letter, the share to map to (selectable from a browse list), the user to connect as, and whether or not to maintain the mapping permanently.

➤ A command line using the UNC name of the share. Here's an example:

```
NET USE <driveletter> \\server\sharename <password>
/USER:<username> /PERSISTENT:YES|NO
```

Default Shares

Windows NT creates special default shares for each of the system's storage volumes each time the computer is booted. The system uses these shares to support network activity and administer internal operations. These default shares—also called "system shares" or "hidden shares"—are not listed in standard browser lists of share resources. The common default shares are:

➤ **ADMIN$** Points to the Windows NT root directory (that is, C:\WINNT)

➤ **IPC$** A share used by InterProcess Communications

➤ **PRINT$** Points to the printer driver directory

➤ **C$, D$, E$, ...** A share for each hard drive volume, pointing to the root directory

Default shares all have a trailing "$" (dollar sign) as part of their name. Default shares can be temporarily disabled, but they cannot be deleted. Windows NT will re-enable all default shares during the next boot. You can map a drive letter to a default or hidden share by providing an Administrator name and password in the map drive dialog box.

You can create your own hidden shares simply by adding a dollar sign to the end of your share name. On Windows NT Server, the Server Manager can be used to display all shares—normal and hidden—but Windows NT Workstation does not offer a similar function. The only indicator of hidden shares on Windows NT Workstation is the small "sharing hand" icon added to the drive or directory within My Computer or Windows NT Explorer. Hidden shares/Administrative cannot be modified in the same way as standard shares. They cannot be deleted.

Permission Combinations

Each time a user attempts to access an object, there are many hurdles his or her security settings must pass in order to reach the object. It is possible for a single user to belong to more than one named group in Windows NT. Access to resources may be assigned to groups or individual users. This makes it possible for a single user or group to be assigned different levels of access for any particular resource. The specified settings of the user account and each group membership must be examined for both the share and the object itself. Here are some items to keep in mind when deciphering permission combinations:

➤ No Access on the share or the object prevents all access, even if Full Control is granted by another group membership.

➤ The permissions from all groups of which a user is a member are cumulative. This applies both to shares and objects.

➤ The most restrictive set of common permissions between a share and an object are used.

Managing Shared Resources

The customary method for sharing files, directories, and resources on Windows NT is by creating what is called a "share." The process is simple. Use the following steps to share a resource or directory:

1. Select the directory or resource you want to share in Windows NT Explorer or through the My Computer icon.

2. Right-click the directory or resource and select Sharing from the drop-down menu (the default is Not Shared).

3. Click the Share As button. When you do this, a dialog box pops up, and Windows NT displays a default share name (this is usually the first eight characters of the selected directory name). You can change the share name if you desire. It is important to note, however, that share names more than eight characters long cannot be accessed from DOS-based clients.

You also can limit access to the share to a maximum number of users on the Sharing tab. It's a good idea to limit the number of users to prevent users from overloading a slow computer or to ensure that other server processes can run unimpeded. Select the Maximum Allowed option if you do not want to impose this limitation. To set the number of allowed users, select the Allow button. A number then appears in the Users box. You can use the up and down arrows to set this number, or you can type a number directly in the Users box.

 Subdirectories inherit the permissions of the parent directories as their default share permissions.

After creating the share, you can assign permission to the share. To do this, select the Permissions button or click the Security tab. Note that the default setting for newly created shares is Full Control for the Everyone group. You have four levels of security available for the purpose of restricting access to server shares: No Access, Read, Change, and Full Control.

 You must always set explicit directory permissions on new shares. The default permissions grant Full Control to the Everyone group.

Securing FAT And NTFS Resources

FAT partitions cannot support local security. However, FAT partitions can use share permissions, which may be imposed when directories are shared on a network. This does not prevent someone who is logged on locally from accessing files located on a particular machine, but it can protect even FAT-based files from unauthorized network access.

For security purposes, NTFS is the wiser choice. NTFS partitions can lock out or limit access both for remote and local users. All files and directories on an NTFS partition can be locked using NTFS security. This means that the only people who can access protected files are the users who have been granted explicit access to them.

Directory shares and NTFS security are controlled by security properties associated with a directory to be shared, or with any NTFS file system object (which can be either a directory or an individual file). By selecting the Properties entry in the File menu, or by right-clicking a file name and selecting the Properties entry in the resulting pop-up menu, users can examine the Sharing (for directories only) and Security (for files and directories) tabs.

The default for the system group Everyone is Full Control for both shares and new NTFS volumes. Only a network administrator, the owner, or a user who has been granted Full Control can reset the access levels on an NTFS or shared resource.

Moving NTFS Secured Files

Higher-level folders usually share NTFS permissions with the files and folders they contain. For example, if you create a folder within a folder in which administrators have Full Control permission and backup operators have Read Only permission, the new folder will inherit those same permissions. The same goes for files that are copied from another folder or moved from a different NTFS partition.

 If you move a folder or a file into another folder on the same NTFS partition, security attributes are not inherited from the new container object. For example, if you move a file from a folder with Read permission for the Everyone group to a folder on the same partition with Full Control permission for the Everyone group, the moved file retains its original Read permission. That's because an NTFS move operation within the same partition changes only the object's location pointer, not any of the object's other attributes (including security information).

These four important rules will help you decide if permissions will be inherited or retained when performing move or copy operations on NTFS objects:

➤ If you move files within the same NTFS partition, they will *retain* their original permissions.

➤ Any NTFS copy operation always *inherits* the new parent folder's permissions.

➤ Other operations, such as file creation or moves across NTFS partition boundaries, inherit their parent folder's permissions.

➤ Other operations, such as file creation, file copy, and moves from one NTFS partition to another, will *inherit* the parent folder's permissions.

➤ All NTFS permissions are lost when files are moved or copied from NTFS to a FAT partition.

Windows NT Backup

Backing up critical data is a very important task for any network administrator. Windows NT 4 ships with a program called NTBACKUP.EXE, for backup functions. Although this program is automatically installed with Windows NT, you must install drivers for your tape backup (performed through the Tape Devices applet) and have a good understanding of how the backup process works to successfully back up and restore important data. In this section, we explain the aspects of NTBACKUP that you need to know.

NTBACKUP Facts

NTBACKUP's advantages include the following:

➤ The program is free; you do not have to purchase a third-party backup utility.

➤ Because NTBACKUP is a native Windows NT program, the chances of the server running into stability problems are slim to none.

➤ NTBACKUP can back up from the two supported file systems— FAT and NTFS. It also can restore just as easily to either file system.

NTBACKUP also has the following disadvantages:

➤ The only acceptable media that NTBACKUP supports is a tape drive; you cannot back up to another hard drive, floppy, or even across the network to a network drive.

➤ There is no built-in scheduler program included with Windows NT backup; to accomplish an unattended backup, you must write a batch file (see the section titled "Scheduling Backups," later in this chapter).

➤ You cannot back up a remote Registry. This task must be done locally. You can, however, back up files both locally and remotely.

➤ NTBACKUP only does a file-by-file backup and not a disk-image backup.

Who Has The Right?

Just like everything else in Windows NT, a user must have the right to perform backups and restorations. All users with Backup Files and Directories permission can back up any file and folder. This right must be granted to the user by selecting User Rights from the Policies menu in the User Manager. To restore files and folders, a user must have the Restore Files And Directories right, which is also granted in the User Manager. By default, only members of the Backup Operator and Administrator groups have these rights.

Backup Types

Table 7.1 lists the different backup types in NTBACKUP.

Performing Backups

Performing backups with NTBACKUP is simple and straightforward. Drives, folders, and individual files are selected through an Explorer-like

Table 7.1 Vital statistics about NTBACKUP's backup types.		
Type Of Backup	**Backs Up**	**Marked?**
Daily copy	Files and folders that have changed during that day	No
Copy	All selected files and folders	No
Differential	Selected files and folders if they have changed since the last backup	No
Incremental	Selected files and folders if they have changed since the last backup	Yes
Normal	All selected files and folders	Yes

interface. Files to be backed up are marked with an X; those that are not to be backed up have an empty checkbox.

Once you have selected which items to back up, you can select different NTBACKUP options from the Backup Information dialog box. Table 7.2 describes each option, along with the description.

After you select the options and type a meaningful description of the backup in the description box, you need to choose the backup type to perform (refer back to Table 7.1).

The last set of options to set is the log information. If you want to create a backup log, simply put a path in the log file line of the Backup Information dialog box. The default is BACKUP.LOG in the %systemroot%\ folder. The three options under Log Information are shown in Table 7.3.

Table 7.2 Vital statistics about NTBACKUP's tape options.	
Option	**Description**
Operation: Append	Adds new backup set after the last backup set on the tape.
Operation: Replace	Overwrites all data on the tape.
Verify After Backup	Confirms that files/folders were backed up.
Backup Registry	This option is available only if you have selected at least one other file. You *cannot* back up only the Registry.
Restrict Access To Owner/Administrator	Limits access to users with the correct permissions. When backing up the Registry, you should always choose this option.
Hardware Compression	If your tape drive supports data compression, select this option.

Table 7.3   Vital statistics about Log Information options.

Option	Description
Full Detail	Logs all backup information, including the names of all of the files and folders backed up and skipped.
Summary Only	Logs only the major backup operations, such as loading and unloading the tape and starting backup.
Do Not Log	No log is created.

Scheduling Backups

There isn't a scheduler inside the NTBACKUP program, but you can write a batch file to start the Windows NT backup process. The syntax follows:

```
NTBACKUP.EXE BACKUP [pathname[options]]
```

Table 7.4 shows the options or switches you can use with this command line process.

Table 7.4   Vital statistics about NTBACKUP options.

Option/Switch	Description
/a	This is not available for a blank tape. This appends the backup set to any existing backup set.
/b	Backs up the local Registry.
/d *text or description*	Allows for a backup description.
/e	Logs exceptions; similar to a summary log.
/l *file name*	Assigns a log file name.
/r	Limits the rights of the backup operation to Administrators, Backup Operators, or Owners.
/t{normal|copy|incremental|differential|daily}	Allows you to specify which type of backup to perform.
/v	Confirmation of backup.
/hc: {on|off }	Enables or disables hardware compression (if your tape drive will support it). The default is off.
Cmd /c net use x:	Connects to a remote share. Use this to connect to a remote machine.
Cmd /c net use x: /delet e	Disconnects from remote shares.

NTBACKUP can be scheduled through batch files and the Scheduler service **AT** command.

Once you have a batch file with the NTBACKUP link included, you can use AT.EXE to schedule the batch file to run at a specific time (see Table 7.5 for AT command options). AT.EXE schedules commands to be run by the scheduling service in Windows NT. The scheduling service must be running on the machine that will run the scheduled task. The syntax for the AT command is as follows:

```
AT [\\computername] [id] [/delete] time [interactive]
[/every: date[,...]| next; date[,...] "command"
```

Restoring With NTBACKUP

Restoring data with the NTBACKUP program is quite simple. You can restore data to the same system or a completely different system, which is a great advantage. (Remember that a Registry cannot be backed up or restored remotely.) The restore process is the reverse of the backup process, with a few different options. (These options are detailed in Table 7.6.)

Note: Restoring files to an NTFS partition will ensure that the ACLs of each file and folder remain intact. However, restoring files to a FAT partition will result in files and folders with no security restrictions.

Table 7.5   Vital statistics about AT.EXE options.

Option	Description
computer name	Specifies a remote machine.
id	Assigns an ID number to a scheduled command.
/delete	Cancels a scheduled command. If the ID is omitted, all the scheduled commands are deleted.
time	Expresses time in hour:minute mode; runs from 00:00 through 23:59.
/interactive	Allows the user to see network activity in realtime.
/every: date[,...]	Specifies the days for the command to run.
/next:date[,....]	Specifies the next day of the month the command is to run.
"command"	Specifies the actual command to be run (for example, NTBACKUP).

Table 7.6   Vital statistics about restoration options and their descriptions.

Option	Description
Restore Local Registry	If you backed up the Registry, this option will restore the local Registry.
Restore File Permissions	Restores NTFS permissions. If this is not selected, the files and folders will follow the general rule of inheriting the new parent directory permissions.
Verify After Restore	Does a check of the tape against the files on the hard drive.

Other NT Security Issues

Two other important aspects of Windows NT security are auditing and transaction logging. In the next two sections, we give you an overview of these issues.

Auditing

On a computer running Windows NT, the administrator has the option to audit access to resources such as directories, printers, and shares. The audit will inform the administrator if someone attempts to access secured resources or just how often a particular resource is accessed. The information gathered by Windows NT's auditing system can be brought to bear against performance problems, security risks, and expansion planning.

The auditing system is designed to watch every event occurrence on your entire network. To simplify the act of fine-tuning the areas you want to audit, there are three levels of switches with which you'll need to work. The master switch is the Audit These Events radio button located on the Audit Policy dialog box (see Figure 7.4). This dialog box is accessed through the User Manager's Policies pull-down menu. This master switch turns on or off NT's entire audit system. By default, this switch is set to Do Not Audit.

The second level of switches becomes available when you set the master switch. Seven event types are listed in the Audit Policy dialog box. Each of these event types can be audited by tracking their success and/or failure. Here are the seven event types and descriptions of the events they control:

➤ **Logon And Logoff** Tracks logons, logoffs, and network connections.

➤ **File And Object Access** Tracks access to files, directories, and other NTFS objects. This includes printers.

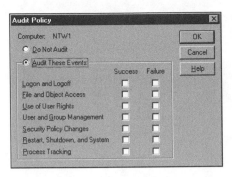

Figure 7.4   The Audit Policy dialog box.

➤ **Use Of User Rights** Tracks when users make use of user rights.

➤ **User And Group Management** Tracks changes in the accounts of users and groups (password changes, account deletions, group memberships, renaming, and so forth).

➤ **Security Policy Changes** Tracks changes of user rights, audit policies, and trusts.

➤ **Restart, Shutdown, And System** Tracks server shutdowns and restarts and also logs events affecting system security.

➤ **Process Tracking** Tracks program activation, program termination, and other object/process access.

The third level of audit switches is on the object level. This level of control only applies to File And Object Access events. These switches reside within the properties of each NTFS-based object, such as files, directories, and printers. Figures 7.5 through 7.7 show the Audit switch screens for file, directory, and print access. Note the differences in the tracking events among the object types: Both the file and directory have Read, Write, Execute, Delete, Change Permissions, and Take Ownership, but the printer object has Print, Full Control, Delete, Change Permissions, and Take Ownership.

A second, important difference applies to the directory object. The directory object allows you to change the files and/or subdirectories within the current directory to the same audit settings. Although this is convenient, you should use it with caution, because any current audit settings on these objects will be cleared and replaced with the new settings.

To get to these dialog boxes, right-click over the object, select Properties from the pop-up menu, select the Security tab, and then click the Auditing button. Remember, object auditing is only available for NTFS objects, not FAT objects.

Figure 7.5 The File Auditing dialog box.

> *Note: By default, the object-level audit switches are all blank with no users or groups present in the Name field. We added the Everyone group before capturing these images so the Events list at the bottom of these dialog boxes would become readable instead of their default near-invisible gray.*

Figure 7.6 The Directory Auditing dialog box.

Figure 7.7 The Printer Auditing dialog box.

The object-level audit dialog boxes allow you to set the same success/failure event tracking for all users and groups listed in the Names field. You cannot track success for one group and failure for another.

Let's repeat the steps required to audit:

1. Turn on the master Audit These Events switch.

2. Select one or more of the event types to track success or failure.

3. If you choose the File And Object Access option, you must also edit the auditing settings for each NTFS object.

The activity of auditing system events demands large amounts of computing overhead, especially if the event monitored, such as file access, occurs often. It is not wise to audit any event or object any more than is absolutely necessary to track a problem or test equipment. Otherwise, your system will run more slowly.

The information gathered by Windows NT's auditing system is stored in the Security log. You can view this log using the Event Viewer. The Event Viewer lists detailed information about each tracked event. Some of the data recorded includes the user logon identification, the computer used, the time, the date, and the action or event that instigated an audit.

When numerous objects or events are audited, the Security log can grow large quite quickly. You need to monitor the size of this log and possibly implement a size restriction and/or an automated new file creation to prevent data loss and maximize the usefulness of the gathered data.

Transaction Logging

Windows NT automatically records a log of all activities performed on NTFS volumes. This includes writes, modifications, renaming, deletions, attribute changes, index alterations, and hot-fix activities. This log of NTFS transactions is a fault tolerance feature that enables the reconstruction of disk activities in the event of an error, data loss, or system error.

Practice Questions

Question 1

> You want to use NTBACKUP.EXE to back up some local files. What type of media can the NTBACKUP program use?
>
> ○ a. Floppy
>
> ○ b. Tape
>
> ○ c. Writable CDs
>
> ○ d. A hard drive across the network

Answer b is correct. The only backup media type that NTBACKUP.EXE supports is a tape drive. NTBACKUP does not support floppy, writable CDs, or network drive backups. Therefore, answers a, c, and d are incorrect.

Question 2

> You suspect that an Account group member is accessing a directory that the user should be prevented from reaching. This might mean that you've set up the group memberships incorrectly. You aren't sure who it is, but you do know what directory is being accessed. What feature of Windows NT will let you track who gains access to this directory?
>
> ○ a. NTFS file activity logging
>
> ○ b. Event auditing
>
> ○ c. Event Viewer
>
> ○ d. Account lockout

Answer b is correct. Event auditing will track the activity around any object within Windows NT. The NTFS file activity logging is a fault tolerance feature used to ensure the integrity of stored data. It cannot be used to track access. Therefore, answer a is incorrect. The Event Viewer is used to review the Security log created by the auditing system, but it is not the feature that does the actual tracking. Therefore, answer c is incorrect. Account lockout is the feature used to prevent compromised accounts from being used. Therefore, answer d is incorrect.

Question 3

User JimBob is a member of the Accounting, Managers, and Print Operators groups. For a share named SalesFeb, these groups have the following share permissions:

- Accounting: Change

- Managers: Read

- Print Operators: Full Control

In addition, JimBob's NTFS permission for the SalesFeb directory and its contents is Read. What is JimBob able to do with files from the SalesFeb directory when he accesses them through the share?

- ○ a. Nothing, he has no access.

- ○ b. Read and execute.

- ○ c. Read, write, execute, and delete.

- ○ d. Read, write, execute, delete, change permissions, and take ownership.

Answer b is correct because Read access includes both read and execute. The less permissive of Read and Full Control is Read, so Bob's effective permission to SalesFeb is Read. To calculate share and NTFS permissions combined, take the most permissive of each kind and then the least permissive of the remaining share and NTFS permissions. If No Access appears anywhere, the resulting permission will always be No Access. Of the three share permissions that pertain to SalesFeb by virtue of JimBob's group memberships, Full Control is the most permissive, so that becomes his share permission. His NTFS permission is Read.

Question 4

> JimBob remains a member of the Accounting, Managers, and Print Operators groups, but he has been added to the Dangerous group by an annoyed boss. For the SalesFeb share, these groups have the following share permissions:
>
> - Accounting: Change
> - Managers: Read
> - Print Operators: Full Control
> - Dangerous: No Access
>
> In addition, JimBob's NTFS permission for the SalesFeb directory and its contents is Read. What is JimBob able to do with files from the SalesFeb directory when he accesses them through the share?
>
> ○ a. Nothing, he has no access.
> ○ b. Read and execute.
> ○ c. Read, write, execute, and delete.
> ○ d. Read, write, execute, delete, change permissions, and take ownership.

Answer a is correct. Because No Access always takes precedence over everything, JimBob has no access to SalesFeb and its contents due to his membership in the Dangerous group. Remember, No Access always wins.

Question 5

> Which of the following are attributes of an object? [Check all correct answers]
>
> ❑ a. Data
> ❑ b. ACL
> ❑ c. Services
> ❑ d. Name

Answers a, b, and d are correct. The data of an object is an attribute. The ACL of an object is an attribute. The name of an object is an attribute. The services of an object are services, not attributes. Therefore, answer c is incorrect.

Question 6

> Where should you check to see if NTBACKUP ran successfully?
>
> ○ a. User Manager
>
> ○ b. Server Manager
>
> ○ c. Backup log
>
> ○ d. Registry

Answer c is correct. To find out whether a backup was successful, you must check the Backup log in NTBACKUP. The User Manager is where most administration takes place for Windows NT—such as adding users and changing their passwords. Backup is not affected directly by User Manager. Therefore, answer a is incorrect. (You do, however, assign backup rights in User Manager.) Server Manager is not a utility found on Windows NT Workstation, but even on Windows NT Server this utility does not offer details about successful backups. Therefore, answer b is incorrect. You wouldn't look for successful backup information in the Registry. Therefore, answer d is incorrect.

Question 7

> Which of the following is not a standard directory or file permission?
>
> ○ a. Read
>
> ○ b. List
>
> ○ c. Create Directory
>
> ○ d. Change
>
> ○ e. Add

Answer c is correct. Create Directory is not a permission. Read is both a directory and a file permission. Therefore, answer a is incorrect. List is a directory permission. Therefore, answer b is incorrect. Change is both a directory and file permission. Therefore, answer d is incorrect. Add is a directory permission. Therefore, answer e is incorrect.

Question 8

> You want to track the activity around a new high-speed color laser printer so you can use the tracking information to restrict and grant privileged and priority access. Which of the following are required steps to implement printer auditing? [Check all correct answers]
>
> ❑ a. Set the auditing switches on the printer object to track the successful print events for the Everyone group.
>
> ❑ b. Grant the Everyone group the auditing right through the User Rights policy.
>
> ❑ c. Set the Audit policy to Audit These Events through the User Manager.
>
> ❑ d. Set the audit switch of File And Object Access to Success under Audit These Events.
>
> ❑ e. Set the priority of the printer to 99 (maximum) under the Scheduling tab on the printer's Properties dialog box.

Answers a, c, and d are correct. Setting the auditing switches on the object is required to enable printer tracking. Therefore, answer a is correct. Setting the master auditing switch to Audit These Events is required to track printer access. Therefore, answer c is correct. Setting the event type switch of File And Object Access to Success is required to track printer usage. Therefore, answer d is correct. There is no auditing user right. Therefore, answer b is incorrect. Setting a printer's priority has nothing to do with tracking access. Therefore, answer e is incorrect.

Question 9

> You need access to a file named VENDORS.TXT in the newly
> created \\Sales\Documents share in the Sales domain. You are a
> member of the Marketing group in the Sales domain. What addi-
> tional settings must be made to allow you access to the
> VENDORS.TXT file?
>
> ○ a. The Read permission on the Documents share must be
> set to your user account.
>
> ○ b. Your user account must be added to the Everyone group
> in the Sales domain.
>
> ○ c. None, Full Control to all users is the default on all new
> shares.
>
> ○ d. A new Sales group must be created and your account
> added as a member.

Answer c is correct. No action is required because your account is a member
of the Sales domain's Everyone group, which has Full Control to new shares
by default. Assigning specific permissions for the object to your user account
is not required because your account is a default member of the Everyone
group and a new share offers Full Control to this group by default. Therefore,
answer a is incorrect. Your user account automatically becomes a member
of the Everyone group when it is created. Therefore, answer b is incorrect.
A new group is not required to gain access to the new share. Therefore,
answer d is incorrect.

Question 10

> When you installed Windows NT Workstation, you noticed that
> the backup utility was installed automatically. When you try to use
> your tape drive, nothing happens. What could be the cause of this?
>
> ○ a. Even though Windows NT installs the NTBACKUP
> program, you still must install the drivers for the tape
> drive.
>
> ○ b. You have to shut down your machine before you can run
> NTBACKUP.
>
> ○ c. You must have the RAS service running.
>
> ○ d. You must have CSNW installed.

Answer a is correct. When Windows NT is installed, NTBACKUP is installed automatically. However, you must still install the drivers for the tape backup. A workstation must be operating to provide access to its storage drives for a backup. Therefore, answer b is incorrect. Windows NT's Remote Access Service is a communications program and has nothing to do with backups. Therefore, answer c is incorrect. The Client Service For NetWare is required for clients to communicate with a NetWare server; it has nothing to do with backups. Therefore, answer d also is incorrect.

Question 11

In what ways can the NTFS permission settings of a file be changed, altered, or modified? [Check all correct answers]

❑ a. Through the CACLS command utility

❑ b. By moving the file to a new partition

❑ c. Through the Share Properties tab

❑ d. By taking ownership

❑ e. Through the Permissions button on the Security
        Properties tab

Answers a, b, and e are correct. The CACLS command line utility is used to change the ACLs or permission settings on files and folders. Therefore, answer a is correct. Moving a file to a new partition causes the file to take on the settings of its new container, thus, its permissions are changed. Therefore, answer b is correct. The Permissions button on the Security Properties tab is the most common and easiest to use method of changing NTFS permissions. Therefore, answer e is correct. The Share Properties tab can only change the permissions of a share, not the NTFS permissions of a file. Therefore, answer c is incorrect. Taking ownership gives a user the ability to change permissions, but the act of taking ownership does not alter the permissions on a file. Therefore, answer d is incorrect.

Question 12

You attempt to add new information into a document stored on a remote server. Using the Documents share, you are able to locate and open the document into your word processor. You have Full Control of the object. You are a member of the Sales group. The Sales group has Read access to the Documents share. You are unable to save your changes to the file, why?

○ a. You cannot edit documents over a network.

○ b. Your resultant permission for the file object is just Read.

○ c. The Sales group has the Save privilege revoked.

○ d. Only administrators can save files over the network.

Answer b is correct. Accessing objects through shares results in the most restrictive combination of share and object ACL permissions. It is possible to edit documents over a network—the only stipulation is you must have the proper access level to modify remote objects. Therefore, answer a is incorrect. There isn't a Save privilege in the Windows NT environment—the Sales group merely has Read access to the share. Therefore, answer c is incorrect. The ability to save documents (in other words, modify objects), is not limited to administrators. Therefore, answer d is incorrect.

Question 13

An important, new custom application is conflicting with an existing utility. The conflict seems to cause both programs to terminate prematurely. Which audit event type should be tracked to record some information about the conflict and which programs are affected?

○ a. File And Object Access

○ b. Security Policy Changes

○ c. Restart, Shutdown, And System

○ d. Process Tracking

○ e. Application Activity

Answer d is correct. Process Tracking tracks threads and processes (that is, applications). File And Object Access is for tracking NTFS objects such as files and printers. Therefore, answer a is incorrect. Security Policy Changes tracks modifications to security and policies. Therefore, answer b is

incorrect. Restart, Shutdown, And System tracks system restarts. Therefore, answer c is incorrect. Application Activity is not a valid selection.
Therefore, answer e is incorrect.

Question 14

You attempt to access a file in the NTFS directory share \UserGuide.
Sales has Change access to the share. Marketing has Read access to the share. Accounting has No Access to the share. You
have Full Control of the object. You are a member of all three
groups. What is your resultant access privileges?

○ a. No Access

○ b. Read

○ c. Change

○ d. Full Control

Answer a is correct. No Access results if any group of which you are a
member has No Access. Read is the access for the Marketing group, but
you are also a member of the Accounting group, which has No Access.
Therefore, answer b is incorrect. Change is the access for the Sales group,
but you are also a member of the Accounting group, which has No Access.
Therefore, answer c is incorrect. You have Full Control of the object only
when accessing it directly, but by using a share, you are restricted by your
group settings that result in No Access. Therefore, answer d is incorrect.

Question 15

Sheila is a member of the local group called Sales. She can back
up files that she reads on a daily basis, but she cannot restore any
files. What is the problem?

○ a. Sheila is not a member of Power Users.

○ b. Sheila is not a member of the Backup Operators, Users,
and the Replicator group.

○ c. Sheila is not a member of the Backup Operators or the
Administrator group.

Answer c is correct. You must be granted a right to restore data. Backup
Operators and the Administrator groups both have the right to do this by
default. Remember, if users can read a file, they can back up the file; but to
restore the file, they must have the Restore Files And Directories right.

The Power Users group does not have the right to restore files. Therefore, answer a is incorrect. The Users and Replicator groups do not have the right to restore files, thus, the stipulation of belonging to all three of these groups does not add the restore right to Sheila. Therefore, answer b is incorrect.

Need To Know More?

 Perkins, Charles, Matthew Strebe, and James Chellis: *MCSE: NT Workstation Study Guide, 2nd Edition.* Sybex Network Press, San Francisco, CA, 1998. ISBN 0-7821-2223-X. Chapter 6 contains detailed information about NT file and directory security, including shares, auditing, and backups. Also, Chapter 7 discusses object and ACL issues.

Tittel, Ed, Christa Anderson, and David Johnson: *NT Workstation 4 Exam Prep* Coriolis, Scottsdale, AZ, 1998. ISBN 1-57610-238-6. Chapter 6 covers file and directory security.

 Search the TechNet CD (or its online version through **www.microsoft.com**) and the *Windows NT Workstation Resource Kit* CD using the keywords "NTFS," "share," "backup," "audit," "ACL," and "permissions."

Windows NT System Security

8

Terms you'll need to understand:

- √ Windows NT security model
- √ Access control list (ACL)
- √ Access token
- √ Logon authentication
- √ WINLOGON
- √ Account policy
- √ User rights policy
- √ Auditing
- √ Customizable environment options
- √ Security Accounts Manager (SAM)

Techniques you'll need to master:

- √ Understanding the Windows NT security model
- √ Learning how user logons are authenticated
- √ Creating customized settings for users

We've already introduced you to many of the security features built into Windows NT Workstation. NTFS and share security, ACLs, and logon authentication were detailed in Chapters 6 and 7. Security and system policies were examined in Chapter 4. However, a few important aspects of Windows NT security have not yet been addressed. Therefore, we include a "grab bag" of security issues in this chapter.

The Windows NT Security Model

The Windows NT security model is designed to control access to data. As you know, security is often not a single barrier or restriction, but a collection of measures designed to prevent data loss of any kind. This includes theft, unauthorized disclosure, virus infection, and destruction of any kind—such as deletion, overwriting, and hardware failures. A security scheme is not impenetrable, but instead, a solid security deployment is one that makes gaining unauthorized access so difficult that it is easier to go elsewhere. Windows NT provides numerous security features that make implementing an effective security scheme straightforward.

The security features of Windows NT include access control lists (ACLs), access tokens, logon authentication, account policies, user rights policies, auditing, and customizable environment options. Many of these topics have already been mentioned or discussed in other chapters, but we'll at least review them here to give you a complete picture of Windows NT security.

Logon Authentication

Windows NT security starts with logon authentication. This is the process that goes on behind the scenes when Ctrl+Alt+Del is pressed at the Windows NT splash screen and a user attempts to gain entry to the system. As discussed in Chapter 7, logging on to the system is controlled by the WINLOGON process and its communication with the security manager in the Executive Services of the Kernel.

There are four distinct parts to the logon process:

➤ **Mandatory logon** To gain access to the system, you must log on with a valid user account. Even if logon is automated by providing this information in the Registry (see the section titled "Customizing The Logon Process," later in this chapter), the logon process still occurs. The reason for this restriction is so that the access token for the user can be built.

➤ **User mode only** Without a valid logon with a current user account, no applications can be accessed or launched. This prevents the activation of Trojan Horse viruses that imitate the logon screen and steal passwords.

➤ **Physical logon** Windows NT requires the Ctrl+Alt+Del keystroke to activate the WINLOGON dialog box. This keystroke combination activates a specific hardware interrupt that can only be generated from the keyboard, thus forcing users to be physically present at a computer to attempt logons.

➤ **User settings and preferences** A valid user account and password will grant a user entry to the system. From the account, NT will restore previously saved desktop and environmental settings, as well as generate an access token.

Access Tokens

When a valid user successfully logs in to Windows NT, an access token is generated by the security subsystem. This access token is used to launch the user's shell and establish the security context. The access token defines the user's access privileges and restrictions for his or her current logon session. Each time an object is accessed, the user's access token is compared to the object's ACL to verify the validity of the access requests.

An access token is built from three types of user data stored in the SAM database:

➤ **Security ID (SID)** The SID is a number assigned to each user, group, Windows NT system, and many other objects that correlate to an entry in the SAM database. Each and every SID within a domain is unique. If a user or group is deleted, that specific SID is never reused. New groups or users with the same name and configuration will not regain the original SID or the previously granted permissions.

➤ **Group ID** A group ID is similar to a SID, except that it is not user specific—it's group specific. When a user joins a group, the group ID is added to that user's security list and included in the data used to create the access token. The group ID is linked to a group's security privileges and is compared to an object's ACL to grant or deny access.

➤ **Permissions** Permissions are specific access control settings granted to or restricted from a single user. If an object's ACL contains a specific user's SID, an additional element is added to a user's access token granting the specified access level to the object.

Each time a user logs in to Windows NT, he or she is assigned an access token generated from the current settings found in the SAM database. This access token is created by the Security Accounts Manager (SAM) and is returned to the WINLOGON process in the User mode. Once a valid access token is delivered to WINLOGON, that token is used to launch the user's primary process—the shell. Then, this process inherits the access token. WINLOGON removes itself from control and gives control to the user.

Each process launched by the user (or any user-controlled application or process) is governed by the access token inherited from the parent process. This inheritance scheme ensures that no process can be started with a higher security level than the parent. Thus, Windows NT maintains control over user access levels through the initial access token assignment.

Objects And ACLs

We've already discussed objects and ACLs in Chapter 7. These are key features of the Windows NT security system. If you are not already familiar and comfortable with the notion of objects and their associated ACLs, please review those sections in the previous chapter.

Customizing The Logon Process

The WINLOGON process has several customizable options to improve overall logon security and to force Windows NT Workstation into compliance with your organization's security policy. All of these configuration settings must be made through the Registry in the WINLOGON key located at:

```
\HKEY_LOCAL_MACHINE\SOFTWARE\Microsoft\WindowsNT
\CurrentVersion\WinLogon
```

The available configuration changes for the Windows NT logon process are detailed in the next five sections.

Removing The Default Username

By default, the user name of the last person to successfully log on to Windows NT is displayed in the WINLOGON dialog box. Because a valid username is half of the information needed by an intruder to gain access to your system, you can improve the security of your system by disabling the display of the last user's account name. You can set this feature by adding a **DontDisplayLastUserName** string value in the Registry. Setting this entry to a value of 1 will display a blank username field; setting this entry to a value of 0 will display the last username.

Display A Security Warning Message

Some security policies require a message to be displayed about the ramifications of gaining unauthorized access to the computer system. Windows NT can display a pop-up warning message just before displaying the WINLOGON dialog box. Each time a user presses Ctrl+Alt+Del, the warning will appear and the OK button must be clicked before logon can be attempted. Even if your security does not specify such a message, it is a good idea to help establish the culpability of intruders for criminal prosecution.

This feature is enabled through two entries to the Registry. The first is the title of the pop-up window for the message—it is called **LegalNotice Caption**. The second is the text to be displayed within the display window—it is called **LegalNoticeText**. These entries are already present in the Registry, but they are blank. To terminate the warning display, clear the contents of each value.

Designating The Shell

A shell is the foundation interface for a user environment. For Windows NT, the default shell is Windows NT Explorer, but you can change the shell to some other custom or third-party application, depending on your needs or security policy. One common replacement for the default shell is the Program Manager (PROGMAN.EXE), a tool often more familiar to Windows NT 3.51 and Windows 3.x users. However, by changing the default shell, the ability to access special Windows NT 4 features such as My Computer, the Start menu, and the Taskbar will be severely limited.

To change the shell, modify the Registry entry named **Shell** to reflect the executable for the new shell. If the executable is not in the root Windows NT directory, you must provide a complete path.

Disabling The Shutdown Button

The WINLOGON prompt for Windows NT Workstation displays the Shutdown button, by default. This same button is disabled, by default, on Windows NT Server. You can choose which setting you prefer or require. The Registry entry that governs this button is **ShutdownWithoutLogon**. A value of 1 enables the button, and a value of 0 disables the button.

Logon Automation

Even though the logon process cannot be bypassed, it can be automated to eliminate the need to press Ctrl+Alt+Del, type in a username and password, and then click Logon. If security is not an issue, this can simplify your computing experience, especially if you reboot often. To enable this feature, add three string values to the Registry: **DefaultUserName**, **DefaultPassword**, and **AutoAdminLogon**. The first two entries should be set to meet the standards set by your corporate security policy. **AutoAdminLogon** should be set to 1 to automate logon or 0 to disable.

Once enabled, the Shift key must be pressed during reboot or logoff to display the WINLOGON dialog box for an alternate user to gain access.

Practice Questions

Question 1

A security scheme is put in place for which of the following reasons? [Check all correct answers]

❑ a. To prevent unauthorized disclosure

❑ b. To protect against virus infection

❑ c. To support privacy

❑ d. To deter unauthorized access

❑ e. To avert data loss

Answers a, b, c, d, and e are all correct. A security scheme should be put in place for any or all of these reasons.

Question 2

Why is mandatory logon required by Windows NT?

○ a. To force compliance with password policies

○ b. To initiate the generation of an access token

○ c. To enable user activity logging

○ d. To grant user access to shut down a machine

Answer b is correct. The only correct answer is the initiation of access token generation. Forcing password policy compliance, enabling user activity logging, and granting shutdown access are not reasons for mandatory logon. Therefore, answers a, c, and d are incorrect.

Question 3

> Which of the following components is responsible for the logon process?
>
> ○ a. SAM database
>
> ○ b. Executive Services
>
> ○ c. WINLOGON
>
> ○ d. User Manager
>
> ○ e. User mode

Answer c is correct. The WINLOGON process is responsible for the logon process. The SAM database is used by the security manager in the Executive Services when the WINLOGON process submits a username and password for validation, but it is not in control of the logon process. Therefore, answer a is incorrect. The Executive Services are involved in the logon process, but they are not responsible for it. Therefore, answer b is incorrect. The User Manager is not associated with logon; it is used to manage user and group accounts. Therefore, answer d is incorrect. User mode is the section of the OS environment where WINLOGON operates, but it is not in control of the logon process. Therefore, answer e is incorrect.

Question 4

> Which of the following are components of Windows NT security? [Check all correct answers]
>
> ❑ a. Sound schemes
>
> ❑ b. ACLs
>
> ❑ c. User rights
>
> ❑ d. Performance counters
>
> ❑ e. Auditing

Answers b, c, and e are correct. ACLs, user rights, and auditing are all features of Windows NT security. A sound scheme is not a security device. Therefore, answer a is incorrect. Performance counters are not security devices. Therefore, answer d is incorrect.

Question 5

An access token is generated when a user successfully logs on to Windows NT. What is the first action the access token performs?

- ○ a. To load user preferences
- ○ b. To launch the shell
- ○ c. To initiate the User mode
- ○ d. To allocate a virtual machine for applications

Answer b is correct. Launching the shell is the first action performed by the access token. Loading user preferences occurs after a shell has been launched. Therefore, answer a is incorrect. The User mode is initiated by the system during bootup and is only accessible after a successful logon. Therefore, answer c is incorrect. Virtual machines are created by the Executive Services, and processes within a virtual machine have the user's access token attached to them. Therefore, answer d is incorrect.

Question 6

What are the four parts or aspects of the logon process? [Check all correct answers]

- ❑ a. Physical logon
- ❑ b. User mode only
- ❑ c. ACLs
- ❑ d. Mandatory logon
- ❑ e. User preferences

Answers a, b, d, and e are correct. Physical logon, user mode only, mandatory logon, and user preferences are the four aspects of the logon process. ACLs are the permission settings on objects. Therefore, answer c is incorrect.

Question 7

An access token is generated by the security manager by pulling data, such as SID, group ID, and special permissions, from the SAM database.

○ a. True

○ b. False

Answer a is correct. This is a true statement.

Question 8

Which setting of **AutoAdminLogon** is required to terminate the automatic logon process?

○ a. 1

○ b. 0

Answer b is correct. A value of 0 will disable the automatic logon feature of Windows NT.

Question 9

Which of the following are options of the logon process? [Check all correct answers]

❑ a. Prevent task list display

❑ b. Display warning message

❑ c. Remove pull-down list of user names

❑ d. Launching of an alternate shell

❑ e. Automating logon

Answers b, d, and e are correct. Displaying a warning message is a customization option of the logon process. Therefore, answer b is correct. Launching an alternate shell and automating logon are two logon options. Therefore, answers d and e are correct. There is no such control to prevent a task list display associated with the logon process. Therefore, answer a is incorrect. There is no such control to remove a pull-down list of usernames. Therefore, answer c is incorrect.

Question 10

By default, Windows NT Workstation does not enable the Shut-down button found on the WINLOGON dialog box.

❍ a. True

❍ b. False

Answer b is correct. Windows NT Workstation does enable the Shutdown button, by default. Windows NT Server disables this button, by default.

Need To Know More?

Perkins, Charles, Matthew Strebe, and James Chellis: *MCSE: NT Workstation Study Guide, 2ⁿᵈ Edition.* Sybex Network Press, San Francisco, CA, 1998. ISBN 0-7821-2223-X. Chapter 7 discusses the Windows NT security features found in this chapter and those subjects referenced in the previous chapter.

Search the TechNet CD (or its online version through **www.microsoft.com**) and *the Windows NT Workstation Resource Kit* CD using the keywords "security," "access token," "ACL," "logon authentication," and "WINLOGON."

Windows NT Networking

Terms you'll need to understand:

√ Protocol

√ Network Basic Input/Output System (NetBIOS)

√ NetBIOS Extended User Interface (NetBEUI)

√ Transmission Control Protocol/Internet Protocol (TCP/IP)

√ NWLink Internetwork Packet Exchange/Sequenced Packet Exchange (IPX/SPX)

√ Data Link Control (DLC)

√ AppleTalk

√ Windows Sockets

√ Remote Procedure Calls (RPC)

√ Network Dynamic Data Exchange

√ Frame type

√ Redirectors

√ Protocol binding

Techniques you'll need to master:

√ Installing and configuring network protocols

√ Familiarization with the Network applet in Control Panel

√ Implementing services that complement certain protocols

√ Understanding and configuring protocol bindings

√ Adjusting frame type settings

To enable communications on a computer network, you must tell Windows NT how it's supposed to "talk" to other computers and peripheral devices. In the networking world, this is established through the use of protocols. Basically, a protocol is an agreed-upon set of standards that define how computers communicate. In this chapter, we explain what protocols are available with Windows NT and when to use which protocol, as well as the properties of each protocol.

Microsoft Network Component Architecture

The networking architecture implemented by Windows NT can be mapped to the International Standards Organization (ISO) model of networking in a near one-to-one relationship. There are a few items within a handful of the components that you need to be aware of.

The Programming interface layer—which provides a standard for interaction between applications and the file system drivers and network services—supports important APIs. These include the following:

➤ **NetBIOS** All basic network communications within Windows NT are performed using NetBIOS.

➤ **Windows Sockets** Provides a standard for application interaction with transport protocols such as TCP/IP over PPP.

➤ **Remote Procedure Calls** Handles network interprocess communications.

➤ **Network Dynamic Data Exchange** Supports DDE applications over a network; developed by Microsoft.

The File System Drivers layer supports all the storage types for Windows NT, including the following:

➤ NTFS

➤ FAT

➤ CDFS

These topics are discussed in detail in Chapter 6, "Windows NT File Systems And Structures."

The Network Driver Interface layer complies with Network Device Interface Specification (NDIS) 3.0. This allows multiple protocols to be bound to multiple adapters, and vice versa.

When Windows NT Workstation is installed, a few network system components are installed automatically. These are present to support both standalone operation and most of the low-level activities when connected to a network. Here are the default components:

➤ **NetBIOS interface** Supports Windows NT's low-level system operation.

➤ **TCP/IP protocol** The default protocol.

➤ **Workstation service** Allows a machine to access network resources.

➤ **Server service** Allows other machines to access local resources and share resources.

➤ **Computer browser** Enables interaction with resource lists.

➤ **NIC driver** Enables Windows NT to communicate with the network adapter.

➤ **RPC service** Manages network interprocess communications.

Built-In Windows NT Protocols

Windows NT Workstation comes with a number of protocols that can be enabled for interoperability and communication:

➤ NetBIOS Extended User Interface (NetBEUI)

➤ Transmission Control Protocol/Internet Protocol (TCP/IP)

➤ NWLink Internetwork Packet Exchange/Sequenced Packet Exchange (IPX/SPX)

➤ Data Link Control (DLC)

➤ AppleTalk

We define and explain all of these protocols and their uses in the following sections.

NetBEUI

NetBEUI is a simple Network layer transport broadcast protocol developed to support NetBIOS networks. NetBEUI is not routable, so it really has no place on an enterprise network. NetBEUI is the fastest transport protocol available to Windows NT. The benefits of NetBEUI include its speed as well as good error protection; also, it is easy to implement, with low memory overhead. The disadvantages of NetBEUI include the fact that it's not routable, there is very little support for cross-platform applications, and there are very few troubleshooting tools.

TCP/IP

TCP/IP is the most widely used protocol in networking today (due in part to the vast growth of the global Internet, which is a TCP/IP-based network). TCP/IP is the most flexible of the transport protocols and is able to span wide areas. In addition, it has excellent cross-platform support as well as routing capabilities. Also, TCP/IP has support for the Simple Network Management Protocol (SNMP), the Dynamic Host Configuration Protocol (DHCP), the Windows Internet Name Service (WINS), the Domain Name Service (DNS), as well as a host of other useful protocols, which are discussed in Chapter 10, "TCP/IP." On the other hand, TCP/IP is difficult to configure and demands a significant amount of overhead.

NWLink (IPX/SPX)

NWLink is Microsoft's "clean room" implementation of Novell's IPX/SPX protocol suite for NetWare networks. This protocol was included with Windows NT to enable communication with NetWare servers. With NWLink, NT clients can access resources located on a NetWare server, and vice versa.

Put simply, Windows NT requires that NWLink be installed to enable communications with NetWare clients and servers. In addition, the File And Print Services For NetWare is also required for NetWare clients and servers to access Windows NT files and printers. The Client Service For NetWare is designed for Windows NT Workstation computers that require a direct link to NetWare servers. The Gateway Service For NetWare lets Windows NT Servers map a drive to a NetWare server, which provides access to NetWare server resources for Windows NT Workstations (via a gateway). Additional information about NWLink can be found in the section titled "NWLink Connectivity Issues" later in this chapter.

DLC

Windows NT uses the Data Link Control (DLC) protocol primarily for connectivity to Systems Network Architecture (SNA) gateways, and more importantly, for connecting to network-attached printers, such as the

Hewlett-Packard JetDirect interface. The use of DLC for network printing is detailed more in Chapter 14, "Windows NT Printing."

AppleTalk

It should come as no surprise that the AppleTalk protocol is used for communication with Macintosh computers. By enabling AppleTalk, you allow Mac clients to store and access files located on a Windows NT Server, print to Windows NT printers, and vice versa. The Windows NT Server service (known as Services for Macintosh) is only required when Macintosh and Windows NT clients need to share files and printers. Otherwise, AppleTalk can be installed on Windows NT Workstation or a network independent of this service to support cross-platform applications, Ethernet file transfer, or remote debugging. The only real benefit to Windows NT users from the AppleTalk protocol is the ability to print to Macintosh color printers hosted on Macintosh computers. Windows NT Workstation does not support AppleTalk directly, except for printing.

NetBEUI Connectivity Issues

NetBEUI is by far the easiest protocol to install and configure on a Windows NT network. To install this protocol, perform the following steps:

1. Open the Control Panel (Start|Settings|Control Panel).

2. Double-click the Network icon.

3. In the Networks window, click the Protocols tab.

4. Click the Add button.

5. Select NetBEUI from the list of available protocols and click OK.

6. Enter the path to the installation CD or the location of the installation files.

7. If you have RAS installed, Windows NT asks if you want to support it with this protocol. Click Cancel to leave it unsupported.

8. In the Network window, click the Close button.

9. Select Yes when Windows NT asks to restart the computer.

NWLink Connectivity Issues

Put simply, NWLink is IPX for Windows NT: IPX is the protocol, and NWLink is the networking component that provides the protocol. NWLink is provided for connectivity to NetWare networks—both to allow NetWare clients to access Windows NT Servers and to allow Windows NT clients to access NetWare servers. It is important to note, however, that NWLink by itself does not enable this type of communication; you must first install Gateway Service For NetWare (GSNW) on Windows NT Server or Client Service For NetWare (CSNW) on Windows NT Workstation. Basically, CSNW is a redirector, whereas GSNW is what makes file and print sharing on NetWare servers available to Microsoft clients.

IPX has a number of benefits: It supports routing between networks, it's faster than TCP/IP, and it's easy to install and maintain. Unfortunately, IPX doesn't have a sufficient central addressing scheme to prohibit multiple networks from making use of identical addresses, and it doesn't support the Simple Network Management Protocol (SNMP).

Installing NWLink

Installing the NWLink protocol is much like installing other protocols in Windows NT. There are, however, some special issues. To install NWLink, perform the following steps:

1. Open the Control Panel (Start|Settings|Control Panel).

2. Double-click the Network icon.

3. Click the Protocols tab in the Network dialog box.

4. Click the Add button.

5. Select NWLink IPX/SPX Compatible Transport from the list of available protocols.

6. Enter the path to the Windows NT installation CD in the path field of the setup dialog box. Click Continue.

    If you have installed Windows NT's Remote Access Service (RAS), Windows NT then asks if you want to bind NWLink to RAS. Either click OK to enable binding or click Cancel.

7. Click the Close button, and then click Yes when Windows NT asks if you want to restart the computer.

 Although, in most cases, it's fine to leave the default frame type (Auto) as is, some Ethernet adapters don't work well with this setting. For new installations, the Ethernet 802.2 setting is recommended.

To change the Ethernet frame type and IPX network number, perform the following steps:

1. Open the Control Panel (Start|Settings|Control Panel).

2. Double-click the Network icon.

3. Click the Protocols tab in the Network dialog box.

4. Double-click NWLink IPX/SPX Compatible Transport from the list of available protocols.

5. Click the Manual Frame Type Detection button.

6. Click the Add button.

7. Select your preferred frame type.

8. Type in the IPX network number for the adapter in the Network Number field.

9. Click the Add button.

10. Repeat the previous three steps for each frame type.

11. Click OK and then click the Close button.

12. Click Yes when asked to restart the computer.

There are more issues to consider when establishing communications between Windows NT and NetWare networks. These details are covered in Chapter 11, "NetWare Connectivity."

TCP/IP Connectivity Issues

TCP/IP currently is the most-used networking protocol, as well as the standard protocol of the Internet. The beauty of the TCP/IP protocol suite lies in its ability to link many disparate kinds of computers and peripheral devices. Using this protocol stack, you enable most TCP/IP clients to access Windows NT-based resources, and vice versa.

Because the following chapter is devoted to TCP/IP, the discussion of TCP/IP connectivity and configuration is not repeated here. Please refer to Chapter 10, "TCP/IP," for all of the details on TCP/IP.

InterProcess Communications

InterProcess Communications (IPC) provides a common communication path and language for clients to request resources and for servers to respond to requests. IPC is comprised of two types of elements: file systems and programming interfaces. The IPC file systems are named pipes and mail slots. These are connection-oriented and connectionless (respectively) communication channels.

Redirectors

A redirector is a software service that intercepts requests for resources and directs those requests to the correct server hosting the required resource, whether local or over the network. There are four standard redirectors in Windows NT:

➤ **Workstation service** Enables a client to request resources.

➤ **Server service** Enables a server to offer resources.

➤ **Multiple Universal Naming Convention Provider (MUP)** Links UNC requests, other redirectors, and applications together, thus isolating the redirection process from users and applications.

➤ **Multi-Provider Router** Handles non-UNC Win32 API naming convention resource requests (for example, C:\TEMP\ LEGAL.DOC).

Network Configuration

Most (if not all) configuration of Windows NT's network capabilities is done through the Network applet of the Control Panel. Some services provide additional utilities and applets, but they must first be installed through the Network applet. Each tab of this applet has important features and abilities.

Identification Tab

The Change button brings up the Identification Changes dialog box (see Figure 9.1). Here you can do the following:

➤ Change the name of the workstation.

➤ Switch membership between domain(s) and/or workgroup(s).

Figure 9.1   The Identification Changes dialog box.

➤ If a domain account does not already exist, you can input the name of the Administrator account and its password so Windows NT will create a computer account for this computer.

These changes do not alter the SID of the workstation; therefore, returning to a domain should not be a problem as long as the computer's account is not deleted.

Services Tab

On this tab, services can be added, removed, and configured. Each service has a different properties and configuration window. There is also an Update button to install new versions of services from Microsoft or from third parties.

Protocols Tab

On this tab, protocols are added, removed, and configured. Earlier in this chapter, details on installing and configuring the three central protocols of Windows NT—TCP/IP, NWLink, and NetBEUI—were discussed in detail.

Adapters Tab

On this tab, network interface card drivers are installed. Because Windows NT is not Plug and Play compatible and the user environment is isolated from the hardware, very little, if any, configuration changes can be made to a NIC through this tab.

Bindings Tab

Protocol binding is the process Windows NT uses to link network components from various levels of the network architecture to enable communication between those components. This tab is where the bindings for installed network components are listed in order of upper-layer services and protocols to lower-layer network adapter drivers. By default, Windows NT enables all possible bindings between services, protocols, and adapters.

Binding should be ordered to enhance the system's use of the network. For example, if your network has both TCP/IP and NetBEUI installed, and most network devices use TCP/IP, workstation bindings should be set to bind TCP/IP first and NetBEUI second. In other words, the most frequently used protocol should be bound first. This speeds network connections. Because servers use whatever protocol is sent to them by each workstation, the binding order needs to be changed on the workstations only. Network speed is affected by the binding order on the workstations, but not on the servers.

Practice Questions

Question 1

> Which of the following are supported IPC elements? [Check all correct answers]
>
> ❏ a. NetBIOS
>
> ❏ b. Multi-Provider Router
>
> ❏ c. NetDDE
>
> ❏ d. Windows Sockets
>
> ❏ e. RPC

Answers a, c, d, and e are correct. The programming interface elements of IPC are NetBIOS, NetDDE, Windows Sockets, and RPC. Multi-Provider Router is a redirector and not an IPC element. Therefore, answer b is incorrect.

Question 2

> What protocols or services are installed by default in Windows NT Workstation? [Check all correct answers]
>
> ❏ a Server service
>
> ❏ b. DLC
>
> ❏ c. RPC
>
> ❏ d. NetBIOS
>
> ❏ e. RAS

Answers a, c, and d are correct. The Server service, RPC, and NetBIOS are all installed by default. DLC and RAS are not automatically installed. Therefore, answers b and e are incorrect.

Question 3

> Your network uses multiple protocols. Where in Windows NT may the binding order of the protocols be changed to increase network speed?
>
> ○ a. On the domain controllers only
>
> ○ b. On the workstations only
>
> ○ c. On the servers only
>
> ○ d. On both the workstations and servers (including the domain controllers)

Answer b is correct. Because Windows NT Servers use the protocol sent to them by workstations, the binding order needs only to be changed on the workstations. Network speed is affected by the binding order on the workstations, but not on the servers. Therefore, answers a, c, and d all are incorrect.

Question 4

> Where is the workgroup membership for Windows NT Workstation defined?
>
> ○ a. Workgroup applet
>
> ○ b. Network applet, Identification tab
>
> ○ c. Services applet, StartUp button
>
> ○ d. Server Manager, machine properties

Answer b is correct. The Identification tab of the Network applet is where workgroup membership is defined. There is no such utility as the Workgroup applet. Therefore, answer a is incorrect. The StartUp button applies to services, not workgroup membership. Therefore, answer c is incorrect. The Server Manager is not used to alter the workgroup membership. Therefore, answer d is incorrect.

Question 5

> Your Windows NT Workstation and the Windows NT Server have
> TCP/IP, NWLink, and NetBEUI protocols installed. Which protocol
> should you bind first to maximize throughput?
>
> ○ a. TCP/IP
>
> ○ b. NWLink
>
> ○ c. NetBEUI

Answer c is correct. NetBEUI uses the least overhead of the other protocols,
and by binding it first, it will be the protocol used by both the client and server
to transfer files. TCP/IP and NWLink are both larger and more resource
intensive than NetBEUI. Therefore, answers a and b are incorrect.

Question 6

> You want to print a document to a color printer hosted on a
> Macintosh client in your workgroup. What protocol is required to
> support this activity?
>
> ○ a. DLC
>
> ○ b. NWLink
>
> ○ c. NetBEUI
>
> ○ d. AppleTalk

Answer d is correct. The AppleTalk protocol is required to support
Macintosh printing. DLC is used for network attached printers. Therefore,
answer a is incorrect. NWLink and NetBEUI cannot be used to communicate with a Macintosh printer. Therefore, answers b and c are incorrect.

Question 7

> The Network Driver Interface, being NDIS 3.0 compliant, enables
> multiple protocols to be bound to multiple network adapters.
>
> ○ a. True
>
> ○ b. False

Answer a is correct. The NDIS 3.0 standard enables Windows NT's Network Driver Interface to bind multiple protocols with multiple adapters.

Question 8

> IPC is a Windows NT mechanism used to support client/server communications.
>
> ○ a. True
>
> ○ b. False

Answer a is correct. IPC enables clients and servers to interact using a common language.

Question 9

> What is the unified Windows NT interface that isolates redirection and network processes from the user and application?
>
> ○ a. NetBIOS Extended User Interface (NetBEUI)
>
> ○ b. Multiple Universal Naming Convention Provider (MUP)
>
> ○ c. InterProcess Communications (IPC)
>
> ○ d. Internetwork Packet Exchange/Sequenced Packet Exchange (IPX/SPX)

Answer b is correct. MUP is the unified redirector hiding interface. NetBEUI is a protocol used by Windows NT, but it is not the unified redirector hiding interface. Therefore, answer a is incorrect. IPC is not a redirector. Therefore, answer c is incorrect. IPX/SPX is the Novell protocol that Microsoft re-created as NWLink, and it is not a redirector. Therefore, answer d is incorrect.

Question 10

> Which network component is required for printer sharing on Windows NT?
>
> ○ a. AppleTalk
>
> ○ b. Server
>
> ○ c. DLC
>
> ○ d. Workstation

Answer b is correct. The Server service is required to offer resources over the network. AppleTalk is needed to access Macintosh hosted printers, but it is not required for printer sharing on Windows NT. Therefore, answer a is incorrect. DLC is used to interact with network connected printers, but it is not required to create a printer share. Therefore, answer c is incorrect. The Workstation service is only required to access a share, not to share a printer. Therefore, answer d is incorrect.

Need To Know More?

 Perkins, Charles, Matthew Strebe, and James Chellis: *MCSE: NT Workstation Study Guide, 2ⁿᵈ Edition*. Sybex Network Press, San Francisco, CA, 1998. ISBN 0-7821-2223-X. Chapter 8 has complete coverage of the networking systems of Windows NT Workstation.

Search the TechNet CD (or its online version through **www.microsoft.com**) using the keywords "protocol management," "TCP/IP," "NWLink," "NetBEUI," and "internetworking."

Tittel, Ed, Christa Anderson, and David Johnson: *NT Workstation 4 Exam Prep*. Coriolis, Scottsdale, AZ, 1998. ISBN 1-57610-238-6. Chapter 8 covers Windows NT Network Architecture in more detail, and includes lots of information about network protocols and servers.

 The *Windows NT Workstation Resource Kit* contains a lot of useful information about networking and protocols. You can search the TechNet (either CD or online version) or the *Resource Kit* CD using keywords such as "protocols," "binding," and "networking services."

10

TCP/IP

Terms you'll need to understand:

- √ Transmission Control Protocol/ Internet Protocol (TCP/IP)
- √ Dynamic Host Configuration Protocol (DHCP)
- √ Windows Internet Name Service (WINS)
- √ Domain Name Service (DNS)
- √ Serial Line Internet Protocol (SLIP)
- √ Point-to-Point Protocol (PPP)
- √ Point-to-Point Tunneling Protocol (PPTP)
- √ World Wide Web (WWW)
- √ File Transfer Protocol (FTP)
- √ Address Resolution Protocol (ARP)
- √ HOSTNAME
- √ IPCONFIG
- √ NBTSTAT
- √ NETSTAT
- √ PING
- √ ROUTE
- √ TRACERT
- √ Peer Web Services

Technique you'll need to master:

- √ Installing and configuring TCP/IP

TCP/IP is a large, complex, and multifaceted subject, especially in relation to networking with Windows NT. In this chapter, we give you an overview of TCP/IP in the world of Windows NT, plus the specifics that apply to Windows NT Workstation.

The TCP/IP Protocol Suite

Windows NT provides a number of useful TCP/IP services. Included are the following:

➤ **Dynamic Host Configuration Protocol (DHCP)** This service enables the assignment of dynamic TCP/IP network addresses on a first come-first-served basis, based on a specified pool of available addresses. When a network client configured for DHCP logs on to the network, the DHCP service assigns the next available TCP/IP address for that network session. This really simplifies address administration. The DHCP server is only available on a Windows NT Server machine; however, both Windows NT Server and Windows NT Workstation (as well as any other TCP/IP client) can request data from a DHCP server.

➤ **Windows Internet Name Service (WINS)** This service enables the resolution of network names to IP addresses (similar to the Unix DNS). This way, you don't have to remember the IP address of the client with whom you are trying to communicate—you can enter the network name, and Windows NT does the rest. Also, if a TCP/IP-based network does not have a WINS server, each time one computer tries to access another, it must send a b-node broadcast, which creates unnecessary network traffic and can slow a busy network to a crawl. WINS servers provide "computer name to IP address" resolution, reducing these broadcast messages and improving network performance. The WINS server is only available on a Windows NT Server machine; however, both Windows NT Server and Windows NT Workstation (as well as any other TCP/IP client) can use WINS server to resolve NetBIOS names.

➤ **Serial Line Internet Protocol (SLIP)** SLIP originally was developed for the Unix environment and is still widely used among Internet providers. Although SLIP provides good performance with little system overhead requirements, it does not support error checking, flow control, or security features. SLIP is good for connecting to Unix hosts or Internet providers. This protocol is quickly being replaced by

PPP. SLIP is present on Windows NT Workstation only for the purpose of connecting to a Unix server; it cannot be used for inbound RAS sessions.

➤ **Point-to-Point Protocol (PPP)** PPP addresses many of the insufficiencies of SLIP, such as providing the capability to encrypt logons as well as support for additional transport protocols, error checking, and recovery. In addition, PPP is optimized for low-bandwidth connections and, in general, is a more efficient protocol than SLIP. PPP is present on Windows NT Workstation and is the preferred WAN protocol for RAS connections.

➤ **Point-to-Point Tunneling Protocol (PPTP)** Simply stated, PPTP is a protocol that creates secure connections between private networks over the Internet. Benefits of PPTP include lower administrative, transmission, and hardware costs than other solutions for this type of connectivity. PPTP on Windows NT Workstation can connect to any system supporting a compatible PPTP implementation.

➤ **World Wide Web (WWW)** This service comes as a part of Peer Web Services (PWS). WWW makes it possible to publish Web pages, whether for an Internet-based Web site or for an internal intranet. It uses Hypertext Transfer Protocol (HTTP) to transfer Web documents and resources.

➤ **File Transfer Protocol (FTP)** This protocol is great for the fast transfer of files to and from a local hard drive to an FTP server located elsewhere on another TCP/IP-based network (such as the Internet). This service/protocol is part of Peer Web Services.

➤ **Gopher** This service, which predates HTTP (the Web protocol), serves text and links to other Gopher sites. Although Gopher sites are still out there, its use has been lessened because HTTP handles information transfer better than this outdated method. This service/protocol is part of Peer Web Services.

Installing And Configuring TCP/IP

You need to have a few items on hand when you install TCP/IP. The following list describes these items:

➤ **Your workstation's IP address** This is the unique address that identifies a particular computer on a TCP/IP network. This number consists of four numbers, separated by periods (for example, 125.115.125.48). The first one to three numbers identify the network on which the computer is located, and the remaining numbers identify the computer on that network. If you do not have a permanent IP address assigned to you, you can configure your Windows NT Workstation to poll a DHCP server to request an address.

➤ **Your network's subnet masks for each network adapter on the network** The subnet mask is a number mathematically applied to the IP address. This number determines which IP addresses are a part of the same subnetwork as the computer applying the subnet mask. This detail can also be requested from a DHCP server.

➤ **Your default gateway** The gateway is the computer that serves as a router or a security filter for a network. If the default gateway is not defined, the computer will be unable to communicate with machines outside its subnet. This detail can also be requested from a DHCP server.

➤ **The domain name server (DNS) for the network** This is a computer that serves as an Internet host and performs translation of fully qualified domain names (FQDNs) into IP addresses.

➤ **Any DHCP and WINS information about your network** These nonmandatory name resolution services can expand the range of reachable services from your Windows NT Workstation.

If you did not install TCP/IP when you first installed Windows NT Workstation, you must perform the following steps to install and configure this protocol suite:

1. Open the Control Panel (Start|Settings|Control Panel).

2. Double-click the Network icon.

3. In the Networks window, click the Protocols tab.

4. Click the Add button.

5. Select TCP/IP from the list of available protocols. Windows NT may request the installation CD or the location of the installation files.

6. In the Network window, click the Close button.

7. Either enter the TCP/IP address of the computer or select Obtain An IP Address From A DHCP Server, whichever is appropriate for this installation. Then, specify the subnet mask and default gateway.

8. If your network has a DNS server or a constant Internet connection, click the DNS tab and enter the DNS address.

9. If your network has a WINS server, click the WINS tab and enter the WINS address.

10. Restart the computer.

Once your system reboots, TCP/IP will be fully installed. You can always return to the Protocols tab of the Network applet to modify the configuration of TCP/IP.

TCP/IP Tools

Once TCP/IP is installed and properly configured, you have access to a handful of TCP/IP utilities. These utilities are divided into two categories—diagnostic and connectivity.

Diagnostic commands:

➤ **ARP** Displays and modifies address translation tables used by the Address Resolution Protocol

➤ **HOSTNAME** Displays the name of the host

➤ **IPCONFIG** Displays all of the current local TCP/IP configuration values, including IP address, subnet mask, and WINS and DNS configuration

➤ **LPQ** Displays print queue status of an LPD printer

➤ **NBTSTAT** Displays protocol statistics and current TCP/IP connections using NetBIOS over TCP/IP

➤ **NETSTAT** Displays protocol statistics and current TCP/IP network connections

➤ **PING** Verifies existence of remote host

➤ **ROUTE** Modifies routing tables

➤ **TRACERT** Displays route taken by an Internet Control Message Protocol (ICMP) to a remote host

Connectivity commands:

➤ **FINGER** Displays information about a user (server must be running a FINGER service)

➤ **FTP** Used to transfer files to and from an FTP server

➤ **LPR** Sends files to an LPD printer

➤ **RCP** Used to copy files between a client and server running the RSHD service (remote shell)

➤ **REXEC** Executes commands on a remote system running the REXECD service

➤ **RSH** Executes commands on a remote system running the RSHD service

➤ **Telnet** A terminal emulator for interacting with remote systems

➤ **TFTP** Transfers files using the Trivial File Transfer Protocol service (similar to FTP)

You can obtain the complete details of the syntax and usage of these commands by typing "/?" after their names at a command prompt or through Windows NT's Help system.

Windows NT Names And Name Services

Computers interact with each other using long strings of complicated address numbers. Fortunately, Windows NT hides most of these unfriendly references behind easy-to-remember names. Name resolution is the activity of transforming a user-friendly name for a computer or network share into a computer-friendly network address. This process enables networks to quickly locate and request resources while shielding users from complicated and difficult-to-remember—much less type in—hardware-level addresses. Within Windows NT, there is a base resolution service (NetBIOS), three protocol-specific services (NetBEUI, NWLink, and TCP/IP), and additional services for TCP/IP (DHCP, DNS, and WINS).

> *Note: NetBEUI and NWLink name resolution is included in this chapter for convenience. They comprise too small a section to have placed them elsewhere.*

NetBIOS Names In Windows NT

NetBIOS is automatically installed during Windows NT installation. It is the underlying communication mechanism for many basic Windows NT functions, such as browsing and interprocess communications between network servers. NetBIOS is an extremely fast protocol that requires very little communications overhead, which is why it's used by Windows NT for basic operations. NetBIOS is an API used by all Windows NT applications. It provides a uniform set of commands to access common low-level services.

All Windows NT resources are identified by a unique NetBIOS name consisting of 15 characters or less. The NetBIOS namespace is not hierarchical, but flat. Therefore, every machine on the same network must have a unique NetBIOS name, even if the machines are in different domains. Each time a computer connects to the network, it broadcasts its presence by "shouting" its NetBIOS name. The Master Browser "hears" this broadcast and attempts to register the new machine. If another machine is already using the name that was broadcast by the newcomer, the registration is denied. That computer cannot go online until its NetBIOS name is changed or the other computer currently using the name goes offline.

A NetBIOS name is not the same as a host name. A host name is a substitute for a four-segment decimal notation IP address of an Internet host. These names are required for communication with the aliased machine (for example, www.microsoft.com equals 207.68.156.53). A NetBIOS name is a mandatory, unique name used by Windows NT for most network functions. Each time an Explorer interface such as an Open File dialog box is activated, you are interacting with NetBIOS names.

As we discuss in Chapter 12 in the section on browsers, NetBIOS names are used to identify and list the resources currently available on a network. A computer announces itself and its resources upon booting up and once every minute thereafter. As it remains up and running, the interval increases to every 12 minutes. If a computer is gracefully shut down, it announces the removal of its resources as it leaves. If a computer goes offline otherwise, its resources can remain listed in the browser service for up to 51 minutes until the Master Browser removes the entries and the backup browsers are updated. Computers rebroadcast their existence and all their resources every 12 minutes, so the level of traffic can be quite high, even for a small network.

NetBEUI And Name Resolution

All name resolution over NetBEUI is done through NetBIOS. Therefore, there is no further configuration or installation required. Both users and computers use the NetBIOS name to call and access network system objects.

With NetBEUI, most of the network overhead is consumed by the NetBIOS announcement broadcasts. This is one of many reasons why NetBEUI should not be used on anything but the smallest of networks.

IPX And Name Resolution

IPX/SPX, or NWLink, uses NetBIOS Over IPX (NBIPX) to resolve NetBIOS names into IPX addresses. Because IPX addresses contain the MAC address of the host, no further resolution is required. NWLink caches NetBIOS names to perform the IPX address mappings. NWLink does not use an address mapping file or name service. Unlike Novell's implementation of IPX/SPX, NWLink from Microsoft does not issue Service Advertisement Protocol (SAP) broadcasts. Therefore, network overhead is greatly reduced.

IP And Name Resolution

Name resolution under TCP/IP is a complex but important issue. The resolution methods for IP include Dynamic Host Configuration Protocol (DHCP), Domain Name Service (DNS), and Windows Internet Name Service (WINS). These methods are discussed in the upcoming sections.

DHCP

DHCP is not exactly a name resolution system. Instead, it is an IP address–leasing system where a limited number of IP addresses can be shared among numerous computers, usually clients. DHCP dynamically assigns IP addresses to clients on a local subnet.

DHCP server is only available on Windows NT Server. However, you need to be familiar with a few terms and the basic method of operation of DHCP.

When a client boots, it broadcasts a message requesting data from a DHCP server. The receiving DHCP server responds with an IP address assignment for a specified period of time (called a lease period). The client receives the data, integrates the data into its configuration, and completes the boot process.

A DHCP server can also distribute subnet masks and default gateway addresses. Each assignment from a DHCP server is for a predetermined length of time, called a lease period. When a lease expires, a DHCP server can reassign the address to another computer. An operating client can extend its lease simply by indicating that it is still using the address. When half of a lease period is reached, a client requests a lease extension, if needed. It continues to request an extension from the leasing DHCP server until 87.5 percent of its time period has expired. Then, it broadcasts the extension request to all DHCP servers. If no server responds by the time the lease expires, all TCP/IP communications from that client will cease.

A client's IP configuration and lease information can be displayed using **IPCONFIG** with the /**all** parameter. This utility can also end a lease by using the /**release** parameter or renew a lease by using the /**renew** parameter.

Configuring a client to access a DHCP server is simple. To configure a client, all you have to do is open the TCP/IP Properties dialog box from the Protocols tab of the Network applet. Then, on the IP Address page, select the radio button labeled Obtain An IP Address From A DHCP Server.

If your DHCP server is located across a router, you'll need to use the DHCP Relay Agent to forward DHCP broadcasts. Using Windows NT Server's DHCP Relay Agent, a single DHCP server can support multiple subnets connected by the Windows NT Multi-Protocol Router (MPR). Without the DHCP Relay Agent, routers filter out the DHCP broadcasts instead of passing them through. The Relay Agent intercepts the DHCP broadcasts and then transmits the broadcasts directly to the DHCP server. The router still filters out the DHCP request, but the added agent intervenes and sends the important boot message to the supporting server.

The following steps describe how to install the DHCP Relay Agent on a Windows NT Server:

1. Add the DHCP Relay Agent through the Services tab of the Network applet in the Control Panel.

2. Specify the IP address of the DHCP server in the IP Address tab of the TCP/IP Properties dialog box.

   The DHCP Relay Agent is enabled automatically and installed as a service.

3. Choose the DHCP Relay tab in TCP/IP Properties dialog box to change default values for the DHCP Relay Agent. The values are Seconds Threshold, Maximum Hops, and List Of DHCP Server Addresses.

DNS

DNS is used to resolve fully qualified domain names (FQDNs) into IP addresses. FQDNs are user-friendly conveniences that represent the dotted decimal notation of IP addresses that are not required for the operation of communication, unlike NetBIOS names. An FQDN, such as www.microsoft.com, is much easier to remember than its IP address (207.68.156.51).

DNS server is only available on Windows NT Server. However, you need to be familiar with a few terms and the basic method of operation of DNS.

Early DNS used a lookup table stored on every machine in a file called "HOSTS." As networks expand, maintaining an updated and correct HOSTS file is increasingly difficult. To ease administration, centralized DNS was developed. A single server hosts the DNS data for the networks it supports, a hierarchy table of domains, and a list of other DNS servers to which it can refer requests.

DNS operates on user-friendly, FQDNs to determine the location (IP address) of a system. For example, ftp2.dev.microsoft.com could represent the server named "FTP2" located in the ".dev" subdomain under the ".microsoft" domain within the ".com" top-level domain. This hierarchy structure enables DNS to quickly traverse its database to locate the correct IP address for the host machine.

DNS is essential on large networks, including the Internet. A client is configured to use a DNS server through the TCP/IP Properties dialog box. The DNS tab contains fields to define the host name of the client, the domain where the client resides, the IP addresses of DNS servers, and a search order of domains.

The configuration of a DNS server is a complicated and convoluted endeavor. Microsoft has done an excellent job of simplifying this task, but it is still difficult. Unix-based DNS, such as that most commonly used on the Internet, can be likened to building an Apollo rocket. Microsoft Windows NT-based DNS can be likened to building a high-performance race car.

WINS

WINS is a name resolution service for Windows NT-based TCP/IP networks. Similar to DNS, WINS maps NetBIOS names to IP addresses. But unlike DNS, WINS dynamically maintains the mapping database. The main WINS functions include:

➤ Mapping NetBIOS names to IP addresses

➤ Recognizing NetBIOS names on all subnets

➤ Enabling internetwork browsing

WINS server is only available on Windows NT Server. However, you need to be familiar with a few terms and the basic method of operation of WINS.

WINS reduced NetBIOS background tracking by eliminating the NetBIOS broadcasts. A WINS client communicates directly with a WINS server to send a resource notification, release its NetBIOS name, or locate a resource.

The original Microsoft solution to reduce NetBIOS broadcast traffic was the LMHOSTS file. This was a static file stored on each client that associated IP addresses with NetBIOS names. Just as with the DNS HOSTS file, it had to be manually maintained. Unfortunately, an LMHOSTS file is useless in a DHCP environment where relationships between IP addresses and NetBIOS names change.

WINS and DHCP work well together. Each time a DHCP client goes online, it can inform the WINS server of its presence. Thus, the dynamic relationship between IP addresses and NetBIOS names can be fully managed by these automatic services.

WINS clients are configured through the TCP/IP Properties dialog box of the Protocols tab of the Network applet. The WINS Address tab enables you to configure two WINS servers. The second server is for fault tolerance.

WINS Vs. DNS

WINS and DNS, although similar, have significant differences that define when each should be used for name resolution. Table 10.1 displays a comparison chart to highlight the differences between WINS and DNS.

Within many private networks, both DNS and WINS are installed. This provides support for both NetBIOS and FQDN resolution. Both DNS and WINS can be configured to pass resolution requests to the opposing

Table 10.1 Differences between WINS and DNS.	
WINS	**DNS**
Maps NetBIOS names to IP addresses	Maps fully qualified domain names (FQDNs) to IP addresses
Automatic client data registration	Manual configuration
Flat database namespace	Uses FQDN's hierarchical structure
Used on Microsoft clients and networks networks	Used on TCP/IP-based hosts and
Only one entry per client	Each host can have multiple aliases
Enables domain functions such as logon and browsing	N/A

resolution service if the referenced name is not listed in the respective database.

Peer Web Services

Another important component of Windows NT that you need to be aware of is the Peer Web Services (PWS). PWS is Windows NT Workstation's equivalent of Windows NT Server's Internet Information Server (IIS). The only significant difference between PWS and IIS is that PWS is limited to 10 simultaneous connections due to the licensing restrictions of Windows NT Workstation.

Windows NT Workstation ships with PWS version 2, but version 3 is the current standard for real-world implementation.

PWS is a file and application server that provides Web, FTP, and Gopher services. If you are not already familiar with the Internet and these three services, you should reference the following resources:

➤ *Internet For Dummies*, by John R. Levine, Carol Baroudi, and Margy Levine-Young, IDG Books Worldwide, 1996. ISBN: 0-76450-106-2.

➤ *The Internet Complete Reference*, by Harley Hahn, Osborne McGraw-Hill, 1996. ISBN: 0-07882-138-X.

PWS can be used to support the Internet services of Web, FTP, and Gopher within a private TCP/IP-based network or over the Internet. You need to be aware of the Web, FTP, and Gopher services to fully understand PWS.

Web

The Web, or World Wide Web, is a service based on the Hypertext Transfer Protocol (HTTP). HTTP is a client/server interprocess communications protocol that employs text and graphics as content. A Web server, such as PWS, sends out requested documents to a Web client, such as Microsoft Internet Explorer. PWS offers numerous configuration options, including the following:

➤ Anonymous access

➤ Windows NT user account restricted access

➤ Activity logging

➤ IP or domain name restricted/granted access

➤ Virtual server configuration

One important configuration feature of PWS is custom directory roots and virtual servers. Multiple Web sites can be hosted from a single installation of PWS. Each Web site is stored in its own root directory. In addition, each hosted Web site can be identified with its own FQDN and IP address. To host multiple IP addresses on the same PWS server, additional IP addresses are assigned to the server's NIC through the TCP/IP properties.

If PWS is used on a network with Internet connectivity, no additional services are required. DNS is handled by Internet-based servers, and WINS will not be needed at all. However, if PWS is used within a private isolated network, both DNS and WINS might need to be installed somewhere on the network to support local name resolution.

FTP

The File Transfer Protocol (FTP) is the service and protocol used on the Internet to transfer files from one machine to another. PWS offers this service to improve file distribution over the Internet and within large private networks. PWS's FTP service can host multiple sites, each stored in a separate directory; however, they must all be referenced by a common base domain name. Version 2 of PWS does not support FTP virtual servers, so you might need to look elsewhere if you want to provide FTP services to your users (or get the newest version of PWS).

Gopher

Gopher is a text-based, menu-like hierarchical organization of data. This service was extremely popular before the development of the Web. Because of this, bastions of Gopher sites can still be found on the Internet. No compelling reason exists for using Gopher within a private network. Like FTP, multiple Gopher sites can exist, but they are all referenced by a common base domain name.

Practice Questions

Question 1

What is the primary function of DHCP?

○ a. To maintain a dynamic relationship database between IP
    addresses and NetBIOS names

○ b. To route IP packets across routers to other subnets

○ c. To assign IP addresses to clients

○ d. To resolve FQDNs into IP addresses

Answer c is correct. The service that assigns IP addresses to clients is DHCP.
The service that maintains a dynamic relationship database between IP
addresses and NetBIOS names is WINS. Therefore, answer a is incorrect.
The service that routes IP packets is RIP For IP. Therefore, answer b is
incorrect. The service that resolves FQDNs to IP addresses is DNS. Therefore, answer d is incorrect.

Question 2

What is an advantage of SLIP over PPP?

○ a. SLIP supports security, whereas PPP does not support
    security.

○ b. SLIP supports error checking, whereas PPP does not
    support error checking.

○ c. SLIP supports flow control, whereas PPP does not
    support flow control.

○ d. SLIP requires less system overhead than PPP.

Answer d is correct. SLIP requires less system overhead than PPP. SLIP
does not support error checking, flow control, or security—these are features of PPP. Therefore, answers a, b, and c are incorrect.

Question 3

> You want to install TCP/IP on a Windows NT Workstation in a nonrouted network. You have already assigned an IP address manually to the machine. What other parameter must you specify to install TCP/IP on the workstation?
>
> ○ a. The subnet mask
>
> ○ b. The default gateway
>
> ○ c. The DHCP server IP address
>
> ○ d. The WINS server IP address

Answer a is correct. When installing TCP/IP on a nonrouted network, the IP address and subnet mask parameters must be specified. If a default gateway is not specified, the machine can only communicate with other machines within its subnet; however, it is not a mandatory element. Therefore, answer b is incorrect. DHCP and WINS are not mandatory fields. Therefore, answers c and d are incorrect.

Question 4

> A DNS server links what types of information together? [Check all correct answers]
>
> ❑ a. NetBIOS names
>
> ❑ b. FQDNs
>
> ❑ c. Subnet masks
>
> ❑ d. IP addresses
>
> ❑ e. MAC addresses

Answers b and d are correct. DNS maintains a relationship between FQDNs and IP addresses in such a way that both forward and reverse lookups are possible. NetBIOS names are stored by WINS. Therefore, answer a is incorrect. Subnet masks can be distributed by a DHCP server, but a link table does not exist. Therefore, answer c is incorrect. MAC addresses are linked through NWLink's and NetBIOS's cached name resolution. Therefore, answer e is incorrect.

Question 5

You need to set up two new virtual Web servers to be hosted on your small private network using only a single installation of PWS. Each Web site will require its own directory, a unique URL, and a unique IP address. What should you do to implement this configuration? [Check all correct answers]

- ❏ a. Install RIP For IP on the PWS server.
- ❏ b. Assign each of the IP addresses to be used to the NIC in the PWS server; then, associate each IP address with the appropriate Web directory.
- ❏ c. Set up the DHCP Relay Agent.
- ❏ d. Configure DNS so it contains the FDQN for each site and correlates that name to its IP address.
- ❏ e. Configure WINS by adding the NetBIOS names and IP addresses of the sites to the static list of sites.

Trick! question

Answers b, d, and e are correct. Assigning the additional IP addresses to the server's NIC is an important step. Therefore, answer b is correct. Because this site is within a private network, you'll need both DNS and WINS to support name resolution. Therefore, answers d and e are correct. RIP For IP should not be used in this situation, plus, you do not know if there is more than one NIC in the server. Therefore, answer a is incorrect. The DHCP Relay Agent does not apply to this situation. Therefore, answer c is incorrect. The trick to this question is realizing that even though Windows NT Workstation does not host DNS or WINS servers, it can be the subject of a reference in a DNS or WINS server resolution database.

Question 6

What are the functions of WINS? [Check all correct answers]

- ❏ a. Enables internetwork browsing
- ❏ b. Maps FQDNs to IP addresses
- ❏ c. Maps NetBIOS names to IP addresses
- ❏ d. Maps NetBIOS names to MAC addresses
- ❏ e. Assigns clients IP addresses

Answers a and c are correct. Enabling internetwork browsing and mapping NetBIOS names to IP addresses are two of the three functions of WINS; the third function is recognizing NetBIOS names on all subnets. Mapping FQDNs to IP addresses is a function of DNS. Therefore, answer b is incorrect. Mapping NetBIOS names to MAC addresses happens in both NWLink and NetBEUI. Therefore, answer d is incorrect. Assigning clients IP addresses is a function of a DHCP server. Therefore, answer e is incorrect.

Question 7

What is an LMHOSTS file?

◯ a. A static list of NetBIOS names mapped to IP addresses

◯ b. A dynamic list of NetBIOS names mapped to IP addresses

◯ c. A static list of FQDNs mapped to IP addresses

◯ d. A dynamic list of FQDNs mapped to IP addresses

Answer a is correct. LMHOSTS is the predecessor to WINS and is a static list of NetBIOS names mapped to IP addresses. A dynamic list of NetBIOS names mapped to IP addresses is WINS. Therefore, answer b is incorrect. The HOSTS file is a static list of FQDNs mapped to IP addresses. Therefore, answer c is incorrect. There is no dynamic list of FQDNs mapped to IP addresses. Therefore, answer d is incorrect.

Question 8

You need users to access the office Windows NT network across the Internet. How can you establish Internet-based access without compromising security?

◯ a. Implement the SLIP protocol

◯ b. Implement the FTP protocol

◯ c. Implement the Point-to-Point Protocol

◯ d. Implement the Point-to-Point Tunneling Protocol

Answer d is correct. The Point-to-Point Tunneling Protocol (PPTP) uses the Internet as a connection medium while still maintaining network security. SLIP cannot be used to connect to a Windows NT system. Therefore, answer a is incorrect. The FTP protocol cannot be used to establish a network connection between Windows NT systems; it is only used to transfer files between TCP/IP systems supporting the FTP protocol. Therefore, answer b is incorrect. PPP will only encrypt the initial password, and all other data is not encrypted. Therefore, answer c is incorrect.

Question 9

Which of the following TCP/IP utilities are useful for troubleshooting connections between your Windows NT Workstation and a remote system by providing connection diagnostic details? [Check all correct answers]

❑ a. IPCONFIG

❑ b. TRACERT

❑ c. FINGER

❑ d. PING

❑ e. Telnet

Answers b and d are correct. The TRACERT utility displays the route taken by packets to the remote system. Therefore, answer b is correct. The PING utility indicates whether or not a remote system is currently online. Therefore, answer d is correct. The IPCONFIG utility is only useful for identifying local TCP/IP configurations. Therefore, answer a is incorrect. The FINGER utility is used to obtain user information; it does not offer connection diagnostics. Therefore, answer c is incorrect. The Telnet utility is used to establish a terminal emulation session with a remote system; it does not offer connection diagnostics. Therefore, answer e is incorrect.

Question 10

How are the HOSTS and LMHOSTS files different?

○ a. A HOSTS file maps host names to IP addresses; an LMHOSTS file maps NetBIOS names to IP addresses.

○ b. An LMHOSTS file maps host names to IP addresses, whereas a HOSTS file maps NetBIOS names to IP addresses.

○ c. A HOSTS file maps host names to IP addresses, whereas an LMHOSTS file maps host names to NetBIOS names.

○ d. An LMHOSTS file maps host names to IP addresses, whereas a HOSTS file maps host names to NetBIOS names.

Answer a is correct. A HOSTS file maps host names to IP addresses, whereas a LMHOSTS file maps NetBIOS names to IP addresses.

Need To Know More?

Bisaillon, Teresa and Brad Werner: *TCP/IP With Windows NT Illustrated.* McGraw Hill, New York, NY, 1998. This is the best all around resource on TCP/IP for Windows NT we know of.

Perkins, Charles, Matthew Strebe, and James Chellis: *MCSE: NT Workstation Study Guide, 2nd Edition.* Sybex Network Press, San Francisco, CA, 1998. ISBN 0-7821-2223-X. Chapter 19 discusses most of the TCP/IP issues raised in this chapter.

Search the TechNet CD (or its online version through **www.microsoft.com**) and the *Windows NT Workstation Resource Kit* CD using the keywords "TCP/IP," "name resolution," "Peer Web Services," "DNS," "WINS," "LMHOSTS," "HOSTS," and "DHCP."

NetWare Connectivity

Terms you'll need to understand:

√ NetWare

√ NWLink Internetwork Packet Exchange/Sequenced Packet Exchange (IPX/SPX)

√ Client Service For NetWare (CSNW)

√ Gateway Service For NetWare (GSNW)

√ File And Print Services For NetWare (FPNW)

√ Frame type

Techniques you'll need to master:

√ Installing, configuring, and enabling NWLink (IPX/SPX)

√ Installing, configuring, and enabling CSNW

√ Installing, configuring, and enabling GSNW

√ Implementing FPNW

√ Adjusting frame type settings

By making NetWare connectivity part and parcel of Windows NT, Microsoft has made it possible to integrate its products directly and easily with existing networks all over the world. Considering the built-in NetWare access capabilities as well as the add-ins available at low cost from Microsoft for Windows NT to enhance these capabilities, it's clear that NetWare interoperability is an important concern in Redmond.

Even if you don't have any NetWare servers on your Windows NT network, you must still understand what Microsoft offers by way of NetWare compatibility and access. Although much of this material will be old hat to those who work in hybrid NetWare–Windows NT environments, those who don't have the benefit of direct exposure should study this chapter carefully.

You might find the detail in this chapter a bit overwhelming. We've included as much information as possible to give you a solid understanding of everything going on when interoperating with NetWare.

Protocols And Compatibility Issues

To avoid paying royalties to Novell, Microsoft built its own implementation of the Internetwork Packet Exchange/Sequenced Packet Exchange (IPX/SPX) protocol suite, called "NWLink" (to avoid infringing on Novell trade names). Surprisingly, some comparisons between Novell's IPX/SPX client implementations and Microsoft's NWLink have shown the latter implementation to be slightly faster than the former. In other words, these guys are serious about their NetWare compatibility, and they have done a pretty good job.

Although NetWare supports multiple protocols—primarily IPX/SPX and TCP/IP—it's most common to find IPX/SPX used to communicate between NetWare's clients and its servers. In fact, Novell does not support any protocols other than IPX/SPX for versions of NetWare older than 3.x (which usually means version 2.2).

IPX/SPX is the protocol used to communicate between the NetWare server and its clients in NetWare 2.2.

When Novell implemented IPX/SPX, it also elected to use a special frame format for the protocol on Ethernet and other network types. Even though the emerging standard at the time (which has since become the official standard) was to use 802.2 frame formats for networked communications, Novell elected to use what's often called a "raw 802.3" frame format for its implementation of IPX/SPX on Ethernet.

To make a long and complex story as short as possible, the upshot of Novell's initial decision, and its subsequent divergence from industry standard frame types, introduced the possibility of a frame type mismatch when using IPX/SPX (or NWLink). You need to be aware of problems communicating on a network and understand NWLink's ability to detect IPX frame types automatically on a Windows NT machine.

Here's what you need to know about IPX frame types:

➤ Although NWLink is provided primarily for NetWare access and interoperability, Windows NT-based networks can run using only NWLink, even if NetWare is not present.

➤ Until NetWare 3.12 shipped, NetWare's default frame type was raw 802.3, which Microsoft calls simply "802.3 frame type."

➤ For NetWare 3.12 and all 4.x versions (including IntranetWare), the default frame type uses 802.2 headers atop the native frame type for the network technology in use. Microsoft calls this the "802.2 frame type," without regard to technology.

➤ The total battery of frame types you're most likely to encounter is:

➤ 802.2 frame type (industry standard; default for NetWare 3.12 and higher-numbered versions)

➤ 802.3 frame type (so-called "raw 802.3 header" format, developed by Novell; default for older, pre-3.12 versions of NetWare)

➤ 802.3 with SNAP header (sometimes called "Ethernet_SNAP frame type" in Microsoft terminology)

➤ 802.5 frame type (the native format for Token Ring networks)

➤ 802.5 frame type with SNAP header (sometimes called "Token_Ring_SNAP" in Microsoft terminology)

Note: SNAP stands for SubNetwork Access Protocol, and it provides a mechanism that permits nonstandard, higher-level protocols to appear within a standard IEEE logical link control frame like the frame types previously mentioned. It's often used to transport AppleTalk or SNA in IP network environments. It's not necessary to understand the subtleties of this technology.

➤ If any workstation (or server) is configured for an incorrect IPX frame type (that doesn't match the rest of the population), an improperly configured machine will not be able to interact with the network. This can occur even though the network may otherwise work properly, and all other machines are able to communicate successfully.

➤ NWLink's auto detect type setting defaults to 802.2. If the initiation broadcast does not receive an 802.2 response, but does get some other frame type, then Windows NT will attempt to use 802.3, Ethernet II, then SNAP in an attempt to detect the correct frame type in use. If a match is found, the default auto detect setting is set to the determined type. However, auto detect can only select a single frame type—namely, the first frame type is sees.

➤ For client/server applications, such as SQL Server database access, or NetBIOS-based applications, native NetWare clients using IPX/SPX can communicate directly with Windows NT running such an application without requiring anything other than NWLink and the server side of the application to be installed on that machine. In essence, the client side of the client/server application supplies everything the client and server need to communicate, as long as they have a protocol in common. Because the assumption is that native NetWare clients use IPX/SPX, a Windows NT machine must install NWLink to communicate with such clients across the network.

Gateway Service For NetWare

Microsoft often refers to Gateway Service For NetWare by its acronym—GSNW. But there's more to this component than meets the eye, and this can lead to some confusion. The complete name of the software component as it appears in the Add dialog box on Windows NT Server, generated from Control Panel|Network applet|Services is Gateway (And Client) Services For NetWare.

You may be surprised to learn that GSNW includes Client Service For NetWare (CSNW; discussed later in this chapter) in its capabilities and functionality. In English, this means that any Windows NT Server with GSNW installed also can function as a client to a NetWare server. This explains why you must remove existing NetWare client software—especially Novell's NetWare Client For Windows NT—from any Windows NT Server before installing GSNW on that machine.

 Keep in mind that the Gateway Service For NetWare is not a service available in Windows NT Workstation; rather, it is a Windows NT Server service. Therefore, the following discussion is from the Server standpoint, not Workstation.

Understanding GSNW

Generically speaking, the term "gateway" refers to a software component permitting computers that do not share a common set of protocols and services to communicate with one another. In other words, the gateway translates from one protocol and service world to another, and vice versa.

GSNW is no exception: What GSNW does is make it possible for ordinary Microsoft Network clients (PCs running Windows 3.x, Windows 95, Windows 98, or even Windows NT Workstation or Server) to access resources on a NetWare server by translating requests from those clients stated in Microsoft Network terms into NetWare terms, and then translating the accompanying responses from the NetWare server from NetWare terms back into Microsoft Network terms. The gateway is in the middle of these communications.

Here's the "trick" that makes this work: The Windows NT computer where GSNW runs imports a logical volume from the NetWare server through the gateway that Microsoft Network clients can access as if it were any other Windows NT-based network share. The gateway also can create a similar function for NetWare-based printers and make NetWare-based print services available to Microsoft Network clients. The chief selling point for GSNW is that it provides access to NetWare resources for Microsoft Network clients without requiring any additional software (or software changes) to be made to those clients themselves.

Installing, Configuring, And Enabling GSNW

The details of GSNW installation are listed here to help you gain a more rounded understanding of this interoperability service from Microsoft.

Gateway Service For NetWare is an optional network service included as part of Windows NT Server: This means it's included with the distribution media for Windows NT Server, but not installed by default whenever you install the core operating system. To install GSNW, you must open the Network applet in Control Panel, select the Services tab, and then click the

Figure 11.1   You can install GSNW (and CSNW) on Windows NT Server through the Select Network Service dialog box in the Network applet in Control Panel.

Add button in the resulting display. This produces the Select Network Service screen shown in Figure 11.1, where GSNW appears as the second choice in the list. To begin the process of installing GSNW, highlight its entry and then click the OK button at the bottom of the window. This brings up a prompt for the Windows NT Server CD.

> It's important to note that if you elect to install GSNW on a Windows NT Server that does not already have NWLink running, NWLink will be installed automatically as a part of the GSNW installation process. Thus, although NWLink is required for GSNW to run, it's not necessary to install it in advance, nor is it a problem if NWLink has already been installed.

Here's a high-level overview of the GSNW installation process, emphasizing those elements and information that must be supplied during installation:

1. Before installing and configuring GSNW, you must create the following accounts on the NetWare server where the gateway will connect:

   a. A user account on the NetWare server with rights to the NetWare file system directories that gateway users from the Windows NT side will need.

   b. A group account named NTGATEWAY on the NetWare server with rights to all file and print resources that gateway users will need.

   Note: All users who go through a single GSNW gateway have the same access and the same rights to the NetWare resources; the only way to create different collections of accesses and rights is to set up multiple gateways—only one instance of GSNW per individual Windows NT Server is permitted.

2. To install GSNW, you must log on to Windows NT Server as an administrator. In the Network applet in Control Panel, select the Services tab, click the Add button, and then select Gateway (and Client) Services For NetWare (as shown in Figure 11.1). Supply the Windows NT installation CD or point to a copy of the \i386 directory where the necessary source code files reside. The software will more or less install itself.

3. To configure GSNW, double-click the GSNW icon in Control Panel. The Gateway Service For NetWare dialog box appears.

   a. Click the Gateway button to elicit the Configure Gateway dialog box.

   b. Check the Enable Gateway box to enable the Gateway Service.

   c. In the Gateway Account field, enter the NetWare username you created in Step 1a. Enter the password into the Password field and then confirm that password in the Confirm Password field.

   d. Click the Add button to create a NetWare share for use by Microsoft networking clients. The New Share dialog box appears.

   e. In the Share Name field, enter a name through which the NetWare directory will be shared.

   f. In the Network Path field, enter a UNC name for the NetWare directory that's being shared. For the SYS:Public directory on a server named NETONE, the syntax is \\NETONE\SYS\ PUBLIC.

   g. In the Comment field, you can add an optional descriptive phrase that will appear in the Browse window for Microsoft Clients on the network.

   h. In the Use Drive field, select a drive letter on the Windows NT Server to be assigned to the NetWare directory. This drive letter remains taken as long as GSNW runs on the Windows NT Server (by default, Z is the letter assigned to the first such share name).

   i. The User Limit box permits administrators to limit the number of users who can access the NetWare share simultaneously. Because the gateway bogs down under increasing load, it's a good idea to limit the number of users to 10 or so (unless the server is extremely fast or only lightly loaded).

   j. Click OK to save all changes. You'll return to the Configure Gateway dialog box. Click OK again to exit the Gateway Service For NetWare dialog box. All changes will take effect upon the next system logon.

4. The only way to create NetWare shares is through the interface described in Steps 3d through 3j (not through Explorer or My Computer, as is the case for normal Windows NT shares). Likewise, you must use the GSNW applet in Control Panel to set permissions for NetWare shares. Here's how:

    a. From an administrative logon, launch the GSNW applet from Control Panel.

    b. When the Gateway Service For NetWare dialog box appears, choose the Gateway button.

    c. In the Configure Gateway dialog box, highlight the NetWare share name and choose the Permissions button. Use this interface to set permissions for the NetWare share.

5. Using NetWare Print Resources through the Gateway requires none of the shenanigans needed to establish and set permissions for the NetWare shares. Instead, configure NetWare print queues through the Printers icon in Control Panel (as with any other Windows NT Server-attached printer). Here's what's involved:

    a. From an administrative logon, launch the Printers applet. Select the Add Printer icon. This displays the Add Printer Wizard window.

    b. Select the Network Printer radio button and then click the Next button. This brings up the Connect To Printer dialog box.

    c. In this dialog box, you'll see two icons: one labeled NetWare Or Compatible Network and the other labeled Microsoft Windows Network. You can expand and navigate the NetWare Or Compatible Network directory tree the same way you would the Microsoft Windows Network tree: Open Network Neighborhood, double-click Network, select a server, and then double-click and select the printer you want to manage.

    Otherwise, the procedure is exactly the same as installing an ordinary Windows NT network printer. (This is covered in Chapter 14.)

Remember that it is necessary to map a drive on the Windows NT computer for the NetWare share, and that NetWare shares and their permissions only can be managed through the GSNW applet, not through ordinary file management tools. NetWare printers, on the other hand, can be handled like any other network printer (that is, through the Printers applet), after GSNW has been installed in Windows NT.

Client Service For NetWare

GSNW makes NetWare resources available to ordinary Microsoft Network clients, but CSNW works only with Windows NT machines to make them act as native clients to NetWare servers elsewhere on the network. This system component is called CSNW only on Windows NT Workstation 4, which ships without GSNW; however, CSNW is part and parcel of GSNW on Windows NT Server 4 machines. In either case, its job is to let Windows NT machines link up to and browse NetWare resources alongside Microsoft Windows Network resources.

CSNW is installed through the Services tab of the Network applet. Once it's installed and your system is rebooted, you can configure the service. A new applet called CSNW appears in the Control Panel, which is where all the configuration of this service takes place. This includes selecting and defining a preferred server (for NetWare 3.12 servers and below) or default tree and context (for NetWare 4.x servers), setting print options (add form feeds, notify print completion, and print banner), and whether or not to run logon scripts. If no settings are made, Windows NT attempts to log in to the closest NetWare server it can find.

The first time you attempt to access a NetWare resource, you'll need to provide an account and password valid on that NetWare network/server. Windows NT should remember this information for all future accesses and perform automatic validation (like the RAS AutoDial feature) the next time NetWare resources are requested.

Due to this auto-reconnect feature, you might need to rearrange your redirector bindings to force Windows NT to search local or Windows NT networks first before NetWare networks. This is done through the Network applet on the Services tab. After CSNW is installed, an additional button is present at the bottom of this tab. The Network Access Order button displays the known networks; through this dialog box, you can reorder networks so that Microsoft networks are searched before NetWare networks.

Resources hosted from a NetWare server appear to Windows NT clients the same as any other Windows NT-hosted resource. CSNW and GSNW hide the translation between the differing networks from the user by listing NetWare resources in standard browser lists. Printing from Windows NT to a NetWare-hosted printer is no different than printing to any other type of network printer. Simply create a new printer using the Add Printer wizard and link to the network-shared device. Windows NT handles all the issues related to NetWare print servers, drivers, and queues, making the use of non-Windows NT network resources seamless.

File And Print Services For NetWare

FPNW, as it's usually called, is not included with Windows NT 4; it must be purchased separately (at the time of writing, it costs $149 in the U.S. market). What GSNW is to Microsoft Network clients, FPNW is to native NetWare clients: It makes resources from a Windows NT Server available to NetWare clients, without requiring any additional software or configuration changes to those clients. In other words, FPNW makes a Windows NT Server look like a NetWare 3.11 server to any native NetWare clients on a network.

NetWare-Aware Applications

Some NetWare-aware applications can be used on Windows NT. If they require only those DLLs for NetWare, they are provided by the NetWare client for Windows, CSNW, or GSNW. Some NetWare-aware utilities will only function if the NetWare link has already been established. The only way to really know is to test the applications yourself.

Several of the NetWare administration tools will not function from Windows NT, but there are command prompt equivalents that can be used instead (see Table 11.1).

However, there are many utilities that can be launched from Windows NT, without significant problems. These include the following:

CHKVOL, COLORPAL, DSPACE, FLAG, FLAGDIR, FCONSOLE, FILER, GRANT, HELP, LISTDIR, MAP, NCOPY, NDIR, PCONSOLE, PSC, PSTAT, RCONSOLE, REMOVE, REVOKE,

Table 11.1	The unsupported NetWare commands and their Windows NT equivalents.
Unsupported NetWare Command	**Windows NT Equivalent**
ATTACH	NET USE
CAPTURE	NET USE
LOGIN	NET LOGON
LOGOUT	NET LOGOFF
SLIST	NET VIEW

RIGHTS, SECURITY, SEND, SESSION (search mapping not supported), SETPASS, SETTTS, SYSCON, TLIST, USERLIST, VOLINFO (slow execution if interval=5), and WHOAMI.

NetWare Troubleshooting

Detailed troubleshooting of NetWare interoperability problems is a bit beyond the scope of this book. Basic familiarity with troubleshooting techniques and a handful of NetWare-resource-specific fixes will suffice for most purposes.

The first step is to determine where the difficulty is occurring. Is it with the hardware, the network connection, the Windows NT network, or the NetWare network? If the location can be isolated, you can apply the appropriate measures to eliminate the issue.

If the problem lies with NetWare, here are a few things to try:

1. Make sure the NetWare server is booted and functioning.

2. Verify that the workstation can connect to other Microsoft-hosted resources.

3. Double-check that NWLink and CSNW are installed properly on the Windows NT Workstation or that GSNW is on the Windows NT Server.

4. Check the preferred server and tree/context settings.

5. Reset frame types and network numbers for both the NetWare systems and the Windows NT systems.

Unless you work in a mixed NetWare/Windows NT environment, you'll want to review the basics about GSNW, CSNW, FPNW, and NWLink to fully understand these services. If these sound like gibberish, check the Glossary first; then, reread this chapter (and at least one of the references in the "Need To Know More?" section at the end of the chapter). For those who feel like they're better prepared, here are some questions for you to study.

Practice Questions

Question 1

> At XYZ Corp., a handful of NetWare 3.11 clients remain in use. These machines need access to files on a newly installed Windows NT subnet. To support such access without changes to the existing clients, which of the following services and/or protocols must be available on Windows NT? [Check all correct answers]
>
> ❑ a. Gateway Service For NetWare (GSNW)
>
> ❑ b. Client Service For NetWare (CSNW)
>
> ❑ c. File And Print Services For NetWare (FPNW)
>
> ❑ d. The NWLink protocol

Answers c and d are correct. File And Print Services For NetWare makes a Windows NT server look like a NetWare server to NetWare network clients, so it's what provides file access. Therefore, answer c is correct. Native NetWare 3.x clients need IPX/SPX to access real NetWare servers, or Windows NT computers running FPNW. Because NWLink is Microsoft's implementation of IPX/SPX, answer d is also correct. GSNW provides mediated access to NetWare services for Microsoft Network clients. Therefore, it's not required, meaning answer a is incorrect. Likewise, CSNW makes it possible for Windows NT Workstations and Servers to obtain direct access to a NetWare server. Therefore, answer b is also incorrect.

Question 2

> You have CSNW installed on your Windows NT Workstation. You also have a logical printer defined for a NetWare-hosted HP LaserJet. You have numerous small documents to print, but you share the printer with many other users. How can you force each print job to be labeled so that your documents are easily identified after printing?
>
> ○ a. Define a separator page within the properties for the logical printer.
>
> ○ b. The NetWare print server must be configured to print separator pages.
>
> ○ c. The Print Banner option should be selected in CSNW.
>
> ○ d. Enable the sort option on the print device.

Answer c is correct. Enabling the Print Banner option in CSNW is the best way to force NetWare to print a separator page before each of your print jobs. The logical printer on your Windows NT Workstation does not have the ability to alter the control of a NetWare-hosted printer. Therefore, answer a is incorrect. The NetWare print server may offer a print separator page option, but you do not need to enable this feature for everyone. Therefore, answer b is incorrect. Most printers do not have a sort option, and this option would not be useful or practical in this situation. Therefore, answer d is incorrect.

Question 3

> With CSNW installed on a Windows NT Workstation, which of the following NetWare command-line utilities does Microsoft support?
>
> ○ a. SLIST
>
> ○ b. LOGOUT
>
> ○ c. SYSCON
>
> ○ d. CAPTURE
>
> ○ e. ATTACH

Answer c is correct. The only utility from this list that can be launched from Windows NT is SYSCON. All of the other utilities are not supported by Windows NT, but their functions can be performed using Windows NT's NET command equivalents. Therefore, answers a, b, d, and e are incorrect. Note that this is not a question about which utilities work or not, but is intended to elicit your knowledge about which such utilities Microsoft says it supports when using CSNW.

Question 4

One of the PCs on a network is unable to establish a working connection, but all other computers are working correctly. The only protocol in use on the network is NWLink. Of the following possibilities, which is the most likely to be the cause of this problem?

○ a. Faulty network interface devices

○ b. A protocol mismatch

○ c. A PC memory conflict

○ d. An incorrect IPX frame type

Answer d is correct. The clue to answering the question correctly lies in the statement "the only protocol in use on the network is NWLink." Because IPX does not require a fixed frame type, but works with multiple frame types, a frame type mismatch easily can render a machine unable to communicate successfully with the network, even though the hardware is working correctly. The key to answering this question correctly is careful reading. Anyone who knows anything about networks knows that loose connections are the most common cause of problems, but that appears nowhere in this list of choices. Because the problem statement includes an indication that only *one* PC is having problems and gives "faulty network interface *devices*" as a possibility, this knocks out what typically might be the next most obvious cause, namely a faulty network interface card, thereby eliminating answer a from further consideration. Answer b patently is false because the only protocol in use is NWLink (or IPX/SPX, if you prefer). Answer c is possible, but unlikely, because most memory conflicts will cause a machine to crash rather than simply rendering network access inoperative.

Question 5

On a network that contains multiple versions of NetWare, some clients are configured for NetWare 2.2, while others are configured for NetWare 4.11. Among other protocols, NWLink is in use on this network. The NetWare 2.2 clients use an 802.3 raw frame type, whereas the NetWare 4.11 clients use the 802.2 frame type. What kinds of information must be supplied in the NWLink IPX/SPX Properties dialog box to allow the same Windows NT Workstation to recognize both flavors of NetWare clients on this network?

○ a. Select Auto Frame Type Detection and add the clients' IPX network numbers and frame types to the frame type configuration list.

○ b. Select Manual Frame Type Detection and add the network numbers and frame types for both 2.2 and 4.11 clients to the frame type configuration list.

○ c. Select only Auto Frame Type Detection; the rest is automatic.

○ d. Select Manual Frame Type Detection and add the 2.2 clients' network numbers and frame types to the frame type configuration list.

Answer b is correct. The secret to answering this question is to understand how automatic frame type detection works in Windows NT. As long as the only one frame type is in use, automatic detection works fine. But because older NetWare clients—especially NetWare 2.2 clients—use only 802.3 frames, Manual Frame Type Detection must be selected during the configuration process. This eliminates answers a and c. Answer d is incorrect because Manual Frame Type Detection requires entry of all frame types and network numbers in use. Only answer b covers all these requirements and is therefore the only correct choice.

Question 6

> Widgets Corp. seeks to make its Windows NT Workstation and Windows 95 clients able to access a NetWare server without installing NetWare client software on their machines. How can this objective be met most effectively?
>
> ○ a. Install Gateway Service For NetWare on a Windows NT server on the same network.
>
> ○ b. Install NWLink on the Windows NT Workstation and Windows 95 computers.
>
> ○ c. Install Gateway Service For NetWare on the NetWare Server.
>
> ○ d. Install File And Print Services For NetWare on a Windows NT Server on the same network.

Answer a is correct. The whole point of a gateway is to permit clients to access services that their current configurations would otherwise make inaccessible. For that reason, answer a is the only correct answer, because it opens a gateway for the Windows NT Workstation and Windows 95 clients to access NetWare resources with no change to their current configurations. Answer b is incorrect, because by adding NWLink to the clients, it not only violates the requirement that no NetWare client software be added to those machines, it does not do the complete job (additional software is necessary for these machines to communicate with a NetWare server). Answer c mentions the right software product, but puts it on a NetWare server rather than on a Windows NT Server, where it was designed to be run. Finally, File And Print Services For NetWare lets native NetWare clients access Windows NT, not native Microsoft Networking clients access NetWare (thus completely missing the point of the question).

Question 7

On a NetWare network, your Windows NT Workstation is configured to Auto Detect, which detects the IPX frame types in use. What is the frame type NWLink will default to if it fails to detect a frame time within a specified time? [Check all correct answers]

❑ a. 802.2 frame type

❑ b. 802.3 frame type

❑ c. 802.3 frame type with SNAP header

❑ d. 802.5 frame type

❑ e. 802.5 frame type with SNAP header

Answer a is correct. 802.2 is the frame type used by NWLink by default when a frame type is not detected automatically.

Question 8

Once you've successfully installed CSNW, what additional configuration steps are necessary to actually access NetWare resources?

○ a. Define a tree and context.

○ b. Set the preferred server.

○ c. Select printer options.

○ d. Enable or disable logon scripts.

○ e. No additional steps are necessary.

Answer e is correct. After CSNW is installed, no additional steps are necessary to connect to a NetWare server. An account and password are required, but these are not defined through CSNW. Windows NT will attempt to connect to the nearest NetWare server without any additional settings. Defining a tree and context and setting a preferred server are not required, and they are mutually exclusive. Therefore, answers a and b are incorrect. Setting printer and logon script options are also not required in order to use CSNW. Therefore, answers c and d are incorrect.

Question 9

> Which of the following software elements and/or protocols are required for a Windows NT Workstation running Client Service For NetWare to successfully access NetWare-based resources? [Check all correct answers]
>
> ❑ a. Gateway Service For NetWare
>
> ❑ b. File And Print Services For NetWare
>
> ❑ c. NWLink
>
> ❑ d. A valid account on a NetWare server
>
> ❑ e. Membership in the NTGATEWAY group on the NetWare server to which Gateway Service For NetWare connects

Answers c and d are correct. Answer c supplies the necessary protocol to communicate from client to server, and answer d provides the necessary permission to access the NetWare server once communication commences. With CSNW in use, the Windows NT Server service of GSNW is not required to connect to NetWare resources. Therefore, answer a is incorrect. Answer e is also incorrect because no membership in the GSNW NTGATEWAY group is needed. File And Print Services For NetWare is an add-on to enable NetWare clients to access Windows NT resources this is also not required for a Windows NT Workstation to access NetWare resources. Therefore, answer b is incorrect.

Need To Know More?

Gaskin, James E.: *The Complete Guide to NetWare 4.11/ IntranetWare, 2nd Edition.* Sybex Network Press, Alameda, CA, 1997. ISBN 0-7821-1931-X. For a comprehensive look at NetWare networking, there's no better reference than this one. Use it to deal with NetWare specifics and the NetWare side of any NetWare-to-Windows NT connection.

Heywood, Drew: *Inside Windows NT Server, 2nd Edition.* New Riders, Indianapolis, IN, 1998. ISBN 1-56205-860-6. Chapter 16, "Windows NT Server and NetWare," explains the salient software, communications issues, and connectivity concerns.

Minasi, Mark, and Peter Dyson: *Mastering Windows NT Server 4, 5th Edition.* Sybex Network Press, Alameda, CA, 1997. ISBN 0-7821-2163-2. Minasi's been a Windows NT guru ever since the product appeared; his experience and practical orientation show in Chapter 13, "Novell NetWare in an NT Server Environment." This book is worthwhile because of the tips and tricks it provides, and it's a good overview as well.

Perkins, Charles, Matthew Strebe, and James Chellis: *MCSE: NT Workstation Study Guide, 2nd Edition.* Sybex Network Press, San Francisco, CA, 1998. ISBN 0-7821-2223-X. Chapter 10 has a detailed account of Windows NT Workstation interoperability with NetWare resources.

Siyan, Karanjit S.: *Windows NT Server 4 Professional Reference, 2nd Edition.* New Riders, Indianapolis, IN, 1997. ISBN 1-56205-805-3. Chapter 12, "Integrating NetWare with Windows NT Server," brings Siyan's usual depth of coverage and details to this topic; this is the best available preparation material for NetWare topics.

Strebe, Matthew, Charles Perkins, and James Chellis: *MSCE: NT Server 4 Study Guide, 2nd Edition.* Sybex Network Press, San Francisco, CA, 1998. ISBN 0-7821-2221-3. Chapter 13, "Interoperating with NetWare," covers this ground well (only Siyan offers more depth and details).

Search the TechNet CD (or its online version through **www.microsoft.com**) using the keywords "NetWare," "NWLink," "Gateway Service," and related product names. The *Windows NT Concepts and Planning Manual*, which is also on TechNet, also includes useful information on making Windows NT-to-NetWare connections, and vice versa.

The *Windows NT Workstation Resource Kit* contains a lot of useful information about NetWare and related topics. You can search the TechNet (either CD or online version) or the CD accompanying the *Resource Kit*, using the keywords "NetWare," "NWLink," and "Gateway Service." Useful NetWare-related materials occur throughout the *Networking Guide* volume.

Workgroups, Domains, And Browsers

12

. . . .

Terms you'll need to understand:

√ Workgroups

√ Domain

√ Primary Domain Controller (PDC)

√ Backup Domain Controller (BDC)

√ Trusts

√ Browsers

√ Logon scripts

√ Replication

Techniques you'll need to master:

√ Understanding the workgroup concept

√ Learning and implementing domain controllers

√ Implementing trusts between domains

√ Exploring the Windows NT Browser Service

There are two types of networks within the Windows NT networking world —workgroups and domains. In addition to network type, Windows NT uses a resource list called the "browse list" to inform users and computers about available resources. In this chapter, we introduce you to these concepts so that you gain a full understanding of Windows NT networking.

Workgroups

A workgroup is a network of computers in which no single machine has control over the operation, activity, or access to the entire network. Within a workgroup, each machine is a peer—meaning that each machine has equal administrative control. A workgroup computer is only able to regulate access to the resources it hosts—it is not able to restrict access to resources hosted by other peers.

Here are a few important points to remember about workgroups:

➤ No central control

➤ Share-level security

➤ All user accounts must be created on each member

A workgroup is a useful networking type, but only if you have 10 computers or fewer to connect. Windows NT Workstation can participate in a workgroup simply by defining the workgroup name in the appropriate place. That place is the Identification tab of the Network applet. Clicking the Change button on that tab causes the Identification Changes dialog box to appear (see Figure 12.1). By selecting the Workgroup radio button and defining the name of the workgroup, you can transform Windows NT Workstation from a client in a domain to a peer in a workgroup.

The process is easily reversed by redefining the domain using the same dialog box. However, for either change, you'll need to reboot the computer for the changes take effect. Also, a workstation cannot be a member of both a workgroup and a domain simultaneously, but it can switch back and forth as needed.

A Simple Look At Domains And Controllers

Put simply, a domain is a collection of networked workstations and servers that are managed as a group. In Windows NT, each domain must have a

Identification Changes   ? ✕

Windows uses the following information to identify your computer on the network. You may change the name for this computer, the workgroup or domain that it will appear in, and create a computer account in the domain if specified.

Computer Name: NTW1

Member of

○ Workgroup:

● Domain: LANW

☐ Create a Computer Account in the Domain

This option will create an account on the domain for this computer. You must specify a user account with the ability to add workstations to the specified domain above.

User Name:

Password:

OK   Cancel

Figure 12.1   The Identification Changes dialog box.

domain controller to administer user rights for that domain. The first Windows NT Server installed in a domain is the Primary Domain Controller (PDC). The PDC houses the security policy and database for the domain; therefore, the server is responsible for authenticating that domain's users at logon.

The next Windows NT Server to be installed should take on the role of Backup Domain Controller (BDC). The BDC maintains a copy of the security policy and domain database (it synchronizes with the PDC at specified intervals to maintain up-to-date copies of these security features). If the PDC goes down for any reason, the BDC continues to authenticate users. A BDC can be promoted to a PDC, but this is not an automatic process. Although it is not required that you have a BDC on a Windows NT network, we highly recommend it.

You can promote a BDC to a PDC manually if you need to take the PDC down for maintenance purposes. It is important, however, to promote the BDC *before* the PDC goes down; otherwise, some account information that might not have yet been replicated between the controllers may be lost. BDC promotion is performed with the Server Manager tool found only on Windows NT Server.

Note: When a PDC is not present in a domain, no changes to the security database can be made. A BDC can only authenticate—it cannot modify or create entries in the security database.

Obviously, Microsoft's description of a domain is highly colored by its configuration and construction of a domain. Here are a few more tidbits to remember about domains:

➤ They provide central control and administration.

➤ They only have user-level security.

➤ User and group accounts are created once and used across the network.

According to Microsoft, a domain should be used when you have more than 10 users/computers.

Workstations And Domains

Workstations can become members of a domain in two ways. The first way is to create a computer account in the domain for the workstation. This is performed in the Windows NT Server utility Server Manager. Once an account is created, the workstation joins the domain simply by being named the same name as the account that was created. Once it joins, the domain controller records that machine's SID so that no other machine can impersonate it. The second way for a workstation to join a domain is to supply an administrative account and password during the installation. This account is used by the setup program to log onto the PDC and create a computer account when it is needed.

Trusts

PDCs and BDCs control access to resources on a particular domain, but what if a user needs access to a resource on another domain? Then you must establish a trust relationship between domains.

By establishing trust relationships, you allow secure access between domains. However, users in one domain are not required to be defined in another domain. Trusted domains make Windows NT a more scalable network scheme, especially in enterprise-wide networks. If it weren't for the use of trusted domains, large Windows NT-based networks would not be workable due to the huge amount of administration involved. With the trusted-domain concept, for example, the Sales department can have its own little part of the network, separate from the rest of the network. If it's necessary for the Sales domain to share information and resources with the Marketing department domain, Windows NT can easily provide the cross-access needed via domain trusts.

Creating trusts requires access to the User Manager For Domains utility. To use this utility on Windows NT Workstation, you must install it from Windows NT Server files, either manually or with Server's Network Client Administrator.

It is important to note that trusts are "one way" by default. This means that although the Production domain (the trusting domain) grants a trust to the Engineering domain (the trusted domain) to access the Design share, Production does not have any additional rights to the Engineering domain unless this is defined in the Trust Relationships dialog box in the User Manager For Domains. Two-way trusts are simply two one-way trusts between domains.

Workstation Logon

To log onto a workstation, you must press Ctrl+Alt+Del to access the WinLogon dialog box. By providing a valid name and password, you may obtain access. However, the type of access depends on the type of user account used to log in. Windows NT Workstation can support logons of two types—workstation and domain. A workstation account is a user account that only exists on the local computer. This is the type of user account used in a workgroup, but it can still be created if a workstation is a member of a domain. When a workstation account is used, the user is limited to local resources and may not access anything on the network. A domain account is a user account that the domain controller handles, thus it grants the user access to all network resources (or at least the ones to which he or she has authorized access).

In instances where both a workgroup and a domain account share the same name, the account type may be selected by choosing the local computer name or the domain name in the bottom box of the WinLogon logon window labeled From. If the account name and the password are the same for both types of accounts, then local and network access will be granted regardless of which account is designated in the WinLogon window.

Browsers

The Windows NT Browser Service maintains a list of all network resources within a domain and provides lists of these domains, servers, and resource objects to any Explorer-type interface that requests them (for example, browse lists).

Each computer within a domain participates in the Browser Service. Each time a computer is brought up within the domain, it announces itself and the resources it has to share (if any). This is the most common level of participation for computers within a domain. The most important role within the Browser Service is that of the Master Browser. The Master Browser maintains the main list of all available resources within a domain (including links to external domains).

> *Note: On some TCP/IP networks, another role—the Domain Master Browser (DMB)—is used to enable resource lists to be communicated across subnets within the same domain. By default, the DMB is the PDC. Also, a Master Browser must reside within each subnet.*

 Two other important roles are the Backup Browser and the Potential Browser. The Backup Browser maintains a duplicate list of the resources and acts like a BDC for the Browser Service. The Backup Browser can serve lists of resources to clients. A Potential Browser may be any machine capable of becoming a Backup or Master Browser. As needed, the Browser Service changes the role of a machine from Potential Browser to Backup Browser. Within any domain, the Browser service attempts to maintain a maximum of three Backup Browsers, but any number of Potential Browsers can exist.

Only the following OSs can serve as Potential Browsers:

➤ Windows NT Server 3.5 or higher

➤ Windows NT Advanced Server 3.1

➤ Windows NT Workstation 3.1 or higher

➤ Windows 95

➤ Windows 98

➤ Windows For Workgroups 3.11

Any of these platforms can also be set to be non-browsers so that they do not participate in supporting the browser lists, except to announce themselves upon bootup.

In the next few sections, we continue our discussion of the Browser Service. This includes how Master Browsers are chosen (elected), in addition to how the browse list is maintained and how it can be managed through the Windows NT Registry.

Browser Election

When a Master Browser goes offline, or when another machine that has the capability to claim the role of Master Browser comes online, an election occurs. The results of the election determine which machine becomes the active Master Browser. An election packet is transmitted by the new computer or by a Backup Browser once the Master Browser is no longer detected. This packet travels to each Potential Browser within the domain. The winner of the election is determined by the following hierarchy of criteria (presented in order of priority):

➤ **Operating system** Windows NT Server, Windows NT Workstation, Windows 95, Windows 98, Windows For Workgroups

➤ **Operating system version** Windows NT versions 4, 3.51, and 3.5; Windows 95 and Windows 98; and Windows For Workgroups 3.11

➤ **Current browser role** Master Browser, Backup Browser, Potential Browser

➤ **Alphabetical** Further election is resolved through the alphabetical order of the computer names

List Maintenance

When a computer comes online, it announces itself. Initially, it announces itself once a minute, with the interval decreasing to once every 12 minutes. This repeated announcement is used by the Master Browser to determine if a resource is still available. The Master Browser maintains the list of resources for any machine for three missed announcements to accommodate performance dips and communication bottlenecks. Therefore, after a machine has been up and running for a reasonable time and then goes offline, its resources can remain in the Master Browser's list for up to 36 minutes.

Backup Browsers poll the Master Browser every 15 minutes to request an updated version of the browse list. Therefore, a failed resource can remain in the Backup Browser's list for up to 51 minutes. If a Backup Browser requests an update from the Master Browser and receives no response, it initiates an election.

Browser And The Registry

The status of any Potential Browser can be altered through two Registry parameters. The parameters are located in HKEY_LOCAL_MACHINE\

SYSTEM\CurrentControlSet\Services\Browser\Parameters. The first value, **MaintainServerList,** determines whether a machine can be a Potential Browser. It can have a value of **No, Yes,** or **Auto. No** sets the machine to be a non-browser. **Yes** forces the machine to be a Master Browser or Backup Browser. And, **Auto** allows the Browser service to determine that machine's role as needed. The second value, **IsDomainMaster,** sets the machine to be the Master Browser. It can have a value of **True** or **False.**

Logon Scripts

Windows NT Workstation (and Server, for that matter) allow you to use logon scripts to define and maintain a consistent collection of network connections. Logon scripts also provide a way to migrate users from NetWare to Windows NT, because the logon script processor for Windows NT can execute native NetWare logon scripts without alteration. Logon scripts are most common for users coming from older legacy systems, and aren't that common for experienced Windows NT Workstation users. Logon scripts can take the form of either a DOS-style .BAT file or an executable file under Windows NT 3.5 and later versions.

Windows NT Workstation As Replication Partner

Windows NT Server includes a built-in replication service called the Directory Replication Service, which is found in the Services tab of the Network applet. This service may be used to distribute copies of important files, such as LMHOSTS, user profiles, logon scripts, and so forth, from a master copy in a special share called REPL$ to a number of designated targets on a regularly scheduled basis. Windows NT Workstation cannot originate replication of such data (this role is called the export server), but it can receive replicated files from an export server (not surprisingly, the receiving role is called the import server).

 Windows NT Workstation can act as an import server for the Directory Replication Service, but it cannot act as an export server for that service.

Practice Questions

Question 1

> Which of the following characteristics are true of workgroups?
> [Check all correct answers]
>
> ❑ a. No central control
>
> ❑ b. Share-level security
>
> ❑ c. Requires a PDC
>
> ❑ d. All user accounts must be created on each member
>
> ❑ e. Recommended for more than 10 users/computers

Answers a, b, and d are correct. Workgroups have no central control, use share-level security, and user accounts must be created on each member. Workgroups do not require a PDC and are recommended for 10 or fewer users/computers. Therefore, answers c and e are incorrect.

Question 2

> A Windows NT Workstation can be a member of a domain and a workgroup member at the same time.
>
> ○ a. True
>
> ○ b. False

Answer b is correct. A workstation can be a member of either a workgroup or a domain at any given time, but not both simultaneously.

Question 3

> Which fields are required to log into Windows NT Workstation locally? [Check all correct answers]
>
> ❑ a. User account name
>
> ❑ b. Domain name
>
> ❑ c. IP address
>
> ❑ d. Password
>
> ❑ e. Workstation name

Answers a, d, and e are correct. To successfully log into a Windows NT Workstation locally, you need a user account, the local computer name, and a password for your user account. A domain name is only needed when you're logging into a domain, an action not requested by this question. Therefore, answer b is incorrect. An IP address is never an item required for Windows NT logon. Therefore, answer c is incorrect.

Question 4

Which of the following computer systems can act as a Potential Browser? [Check all correct answers]

❑ a. Windows NT Server 4

❑ b. Windows NT Advanced Server 3.1

❑ c. Windows NT Server 3.1

❑ d. Windows For Workgroups 3.11

❑ e. Windows NT Workstation 3.5

❑ f. OS/2 Warp

Answers a, b, d, and e are correct. Windows NT Server 4, Windows NT Advanced Server 3.1, Windows For Workgroups 3.11, and Windows NT Workstation 3.5 are all valid system types that can be Potential Browsers. Windows NT Server 3.1 and OS/2 Warp are invalid system types for Potential Browsers. Therefore, answers c and f are incorrect. In addition, Windows 95 and Windows 98 can also be Potential Browsers.

Question 5

When the PDC on a domain fails, what can you do with your Windows NT Workstation? (Assume a BDC is available) [Check all correct answers]

❑ a. Log on locally to the Workstation

❑ b. Maintain a current active session on the network

❑ c. Change your password

❑ d. Log on to the network

Answers a, b, and d are correct. Without a PDC, you can still log on locally, maintain current network access, and log on to the network (through BDC authentication). You cannot change your password because a BDC cannot modify the SAM database. Therefore, answer c is incorrect.

Question 6

A Windows NT Workstation can participate as a Master Browser.

O a. True

O b. False

Answer a is correct. A Windows NT Workstation can be a Master Browser; however, it is unlikely because any Windows NT Server within a domain will have a better chance of winning the browser election due to its OS type.

Question 7

If a client hosting a network printer goes offline, how long could the browser list entry for that printer remain before it is removed from a Master Browser's resource list?

O a. 12 minutes

O b. 15 minutes

O c. 36 minutes

O d. 51 minutes

Answer c is correct. Thirty-six minutes is the maximum length of time a missing resource can remain in a Master Browser's list. Twelve minutes is the interval of how often a machine announces itself to the Master Browser; it takes three intervals before the Master Browser removes a missing resource from its list. Therefore, answer a is incorrect. Fifteen minutes is the interval of how often a Backup Browser polls the Master Browser for a list update. Therefore, answer b is incorrect. Fifty-one minutes is the maximum length of time a missing resource can remain in a Backup Browser list, because it polls for an updated list every 15 minutes and a Master Browser can have a bad resource listed for 36 minutes. Therefore, answer d is incorrect.

Question 8

What is the process by which a computer becomes a Master Browser?

○ a. Domain synchronization

○ b. Browser election

○ c. Replication

Answer b is correct. A browser election is the process by which a computer can become a Master Browser. Domain synchronization is the process by which the SAM of a PDC is duplicated to all BDCs in the domain. Therefore, answer a is incorrect. Replication is the process by which logon files are distributed across a network to speed authentication. Therefore, answer c is incorrect.

Question 9

Which of the following characteristics are true of domains? [Check all correct answers]

❑ a. Central control and administration

❑ b. User-level security

❑ c. Requires a PDC

❑ d. All user accounts must be created on each member

❑ e. Recommended for 10 or fewer users/computers

Answers a, b, and c are correct. Domains have central control and administration, user-level security, and require a PDC. Domains do not require accounts to be created on each member and are recommended for more than 10 users/computers. Therefore, answers d and e are incorrect.

Question 10

If no domain controller of any type is present, a Windows NT Workstation can still be logged on to locally.

○ a. True

○ b. False

Answer a is correct. If no PDC nor BDCs are present, a Windows NT Workstation can be logged on to locally if a user account has been created to do so. Workstations can maintain local accounts separate and distinct from domain accounts used to access the network.

Need To Know More?

 Perkins, Charles, Matthew Strebe, and James Chellis: *MCSE: NT Workstation Study Guide, 2nd Edition*. Sybex Network Press, San Francisco, CA, 1998. ISBN 0-7821-2223-X. Chapter 11 discusses workgroups, domains, and browsing.

Tittel, Ed, Christa Anderson, and David Johnson: *NT Workstation 4 Exam Prep*. Coriolis, Scottsdale, AZ, 1998. ISBN 1-57610-238-6. Chapter 10 includes a detailed examination of the Windows Browser Service, and related topics.

 Search the TechNet CD (or its online version through **www.microsoft.com**) and the *Windows NT Workstation Resource Kit* CD using the keywords "workgroup," "domain," and "browser."

Remote
Access
Service (RAS)

13

Terms you'll need to understand:

√ Remote Access Service (RAS)

√ RAS clients

√ Telephony Application Programming Interface (TAPI)

√ RAS Phonebook

√ Encryption

√ AutoDial

√ Logging

√ Null modem

√ Name resolution

Techniques you'll need to master:

√ Installing and configuring RAS

√ Configuring the RAS Phonebook

√ Implementing RAS security measures

Remote Access Service (RAS) is a secure and reliable method of extending a network across communication links to remote computers. Modems and other communication devices act just like a network interface card (NIC) over a RAS connection. A remote RAS client can access and operate everything a standard network-attached client can.

Windows NT RAS

RAS in Windows NT 4 is a significant improvement over the communications capabilities of version 3.51. Many of its advances were borrowed from Windows 95, including the ease of installation, process of configuration, and the look and feel of the service itself. Windows NT Server RAS is able to support 256 simultaneous connections, act as a firewall, gateway, or router; and maintain tight security; Windows NT Workstation RAS is limited to a single connection, whether inbound or outbound.

The communication links through which RAS can connect include the following:

➤ Public Switched Telephone Network (PSTN)

➤ Integrated Service Digital Network (ISDN)

➤ X.25 packet switching network

Standard LAN protocols are used over the RAS connection. Thus, TCP/IP, IPX/SPX, or NetBEUI can be used for network communication over the link established by RAS. Because the actual network protocol is used, the remote RAS client acts just as if it were connected to the network locally. The only difference is that the speed of data transfer is slower over the RAS connection than it would be if the computer accessing the server were physically attached to the network. Always remember that a client is a client is a client, whether locally connected or using RAS.

RAS Clients

A RAS client is any machine that is able to dial in or connect to a RAS server and establish an authorized connection. Although optimized for the integration of Microsoft-based operating systems, other system types can gain access with the proper software, protocols, and configuration.

The links established between a client and a server using RAS are called wide area network (WAN) links. Because RAS is most often used to connect a computer (or an entire LAN) to a centrally located network over a long distance, it is considered to create a WAN link. The communication protocols used to establish a RAS connection are called WAN protocols. Windows NT supports two WAN protocols:

➤ **SLIP** The Serial Line Internet Protocol connection supports TCP/IP, but it does not support IPX/SPX or NetBEUI. Every client that uses SLIP must have a statically assigned IP address. SLIP does not support encrypted passwords, either. This protocol is provided only as a means for a Windows NT Server to act as a client when dialing in to a Unix server; it cannot be used to accept inbound connections on Windows NT.

➤ **PPP** The Point-to-Point Protocol supports several protocols, including AppleTalk, TCP/IP, IPX/SPX, and NetBEUI. It was designed as an improvement to SLIP. PPP supports DHCP, PPTP, and encrypted passwords. PPP is the most common and widely supported WAN protocol.

Windows NT Workstation can act as a RAS client whenever it dials out over a modem (or other communication link device) to establish a connection with a Windows NT Server or some other type of computer system. The most common situation in which Windows NT is a RAS client is when it connects to the Internet.

RAS Servers

Windows NT Workstation can support only one incoming RAS connection. (Windows NT Server can support up to 256.)

Important points to remember about Windows NT as a RAS server include the following:

➤ Windows NT only supports PPP clients—SLIP is not supported for dial-up.

➤ A NetBIOS gateway is established between the RAS server and PPP-attached RAS client to sustain standard Windows NT network operations.

➤ RAS supports both IP and IPX routing.

➤ RAS supports NetBIOS and Windows Sockets applications.

➤ Windows NT supports Point-to-Point Tunneling Protocol (PPTP) connections, which makes it possible for Windows NT computers to communicate securely over the Internet. In addition, it also supports Multilink PPP (MP), where numerous connections can be aggregated to create a larger amount of bandwidth.

Point-To-Point Tunneling Protocol (PPTP)

PPTP enables "tunneling" of IPX, NetBEUI, or TCP/IP inside PPP packets to establish a secure link between a client and server over the Internet. PPTP connections are useful for establishing virtual private networks (VPNs) in small companies that cannot afford expensive leased lines for network communications over long distances. PPTP enables users anywhere in the world to connect to the home office's network. PPTP uses a powerful encryption security scheme that is more secure than standard communications over the network itself. Thus, all traffic over the Internet using PPTP is safe.

Like all other network protocols, PPTP must be installed through the Protocols tab in the Network applet.

Multilink PPP (MP)

Windows NT has the capability to combine the bandwidth of multiple physical links, which increases the total bandwidth that could be used for a RAS connection. This aggregation of multiple communication links can be used as an inexpensive way to increase the overall bandwidth with the least amount of cost. MP must be supported by both the client and server systems. MP cannot be used with the callback security feature (discussed in detail later in this chapter in the section entitled "RAS Callback").

Multilink PPP can be used for dial-out connection only from Windows NT Workstation. Only Windows NT Server can support inbound Multilink PPP connections.

For the test, you can assume MP can aggregate different types of links, such as a regular telephone link and ISDN, into a single pipeline. However, in reality, MP only works when all of the links are of the same type.

Telephony API (TAPI) Properties And Phonebooks

In Windows NT, the Telephony Application Programming Interface (TAPI) provides a standard method of controlling communications over voice, data, and fax. Although the hardware is not provided with Windows NT, TAPI can be used to control many PBX systems and communication devices for automated activity.

When you install a modem or the RAS components of Windows NT, TAPI is installed automatically. TAPI is required to control any communications device. Each time a dial-out connection is attempted, TAPI controls the modem and moderates the connection. Once the connection is established, TAPI continues to oversee the operation of the communication link.

The Dialing Properties dialog box (reached through the Modems applet in Control Panel) controls how TAPI uses your modem to place calls. You can control long-distance dialing, calling card use, prefix numbers, and tone/pulse dialing. You can also define multiple configurations based on physical location. If you travel with a Windows NT Workstation notebook, you can define a dialing property profile for each of the cities you visit regularly.

TAPI is also the controlling entity for the Phonebook entries used to establish RAS connections. All of the functions and features of the modem and the communication types established over a modem are configured through a TAPI-controlled interface.

Installing RAS

RAS is installed through the Services tab of the Network applet. Installing RAS correctly does take some preparation and know-how. When performing the installation, you must remember the following:

1. Physically install or attach the modem or adapter first. During installation, if a modem has not been installed, you will be forced to install one.

2. Install RAS through the Services tab of the Network applet.

3. Select the communications port.

4. Add an installed modem as a RAS device.

5. Configure the port for one of the following:

   ➤ Dial Out Only

   ➤ Receive Calls Only

   ➤ Dial Out And Receive Calls

6. Select the LAN network protocols (see Figure 13.1).

   ➤ If Dial Out Only was selected, only the outbound protocols can be chosen.

   ➤ If Receive Calls Only was selected, only the inbound protocols can be configured.

Figure 13.1 The Network Configuration dialog box for RAS.

> ➤ If Dial Out And Receive Calls was selected, both outbound and inbound protocols can be configured.

7. Select protocol-specific configuration for each inbound protocol (see Figures 13.2 and 13.3).

After RAS is installed, you need to check your port and modem configuration through the Ports and Modems applets of the Control Panel. If RAS is configured to receive calls, the port and modem cannot be used by any

Figure 13.2 The RAS Server TCP/IP Configuration dialog box.

Figure 13.3   The RAS Server IPX Configuration dialog box.

other application. RAS locks the port to maintain control to remain ready to receive.

RAS Routing, Gateway, Firewall

You can select whether to let RAS clients using network protocols access just the RAS server or the entire network. When you limit RAS clients to the RAS server, you are using RAS as a firewall; no access of any kind off the RAS server is permitted. If you allow RAS clients to access the entire network, you are using RAS as a router. If NetBEUI is the only protocol in use, RAS acts as a gateway to enable (a nonroutable protocol) NetBEUI to access the network.

RAS Phonebook

RAS dial-out capabilities are controlled and accessed through the RAS Phonebook. This utility, Dial-Up Networking (DUN), is found in the Programs|Accessories folder of the Start menu. The first time DUN is launched, the RAS Wizard appears to help you create your first Phonebook entry. Every time after that, the Phonebook dialog box appears. Through this interface, you can create and modify dial-up parameters for every RAS connection.

Phonebook entries consist of the following:

➤ Name, phone number, and modem to use

➤ Server type and protocol settings

➤ Connection scripts

➤ Security settings

➤ X.25 settings (if applicable)

RAS Security

RAS has numerous levels and types of security that protect your network from unauthorized remote access. The following sections highlight these security features.

RAS Encryption

Windows NT can be configured to increase or decrease connection security through the following:

➤ The Security tab of a Phonebook entry for outbound RAS links

➤ The Network Configuration dialog box for inbound RAS links (as shown in Figure 13.1)

Here are the three settings available for RAS data encryption:

➤ **Allow Any Authentication Including Clear Text** This is the most permissive setting. It should be used when the user is not concerned about passwords. This option allows a connection using any authentication provided by the server; therefore, it is useful when connecting to a non-Microsoft server.

➤ **Require Encrypted Authentication** This option is beneficial when the transmission of clear text password is not desired and when you are connecting to a non-Microsoft server.

➤ **Require Microsoft Encrypted Authentication** For this setting, the Microsoft Challenge Handshake Authentication Protocol (MS-CHAP) must be used; therefore, it is useful when calling a Microsoft server. If the Require Encrypted Authentication box is checked, all clients are required to use encryption during authentication (i.e., clear text authentication is not allowed). Data encryption is provided by Windows NT using the Rivest-Shamir-Adleman (RSA) Data Security Incorporated RC4 algorithm. If the data sent fails to encrypt, the connection is terminated automatically.

RAS Callback

Callback is a security feature in which a RAS connection is established only after the server has disconnected the inbound call and then has called the user back. Setting callback is performed via the User|Properties option in User Manager or the User|Permissions command of the Remote Access Manager, by selecting from the following:

➤ **No Call Back** This is the default setting. It means that when a user is establishing a RAS connection, he or she will not be called back.

➤ **Set By Caller** Callback can be set by the user. This is a good way to save on long-distance charges, because the server calls the client back at the number set by the caller.

➤ **Preset To** You can configure the callback for a preset number. This heightens security because the user must call from a predetermined phone number.

The RAS Logon Process

With Windows NT, you can log on to a domain via RAS at the Logon prompt by selecting the Connect Via Dial-In option and providing the proper domain. This allows you to establish a RAS connection to the remote network without requiring you to log on locally first.

 When you are using TCP/IP via a slow RAS connection, an LMHOSTS file might speed up network access and name resolution. Place an LMHOSTS file on the RAS client. Ensure that LMHOSTS entries include the **#PRE** tag so that the IP addresses will be cached.

Additional RAS Features

There is much more to RAS than is covered in this chapter. You'll need to review the reference materials listed at the end of this chapter for more RAS information. However, we have included a short list of important RAS features or options.

AutoDial

AutoDial provides Windows NT's ability to remember the location of resources accessed over a RAS connection. AutoDial maintains a map that correlates a network address to a Phonebook entry. When that resource is referenced, RAS reestablishes the WAN connection to regain access to that resource without additional user interaction. AutoDial is enabled by default. AutoDial does not yet function over IPX/SPX, but it works with TCP/IP and NetBEUI.

DUN Monitor

Once you've established a RAS connection so that your Windows NT Workstation is a client on another network, you can obtain realtime status information about the connection using the DUN Monitor. It appears, by default, in the taskbar, but it can be set to appear as an icon in the system tray (the area next to the time on the taskbar). Device statistics, connection statistics, and errors are some of the data sets presented by the utility. This is often the first place you should start when troubleshooting a RAS connection because data about connection speed, duration of link, users connected, protocols in use, and the RAS device are clearly listed.

Logging

Troubleshooting RAS difficulties is much simpler when it's logging capabilities are employed. Two logging features record RAS-related activities. The first is the MODEMLOG.TXT file, which records the activities of the modem. This is enabled through a modem's properties in the Modems applet in the Advanced Connections Settings area. This file is placed in the Windows NT root directory.

The second log file is DEVICE.LOG. This file can be enabled only through the Registry. The "Logging" value located in \HKEY_LOCAL_ MACHINE\SYSTEM\CurrentControlSet\Services\RasMan\Parameters should be set to 1. The DEVICE.LOG file is stored in the %systemroot%\ system32\ras directory by default.

A PPP log (ppp.log) can be recorded to aid in diagnosing connectivity problems. To enable this log, edit the logging value in the HKEY_ LOCAL_MACHINE\SYSTEM\CurrentControlSet\Services\RasMan\ PPP Registry key. Set the logging value to 1 to enable logging, and to 0 to turn off logging. The ppp.log file is stored in \System32\Ras\.

The Event Viewer captures RAS information that may be useful for troubleshooting and deciphering RAS. By default, all server errors, user connect attempts, disconnects, and so on, are logged in the System Log.

Null Modem

A null modem is a serial cable that enables two computers to connect without the need for a modem. These special cables are common peer-to-peer attachment devices, but they can be used by Windows NT RAS to establish a standard Windows NT network connection. A null modem can be installed through the Modems applet by selecting it from the standard modems. A cable is not actually required for the setup, and this offers you a way out when installing RAS if you don't already have a modem on hand. Once installed, a null-modem cable can be used just like a modem, which is itself used by RAS just as if it were a NIC—that is, a workstation attached via a null-modem cable can fully participate in a domain, but at a slower data transfer rate.

Name Resolution

In situations where static lookups occur, the configuration with optimal resolution speed and WAN link traffic is to store the HOSTS (DNS) and the LMHOSTS (WINS) files on the local hard drives of the RAS clients. This configuration makes it somewhat difficult to maintain the newest version of the files on multiple remote clients but offers the best performance.

Practice Questions

Question 1

> Your Windows NT Workstation is unable to maintain a connection
> to your office RAS server. Where should you start looking to in-
> vestigate this problem?
>
> ○ a. The System Log through the Event Viewer
>
> ○ b. The DUN Monitor
>
> ○ c. The DEVICE.LOG file
>
> ○ d. The Remote Access Admin application located in
>   Start|Programs|Administrative Tools

Answer b is correct. The best place to start investigating RAS connection
problems is the DUN Monitor, because details about connection speed,
protocols, and link duration might instantly pinpoint the problem. The
System Log will contain little if any information about RAS connections.
Therefore, answer a is incorrect. The DEVICE.LOG file is the second
step in RAS troubleshooting, because it focuses on the activity of the RAS
device, which might not be the problem. Therefore, answer c is incorrect.
The Remote Access Admin application is not a tool to use for troubleshooting—it's for monitoring traffic, granting permissions, and controlling
the RAS server. Therefore, answer d is incorrect.

Question 2

> Which of the following statements about PPP and SLIP are true?
> [Check all correct answers]
>
> ❑ a. PPP supports encrypted passwords; SLIP does not.
>
> ❑ b. SLIP supports NetBEUI, IPX/SPX, and TCP/IP; PPP only
>   supports TCP/IP.
>
> ❑ c. PPP supports DHCP; SLIP does not.
>
> ❑ d. SLIP is used to access Unix servers.
>
> ❑ e. PPP is the most commonly used WAN protocol.

Answers a, c, d, and e are correct. PPP supports encrypted passwords; SLIP does not. Therefore, answer a is correct. PPP supports DHCP; SLIP does not. Therefore, answer c is correct. SLIP is used to access Unix servers. Therefore, answer d is correct. PPP is the most commonly used WAN protocol. Therefore, answer e is also correct. PPP supports NetBEUI, IPX/SPX, and TCP/IP, but SLIP only supports TCP/IP. Therefore, answer b is incorrect.

Question 3

Which of the following Windows NT networking activities are supported by a PPP RAS connection? [Check all correct answers]

❑ a. Printer share access

❑ b. Named pipes

❑ c. WinSOCK API applications over TCP/IP

❑ d. InterProcess Communications (IPC)

❑ e. User logon authentication

All answers are correct. Because a RAS-connected client is no different than a direct-connected client (other than in its speed of data transfer), all standard network activities still occur over the WAN link.

Question 4

While connected to the office LAN, you create a shortcut on your desktop that points to a documents folder located on the LAN's file server. After working with a few files from this folder, you close your RAS session. Later, you attempt to reopen the files you edited earlier. What happens?

○ a. Access is denied because no link to the LAN exists.

○ b The file is pulled from the network cache.

○ c A file with a similar name on your local hard drive is accessed instead.

○ d. RAS AutoDial attempts to reconnect to the office LAN.

Answer d is correct. RAS maintains a map list of the resources accessed over WAN links. When one of these resources is referenced, it attempts to use AutoDial to regain a connection to the server hosting the resource.

Answer a would be the result if AutoDial was not enabled, but you always should assume the default configuration for computers unless indicated otherwise. Therefore, answer a is incorrect. Answers b and c are fictitious activities that do not occur.

Question 5

Where can you find information related to RAS problems to aid in troubleshooting? [Check all correct answers]

❑ a. Event Viewer

❑ b. DEVICE.LOG

❑ c. Dr. Watson

❑ d. MODEMLOG.TXT

❑ e. Windows NT Diagnostics

Answers a, b, and d are correct. Event Viewer, DEVICE.LOG, and MODEMLOG.TXT can be useful troubleshooting tools for RAS problems. Dr. Watson does not track RAS events; it focuses on applications. Therefore, answer c is incorrect. Windows NT Diagnostics will not provide useful information related to RAS. Therefore, answer e is incorrect.

Question 6

Your Windows NT Workstation has two ISDN modems, each with two B channels. You need to establish a RAS connection with a Windows NT Server that can permit you to multiplex both modems to create a single logical connection. Assuming that MP is supported on this RAS server, how should you configure your Phonebook entry to maximize throughput on the connection?

○ a. Create four Phonebook entries—one for each of the four B channels of both ISDN modems.

○ b. Create two Phonebook entries—one for each of the two ISDN modems.

○ c. Create a single Phonebook entry that uses all four B channels of both ISDN modems.

○ d. Create a single Phonebook entry for the ISDN modem attached to the lowest COM port address.

Answer c is correct. Creating a single Phonebook entry that uses all of the RAS devices in a Multilink PPP aggregation is how DUN should be configured for maximum throughput. Creating multiple Phonebook entries does not permit separate lines to be aggregated because only a single phonebook entry can be active at any time in RAS. Thus, answers a and b are incorrect. By using only the ISDN modem, you cannot get the maximum bandwidth that would be possible if the second ISDN modem were included in the link. Therefore, answer d is incorrect as well.

Question 7

You have a field technician who travels extensively around the country. Her schedule changes often, and she rarely visits the same place twice. It is important that she is able to connect to the office LAN periodically, but your organization's security policy requires callback security on all RAS connections. How can you configure her account so that she is able to gain access, while also supporting your organization's security?

○ a. Set the callback security to No Call Back only for her account.

○ b. Enable callback security with Set By Caller selected.

○ c. Set the callback security to Preset To with her home phone number.

○ d. Set the callback security to Roaming and give her the page number to configure the callback number remotely.

○ e. Turn on the callback Caller ID capture.

Answer b is correct. Setting the Set By Caller option will allow her to input the callback number each time she needs to connect. Setting the No Call Back option violates the organization's security policy. Therefore, answer a is incorrect. Setting the Preset To number will not allow her to gain access to the network because she is never in the same place. Therefore, answer c is incorrect. There is not a Roaming callback setting. Therefore, answer d is incorrect. Windows NT does not have a Caller ID capture setting, but this can be obtained through third-party software; however, it is not required for this situation. Therefore, answer e is incorrect.

Question 8

> Which protocols can be used over a RAS connection?
>
> ○ a. TCP/IP, NetBEUI, but not NWLink
>
> ○ b. TCP/IP, NWLink, but not NetBEUI
>
> ○ c. Only TCP/IP
>
> ○ d. TCP/IP, NetBEUI, and NWLink

Answer d is correct. TCP/IP, NetBEUI, and NWLink can all be used over RAS. TCP/IP, NetBEUI, but not NWLink is the restriction for the AutoDial feature, but this is not a limitation of RAS as a whole. Therefore, answer a is incorrect. TCP/IP, NWLink, but not NetBEUI are the protocols that can be routed over RAS, but this is not a limitation as to which protocols can be used. Therefore, answer b is also incorrect. Only TCP/IP can be used over SLIP, but RAS is not limited to SLIP. Therefore, answer c is incorrect.

Question 9

> What are the possible uses of a null-modem cable? [Check all correct answers]
>
> ❑ a. Attach a workstation to a domain
>
> ❑ b. Enable subnet routing
>
> ❑ c. Test a RAS server locally
>
> ❑ d. Establish a VPN over the Internet
>
> ❑ e. Temporarily connect two LANs

Answers a, c, and e are correct. Attaching a workstation to a domain is a use for a null-modem cable. Therefore, answer a is correct. A RAS server can be tested using a null-modem cable to simulate a remote client. Therefore, answer c is correct. Two closely adjacent LANs can be connected over a null-modem cable. Therefore, answer e is correct. Subnet routing can be implemented only when two NICs are installed on the same machine. Therefore, answer b is incorrect. A VPN over the Internet can be established only with PPTP and a connection to the Internet, requiring a modem. Therefore, answer d is incorrect.

Question 10

> If static name resolution is used, what is the proper location of the HOSTS and LMHOSTS files to optimize the lookup time?
>
> ○ a. Both HOSTS and LMHOSTS should be stored on the RAS clients.
>
> ○ b. HOSTS should be stored on the RAS server, and LMHOSTS should be stored on the RAS clients.
>
> ○ c. Both HOSTS and LMHOSTS should be stored on the RAS server.
>
> ○ d. HOSTS should be stored on the RAS clients, and LMHOSTS should be stored on the RAS server.

Answer a is correct. The fastest lookup time will occur when the HOSTS and LMHOSTS files are stored on the local hard drive of each RAS client, because no WAN traffic must occur to resolve a resource location. All others answers are incorrect because they discuss storing these files somewhere other than on the client, which increases the lookup time.

Need To Know More?

 Perkins, Charles, Matthew Strebe, and James Chellis: *MCSE: NT Workstation Study Guide, 2nd Edition*. Sybex Network Press, San Francisco, CA, 1998. ISBN 0-7821-2223-X. Chapter 12 focuses on the Remote Access Service. It includes numerous exercises to walk you through the installation process.

 Tittel, Ed, Christa Anderson, and David Johnson: *NT Workstation 4 Exam Prep*. Coriolis, Scottsdale, AZ, 1998. ISBN 1-57610-238-6. Chapter 11 covers Remote Access Services in great detail.

 Search the TechNet CD (or its online version through **www.microsoft.com**) using the keywords "RAS," "Remote Access," "PPP," and "modems."

The *Windows NT Workstation Resource Kit* contains some discussion of RAS in scattered articles. Performing a search on the TechNet (either CD or online version) or the CD accompanying the *Resource Kit* using "RAS" or "Remote Access" will locate these quickly.

Windows NT Printing

. . . .

Terms you'll need to understand:

√ Connecting to a printer

√ Creating a printer

√ Network interface printer

√ Print client

√ Print device

√ Print job

√ Print resolution

√ Print server

√ Print spooler

√ Print driver

√ Printer/logical printer

√ Queue/print queue

√ Rendering

Techniques you'll need to master:

√ Installing and configuring a printer

√ Managing printing clients

√ Managing the print spooler

√ Setting up print priorities

√ Establishing logical printers and printing pools

253

It's the job of the network administrator to make sure that users have access to needed resources—and the printer is one of the most often-used resources. One of the biggest complaints about other network operating systems has been their inability to handle printers effectively and efficiently. Microsoft has developed an intuitive and simple way to manage this much-used resource. This chapter focuses on the Microsoft approach to printing and defines a few Microsoft-specific printing terms.

The Windows NT Print Lexicon

The following list contains Microsoft-specific printing terminology that must be mastered. It is very important for successful exam taking that you know and fully understand all of these terms and concepts. Printing problems can be tricky, especially when they deal with this specialized terminology.

➤ **Client application** A network program that originates print jobs (this can be located on a print server or client computer on the network).

➤ **Connecting to a printer** The process of attaching to a network share that resides on the computer on which the logical printer was created (performed through the Add Printer Wizard, accessed from the Start menu's Printers option).

➤ **Creating a printer** The process of naming a printer, as well as defining settings for, installing drivers for, and linking a printing device to the network. In Windows NT, this process is performed through the Add Printer Wizard.

➤ **Network interface printer** Built-in network interface cards for print devices that are directly attached to the network—for example, the Hewlett-Packard JetDirect.

➤ **Print client** A computer on a network (called a "client computer") that transmits the print jobs to be produced by the physical printing device.

➤ **Print device** Commonly referred to as the "printer." In other words, it is the physical hardware device that produces printed material. This is very confusing to most people. Just remember that the print device is the piece of hardware that actually spits out paper with your material printed on it. But you should also realize that a printer can also be a fax modem, a slide maker, or even a CAD plotter.

➤ **Print job** The code that defines the print processing commands as well as the actual file to be printed. Windows NT defines print jobs by data type, depending on what adjustments must be made to the file for it to print accurately (that is, one data type can be printable as-is, whereas another might need a form feed to conclude the data stream for the print job to execute properly).

➤ **Print resolution** The measurement of pixel density that is responsible for the smoothness of any image or text being printed. This is measured in dots per inch (DPI)—the higher the DPI, the better the quality of the printed material.

➤ **Print server** The server computer that links physical print devices to the network and manages sharing those devices with computers on the network.

➤ **Print Server services** Software components located on the print server that accept print jobs and send them to the print spooler for execution. These components, such as Services For Macintosh, enable a variety of client computers to communicate with the print server to process print jobs.

➤ **Print spooler** The collection of dynamic link libraries (DLLs) that acquires, processes, catalogues, and disburses print jobs. A print job will be saved to disk in a spool file. Print despooling is the process of reading what is contained in the spool file and transmitting it to the physical printing device.

➤ **Printer driver** Programs that enable communications between applications and a specific print device. Most hardware peripherals, such as printers, require the use of a driver to process commands.

➤ **Printer/logical printer** The logical printer (Microsoft calls this "the printer") is the software interface that communicates between the operating system and the physical printing device. The logical printer handles the printing process from the time the print command is issued. Its settings determine the physical printing device that renders the file to be printed as well as how the file to be printed is sent to the printing device (for example, via a remote print share or local port).

➤ **Queue/print queue** In printing terms, a queue is a series of files waiting to be produced by the printing device.

➤ **Rendering** The process by which Windows NT prints is as follows: A client application sends file information to the Graphics Device Interface (GDI), which receives the data, communicates that data to the physical printing device driver, and produces the print job in the language of the physical printing device. The printing device then interprets this information and creates a file (bitmap) for each page to be printed.

Printing With Windows NT Workstation

Windows NT print settings are managed through the Printers folder, which is accessible from the Control Panel or the Start menu (under Settings).

Note: The Printers folder replaces the old Windows NT 3.51 Print Manager.

This approach is extremely straightforward compared to earlier versions of Windows NT and other network operating systems.

Windows NT takes a modular approach to printing, as shown in Figure 14.1. Each component has a specific use and interfaces with the other components in the print architecture.

Figure 14.1 The Windows NT print architecture components work together to render print jobs for the user.

The following defines each component of the printing architecture:

> **Graphics Device Interface (GDI)** The component that provides network applications with a system for presenting graphical information. The GDI works as a translator between the application's print requests and the device driver interface (DDI) to make sure a job is rendered accurately.

> **Print device** The hardware device that produces printed output.

> **Print driver** The software component that enables communication between the operating system and the physical printing device.

> **Print monitor** The component that passes the print job (which has been translated to the print device's language) to the printing device.

> **Print processor** The component that makes any necessary modifications to the print job before passing the job to the print monitor. Windows NT actually has two print processors—one for the Windows platform and one for the Macintosh.

> **Print router** The component that directs the print job to the appropriate printing device.

> **Print spooler** The component that accepts print jobs from the router, calls the processor to make any needed changes to the print job, and transfers the jobs one at a time to the print monitor. It is also called the "print provider."

Printing From Windows NT Clients

This is where Windows NT's approach to printing really shines. Client computers need access to print devices, so they must add the printer via the Add Printer Wizard. Previously, all client computers required that the print driver be installed on each client machine that needed access to a printing device. No more! All that is needed for printing from a Windows NT client is that the driver be installed on the print server. That's it! This simplifies the printing process, because if an updated print driver is released, it just needs to be installed on the server, not on every client machine.

> *Note: The same is true for Windows 95 and Windows 98 clients— they can also download the print driver from a Windows NT print server. Thus, they needn't install print drivers, locally.*

Printer Installation

Configuring or installing printers under Windows NT is extremely simple, even if the drivers for the printer are not on the shipping distribution CD-ROM. There are two types of printer setup—local and network.

A local printer is simply the situation where a print device is physically attached to your workstation. In such a case, your machine will act as the print server. Once you've physically connected the printer, use the Add Printer Wizard from the Printers folder to install the proper drivers. Select the My Computer option at the first prompt. You'll be asked for the port, the printer make and model (if not listed you can click the Have Disk option to load drivers from a floppy), and a name for the printer. If you want to offer access to the printer across the network to other clients, you should select the Shared option and define a share name. By default, the Everyone group will have Print access, Administrators and Power Users will have Full Control, and you'll be the Owner with Manage Document permissions. You should now see a printer icon in the Printers folder (hit Refresh if it does not appear) with a hand under the printer if it has been shared.

A network printer is simply a software redirector that guides print jobs from your workstation to the actual location of the print server and ultimately the printer itself. Attaching to a network printer is simple. Once again, use the Add Printer Wizard from the Printers folder, but select Network Printer Servers at the first prompt. A list of all printer shares on the network will be displayed. Make a selection and opt to print a test page. If the test document prints, you've connected successfully. Please notice that you do not install a printer driver when connecting to a network printer if you are working from a Windows NT client. Instead, the driver is downloaded from the print server each time a print job needs to be created.

Printer Configuration

Once a printer has been installed, you can alter its configuration and setup to better suit your needs. Through the Properties dialog box of the printer, you have numerous features and options. These include General, Ports, Scheduling, Sharing, Security, and Device Settings. You'll need to be familiar with each of these tabs.

General

On the General tab, you can do the following:

➤ Comment about the printer

➤ Describe the printer's location

➤ Change, update, or reinstall the driver for the printer

➤ Define a separator page that prints between print jobs

➤ Set the print processor, such as allowing Unix or Macintosh print jobs, and data type, such as **EMF, RAW, RAW (FF Appended), RAW (FF Auto), TEXT**, and **PSCRIPT**, for the printer

➤ Print a test page

Ports

On the Ports tab, you can do the following:

➤ Set the attached port, including add, delete, and configure ports

➤ Enable bidirectional support so that print jobs and the printer status can be communicated simultaneously

➤ Enable printer pooling

Scheduling

On the Scheduling tab, you do the following:

➤ Set time restrictions where all print jobs sent outside of the valid time period are spooled and printed during the next interval

➤ Prioritize print jobs

➤ Spool documents directly to the printer

➤ Print spooling documents immediately or after the entire job has been spooled

➤ Hold mismatched documents

➤ Print spooled documents first

➤ Keep documents after they have printed

Sharing

On the Sharing tab, you can do the following:

➤ Share or not share

➤ Share name

➤ Select additional Windows 95, Windows 98, or versions of Windows NT drivers to install

Security

On the Security tab, you can do the following:

➤ Set permissions for users and/or groups to Full Control, Manage, Print, or No Access (the settings operate the same way as file and directory permissions)

➤ Set print-related auditing for users and/or groups (the settings operate the same way as file and directory auditing)

➤ Take ownership

Device Settings

On the Device Settings tab, you can set most of the printer-specific settings. These are the settings that you would otherwise interact with through the device's on-board LCD screen and buttons or the manufacturer-supplied configuration software utility. However, the interface is easier to use and displays all possible options, plus it offers some additional help and information.

Print Job Management

Managing print jobs is a fairly simple task with Windows NT. As a print operator, printer owner, or print job owner, you can manipulate a job that is listed in the queue. To do this, open the printer queue window through the main Printers folder. The printer queue window is shown in Figure 14.2. By opening the Properties dialog box for a print job, you can manipulate how it is printed by the printer, its priority, and who to notify when it is completed. Changing a print job's priority alters how quickly it will be sent to the printer. Working with the queue as a whole, you have the privilege of using the following commands from the Document menu to control the queue:

➤ **Pause** Halts a print job.

```
HP LaserJet 5L (Copy 2) - Paused                                    _ □ ×
Printer  Document  View  Help
┌─────────────────┬────────┬───────────┬───────┬──────┬──────────────┬──────┐
│ Document Name    │ Status │ Owner     │ Pages │ Size │ Submitted    │ Port │
├─────────────────┼────────┼───────────┼───────┼──────┼──────────────┼──────┤
│ Microsoft Word - ecw-ch14.doc    │   Administrator │ 11 │ 229KB │ 2:57:43 PM  7/16/97 │
│                                                                             │
│                                                                             │
│                                                                             │
└─────────────────────────────────────────────────────────────────────────────┘
1 document(s) in queue
```

Figure 14.2   The print queue window of a logical printer.

➤ **Resume** Continues printing where paused.

➤ **Restart** Starts current print job over. Any document can be restarted if it has not been deleted from the spooler.

However, you only have the ability to manage your own documents unless you are a printer owner or a member of either the Print Operators or Administrators groups. You can also manage other documents if you have the Manage Documents or Full Control access permission on the printer.

Printer Shares

One of the most useful capabilities of a network is that of sharing a single printer with multiple users. The process of enabling other network users to access a printer is just as simple as giving users network access to a directory or a drive—you create a printer share. This is done through the Sharing command located in the File menu of the main Printers folder or the Printer menu of the individual Printers folder (under Settings). All you need to do is assign a share name and everyone on the network can print to that printer (provided they have the printer drivers available).

To tighten security on a printer, you must access the Permissions button located on the Security tab of a printer's Properties dialog box. The Printer Permissions dialog box acts the same as the File Permissions version. The only real change is the types of access possible with printers:

➤ **No Access** Grants no access other than viewing the NetBIOS name

➤ **Print** Enables users to print and manage their own documents, but they can only see others' documents

➤ **Manage Documents** Allows users to manage print jobs in the queue; does not grant the ability to print

➤ **Full Control** Allows users to print, manage print jobs, change permissions, and install drivers

The default settings for a newly created printer share are:

➤ **Full Control** Administrators and Power Users

➤ **Manage Documents** Creator owner

➤ **Print** Everyone

To restrict access to a printer, you must remove the Everyone group and then add groups and users as needed.

Multiple Printers: Physical And Logical

Many problems that arise with printers involve multiple groups requiring printer access, with one of the groups printing large, nonurgent documents. More often than not, these situations are resolved by defining multiple logical printers for a single physical printer and altering the priority or access times.

Keep in mind that:

➤ Multiple logical printers can serve a single physical printer.

➤ A single logical printer can serve multiple physical printers (pooling).

➤ Multiple logical printers can serve multiple physical printers.

Print Auditing

A printer is just another Windows NT object. Therefore, you can use Windows NT's audit system to monitor access, use, and errors. (For more details about Windows NT's audit system, refer to Chapter 4.) You need to enable File And Object Access-level auditing (Success and/or Failure) to track Printer events. To set the events to Audit By User/Group, go to the Audit button on the Security tab of the Properties dialog box of a printer. This dialog box operates the same way as the File version.

The events you can audit are:

➤ Print

➤ Full Control

➤ Delete

➤ Change Permissions

➤ Take Ownership

Events captured through print auditing are listed in the System or Security log, depending on the nature of the event.

Ownership

The creator of a logical printer is the owner of that printer. Only an administrator or a user with Full Control access can take ownership of a printer (just like every other object within Windows NT). In addition to the ability to change permissions on an owned printer, the owner can also modify form-to-tray assignments, install font cartridges, and adjust the halftone settings.

Spooling

When a user sends out a print job, it goes to the print spooler, which is responsible for tracking the print job through the printing process, routing jobs to the correct ports, and assigning priorities to print jobs.

Print Priorities

By default, the spooler prints jobs in the order in which they are received. It is possible, however, to ensure that print jobs from certain users are printed before any other job. To adjust priority levels for individual users or groups, you must create a different logical printer to a particular printing device (this is discussed in detail in the "Logical Printers And Printing Pools" section, later in the chapter). To assign higher priority to print jobs from certain users, the following steps must be performed on a logical printer:

1. Go to the Printers folder (Start|Settings|Printers).

2. Select the logical printer whose priorities you wish to adjust.

3. From the Printer menu entry in that printer's display window, select the Properties entry.

4. On the Properties window for the printer, select the Scheduling tab.

5. Adjust the slide bar to assign a higher priority (this can be set anywhere from 1 to 99, with 1 being the lowest—as well as the default setting).

Separate Spool Files

If the printers on your network are hit with many print jobs at one time, the print spool can get fairly large. It is important to make sure that the spooler file is big enough to handle all the jobs that are sent to it, the size of this file varies with the capabilities of the printer and its print server. It might become necessary, therefore, to create individual spool files for each printer on the network. This is performed through the Registry by creating files under the following Registry key:

```
HKEY_LOCAL_MACHINE\SYSTEM\CurrentControlSet\Control\Print\Printers\
[Printer Name]
```

It is possible for print jobs to get stuck in the spooler. To remedy this, stop and restart the spooler service by performing the following steps:

1. Go to the Control Panel (Start|Settings|Control Panel).

2. Double-click the Services icon.

3. Highlight the entry labeled Spooler in the list of services.

4. Click the Stop button and confirm that you want to stop the service.

5. Click the Start button.

6. Click Close on the Services dialog box.

Changing The Spool Location

The default directory for the print spooler is %systemroot%\System32\Spool. Here are the steps for changing the location of the spooler directory:

1. Go to the Printers folder (Start|Settings|Printers).

2. Select Server Properties from the File menu.

3. Select the Advanced tab.

4. Enter the path to the new spool directory in the Spool Folder text box.

You may want to change this setting because the drive for the default path has limited space for storing print jobs. (Note that you must restart the print server before these changes take effect.)

Logical Printers And Printing Pools

A logical printer is the software interface that enables communication between Windows NT and the physical printing device. You can create multiple logical printers that send print jobs to a single print device (and, conversely, a single logical printer that sends jobs to multiple print devices).

It is necessary to create different logical printers (with different share names) to assign priorities to various groups and users printing to a single print device. All of this is defined through the Add Printer Wizard in the Printers folder. You simply provide different settings (such as access rights, access times, and priorities) for different shares that attach to the same physical print device.

When a printer services multiple printing devices, it creates what is called a "printer pool." Put simply, a single logical printer spools out jobs to the next available printing device in the printer pool. It is necessary for all of the print devices in a printer pool to be of the same type. With this setup, the printer assigns files to be printed to whichever print device is free in the printer pool.

DLC

The DLC protocol is typically used to interoperate with IBM mainframes, but it is also used to provide connectivity to network-attached print devices. Most commonly, the DLC protocol is used for Hewlett-Packard network-attached printers and/or JetDirect interfaces (for example, a printer NIC).

The DLC protocol is installed using the Protocols tab of the Network Control Panel applet. There are no configuration options; however, the binding order of DLC is important. The order in which adapters are bound (that is, prioritized) to DLC is the reference number used by DLC applications—the first adapter is value 0, the second is value 1, and so on. Windows NT DLC can support up to 16 physical adapters numbered 0 through 15.

To use DLC for printing, you must install both the DLC protocol and the Hewlett-Packard Network Port monitor on the server that is designated as the print server. You can designate any server to be the print server because the print device is attached to the network directly and not through a parallel cable to a computer. The DLC protocol must be installed first, and then the HP Network Port monitor (HPMON.DLL) should be installed through the Add Printer Wizard Add Port command. Once installation is complete, the logical printer on the print server can be shared across the network and used as any other printer.

The Hewlett-Packard Network Port monitor can be configured so that the managed ports are either "job-based" or "continuous connection," which is set at port creation. A job-based setting disconnects from a printer when the print job is complete. Thus, other print servers can connect and print.

A continuous connection setting does not release the printer; therefore, other servers cannot connect.

TCP/IP And Unix Printers

If your network has Unix workstations, you can use the Microsoft TCP/IP Printing service. TCP/IP only needs to be installed on the printer server hosting the physical printer. The path of the TCP/IP Print Services is the Line Printer Daemon (LPD) and Line Printer Remote (LPR). LPD servers and LPR clients are often Unix systems, but these utilities are available for most platforms, including Windows NT.

TCP/IP Print Services is installed through the Services tab of the Network applet in the Control Panel. After installation, you can change its startup settings in the Services applet from Manual (the default) to Automatic. If the printer is hosted on a Windows NT machine, use the New Printer Wizard to create a new port of type LPR Port and direct it to the proper location of the printer, whether a Windows NT print share or a Unix-hosted queue.

Logical printers are created to send documents to the TCP/IP printer through the Add Printer Wizard. This is done by using the IP address print server and the name of the printer, as defined by the print server.

Printer Troubleshooting

When working with printers, there seems to be an infinite number of issues to resolve before normal operation is restored. Many printer problems are either simple or obvious, so check these before moving on to the more complicated solutions:

➤ Always check the physical aspects of the printer—cable, power, paper, toner, and so on.

➤ Check the print queue for stalled jobs on the logical printer on both the client and server.

➤ Make sure the printer driver has not become corrupted by reinstalling it on the print server in a networked environment or on the host in a standalone environment.

➤ Attempt to print from a different application or a different client.

➤ Print using Administrator access.

➤ Stop and restart the spooler using the Services applet.

➤ Check the status and CPU usage of SPOOLSS.EXE using the Task Manager.

➤ Check the free space on the drive hosting the spooler file and change its destination.

Practice Questions

Question 1

Several users are trying to print to a print server. You receive many complaints from the users that they have sent several jobs to the print server, but the jobs have not printed and cannot be deleted. How do you resolve this problem?

- ○ a. Verify that the pause spool option is not checked on the print server.

- ○ b. Delete the stalled printer from the print server, create a new printer, and tell the users to resend their jobs to the new printer.

- ○ c. Delete all files from the spool folder on the print server and tell the users to resend them.

- ○ d. Stop the spooler service and then restart it.

Answer d is correct. This scenario is a quintessential example of a stalled print spooler. To fix the problem, select Services in the Control Panel, stop the spooler service, and then restart it. There isn't a pause spool option. Therefore, answer a is incorrect. There's no need to re-create the printer from scratch. Therefore, answer b is also incorrect. You should never have to involve users in the problem-solving process (other than to gather information from them). Therefore, answer c is also incorrect.

Question 2

> You have an HP LaserJet attached to your Windows NT Workstation that is acting as the print server for 20 other Windows NT computers on your network. Hewlett-Packard has just released an updated printer driver. What must be done to distribute the updated driver to all the computers that print to this print server?
>
> ○ a. Install the updated driver on all client computers; there is no need to update the server.
>
> ○ b. Install the updated driver on the print server and do nothing more.
>
> ○ c. Install the updated driver on the print server and on all client computers.
>
> ○ d. Create a separate logical printer with the updated driver on the print server and tell all the users to print to the new printer.
>
> ○ e. Install the updated driver on the print server and instruct all client computers to download the updated driver from the server.

Answer b is correct. The best way to update a printer driver is to update the driver on the print server. There is no need to update the driver manually on each client computer running Windows NT. Therefore, answer a is incorrect. When a client computer sends a print job to the print server, the updated driver is automatically copied to the client. Therefore, answers c, d, and e are also incorrect.

Question 3

> You run a network for a small consulting firm. You have only a
> single printer on the network. The company executives have asked
> that you configure printing so that all documents from the execu-
> tives print before other documents. How is this performed?
>
> O a. Create a separate logical printer, assign rights to the
>   executive group, and set the printer priority to 1.
>
> O b. Create a separate logical printer, assign rights to the
>   executive group, and set the printer priority to 99.
>
> O c. Create a separate logical printer for the executive group
>   and configure the printer to start printing immediately.
>
> O d. Create a separate logical printer for the executive group
>   and configure the printer to print directly to the physical
>   print device.

Answer b is correct. The highest priority is 99. It is possible to set priorities
between groups of documents by creating different logical printers for the
same physical print device and setting different priority levels on the printers. To set printer priority, select the Scheduling tab in Printer Properties
dialog box. The lowest priority is 1. Therefore, answer a is incorrect. There
is no Start Printing Immediately option. Therefore, answer c is incorrect.
Any Windows NT printer automatically prints to the print device. Therefore, answer d is incorrect.

Question 4

> You just installed a new printer on your print server. You send a
> print job to the printer, but it comes out as pages of nonsense.
> What is the most likely cause of the problem?
>
> O a. The DLC protocol is not installed.
>
> O b. The print spooler is corrupt.
>
> O c. An incorrect printer driver has been installed.
>
> O d. There is not enough hard disk space for spooling.

Answer c is correct. If an incorrect printer driver has been installed, documents might print illegibly. A print job won't print at all if the wrong protocol is used. Therefore, answer a is incorrect. Likewise, nothing will print

without the spooler. Therefore, answer b is incorrect. As in answer b, a print job won't print without proper spooling. Therefore, answer d is incorrect.

Question 5

> You want to create a printer pool with five print devices. Which condition must be present for you to create this printer pool?
>
> ○ a. All print devices must use the same protocol.
>
> ○ b. All physical print devices must be connected to the same logical printer.
>
> ○ c. All print devices must use the same printer port.
>
> ○ d. All print devices must be located in the same room.

Answer b is correct. To create a printer pool, all print devices must be connected to the same print server. It is not necessary for all print devices to use the same protocol. Therefore, answer a is incorrect. All print devices also should be identical. Answers c and d are both incorrect because you don't have to use the same port for multiple printer devices, and printers don't have to be in the same room.

Question 6

> You have a printer pool that consists of Printer 1 and Printer 2. Printer 1 is printing a job and Printer 2 is idle. A paper jam occurs on Printer 1's print device. What will happen to the rest of the job that was being printed?
>
> ○ a. The print job will be completed on Printer 2.
>
> ○ b. The print job will be canceled.
>
> ○ c. The print job will be completed on Printer 2 because Printer 2 has a higher priority level.
>
> ○ d. The print job is held for completion by Printer 1 until the device is fixed.

Answer d is correct. If a physical print device in a printer pool fails in the middle of a print job, the print job is retained at that physical print device until the device is fixed. The print job will not be sent to Printer 2. Therefore, answer a is incorrect. The print job will not be canceled if the device fails. Therefore, answer b is also incorrect. Priority levels have nothing to do with failed devices. Therefore, answer c is wrong as well. Any other print jobs sent to the printer pool will continue to print to other physical print devices in the printer pool.

Question 7

You want to configure a Windows NT computer to be the print server for an HP network interface print device. However, you are unable to locate the option to install a port for the printer. Why is this?

○ a. PostScript printing is enabled on the print device and must be disabled.

○ b. You didn't install the print driver on the print server.

○ c. The print processor is corrupt and must be fixed.

○ d. The DLC protocol is not installed on the print server.

Answer d is correct. For Windows NT to provide support for HP network interface print devices, you must install the DLC (Data Link Control) protocol. PostScript printing has nothing to do with print device installation. Therefore, answer a is incorrect. You can't install a print driver if Windows NT can't recognize the print device. Therefore, answer b is incorrect. The print processor is not involved in the installation of printers. Therefore, answer c is also incorrect.

Question 8

During the printing of a 43-page document, your printer jams on the second page. You pause the printer through the Printers folder. After you remove the jam and reset the physical printer, what command should you enter?

○ a. Open the Printers folder for the printer and select Resume from the Document menu.

○ b. Open the Printers folder for the printer and select Restart from the Document menu.

○ c. Open the Printers folder for the printer and select Resume from the Printer menu.

○ d. Open the Printers folder for the printer and select Restart from the Printer menu.

Answer b is correct. Restart will restart the print process from the beginning. Resume will start printing from the last place in the print job and will not resend the destroyed page or the data lost from the printer buffer. Therefore, answer a is incorrect. Resume is located in the Document menu, not the Printer menu, and it is the wrong command. Therefore, answer c is incorrect. Restart is located in the Document menu (therein lies the "trick"), not the Printer menu. Therefore, answer d is incorrect.

Question 9

What is the advantage of connecting to a printer as opposed to creating a new printer with Windows NT?

○ a. More options over the scheduling of accessibility

○ b. Local spooling of print jobs

○ c. The print driver does not have to be manually installed

○ d. Local print queues

Answer c is correct. Print drivers do not need to be installed locally on each Windows NT Workstation that connects to a network share printer. There are no additional scheduling options in either case. Therefore, answer a is incorrect. There is no local spooling of print jobs for network connection over printers; a logical printer is simply a redirector to the real print server where all spooling takes place. Therefore, answer b is incorrect. The logical printer used to connect to the print share will display a print queue, but it is the entire print queue for the printer as seen by the print server that is displayed. There is not an individual print queue for each local machine; however, only those print jobs owned by the workstation user can be manipulated by that user. Therefore, answer d is incorrect.

Question 10

> You want to share the printer attached to your Windows NT
> Workstation with the rest of the network. There are Windows
> 95, Windows NT 4, and Windows NT 3.51 systems on the net-
> work that need access to your printer. What is the simplest
> way to allow them access?
>
> ○ a. Install printer drivers on each machine.
>
> ○ b. Install the needed drivers on your printer server.
>
> ○ c. Run serial cables to each machine and use a multiport
>   switchbox.
>
> ○ d. Upgrade all machines to Windows NT 4 and then access
>   the print share.

Answer b is correct. Because Windows 95 and Windows NT machines don't
need the drivers, the driver only needs to be installed on the print server.
Installing a print driver on each machine is a waste of time, especially with
these three OS types. Therefore, answers a, c, and d are incorrect.

Need To Know More?

 Heywood, Drew: *Inside Windows NT Server, 2nd Edition.* New Riders, Indianapolis, IN, 1998. ISBN 1-56205-2221-3. Chapter 6, "Managing Print Services," details the issues relating to printing and printer permissions and management.

 Perkins, Charles, Matthew Strebe, and James Chellis: *MCSE: NT Workstation Study Guide, 2nd Edition.* Sybex Network Press, San Francisco, CA, 1998. ISBN 0-7821-2223-X. Chapter 13 has a detailed account of the print system of Windows NT Workstation.

 Siyan, Karanjit S.: *Windows NT Server 4 Professional Reference, 2nd Edition.* New Riders, Indianapolis, IN, 1997. ISBN 1-56205-805-3. A nice discussion of using Windows NT print services is located in Chapter 17, "Windows NT Printing."

Strebe, Matthew, Charles Perkins, and James Chellis: *MSCE: NT Server 4 Study Guide, 2nd Edition.* Sybex Network Press, San Francisco, CA, 1998. ISBN 0-7821-2222-1. Chapter 14 contains detailed information about creating and maintaining your printing environment.

Tittel, Ed, Christa Anderson, and David Johnson: *NT Workstation 4 Exam Prep.* Coriolis, Scottsdale, AZ 1998. ISBN 1-57610-238-6. Chapter 12 is entirely devoted to print-related topices.

 Search the TechNet CD (or its online version through **www.microsoft.com**) using the keywords "printing," "logical printers," "print management," and "print devices."

 The *Windows NT Workstation Resource Kit* contains a lot of useful information about printers and printer management. You can search the TechNet (CD or online version) or the *Resource Kit* CD, using keywords such as "shares," "resource management," and "user management."

Tuning And Monitoring Windows NT Workstation

15

Terms you'll need to understand:

√ Performance Monitor

√ Optimization

√ Objects

√ Counters

√ Baselining

√ Update Interval

√ Task Manager

√ Paging file

√ Priorities

Techniques you'll need to master:

√ Using Performance Monitor

√ Understanding what network characteristics to monitor

√ Viewing network data with Chart view, Alert view, Report view, and Log view

√ Logging network statistics

√ Establishing a baseline

√ Setting administrative alerts

Performance tuning and monitoring on Windows NT Workstation involves numerous applications and configuration screens. In this chapter, we look at many of the tools and methods used to monitor and increase performance. Specifically, we look at the Task Manager, Performance Monitor, and the Windows NT paging file. In addition, we look at managing process priorities and optimizing system settings.

Task Manager

The Task Manager is a new utility in the Windows NT environment. This tool enables you to view and control the processes currently active on your machine. Three types of information are available through the Task Manager (each displayed on its own display tab).

The three types of information available through the Task Manager are:

➤ **Applications** This tab shows a list the applications currently in use and their status, whether running or nonresponsive (see Figure 15.1).

➤ **Processes** This tab displays a list of all processes in memory with details on the CPU and memory usage (see Figure 15.2).

➤ **Performance** This tab shows a graphical and numerical display of system performance metrics—including CPU and memory usage graphs; totals for handles, threads, and processes; physical memory statistics; committed memory changes (memory allocated to the system or an application); and Kernel memory statistics (see Figure 15.3).

The Task Manager can be reached using three different methods:

➤ Press Ctrl+Alt+Del and then click the Task Manager button.

➤ Right-click over a blank area of the taskbar and then select the Task Manager from the pop-up menu.

➤ Press Ctrl+Shift+Esc.

The Task Manager is an invaluable tool used for fast investigation of system activity and instant corrective actions, such as the following:

➤ Identifying nonresponsive applications and terminating them to release their hostage resources (Applications tab).

➤ Identifying runaway processes and terminating them to return the system to normal operational levels (Processes tab).

Figure 15.1   The Task Manager's Applications tab.

➤ Ascertaining the memory usage levels to determine the need for additional RAM (Performance tab).

The Task Manager also enables you to launch new processes, switch to a new foreground application, view separate graphs for each CPU, display the Kernel access time, and alter the priority of processes (see the "Managing Process Priorities" section later in this chapter).

Figure 15.2   The Task Manager's Processes tab.

Figure 15.3 The Task Manager's Performance tab.

Performance Monitor

The Windows NT Performance Monitor (also called PerfMon) is a solid utility that you can use to inspect the performance and activity of processes, resources, physical components, networks, and remote machines. The use and operation of Performance Monitor is rather simple. However, knowing what metrics and counters to watch and what to do about them is not always so easy. We'll take a look at PerfMon's controls and commands and then look into how to use it to evaluate Windows NT's performance.

Performance Monitor has four views: Chart, Alert, Log, and Report.

The four views of the Performance Monitor are:

➤ **Chart view** Allows users to view realtime data in line graph or histogram form (see Figure 15.4).

➤ **Alert view** Allows users to set and view alerts and alert statistics.

➤ **Log view** Allows users to create and save a log of system performance.

➤ **Report view** Allows users to create custom reports of Performance Monitor data. All four views revolve around

Figure 15.4   The Performance Monitor in Chart view, monitoring processor time and memory page swaps.

counters. A counter is a measurable aspect of an object used to evaluate the performance of that object. No matter which view you use, the Add To command in the Edit menu is how you add counters. When you initiate this command, a dialog box appears that allows you to select counters based on the counter's computer, object, and instance.

The following is a list of what information is required to monitor an object:

➤ **Computer** As long as the Network Monitor Agent is installed, for Windows NT/95/98 machines, PerfMon can read counters from those operating systems. PerfMon cannot read counters from non-Microsoft or older Microsoft systems unless third-party software is used.

➤ **Objects** Any component on the specified computer that can be measured, such as the processor, the memory, the physical disk, and so forth, is listed as an object.

➤ **Instances** This identifies which instance of an object should be monitored. Instance 0 is the first or only occurrence of an object, instance 1 is the second occurrence, and so on. If it is not possible for an object to have multiple instances (for example, the Workstation service), then this area is blank.

➤ **Counters** This identifies the available counters for a specific instance of an object on the chosen computer.

A cursory interaction with PerfMon might leave you baffled as to which counters are important. The next section only looks at counters that are used most commonly.

Common Objects And Counters

In the real world of networking, you might have to be familiar with more counters than the ones listed in this section. Fortunately, if you don't quite understand a counter, you can highlight it in the Add To dialog box and click the Explain button to get a brief but helpful definition of that counter.

The following list of Performance Monitor counters only includes these items that are used most frequently.

➤ **Processor: %Processor Time** When you suspect a processor upgrade is necessary, measure this counter. If the processor counter measures 80% or more for an extended period of time, this could be a good indication that the processor is in need of an upgrade.

➤ **System: Processor Queue Length** This can also be measured to determine if a processor upgrade is necessary. If the number of threads waiting to be processed is greater than two, the processor might be a bottleneck for the system.

➤ **Processor: Interrupts/sec.** When you suspect a hardware device is malfunctioning in the system, measure this counter. If the Processor: Interrupts/sec. increases and the processor time does not, a hardware device might be sending bogus interrupts to the processor. Locate the hardware device and replace it.

➤ **Memory: Cache Faults, Page Faults, and Pages/sec.** When you suspect that there is not enough memory in the system, these counters should be measured. They indicate how frequently your system needs to swap pages to the hard disk swap file. If these counters are high, chances are the need for memory is high as well.

➤ **PhysicalDisk/LogicalDisk: %Disk Time** When you suspect the hard disk is a system bottleneck, measure this counter—it shows you how much processor time is being spent servicing disk requests. Measure this counter against Processor: %Processor Time to see if the disk requests are using up a notable amount of processor time.

> ➤ **PhysicalDisk/LogicalDisk: Disk Bytes/Transfer** When you are trying to find out how fast your hard disks are transferring data, measure this counter.

> ➤ **PhysicalDisk/LogicalDisk: Current Disk Queue Length** When you are thinking about upgrading your hard disk, measure this counter. This counter shows you how much data is waiting to be transferred to the disk. If the disk queue is long, processes are being delayed by disk speed.

> *Note:* The PhysicalDisk object counters apply to the entire physical storage device and are best used for suspected hardware troubleshooting. The LogicalDisk object counters focus on a specific volume and are best used for Read/Write performance investigations.

Monitoring Disk Performance

By default, the PhysicalDisk and LogicalDisk counters are not activated. The process of gathering disk counters has a significant effect on the performance of storage devices. To turn on the disk counters, you need to execute **diskperf -y** and then reboot your system. Once you complete your monitoring, turn off the disk counters with **diskperf -n** and then reboot. You must be logged on as Administrator to execute either of these commands. Until **diskperf** is executed, all PhysicalDisk and LogicalDisk counters will display a reading of **0**.

Monitoring Network Performance

Unlike Windows NT Server, Workstation has only a limited capability for analyzing network performance. A network service tool called Network Monitor Agent (NMA) gathers counter readings from network-related objects. These readings can be viewed through the Performance Monitor from the Network Segment object. Without NMA installed, these counters will report null readings. The NMA statistics can also be gathered remotely by a Windows NT Server machine running the built-in or the SMS version of Network Monitor.

Using The PerfMon Views

In the following sections, we explore the various views you can use in Performance Monitor to examine network data. These views include Chart, Alert, Log, and Report.

Using Charts

Once you've selected and added counters to your Chart view, you can make some adjustments through the Options|Chart command. This command brings up a dialog box where you can alter the maximum value of the vertical axis, change between graph and histogram, add grid lines, and change update intervals.

Configuring Alerts

You can use the Windows NT Performance Monitor to configure system alerts. For example, an administrator could be informed when a storage device approaches 85 percent capacity. To work with alerts, you must switch to the Alert view from the View menu. You add counters through the Edit|Add To Alert command (the same way they are added in Chart view). The Add To Alert dialog box is the same as the one for a chart, with the addition of an alert trigger level and program/script to run when an alert occurs.

The remaining alert configuration options are accessed through the Options|Alert command. From there, you can instruct PerfMon to switch to Alert view when an alert is triggered, write the alert in the Application log, and send a notification message to a user or machine.

Working With Logs

The Log view creates a stored record of the performance of one or more objects to be analyzed or compared at another time. You must use the Edit|Add To Log command to add objects for the log to record. Note that the Log view does not offer a selection at the counter level. It records all possible counters for the selected objects.

Once you've selected the objects to log, you need to define the update interval and file name of the log file. This is done through the Options|Log command. You will be prompted for a file name and how often to capture the counters for the objects.

Creating Reports

A report of your gathered metrics can be created through the Report view. Counters to include in a report are added the same way that counters are added in the other views, through the Edit|Add To Report command. After you select the counters to list in the report, you need to set the update interval using the Options|Report command.

Miscellaneous Commands And Controls

All PerfMon view selections have numerous commands in common, including the following:

➤ **File|Save [View] Settings As** Saves a view's settings to be used at another time.

➤ **File|Save Workspace** Saves all view settings in a single file.

➤ **File|Export** Saves the current view's captured data in a tab- or comma-delimited file.

➤ **Add|Edit** Edits the counter's parameters or settings.

➤ **Add|Delete** Removes the counter.

➤ **Options|Data From** Displays data from the active network or from a log file.

> *Note: No matter which view is being used, Performance Monitor must remain up and running (that is, as an active process) to display realtime charts, record logs, send alerts, or create reports.*

Now that we have discussed the Performance Monitor's views, let's move on to the process of baselining.

Baselining

Baselining, or establishing a baseline, is the process of recording the parameters of a fully functional system. This is done through the Log view. Once you've recorded a log of an operating system with "normal" parameters, you can use the log in the future to evaluate the performance of the system. Some objects you should include in your baseline are:

➤ Processor

➤ PhysicalDisk

➤ Memory

➤ System

➤ Any installed protocols

However, just grabbing a short interval of data won't provide a useful baseline for comparison. Instead, you should record a log file for each counter over a 24-hour interval with a counter reading every 5, 10, or 15 minutes. Repeat this process for a few days or even a week. This provides you with a look into the network's performance during an entire day, covering both peak and off-peak hours. Furthermore, it is a good idea to repeat the process of collecting a baseline once a month. This not only establishes a timeline of "normal" performance, but it provides a regular interval to investigate the activity of your network. The regular inspection can help reveal new bottlenecks or failures that you would otherwise fail to notice until production came to a standstill.

Windows NT Paging File

You should remember that Windows NT uses disk space to expand the available memory for the system. The Virtual Memory Manager (VMM) swaps pages from physical RAM to the paging, or swap, file stored on a hard drive. Generally, the VMM handles everything about the paging file automatically, but you can control its maximum size and destination drive.

Changes to the paging file are made through the Performance tab of the System applet in the Control Panel. An area in the middle of this display tab, labeled Virtual Memory, indicates the total size of the pagefile (see Figure 15.5). Click the Change button to alter this setting.

Through the Virtual Memory dialog box, you can change the size of the paging file on any storage device. The paging file can reside on a single drive or in areas on multiple drives. However, the overall speed of Windows NT is determined by how fast the VMM can swap sections of memory from physical RAM to the swap file. Therefore, the speed of the storage device is important.

Figure 15.5 The Virtual Memory dialog box.

The two parameters you must define for each drive that will support a paging file are Initial Size and Maximum Size. The Initial Size is the space VMM initially allocates and uses for the swap file. The Maximum Size is the most space the VMM will use on the drive for the paging file. The VMM is able to expand or shrink the paging file as needed between these two settings. However, neither of these settings guarantees that the disk will have enough free space for a pagefile of the specified size.

 Here are some hints on how to speed up the paging file:

➤ If your system is comprised of multiple physical disks, the paging file may be spread across these disks.

➤ If you move the paging file off the drive that contains the Windows NT system files, it keeps the paging files from competing with the operating system files.

➤ At a minimum, your paging file should be the size of your physical RAM plus 12 MB. Therefore, if your machine has 32 MB of RAM, you should set the pagefile to 44 MB.

➤ While Windows NT is operating, PAGEFILE.SYS (the name of the paging file) cannot be deleted. If for some reason the paging file is deleted, Windows NT will re-create it during boot-up.

If your system is "thrashing"—when the disk drive is in constant activity swapping pages between the drive and physical RAM—you need to take one of the following steps to solve the problem:

➤ Add more physical RAM to your system

➤ Place your paging file on a faster storage device

➤ Spread the paging file across multiple physical disks

Each of these solutions is an inexpensive way to improve performance; the next step is to upgrade your motherboard and CPU.

Managing Process Priorities

Windows NT's multiprocessing environment requires that some processes have a higher execution priority than others. The kernel handles the setting of priorities for each process and has the capability to increase or decrease the priority of a process to improve or alter how it executes. There are 32 priority levels (0 through 31). The higher-numbered priorities are executed before the lower numbered priorities.

Although the system has the capability to use all 32 levels directly, you have only a limited ability to set priorities. By default, all user- and administrator-launched applications are assigned a base priority of **8** (**/normal**). However, users can launch applications with **4** (**/low**) or **13** (**/high**) priority and an administrator can launch with **24** (**/realtime**) priority. To launch an application with an alternate priority level, use the following syntax at a command prompt:

```
start [/low|/normal|/high|/realtime] application
```

Windows NT offers two other priority controls to alter the levels of running processes. The first is a slide bar to control the performance boost for foreground applications. A foreground application is the process that is the active window on your screen, usually indicated by a colored title bar. This slide control is located on the Performance tab in the System applet in the Control Panel. By default, foreground applications have a priority of **10** (maximum). You can move the slider to set foregrounds with an additional priority level of **2** (right tick), **1** (middle tick), or **0** (left tick).

The second control is accessed via the Task Manager. By selecting any of the listed processes on the Process tab, you can change the priority to low, normal, high, or realtime via the Set Priority menu, which is accessed through the right-click pop-up menu.

Practice Questions

Question 1

Which of the following is the best way to establish a baseline for system performance counters?

- ○ a. Capture performance counters from the System object for 30 minutes during nonworking hours.
- ○ b. Capture performance counters from the System object for 30 minutes during the peak hour, capture performance counters from the System object for 30 minutes during a nonworking hour, and then average these two measurements.
- ○ c. Capture performance counters from the System object for 30 minutes each day at a preselected time for a week.
- ○ d. Capture performance counters from the System object at regular intervals throughout the day for three days.

Answer d is correct. It provides an adequate baseline because the data collected will represent all levels of use over a multiple-day period. Answer a will not provide an adequate baseline because the captured data covers only a brief off-peak interval. Therefore, answer a is incorrect. Answer b will not provide an adequate baseline because the captured data represents only a brief off-peak and peak interval. Furthermore, the averaging of the times makes the data even more useless. Therefore, answer b is incorrect. Answer c will not provide an adequate baseline because recording a brief period every day does not reflect the overall picture of the network activity. Therefore, answer c is incorrect.

Question 2

You want to monitor PhysicalDisk performance counters of a local drive. With a standard installation of Windows NT Workstation, what additional operation must be performed to enable the monitoring of the PhysicalDisk counters?

○ a. Install Network Monitor Agent.

○ b. Run the **diskperf** utility with the **-y** option.

○ c. Install Network Monitor Agent and run the **diskperf** utility with the **-n** option.

○ d. No additional operations are required. The PhysicalDisk counters are accessible by default.

Answer b is correct. The **diskperf -y** command is needed to enable the PhysicalDisk counters. The Network Monitor Agent is not required to monitor PhysicalDisk performance counters. It is only needed to access Network Segment object counters. Therefore, answer a is incorrect. The Network Monitor Agent is not required, but the diskperf command is; however the -n option turns off the PhysicalDisk counters. Therefore, answer c is incorrect. The **diskperf** command is required because PhysicalDisk counters are not enabled by default. They must be turned on before PerfMon can access them. Therefore, answer d is incorrect.

Question 3

As a domain user on a Windows NT Workstation, what priority levels can you set for the process you launch? [Check all correct answers]

❑ a. Realtime (**24**)

❑ b. High (**13**)

❑ c. Normal (**8**)

❑ d. Low (**4**)

❑ e. System (**31**)

Answers b, c, and d are correct. As a non-administrator, any user can set a priority process of High, Normal, or Low. Only administrators have the privilege of setting process priority to Realtime. Therefore, answer a is incorrect.

Only the system itself can launch processes with the highest level of priority—System—therefore, answer e is incorrect.

Question 4

> Which of the following utilities can be used to display the current level of CPU utilization? [Check all correct answers]
>
> ❑ a. Performance Monitor
>
> ❑ b. Network Monitor
>
> ❑ c. Task Manager
>
> ❑ d. Windows NT Diagnostics
>
> ❑ e. Server Manager

Answers a and c are correct. The Performance Monitor can display the Processor CPU Utilization counter. Therefore, answer a is correct. The Task Manager displays CPU utilization. Therefore, answer c is correct. Network Monitor and Server Manager are Windows NT Server tools not found on Windows NT Workstation. Therefore, answers b and e are incorrect. Windows NT Diagnostics cannot display CPU utilization. Therefore, answer d is incorrect.

Question 5

> Which view available through Performance Monitor should you use to create a baseline?
>
> ○ a. Chart
>
> ○ b. Log
>
> ○ c. Report
>
> ○ d. Graph

Answer b is correct. Log view records object counters and should be used to create a baseline. Chart view displays the realtime values of counters but cannot record the data as it is gathered. Therefore, answer a is incorrect. Report view creates a snapshot of the performance levels of counters from realtime gathering or a recorded log. Therefore, answer c is incorrect. Graph is not a view but rather a display selection in the Chart view. Therefore, answer d is incorrect.

Question 6

Users on your peer-to-peer network are experiencing up to twice the normal time to access files from your Windows NT Workstation, but all other activities are relatively unaffected. Your system has three physical hard disks with two partitions on each. Which of the following is the best type of object counter to monitor to investigate this problem?

○ a. System object counters

○ b. LogicalDisk object counters

○ c. Server object counters

○ d. PhysicalDisk object counters

○ e. Memory object counters

Answer b is correct. LogicalDisk object counters are the best selection because they provide data on space usage and levels of Read/Write activities on volumes. System, Server, and Memory object counters provide little help toward a storage device performance problem. Therefore, answers a, c, and e are incorrect. PhysicalDisk object counters are useful for hardware troubleshooting and affect an entire drive. The question focuses on the time to access files within a partition and not necessarily the entire drive, making the LogicalDisk counters more effective. Therefore, answer d is incorrect.

Question 7

After an application has been launched, which of the following are possible settings for the priority level on the Processes tab of the Task Manager? [Check all correct answers]

❑ a. Low

❑ b. Realtime

❑ c. System

❑ d. Normal

❑ e. Kernel

❑ f. High

Answers a, b, d, and f are correct. Low, High, Normal, and Realtime are the possible priority settings. There are no System or Kernel priority settings. Therefore, answers c and e are incorrect.

Question 8

> Which are possible functions of the Task Manager? [Check all correct answers]
>
> ❏ a. Switch the foreground application
>
> ❏ b. View committed memory changes
>
> ❏ c. Launch new processes
>
> ❏ d. Set the increase in priority for foreground applications
>
> ❏ e. View multiple CPUs in separate graphs

Answers a, b, c, and e are correct. The Task Manager is able to switch the foreground application, view committed memory changes, launch new processes, and view multiple CPUs in separate graphs. The Task Manger cannot set the increase in priority for foreground applications. This is done through the System applet. Therefore, answer d is incorrect.

Question 9

> You just doubled the size of your server's physical RAM to 128 MB. The pagefile is currently hosted on the same drive as the Windows NT system files, not on the drive containing only your user data files. What change should be made to your pagefile?
>
> ○ a. No change to the pagefile size is recommended, but it should be placed on the data drive.
>
> ○ b. The pagefile should be increased to 140 MB and placed on the data drive.
>
> ○ c. The pagefile should be increased by 12 MB.
>
> ○ d. The pagefile should be increased to 140 MB.

Trick! question

Answer b is correct. The pagefile should be 140 MB and placed on a different drive than the one hosting the system files if possible. You have to read this question carefully to be able to determine that you need to add 12 MB to the 128 MB of installed RAM and that it should reside on a different drive. Always read the questions (and answers) carefully! The pagefile size is recommended to be the size of physical RAM plus 12 MB. Therefore, answer a is incorrect. The pagefile should be the size of physical RAM plus 12 MB. Therefore, answer c is incorrect. The pagefile should be 140 MB and placed on a different drive than the one hosting the system files if possible. Therefore, answer d is incorrect.

Question 10

> What can be done to improve performance on a Windows NT Work-station computer if excessive paging is occurring? [Check all correct answers]
>
> ❏ a. Add more physical RAM.
>
> ❏ b. Reduce the size of the paging file.
>
> ❏ c. Spread the paging file across several drives.
>
> ❏ d. Move the paging file to a drive other than the one hosting the Windows NT system files.

Answers a, c, and d are correct. Adding more RAM, using multiple drives, and avoiding the boot partition are all methods of improving performance due to excessive paging. Reducing the size of the paging file will degrade performance further and possibly prevent the system from functioning properly. Therefore, answer b is incorrect.

Need To Know More?

Perkins, Charles, Matthew Strebe, and James Chellis: *MCSE: NT Workstation Study Guide, 2ⁿᵈ Edition*. Sybex Network Press, San Francisco, CA, 1998. ISBN 0-7821-2223-X. Chapter 14 has detailed information about Performance Monitor and using its features to optimize your system.

Tittel, Ed, Christa Anderson, and David Johnson: *NT Workstation 4 Exam Prep*. Coriolis, Scottsdale, AZ, 1998. ISBN 1-57610-238-6. Chapter 13 covers performance optimization and training for Windows NT Workstation from a number of perspectives.

Search the TechNet CD (or its online version through **www.microsoft.com**) and the *Windows NT Workstation Resource Kit* CD using the keywords "performance," "process priorities," "pagefile," and "Task Manager."

Application Subsystem Architecture

16

. . . .

Terms you'll need to understand:

√ Environment subsystem

√ Win32 subsystem

√ POSIX subsystem

√ OS/2 subsystem

√ Virtual DOS Machine (VDM)

√ Virtual Device Driver (VDD)

√ Windows-On-Windows (WOW)

Techniques you'll need to master:

√ Understanding the Windows NT Workstation system architecture

√ Knowing how older applications run on Windows NT Workstation

Windows NT Workstation is a 32-bit Windows operating system. In addition to supporting Win32 applications, Windows NT can host Win16, DOS, OS/2, and POSIX applications. The range of support varies for each type of application. In this chapter, we examine the details you need to know regarding the application subsystems.

The Windows NT Environmental Subsystems

Windows NT has three environmental subsystems that provide application support (see Figure 16.1): the Win32 subsystem, the POSIX subsystem, and the OS/2 subsystem.

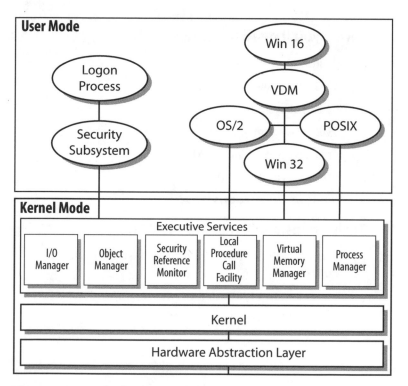

Figure 16.1 The location of the subsystems in the overall architecture of Windows NT.

The Win32 Subsystem

The Win32 subsystem handles support for 32-bit Windows applications (Win32 applications). This subsystem is also called the "CSR" or "client/server" subsystem. Win32 applications run directly in the Win32 subsystem.

This subsystem also maintains the display settings and manages user input from all applications. Character-based screen I/O used by OS/2 and POSIX applications are mapped by their respective subsystems to functions supported by the Win32 subsystem.

The Win32 subsystem boasts the following features:

➤ **32 bit** This system is a 32-bit architecture.

➤ **Threads** Multiple execution threads are supported for each process, and these threads are scheduled preemptively.

➤ **Large address space** Each application within this subsystem is assigned a 2 GB continuous, nonsegmented address space—the actual memory used by a process is controlled by the Virtual Memory Manager (VMM).

➤ **Memory protection** Each Win32 application is protected and separated from every other application in the Windows NT environment. Each application perceives itself as the only process active within the computer.

➤ **OpenGL** An industry software interface standard for 2-D and 3-D graphics.

VDMs or Virtual DOS Machines can exist within the Win32 subsystem. These are Win32 processes that support DOS applications. VDMs are discussed in the next section.

DOS And Virtual DOS Machines (VDMs)

Windows NT supports DOS applications through Virtual DOS Machines (VDMs). A VDM is a Win32 application that creates an operational environment for DOS applications. This environment resembles a DOS-only computer and fools DOS applications into thinking that they have direct and unrestricted access to the computer hardware. Every DOS application is given its own single-threaded VDM, where it perceives itself as the only process on the computer.

However, not all DOS applications can operate within Windows NT. Those DOS applications that make direct hardware-level function calls are not allowed to continue functioning. Only those applications that Windows NT can intercept hardware calls through the use of Virtual Device Drivers (VDDs) can continue operation within a VDM. Therefore, DOS support is limited to the programming method of the application itself.

There are four components used to create and control VDMs:

➤ **NTVDM.EXE** The protected mode executable that translates DOS resource requests into Win32 requests.

➤ **NTIO.SYS and NTDOS.SYS** The Windows NT equivalents of IO.SYS and MSDOS.SYS. These operate within the VDM in real mode.

➤ **VDMREDIR.DLL** The redirector that directs file system and I/O requests to the Win32 subsystem.

The default environment found within a VDM can be configured by modifying the CONFIG.NT and AUTOEXEC.NT files. These are the equivalent to the CONFIG.SYS and AUTOEXEC.BAT files found on MS-DOS machines. However, fine-tuning for each DOS application can be performed through the executable's properties. In effect, you are modifying the application's Program Information File (PIF), which appears as a shortcut for the application. The next time you need to use the DOS application, use the new shortcut to launch the application and your customized settings will be used.

The Properties dialog box for a DOS application has four additional tabs not found on Win32 applications. Basic familiarity with these tabs is essential; these settings are the same as those found on Windows 95 and Windows 98.

The four tabs for the DOS Properties dialog box are:

➤ **Font** Font type of bitmap or True Type is selected along with the font's size for the DOS window.

➤ **Memory** The memory environment is defined, including XMS (expanded), EMS (extended), and DMPI (protected).

➤ **Screen** Sets the window size, toolbar visibility, and performance emulation.

➤ **Misc** A conglomeration of options: screen saver, suspend, mouse control, and reservation of Windows shortcut key sequences.

Each time a DOS application is launched, a VDM is created. When a DOS application terminates, the VDM is not destroyed by Windows NT and its memory and system pointers are maintained. When a subsequent DOS application is launched, it assumes the existing VDM. Therefore, if multiple DOS applications are launched concurrently and then exited, some system resources will be tied up in maintaining each of the VDMs. VDMs are only destroyed by terminating the VDM process itself or rebooting Windows NT.

Within a VDM, a WOW environment can exist that supports Win16 applications. This is discussed in the next section.

Win16 And WOW

Windows 16-bit applications (Win16 applications) are supported through a DOS application called Windows-On-Windows (WOW). WOW executes within a VDM, which itself runs as a Win32 process. This configuration is used to mimic the Windows 3.x environment where Windows runs on top of DOS; thus, the applications are "fooled" into thinking they are operating within a Win16 environment. All Win16 applications operate within a single instance of WOW, unlike DOS applications, which operate within separate VDMs. This mimics the Windows 3.x environment where Win16 applications share a memory space and computer resources. Therefore, just like on Windows 3.x, Win16 applications can interact and interfere with other Win16 applications. If a Win16 application fails or corrupts the system resources of a WOW, this will not affect the operation of Windows NT itself or any other VDMs or Win32 processes.

All applications within a Win16 WOW environment operate in a cooperative, multitasking environment—each app controls processing time until it chooses to release control. However, because WOW is within a VDM, which itself is a single-threaded Win32 process, the entire WOW environment is preemptively multitasked with all other Win32 threads.

WOW is constructed within a VDM, and the components involved in this creation are:

➤ **KRNL386.EXE** A modified version of Windows 3.1 that functions under Windows NT. Most of the system functions are passed to the Win32 subsystem by this component.

➤ **USER.EXE** A modified version of the Windows 3.1 USER.EXE that directs API calls to the Win32 subsystem.

➤ **GDI.EXE** A modified version of the Windows 3.1 GDI.EXE that renders graphic calls into Win32 calls.

➤ **WOWEXEC.EXE** Establishes the Windows 3.1 emulation within a VDM.

Win16 applications are launched within the same instance of WOW by default. However, it is possible to launch Win16 applications in their own individual instances of WOW by modifying their PIFs or indicating this parameter from a Run instruction or command prompt. When multiple WOWs are in use, Clipboard data from one WOW app cannot be transferred into another WOW app because they no longer share resource space.

The OS/2 Subsystem

Windows NT provides a low level of OS/2 support. The support is only for OS/2 1.x applications. There is no support for the popular 2.x+ GUI applications with which most OS/2 users are familiar. An extension component enables some graphics support for the launching of Presentation Manager. The OS/2 subsystem operates alongside the Win32 subsystem, but some system calls are sent to the Win32 subsystem instead of directly to the Executive Services.

The OS/2 subsystem is constructed with the following components:

➤ **OS2SS.EXE** The main component of the OS/2 subsystem. It adapts services provided by Win32 and the Windows NT Executive Services to the OS/2 environment.

➤ **OS2SRV.EXE** Launches OS/2 applications.

➤ **OS2.EXE** A Win32-based program that passes the name of OS/2 applications and any command-line parameters to OS2SRV.EXE.

➤ **NETAPI.DLL and DOSCALLS.DLL** Windows NT files that support OS/2 program APIs.

Some applications are compiled to function within DOS or OS/2—they are called "bound applications." Such programs will be launched into the OS/2 subsystem unless the FORCEDOS.EXE utility is used to force the bound application to be launched into a VDM.

The POSIX Subsystem

Windows NT provides a low level of POSIX support for the purpose of complying with government purchase regulations. The support is only for POSIX.1 character-based applications. Like the OS/2 subsystem, the

POSIX subsystem runs alongside and makes some system calls through the Win32 subsystem.

The POSIX subsystem is constructed with the following components:

➤ **PSXSS.EXE** The main component of the POSIX subsystem. It starts when the first POSIX application is loaded.

➤ **POSIX.EXE** Similar to OS2.EXE, POSIX.EXE is a Win32-based program that passes information between the Executive Services and the subsystem it supports.

➤ **PXSDLL.DLL** Handles communication between each POSIX application and the POSIX subsystem. This dynamic link library (DLL) contains support for the C routines that POSIX applications expect.

To establish the POSIX.1 compliance of Windows NT, the following support was added to the POSIX subsystem:

➤ **Case-sensitive naming** NTFS supports the case-sensitive naming of files though the preservation of file name case. This means that files named Text.txt, TEXT.txt, and text.txt are all different within the POSIX subsystem. Windows NT still views these files as the same, because by default it is not case sensitive.

➤ **Hard links** NTFS also supports the storage of multiple file names for a single file, called hard links.

➤ **POSIX.1 library compliance** POSIX.DLL supports POSIX library compliance for applications making C program calls.

Windows NT has very limited support of POSIX. Therefore, most Unix applications will not operate under the POSIX subsystem.

Practice Questions

Question 1

> Windows NT provides support for what types of applications?
> [Check all correct answers]
>
> ❏ a. POSIX
>
> ❏ b. Win16
>
> ❏ c. DOS
>
> ❏ d. MacOS
>
> ❏ e. Win32
>
> ❏ f. OS/2
>
> ❏ g. Solaris

Answers a, b, c, e, and f are correct. Windows NT provides application support for POSIX, Win16, DOS, Win32, and OS/2. Windows NT does not provide support for MacOS or Solaris applications. Therefore, answers d and g are incorrect.

Question 2

> Which subsystem do all the application subsystems interact with in some form?
>
> ○ a. WOW
>
> ○ b. VDM
>
> ○ c. Win32
>
> ○ d. POSIX
>
> ○ e. OS/2

Answer c is correct. The Win32 subsystem is used or interacted with by all the subsystems within Windows NT. WOW, POSIX, and OS/2 are only used by their respective applications. Therefore, answers a, d, and e are incorrect. VDM is used by WOW, but not by the other subsystems. Therefore, answer b is incorrect.

Question 3

> Which of the following subsystems employ the use of threaded execution? [Check all correct answers]
>
> ❑   a. Win32
>
> ❑   b. WOW/Win16
>
> ❑   c. VDM/DOS
>
> ❑   d. POSIX
>
> ❑   e. OS/2

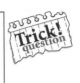

Answers a, b, c, d, and e are correct. All the subsystems within Windows NT are executed through threads. Even though a VDM (and subsequently WOW) uses only a single thread, it is still a threaded execution.

Question 4

> How large is the memory address space assigned to each process by the Win32 subsystem?
>
> ○   a. 32 MB
>
> ○   b. 2 MB
>
> ○   c. 4 GB
>
> ○   d. 2 GB

Answer d is correct. The Win32 subsystem assigns a 2 GB address space to each process it launches.

Question 5

> All DOS applications are launched within a single VDM.
>
> ○   a. True
>
> ○   b. False

Answer b is correct. Each DOS application is launched within its own VDM.

Question 6

> How can the DOS environment of VDMs be modified? [Check all correct answers]
>
> ❑ a. By changing the DOS executable's PIF
>
> ❑ b. By editing the CONFIG.NT
>
> ❑ c. Through the VDM Manager
>
> ❑ d. Through Environment tab in the System applet
>
> ❑ e. By altering AUTOEXEC.NT

Answers a, b, and e are correct. DOS VDM environments can be modified by altering the PIF, CONFIG.NT, and AUTOEXEC.NT. There isn't a VDM Manager, and the System applet does not affect VDMs. Therefore, answers c and d are incorrect.

Question 7

> What other two subsystems are required or used by WOW? [Check all correct answers]
>
> ❑ a. Win32
>
> ❑ b. VDM
>
> ❑ c. POSIX
>
> ❑ d. OS/2

Answers a and b are correct. The WOW subsystem is launched within a VDM, which is itself launched within Win32. POSIX and OS/2 are not associated with WOW in any way. Therefore, answers c and d are incorrect.

Question 8

> If a Win16 application corrupts its memory space and hangs, Windows NT will need to be rebooted to restore the system.
>
> ○ a. True
>
> ○ b. False

Answer b is correct. A Win16 application will only cause other Win16 applications within the same WOW to fail, it will not affect Windows NT or any other separate subsystem. Stalled Win16 applications are resolved by terminating the WOW environment.

Question 9

OS/2 and POSIX support are included in Windows NT, but at what level?

○ a. Complete support for both systems as available at the release of Windows NT

○ b. Full graphical support

○ c. Text-only level or version 1

Answer c is correct. OS/2 and POSIX support is limited to text only or version/level 1.

Question 10

Which of the following is not true about Win16 applications?

○ a. Operates within a VDM

○ b. Can be launched in a separate memory space

○ c. All system calls are handled through the Win32 subsystem

○ d. Direct hardware-level resource requests are possible

Answer d is correct. Win16 applications cannot make direct hardware-level resource requests—this is a limitation of VDM and Windows NT itself. Win16 applications operate within a VDM and can be launched in a separate memory space. Also, all system calls within Win16 application are processed by the Win32 subsystem. Therefore, answers a, b, and c are incorrect.

Need To Know More?

Perkins, Charles, Matthew Strebe, and James Chellis: *MCSE: NT Workstation Study Guide, 2nd Edition*. Sybex Network Press, San Francisco, CA, 1998. ISBN 0-7821-2223-X. Chapter 15 discusses the application support through subsystems found in Windows NT.

Tittel, Ed, Christa Anderson, and David Johnson: *NT Workstation 4 Exam Prep*. Coriolis, Scottsdale, AZ, 1998. ISBN: 1-57610-238-6. Chapter 14 covers the various Windows NT environmental subsystems in-depth and also covers Win16 and VOM details.

Search the TechNet CD (or its online version through **www.microsoft.com**) and *the Windows NT Workstation Resource Kit* CD using the keywords "subsystem," "Win32," "Win16," "WOW," "VDM," "OS/2," and "POSIX."

Booting Windows NT

Terms you'll need to understand:

√ Boot

√ Boot up

√ Bootstrap

√ Bootstrap loader

√ ARC names

√ ARC path names

√ Master Boot Record (MBR)

√ BOOT.INI

√ NTLDR

√ NTDETECT.COM

√ NTBOOTDD.SYS

√ Boot partition or boot drive

√ System partition or system drive

Techniques you'll need to master:

√ How to edit the BOOT.INI file

√ How to interpret and construct Advanced RISC Computer (ARC) device and path names

√ How to troubleshoot the Windows NT boot sequence

Starting up a computer from scratch involves a lot more work, as well as many more parts, than might immediately be expected. Because a computer that won't boot is a dead computer, it's essential to understand the Windows NT boot process and where that process can go awry.

In this chapter, we walk you through the Windows NT boot process, explain the important pieces, and explore some things that can derail this process. Along the way, you'll get to know more about how computers work, in general. You'll also learn what's involved in fully completing Windows NT's intricate boot process.

Bootstrapping A Computer

When you boot a computer that has Windows NT installed, the machine goes through a number of steps before an operating system (OS) can be selected. And if Windows NT is selected, a number of additional steps follow before the login prompt dialog box appears.

The initial phase, called the bootstrap process, covers the steps necessary to turn a computer from a lump of inert metal and plastic into a device that is ready to accept and react to input. For ordinary PCs, this consists of the following steps:

1. **Power-on the computer, or initiate startup** This one is easy. It requires only that the computer be plugged in and that you turn the power switch to on. For Windows NT, the startup process also can be initiated when you click Restart The Computer in the Shut Down Windows dialog box (Start|Shut Down), or when you select the Shutdown tab followed by Shutdown And Restart through the Windows NT Security dialog box, which is always available by pressing Ctrl+Alt+Del while Windows NT is running.

2. **Power-On Self-Test (POST) processing** Once the computer begins its startup process, it performs a number of built-in diagnostics and hardware tests to make sure all its components are working properly. This is driven by firmware on the motherboard through the BIOS (and might involve other BIOSs such as those typically found on graphics adapters) once the on-board BIOS completes its checks. This produces all the messages and status information that flash on your screen while the computer is going through the hardware check stages of startup. POST also determines how much RAM is available on the machine and checks to make sure essential peripherals (keyboard, mouse, and so on) are present and connected.

3. **Initial startup process** Once the hardware has been checked out, the initial startup process exhausts the on-board diagnostics and self-check capabilities of most computers. At this point, some real software must be read from disk to continue the boot process, which requires that an OS establish a runtime environment for the computer to be loaded.

If you are booting from a floppy, the first sector on the disk contains the Partition Boot sector; if you are booting from a hard disk, the first sector contains the Master Boot Record (MBR) and the partition table. These records contain the information that allows the computer to obtain boot information; they also provide a map for how the hard disk (or floppy) is physically arranged.

The MBR is probably the most important record on any hard disk. It contains the partition table that describes a disk's physical layout and arrangement, and it includes a small program that examines the partition table and identifies the system partition. The program then locates the system partition's starting address on disk (sector 0) and loads a copy of the Partition Boot sector into memory.

Once this step is complete, the program transfers execution to the operating system loader and is run from code found in the partition boot sector just loaded. This partition is marked active in the partition table and is thus responsible for the next instructions in the boot process.

Warning! It's essential to recognize that the files that reside in the system partition on a drive are the files needed to boot a computer and some operating systems, whereas the files that reside in what Microsoft calls "the boot partition" on a drive are those files needed to run Windows NT. Therefore, the boot files—that is, NTLDR, BOOT.INI, NTDETECT.COM, and so on—reside in the system partition, whereas the Windows NT OS files—including NTOSKRNL.EXE and the Windows NT Kernel—reside on the boot partition. Get it?

4. **Boot loader process** When the Partition Boot Sector code is loaded, a program runs that brings up a designated operating system—or, as with Windows NT's NTLDR program, it provides a menu of load choices. This starts an execution sequence for full-blown programs from files on-disk (as opposed to code embedded in the MBR or a Partition Boot Sector). This ultimately results in the complete loading of an operating system, after which the computer will be ready to run applications or services on demand.

> Windows NT also runs on RISC CPUs as well as on generic PCs. The boot process differs for RISC machines to some degree. We'll point out these differences in tips as we step through the rest of this process. The primary difference, as far as the bootstrap process is concerned, is that once a RISC computer completes its POST routines, built-in firmware selects a startup disk by reading a boot precedence table from nonvolatile RAM on the machine. This identifies the system partition (where the boot files reside) and indicates if a floppy may be used as an alternative boot selection. The information in nonvolatile RAM also indicates where the OSLOADER.EXE program, which loads Windows NT on a RISC system, resides as well as the folder that contains the OS to be booted.

This marks the point at which the bootstrap process is complete, and the point at which activities specific to the OS to be booted begin. Once NTLDR is loaded into memory, it is possible to choose an OS (or multiple versions of the same OS, one of which is definitely Windows NT). The steps that follow assume Windows NT is selected as the operating system to boot:

1. **Selecting the OS** When NTLDR executes, it reads another important Windows NT boot file, BOOT.INI, which we discuss in detail later. BOOT.INI provides information about choices of operating systems, defines their locations on-disk, and assigns some important default characteristics for the load process. This information makes it possible to boot a Windows NT machine without requiring user intervention; therefore, keyboard input is not strictly required to start up a Windows NT machine. We now will choose a version of Windows NT in the loader menu to begin the process of loading Windows NT.

> At this point in the process for RISC machines, the program that loads is named OSLOADER.EXE. It performs all the functions supplied for PCs by NTLDR, NTDETECT.COM, and BOOTSECT.DOS.

2. **Detecting hardware**   Now the Windows NT program NTDETECT. COM executes. This is a hardware recognition program that collects a list of currently installed components and returns the information to NTLDR. NTLDR will not run, however, unless you select a version of Windows NT on the boot loader screen (or the default selection is Windows NT and the timer times out). The following message appears:

```
NTDETECT V1.0 Checking Hardware . . .
```

3. **Choosing a load configuration**   Once NTDETECT finishes its job, the boot loader resumes control and the following message appears:

```
OS Loader V4.0

Press spacebar now to invoke Hardware Profile/
  Last Known Good Configuration menu.
```

The boot loader waits several seconds to give you time to press the spacebar. If it isn't pressed and only one hardware profile is defined for the computer (which is typical, except for laptops), the boot loader loads Windows NT's default configuration. Otherwise, you can elect to use an alternative hardware profile here (for laptops, this usually means selecting Networked or Detached hardware profiles) or switch to the Last Known Good Configuration menu, which permits you to boot Windows NT using the Registry values defined the last time the machine booted successfully.

4. **Loading the Windows NT Kernel**   Once the configuration or Registry versions have been identified (or chosen by default, as is most often the case), the next step is to load the OS Kernel for Windows NT. A sequence of periods appears on screen as the boot loader loads NTOSKRNL.EXE and the Hardware Abstraction Layer (HAL.DLL) into memory.

On RISC machines, OSLOADER.EXE handles everything through this step. It concludes by loading the appropriate version of NTOSKRNL.EXE and HAL.DLL for the CPU in use. The remaining steps are identical, whether the machine is a PC clone or a RISC computer.

5. **Initializing the Kernel** When the PC's screen turns blue and displays a message similar to the following:

```
Microsoft (R) Windows NT (TM) Version 4.0 (Build 1381)
1 System Processor (64 MB Memory)
```

this indicates that the Kernel has initialized properly and has taken control. At this point, Windows NT is running the computer.

During Kernel initialization, the following tasks are completed:

➤ Initializing low-level device drivers loaded with the Kernel in the preceding step

➤ Loading and initializing other device drivers as needed

➤ Running diagnostic or setup programs such as CHKDSK before loading services

➤ Loading and initializing all services identified with automatic startup in the OS configuration

➤ Creating the paging file for temporary storage and swap space

➤ Starting all subsystems needed for Windows NT (such as the Win32 subsystem, security subsystem, and possibly the OS/2 or POSIX subsystems)

6. **Logging on** When Kernel initialization is complete, the Begin Logon dialog box appears (this contains the message "Press Ctrl+Alt+Delete to log on"). Once a successful logon occurs, Windows writes the values in the Registry to a special backup file that provides the data needed to invoke the Last Known Good Configuration boot option the next time the machine starts up (a successful logon is required to make this change because numerous Registry values will not be updated until the first actual logon occurs).

The Windows NT Boot Components

The most important components of the Windows NT boot process are worth memorizing:

➤ **BOOT.INI** This is the PC information file that describes Windows NT boot defaults as well as operating system locations, settings, and menu selections. This file resides in the root directory of the system partition.

➤ **BOOTSECT.DOS** This MS-DOS boot sector file is used if NTLDR offers the option to boot to some other Microsoft (or near-equivalent) operating system, such as DOS or Windows 95. This file resides in the root directory of the system partition.

➤ **NTDETECT.COM** This is the PC hardware detection program that gathers equipment and configuration information prior to booting Windows NT (to make sure the stored configuration agrees with the detected one). This file resides in the root directory of the system partition.

➤ **NTLDR** This is the PC operating system loader program, which loads Windows NT or another designated operating system and then relinquishes control once loading is complete. This file resides in the root directory of the system partition.

➤ **NTOSKRNL.EXE** This is the executable file for Windows NT that includes all the basic capabilities and components necessary to establish a working run-time environment. This file resides in the %systemroot%\system32 directory on the boot partition.

➤ **OSLOADER.EXE** This is the OS loader program for RISC computers, which performs the same functions as NTLDR does for Intel-based systems.

One other PC-based Windows NT boot file that you should be familiar with is NTBOOTDD.SYS. It must be present when a SCSI drive, with its on-board BIOS disabled, is used as the system partition or the boot partition on a Windows NT system. This file replaces the functions the on-board BIOS would normally provide with a software-based driver. Like the other boot files, NTBOOTDD.SYS resides in the root directory of the system partition.

ARC Names And Attached Hard Drives

To fully understand the ins and outs of the BOOT.INI file, which drives much of NTLDR's behavior during the Windows NT boot process, it is essential to understand what Microsoft calls "Advanced RISC Computer (ARC) names" (and sometimes, ARC path names). ARC represents a common naming convention used within disk controller software to specify the unique combination of disk controller, disk drive, and disk partition that identifies the system and boot partitions for Windows NT. These names appear in the BOOT.INI file and must sometimes be edited, particularly during recovery from failure of the primary member of a mirrored or duplexed drive pair.

ARC names not only provide a method to specify the type and location of the disk controllers, drives, and partitions in use, but they also include pointers to files and directories. Such names typically take one of two forms:

```
scsi(0)disk(0)rdisk(0)partition(1)\path
multi(0)disk(0)rdisk(0)partition(1)\path
```

Here's a breakdown of the terms involved:

➤ **scsi(*) or multi(*)** Most ARC names begin with "multi(*)"; "scsi(*)" appears only when a SCSI controller with its on-board BIOS disabled is in use. **multi(*)** is used for other hard disks of all kinds, including IDE, EIDE, ESDI, and SCSI (where the on-board BIOS is enabled, as is most often the case). The (*) indicates the address of the hardware adapter from which to boot, numbered ordinally, beginning with zero. Controller numbers begin at zero; therefore, the card closest to bus slot zero on the motherboard is the first controller and is assigned the controller number of zero (0); the next card is the second controller and is assigned the controller number of one (1), and so on.

➤ **disk(*)** This portion of the name applies only when the **scsi(*)** keyword appears. In that case, the value of (*) indicates the SCSI bus ID (usually 0 to 6) for the drive where the designated files reside. If the ARC name begins with the **multi(*)** keyword, this value is always **disk(0)**.

➤ **rdisk(*)** This portion of the name applies only when the **multi(*)** keyword appears. It either indicates the SCSI logical unit number (LUN) for the drive or selects the position in the chain of hard disks attached to the controller where the designated files reside. Here again, numbering begins with zero; therefore, the first drive in the chain is named **rdisk(0)**, the second **rdisk(1)**, and so on. If the ARC name begins with scsi (*), this value is always rdisk (0).

➤ **partition(*)** This portion of the name indicates the disk partition that contains the designated files. Unlike the other numbering schemes in

ARC names, partition numbers begin with one; therefore, the first partition is **partition(1)**, the second is **partition(2)**, and so on.

 Please note that for PCs, a maximum of four partitions per drive is allowed. But one of those partitions can be something called an "extended partition," which simply means that more than one logical drive can be created within that partition. The other three (or four, if no extended partition exists) are called primary partitions and can have only one logical drive per partition.

There are two important things to remember about primary and extended partitions. First, only a primary partition can be a system partition (where boot files reside and initial boot phases occur), but Windows NT system files (the boot partition) can reside on a logical drive within an extended partition. Second, on a drive with primary and extended partitions, the extended partition is always numbered the highest. If the Windows NT files reside on an extended partition and a new primary has been defined, this means the partition number for the extended partition increases by one as a result of that new definition.

➤ **\path** Indicates the directory (or subdirectory) on the partition where the operating system files can be found. The default path for Windows NT is \winnt.

Working with ARC names requires understanding the rules by which they're to be applied or interpreted. Remember that **scsi(*)** appears only for SCSI controllers with their on-board BIOSs disabled, and that numbering for **scsi(*)**, **multi(*)**, **disk(*)**, and **rdisk(*)** starts with zero, but numbering for **partition(*)** starts with one. Also, remember that when multi(*) appears, disk(0) is the only valid value, and that when **scsi(*)** appears, **rdisk(0)** is the only valid value. Finally, you can tell which disk term goes with each controller type by counting letters: scsi and disk each have four and go together; likewise, multi and rdisk each have five and go together. These four rules, properly applied, will help you understand the ARC name.

Managing The BOOT.INI File

You can make changes to BOOT.INI from the Startup/Shutdown tab of the System applet or by using a text editor. If problems occur as a result of these changes, always make a backup copy of the file to a floppy. Here's an example of a typical BOOT.INI file (without most of the many possible bells and whistles):

```
[boot loader]
timeout=30
default=multi(0)disk(0)rdisk(0)partition(3)\WINNT
[operating systems]
multi(0)disk(0)rdisk(0)partition(3)\WINNT="Windows NT
Workstation Version 4.00"
multi(0)disk(0)rdisk(0)partition(3)\WINNT="Windows NT
Workstation Version 4.00 [VGA mode]" /basevideo /sos
C:\ = "MS-DOS"
```

Note that this file is divided into two sections labeled **[boot loader]** and **[operating systems]**. The **[boot loader]** section supplies the **timeout** interval after which the default operating system to load (defined in the **default=** line that follows **timeout**) loads automatically. The **[operating systems]** section supplies the complete menu of operating system choices NTLDR displays after the program loads. You can disable the timer before it elapses by striking any arrow or letter key on the keyboard. Then, you can wait as long as you like to make your menu selection.

Using The Control Panel

Using the System applet in the Control Panel to change BOOT.INI is definitely the safest method, but it doesn't expose everything you might need to access. The System applet includes a Startup/Shutdown tab that permits you to choose a default boot selection as well as to set the interval for the delay before the default boot selection is automatically invoked. This delay time corresponds to the **timeout** value in the **[boot loader]** section of the file shown previously. Also, the value assigned to the **default=** statement in that section defines the ARC name for the default OS to be loaded.

Using A Text Editor

BOOT.INI is a plain, pure-ASCII file that should be edited with a plain text editor, such as Notepad or an equivalent program. As with any initialization file, be careful when editing it. Anything between quotation marks in the **[operating systems]** section of the file is fair game, but it is vital that you be careful if you must edit an ARC name. There is no need to create an Emergency Repair Disk (ERD) when making changes to BOOT.INI because the ERD doesn't make a copy of it. You should, however, make a fault-tolerant boot floppy with a working copy of the BOOT.INI, NTLDR, and NTDETECT.com.

BOOT.INI has the following DOS attributes: Read-Only, System, and Hidden. You will need to turn off the Read-Only attribute to make changes to the file, and you'll probably want to turn off the Hidden attribute as well.

It's necessary to restore the file to Read-Only after editing, so be sure to remember this step before you try to reboot.

Troubleshooting The Windows NT Boot Process

There are a lot of ways things can break down and interfere with the Windows NT boot process. Here, we recount those problems—and their fixes—that you're most likely to encounter when dealing with boot problems. While you're troubleshooting, remember that hardware problems are always possible (if not also vexing and unpleasant), and sometimes the computer won't boot because a component has failed, not because of the kinds of software and configuration difficulties we recount here.

That's why the first things to do with a PC that won't boot Windows NT is to insert a DOS boot disk. If the machine will boot DOS, it's easy to run DOS-based diagnostics to check the hardware. This eliminates many potential avenues for problems from further consideration. The next step is to boot the system from a set of Windows NT boot floppies—if this works, it proves the machine will still boot Windows NT, no matter how badly the current configuration is mangled or disturbed.

The next step is to try to boot using the Last Known Good Configuration boot option. If this works, it indicates the problem lies in changes made to the system since the last time it booted successfully. This should narrow the field considerably and let you focus on the most likely causes of the problems. If you can't get to this point, you'll have to get the hardware working before you can proceed.

Common Boot-Related Problems, Causes, And Fixes

Here's a litany of potential woes, with possible causes and definite fixes:

➤ **I/O Error Accessing Boot Sector File** This type of error can occur when a power failure or fluctuation interrupts file system activity or software installation. Sometimes, this occurs when installing another OS over a Windows NT installation. The symptom will be a BIOS-level error message from the computer indicating that the boot sectors are damaged or that the drive is unavailable. The only way to repair this is to boot the PC from a DOS floppy and run the **FDISK/MBR** command to rebuild the MBR.

➤ **Corrupted Partition Tables** This generally won't happen unless you attempt to use some operating system other than Windows NT, or another operating system that's incompatible with the IBM/ Microsoft partitioning scheme, to create or manipulate partitions on a drive. For obvious reasons, Unix can be a culprit. If this happens, a backup is your best bet—you'll have to reformat the drive, reestablish the partitions, and restore the data. If no data was written to the drives following their partition changes, it might be possible to restore the partition table to its prior state and attempt to carry on from there. However, this can be an unbelievable exercise in frustration.

➤ **BOOT: Couldn't Find NTLDR** This error message indicates that NTLDR is corrupt or missing. This can sometimes pop up if the wrong partition has been made active in Disk Administrator, but it is usually remedied by copying a good copy of NTLDR onto the root of the errant drive. The most common situation where this error appears is when a non-bootable floppy has been left in the floppy drive during a reboot. In this case, remove the floppy and try booting again.

➤ **NTDETECT V1.0 Checking Hardware...** If this message appears repeatedly, it means NTDETECT.COM is corrupted or missing. In most cases, putting a fresh copy of the program onto the root of the errant system partition will do the trick. The ERD can help with this.

➤ **Windows NT Could Not Start Because The Following File Is Missing Or Corrupt: %systemroot%\system32\ntoskrnl.exe** This indicates any number of problems, but it generally means NTLDR couldn't find the Windows NT operating system Kernel file needed to complete the OS load. The most frequent cause of this problem is when allocation of free space on a Windows NT drive results in a change to the partition number for the boot partition where the Windows NT system files reside. Properly assigning the partition number for the boot partition usually fixes this problem.

➤ **Could Not Read From The Selected Boot Disk...** This indicates that something is amiss with the boot partition. It could be that a drive is missing or malfunctioning (unlikely, but possible). Otherwise, the disk partition specified in an ARC name might not contain a file system that's recognizable to the NTLDR program. In that case, check to see if partition allocations have changed lately or if someone has been tinkering with BOOT.INI. Restoring the malfunctioning drive or correcting the ARC name should fix the problem.

➤ **STOP: 0x000007E: Inaccessible Boot Device** A STOP error is as fatal as it gets; Windows NT won't go any further until you fix the problem. This error occurs most frequently when a SCSI controller that fails to adhere completely to the SCSI standard is installed in a Windows NT machine. It can also occur if you add a SCSI controller to a Windows NT machine that boots from an IDE hard disk. In that case, make sure no SCSI device is set to SCSI ID 0; otherwise, disable booting from the SCSI drive(s). This prevents the SCSI controller from attempting to boot the disk and stops NTDETECT.COM from assigning the SCSI adapter a bus number equal to zero, which might cause BOOT.INI to point to the wrong partition.

Multiboot Configuration Issues

Windows NT can exist on a system that hosts multiple operating systems. Windows NT Workstation can exist without problems on a computer with Windows 95, Windows 98, Windows For Workgroups, Windows 3.x, or DOS. For such a dual-boot to exist, it is recommended that you install the other OS first and then install Windows NT onto a different partition. The resultant BOOT.INI file will contain the two standard lines for Windows NT's normal and safe boot modes as well as a third entry for the alternative operating system, which is usually labeled "MS-DOS" by default. Keep in mind that other Windows NT OSs will probably not be able to read any data stored on NTFS volumes.

Windows NT can also be installed in a multiboot configuration with other OSs, but the ease of installation and operation will vary. OS/2 is shipped with its own boot manager. When Windows NT is installed onto an OS/2 system, the OS/2 boot manager is disabled in favor of the Windows NT boot manager. You can revert to the OS/2 boot manager by activating the small OS/2 boot manager partition through Disk Administrator. If this change is made, the OS/2 boot manager will be displayed. If DOS or Windows is selected, the Windows NT boot manager is then displayed.

To remove an alternative OS from the boot manager, simply edit the BOOT.INI file and delete the ARC name\path entry.

Practice Questions

Question 1

> A Windows NT PC is configured with two 2.2 GB EIDE hard drives, with both drives attached to a controller built into the motherboard. Each disk contains a single primary partition; the Windows NT system files reside on disk 1, and the boot files reside on disk 2. Which of the following ARC names correctly identifies the boot partition that appears in the BOOT.INI file?
>
> ○ a. multi(0)disk(0)rdisk(0)partition(1)
>
> ○ b. multi(0)disk(1)rdisk(0)partition(1)
>
> ○ c. multi(0)disk(0)rdisk(0)partition(0)
>
> ○ d. multi(1)disk(0)rdisk(0)partition(0)
>
> ○ e. multi(0)disk(0)rdisk(1)partition(1)

Answer a is correct. Because each of the partitions mentioned in this question is the one and only on its drive, it must be "partition(1)." Therefore, answer c is incorrect. The partition that appears in BOOT.INI is the boot partition, which contains the Windows NT system files. This means that the correct answer is the ARC name for disk 1, where the Windows NT system files reside. The options for the first element in an ARC name are either **scsi** or **multi,** but **scsi** applies only to a genuine SCSI drive whose onboard BIOS has been disabled. Because **multi(*)** appears at the start of all five choices, all of them are correct to that point. The number that follows **multi** within the parentheses is the ordinal number of the disk controller to which the drive (or drives) is attached. Ordinal numbers start with 0; because there is only one controller mentioned, that immediately rules out answer d, because it alludes to a second controller (as denoted by multi(1)) to which neither drive in the question is attached. The **disk(*)** element in an ARC name designates the SCSI bus number for a SCSI drive with its BIOS disabled, and it is always zero for a non-SCSI disk. Therefore, answer b is incorrect. The **rdisk(*)** element in an ARC name indicates the SCSI logical unit number (LUN) or selects the drive that contains the operating system. The **rdisk(*)** element is always set to zero when an ARC name starts with scsi—because this one starts with **multi,** it indicates the position in the order in which drives are attached to the controller. Therefore, answer e is incorrect. Furthermore, the question indicates that the Windows NT system files are on the first disk, and boot files on the second disk. Because **rdisk** numbers begin with zero, this means that the Windows NT system files (the boot partition) live on the drive named **multi(0)disk(0)rdisk(0)partition(1)** and that the boot files (the system partition) live on the drive named **multi(0)disk(0)rdisk(1)partition(1)**. One small trick to ARC names is that although **scsi, multi, disk,** and **rdisk** all number ordinally, starting with zero, partition numbers start with 1. Therefore, any valid ARC name will never have zero as a value for **partition(*)**.

Question 2

> Jane has just installed a new device driver for her UPS on her Windows NT client, and now the machine will not boot properly. What is the easiest way to get the system to boot so the driver problem can be fixed?
>
> ○ a. Add the /NoSerialMice option to the BOOT.INI file.
>
> ○ b. Run the emergency repair process to restore the Windows NT Registry.
>
> ○ c. Boot Windows NT from the Emergency Repair Disk (ERD).
>
> ○ d. Select the Last Known Good Configuration option when it appears during the next reboot.

Answer d is correct. Answer d is the only option that really makes sense because it reverts Windows NT to the working configuration in effect the last time it booted successfully. Because this ignores anything changed since then—such as the errant UPS driver that may (or may not) be causing the problem—it brings the machine back up so Jane can try again from a relatively pristine state. First, we can dispense with a couple of red herrings: Answer a has nothing to do with getting an unbootable Windows NT machine running for troubleshooting purposes (even if it might be the fix that's finally enacted for a UPS that resets a PC when its serial port is probed). And, because it's impossible to boot from the ERD, answer c is bogus. Answer b sounds tempting, but it raises interesting questions about how the emergency repair process knows what to fix in the Registry, and how it can change the behavior of possibly damaged or mismatched driver software. It, too, is bogus.

Question 3

> Which ARC name in the following list correctly indicates that Windows NT boot files reside on the fourth partition on a SCSI disk drive whose on-board BIOS is disabled, with a SCSI bus ID of 1 on the first SCSI controller on the Windows NT machine?
>
> ○ a. scsi(0)disk(0)rdisk(0)partition(3)
>
> ○ b. scsi(0)disk(1)rdisk(0)partition(4)
>
> ○ c. scsi(0)disk(1)rdisk(1)partition(4)
>
> ○ d. multi(0)disk(0)rdisk(0)partition(4)

Answer b is correct. By the process of elimination, b must be the right answer. By breaking down the question, we discover that:

➤ The first SCSI controller with BIOS disabled translates into **scsi(0)**.

➤ The SCSI bus ID provides the value for **disk(*)** whenever the BIOS is disabled, which translates into **disk(1)**.

➤ Because the BIOS is disabled, **rdisk(*)** is always **rdisk(0)**.

➤ The value for partition equals its number on the drive; therefore, **partition(*)** translates into **partition(4)**.

Only b matches the entire string.

The secret to answering this question lies in knowing how to "unpack" its contents and what values to assign based on the information it contains. Partitions are numbered ordinally starting from one, so any correct answer must end in **partition(4)**. This automatically disqualifies answer a. Likewise, if the **scsi(*)** keyword begins an ARC name, the value for **rdisk** will always be zero; this disqualifies answer c. Any SCSI hard disk with its onboard BIOS disabled must begin with the string **scsi(*)**. This automatically disqualifies answer d.

Question 4

> Of the choices in the following list, what is the most likely cause of the following Windows NT error message at boot time?
>
> "Boot: Couldn't find NTLDR
> Please insert another disk"
>
> ○ a. An incorrect hard disk partition is set to active.
>
> ○ b. NTLDR is missing or corrupt.
>
> ○ c. A floppy was left in the A drive.
>
> ○ d. The designated system disk is damaged or inaccessible.

Answer c is correct. The most common cause of this error message, by far, is powering down a Windows NT machine with a floppy in the floppy drive. Because many PCs' BIOSs try to boot from any floppy inserted during bootup, this error occurs whenever you forget to remove a floppy before the machine is powered back up. Therefore, answer c is the most likely. Answers a, b, and d are possible, but nowhere near as likely to provoke this error message. When you see this error message, look for (and remove) a floppy and try again.

Question 5

> Windows NT can exist in a multiboot configuration with OS/2.
>
> ○ a. True
>
> ○ b. False

Answer a is correct. Windows NT can exist in a dual-boot system with OS/2.

Question 6

> When the System Administrator at XYZ Corp. tries to boot a newly reconfigured Windows NT machine, she gets an error message that reads:
>
> "I/O Error accessing boot sector file multi(0)disk(0)rdisk(0)partition(2): \bootsect.dos"
>
> What is the most expedient way to fix this problem?
>
> ○ a. Boot from the Last Known Good Configuration.
>
> ○ b. Start the computer from the Windows NT boot disks and copy BOOTSECT.DOS from another machine.
>
> ○ c. Boot the computer from the Emergency Repair Disk and follow the prompts.
>
> ○ d. Start the computer from the Windows NT boot disks and insert the Emergency Repair Disk when prompted.

Answer d is correct. The Windows NT boot disks permit the system to boot completely and the ERD can then regenerate a new BOOTSECT.DOS. Here, full-blown repair is needed because BOOTSECT.DOS stores partition information that is specific to the computer where it is generated. Because the machine won't boot completely, the Last Known Good Configuration option never appears; this eliminates answer a. Any copy of this file from another machine is useless; this disqualifies answer b. Because the ERD is not bootable, answer c is bogus.

Question 7

> Which of the following files must appear in the system partition of an Intel PC-based Windows NT machine if that machine uses one or more SCSI drives with their on-board BIOSs disabled? [Check all correct answers]
>
> ❑ a. BOOT.INI
>
> ❑ b. NTLDR
>
> ❑ c. NTOSKRNL.EXE
>
> ❑ d. NTBOOTDD.SYS
>
> ❑ e. OSLOADER.EXE

Answers a, b, and d are correct. The files that always appear in the system partition on a PC running Windows NT are BOOT.INI, NTDETECT.COM, and NTLDR. When a drive with its on-board BIOS disabled is used as the boot or system partition, an additional file, NTBOOTDD.SYS, is also required. Answer e applies only to RISC machines (that is, non-Intel CPUs) running Windows NT; answer c names a file that appears in the default directory where the Windows NT system files reside (usually specified as winnt_root\system32 or as the common default—winnt\system32).

Question 8

XYZ Corp. has just added a new IDE hard drive and controller to a Windows NT machine. The machine continues to boot from its SCSI drive, which has its BIOS disabled. Each drive has only a single primary partition. Of the following options, which is the correct ARC name for the machine's system partition as listed in the BOOT.INI?

○ a. scsi(0)disk(0)rdisk(0)partition(1)

○ b. scsi(0)disk(1)rdisk(0)partition(0)

○ c. scsi(1)disk(0)rdisk(0)partition(1)

○ d. scsi(1)disk(1)rdisk(0)partition(1)

○ e. scsi(0)disk(0)rdisk(1)partition(1)

Answer a is correct. By default, **disk(0)** is the correct value (because no replacement bus number was specified); this disqualifies answer b (and d). By the process of elimination, this leaves answer a, which can be constructed as follows:

➤ **scsi(*)** becomes **scsi(0)** because the BIOS is disabled, and it is the first and only SCSI controller.

➤ **disk(*)** becomes **disk(0)** because that's the default assignment and no overriding values were supplied.

➤ **rdisk(*)** must be **rdisk(0)** because the BIOS is disabled on a SCSI controller; therefore, this value is ignored.

➤ **partition(*)** becomes **partition(1)** because it is the first and only partition on the drive, and partition numbering begins with one.

Once again, a working knowledge of ARC name construction comes in handy. Because the drive in question is SCSI, but its on-board BIOS is disabled, the ARC name must begin with **scsi(*)**. Because there is only one SCSI controller and numbering begins with zero, it must begin with **scsi(0)**; this disqualifies answers c and d immediately. For ARC names that begin with **scsi(*)**, only the **disk(*)** keyword is significant. In such cases, **rdisk(*)** is always **rdisk(0)**; this disqualifies answer e. Here again, disks are numbered by their SCSI bus numbers, starting with zero.

Question 9

After modifying the Registry, a Windows NT machine will no longer boot. What is the easiest way to get the machine to boot?

○ a. Start the computer from the Windows NT boot disks and restore the Registry from a backup.

○ b. Start the computer from the Windows NT boot disks and select the Emergency Repair option.

○ c. Start the computer from the Emergency Repair Disk and follow the prompts.

○ d. Choose the Last Known Good Configuration option when it appears during boot up.

Answer d is correct. The easiest approach to this kind of problem, be it caused by untoward edits to the Registry or by installation of drivers or new system components, is to choose the Last Known Good Configuration option during bootup. Answers a and b are incorrect; they might produce the same results eventually, but they're not nearly as easy (and perhaps not as up-to-date as the Last Known Good Configuration). Answer c is incorrect because you can't boot from the ERD.

Question 10

> While Windows NT is booting, the following error message appears right after the Last Known Good Configuration prompt:
>
> "Windows NT could not start because the following file is missing or corrupt:
>
> \Winnt\system32\ntoskrnl.exe.
> Please reinstall a copy of the above file."
>
> You're certain this file is present even though the boot process cannot locate it. What's the most likely cause of this error message?
>
> ○ a. Missing NTLDR
>
> ○ b. Missing BOOTSECT.DOS
>
> ○ c. Missing NTDETECT.COM
>
> ○ d. Missing BOOT.INI

Answer d is correct. It's the absence of BOOT.INI that makes the difference because it's the file that indicates where the other files are located. The most common cause of this error is setting an invalid partition as active in Disk Administrator—that is, one that does not include any of the requisite Windows NT boot files. When this happens, none of these files is present on the designated boot partition. This message will also appear if the ARC name for the NTOSKRNL.EXE file is incorrect in BOOT.INI (which is sometimes specified as the **default=** entry in the **[boot loader]** section, and always in at least two entries in the **[operating systems]** section).

Need To Know More?

Perkins, Charles, Matthew Strebe, and James Chellis: *MCSE: NT Workstation Study Guide, 2nd Edition*. Sybex Network Press, San Francisco, CA, 1998. ISBN 0-7821-2223-X. Chapter 16 has complete details on the boot process of NT, including altering the BOOT.INI and multiboot configurations.

Tittel, Ed, Christa Anderson, and David Johnson: *NT Workstation 4 Exam Prep*. Coriolis, Scottsdale, AZ, 1998. ISBN: 1-57610-238-6. Chapter 15 covers the various Windows NT boot process and related topics in great detail.

Search the TechNet CD (or its online version through **www.microsoft.com**) and the *Windows NT Workstation Resource Kit* CD using the keywords "boot," "BOOT.INI," "boot troubleshooting," and "ARC names."

Troubleshooting

· ·

Terms you'll need to understand:

√ Troubleshooting

√ Boot Failures

√ NTLDR

√ NTOSKRNL

√ BOOT.INI

√ BOOTSECT.DOS

√ NTDETECT.COM

√ Event Viewer

√ Last Known Good
   Configuration (LKGC)

√ Registry

√ Emergency Repair
   Disk (ERD)

√ Dr. Watson

√ Kernel Debugger

Techniques you'll need to master:

√ Understanding the troubleshooting process

√ Troubleshooting media errors,
   domain controller communication difficulties, stop
   message errors or halt on blue
   screen, hardware problems,
   and dependency failures

√ Recognizing installation
   failures

√ Troubleshooting boot failures

√ Using Windows NT's built-in
   repair tools

The arena of troubleshooting Windows NT is both extensive and immense. In this chapter, we focus on troubleshooting issues including installation failures, repair tools, printing solutions, and other pertinent issues. Not all the troubleshooting details are listed in this chapter; some useful trouble-shooting details can be found in the chapters that focus on these topics, such as printing and booting.

Installation Failures

During the initial installation of Windows NT, five common types of errors can occur: media errors, domain controller communication difficulties, STOP message errors or halt on blue screen, hardware problems, and dependency failures. The following is a short synopsis of each type of error:

➤ **Media errors** Media errors are problems with the distribution CD-ROM, the copy of the CD-ROM hosted on a network drive, or the communications between the installation and distribution files. The only way to resolve a media error is to attempt to switch media, such as switching from one server's CD-ROM to another or copying the CD-ROM files to a network drive. If media errors are encountered, always restart the installation from the beginning.

➤ **Domain controller communication difficulties** Not being able to communicate with the existing domain controller prevents the current installation from joining the domain. This error is often due to a mistyped name, a network failure, or because the domain controller is offline. Verify the viability of the domain controller directly and with other workstations (if present).

➤ **STOP message errors or halt on blue screen** STOP messages and halting on the blue screen during installation are usually caused by using the wrong driver for a controller card. If any information about an error is presented to you, try to determine if the proper driver is being used. If not (or if you can't tell), double-check your hardware and the drivers required to operate them under Windows NT.

➤ **Hardware problems** Hardware problems should occur only if you failed to verify your hardware with the Hardware Compatibility List (HCL) or if a physical defect has surfaced in previously operational devices. In such cases, replacing the device is the only solution. However, it is not uncommon for a device to be improperly configured or installed. Always double-check your hardware setup before purchasing a replacement.

➤ **Dependency failures** Dependency failures are when one or more dependent services fail due to the absence of a foundation service, hardware, or a driver. An example of a dependency failure is when the Server and Workstation services fail because the NIC fails to initialize properly. If Windows NT boots with such errors, always check the Event log.

Now that we have covered some caveats pertaining to installation, let's move on to discuss Windows NT's built-in repair tools.

Repair Tools

Fortunately, Windows NT does not leave you high and dry when you encounter errors. It has a handful of invaluable tools to repair and correct operational difficulties. In the next few sections, we detail how to use the Event Viewer, Last Known Good Configuration, Registry, and Emergency Repair Disk (ERD).

Event Viewer

The Event Viewer, located in Programs|Administrative Tools, is used to inspect the three logs automatically created by Windows NT. These logs are:

➤ **System** Records information and alerts about Windows NT's internal processes

➤ **Security** Records security-related events

➤ **Application** Records Windows NT application events, alerts, and system messages

Each log records a different type of information, but all the logs collect the same information about each event: date, time, source, category, event, user ID, and computer. Also, each event recorded has either an error code number or a detailed description with a memory HEX buffer capture.

Most system errors, including STOP errors that result in the blue screen, are recorded in the System log. This allows you to review the time and circumstances around a system failure.

Last Known Good Configuration

The Last Known Good Configuration (LKGC) is a recording Windows NT makes of all the Registry settings that existed the last time a user successfully logged on to the server. Every time a logon is completed, Windows

NT records a new LKGC. If a system error occurs or the Registry becomes corrupted so that booting or logging in is not possible, the LKGC can be used to return to a previously operational state. The LKGC is accessed during bootup when the message "Press the spacebar to boot with the Last Known Good Configuration" displays. A menu will appear from which you can se-lect to load using the LKGC (by pressing L) or other stored configurations.

The Registry

Editing the Registry by hand should be the last resort. A single, improperly configured Registry entry can render a Windows NT installation unusable. There are two Registry editing utilities: REGEDIT and REGEDT32. Both of these utilities must be launched from the Run command or a DOS prompt. REGEDIT displays all the hives of the Registry in a single display window, and the entire Registry can be searched at one time. REGEDT32 displays each of the five hives in separate display windows, but it offers more security- and control-related functions.

 It is a good idea to regularly back up your Registry. This can be done using:

➤ Windows NT Backup (on the local machine)

➤ Disk Administrator (**SYSTEM** key only)

➤ Either Registry editing tool (REGEDIT or REGEDT32)

➤ The REGBACK utility from the *Windows NT Workstation Resource Kit*

The best times to make a backup are just before and after any significant changes are made to your system, such as hardware installation, software installation, or service pack application. If Windows NT fails to operate properly but boots up, you can attempt a repair by restoring the Registry from a backup.

You should note a few things about working with the Registry. When you edit the Registry, you are working with it in memory. This means the instant you make a Registry change, it goes into effect. However, in some cases, a reboot is required to correct memory settings and launch applications to fully comply with the changes. It is always a good idea to reboot after editing the Registry. Also, when a key of the Registry is saved (or backed up), you capture all the subcontents of that key. This is important to remember when restoring portions of the Registry from backup. All subkeys below the point at which restoration occurs will also be overwritten by the saved version. All changes made since the backup will be lost in the sections restored.

Emergency Repair Disk

Emergency Repair Disk (ERD) is the miniature first-aid kit for Windows NT. This single floppy contains all the files needed to repair system partition and many boot partition problems. The ERD is most often used to repair or replace files that are critical to Windows NT's boot process. An ERD is usually created during installation, but additional and updated ERDs can be created using the RDISK.EXE utility. At the Run command, **RDISK /S** forces Windows NT to save all current Registry settings in memory to \Winnt\System32\ Config. You are then prompted for a preformatted disk. The ERD contains the files listed in Table 18.1.

The ERD does not contain the entire Registry, but just enough to fix the most common errors. To use the ERD to make repairs, you need the three setup disks used to install Windows NT. The repair process is depicted in the following steps:

1. Reboot the computer using the Windows NT setup disks 1 and 2.

2. Select "R" for repair. A menu appears containing the following options:

   ➤ Inspect Registry files

   ➤ Inspect startup environment

   ➤ Verify Windows NT system files

   ➤ Inspect boot sector

3. Deselect any options you do not wish to use; then continue.

4. Insert disk 3 and the ERD when prompted.

Table 18.1 The contents of an ERD.	
File	**Contents**
SYSTEM._	HKEY_LOCAL_MACHINE\SYSTEM compressed
SOFTWARE._	HKEY_LOCAL_MACHINE\SOFTWARE compressed
SECURITY._	HKEY_LOCAL_MACHINE\SECURITY compressed
SAM._	HKEY_LOCAL_MACHINE\SAM compressed
NTUSER.DA_	Default profile, compressed
AUTOEXEC.NT	Winnt\system32\autoexec.nt
CONFIG.NT	Winnt\system32\config.nt
SETUP.LOG	List of installed files and their checksums
DEFAULT._	HKEY_USERS\DEFAULT compressed

Boot Failures

Boot failures are problems during the startup of Windows NT.

NTLDR Error Message

If the NTLDR is damaged or missing, the following error occurs:

```
BOOT: Couldn't find NTLDR. Please insert another disk.
```

Resolve using ERD to repair or replace.

Boot Error Due To Floppy In Drive A:

If a Windows NT bootable floppy with a defective BOOT.INI is in Drive A:, the following error occurs:

```
BOOT: Couldn't find NTLDR. Please insert another disk.
```

If the floppy is not bootable, the following error occurs:

```
Invalid system disk. Replace the disk, and then press any key.
```

In either case, eject the floppy and then reboot or press any key.

NTOSKRNL Missing Error Message

If NTOSKRNL is corrupt, missing, or the BOOT.INI points to the wrong partition, the following error occurs:

```
Windows NT could not start because the following file is missing
or corrupt:
\winnt\System32\ntoskrnl.exe
Please re-install a copy of the above file.
```

Repair the NTOSKRNL file using the ERD repair process, or edit and correct the BOOT.INI.

BOOT.INI Missing Error Message

If no BOOT.INI is present, NTLDR will launch Windows NT from \winnt of the current partition. If this fails, the following error occurs:

```
BOOT: Couldn't find NTLDR.
Please insert another disk.
```

To alleviate this problem, replace the BOOT.INI file from a backup or use the ERD to repair.

BOOTSECT.DOS Missing Error Message

If the BOOTSECT.DOS file is not present to boot to MS-DOS or another operating system (not Windows NT), the following error message appears:

```
I/O Error accessing boot sector file
multi(0)disk(0)rdisk(0)partition(1):\bootsect.dos
```

This indicates that the BOOT.INI file has been changed, the partition numbering has changed, or the partition is missing, inactive, or inaccessible. To repair or replace the BOOTSECT.DOS file, use the ERD repair procedure.

NTDETECT.COM Missing Error Message

If the NTDETECT.COM file is not present, the following error message appears:

```
NTDETECT V1.0 Checking Hardware...
NTDETECT failed
```

This error must be repaired with the ERD repair process.

Printing Solutions

When you're working with printers, there seems to be an infinite number of issues to resolve before normal operation can be restored after an error. Many printer problems are simple or obvious, so always check the obvious solutions before moving on to more complicated ones. Here is a short list of tasks you can perform when digging for a printer solution:

➤ Always check the physical aspects of the printer—cable, power, paper, toner, and so on.

➤ Check the logical printer on both the client and the server.

➤ Check the print queue for stalled jobs.

➤ Reinstall the printer driver to be sure it hasn't become corrupted.

➤ Attempt to print from a different application or a different client.

➤ Print using Administrator access.

➤ Stop and restart the spooler using the Services applet.

➤ Check the status and CPU usage of SPOOLSS.EXE using the Task Manager.

➤ Check the free space on the drive hosting the spooler file and change its destination.

A number of topics don't fall into any one category; the following sections discuss this hodgepodge of troubleshooting considerations.

Miscellaneous Troubleshooting Issues

Topics included here encompass permissions problems, re-creating setup disks, the Master Boot Record, and other troubleshooting issues.

Permissions Problems

If you suspect a permissions problem, use the Administrator account or temporarily add the user account to the Administrators group. Double-check group memberships for conflicting access levels—especially No Access. Check the access control list (ACL) on the object in question for group and No Access assignments. Check the permissions on the share if appropriate. Check user, group, or computer policies for access restrictions.

Re-Creating The Setup Disks

If you need a new set of installation floppies, run the WINNT.EXE (or WINNT32.EXE) program from the installation CD-ROM with the /ox parameter. This creates the three floppies without initializing the actual installation process. However, you'll need to preformat the disk beforehand.

Master Boot Record

If the Master Boot Record (MBR) fails on the system partition (the section of the disk that contains BOOT.INI, NTLOADER, and NTDETECT), the ERD will not help with its restoration. Instead, you'll need to use the first disk from DOS 6.0 (or higher). Executing **FDISK /MBR** re-creates the MBR and allows the system to boot to DOS. Next, you'll need to boot from the startup disks, select the repair option, and instruct it to rebuild the MBR.

Dr. Watson

Dr. Watson is Windows NT's application error debugger. It detects application errors, diagnoses such errors, and logs the diagnostic information. Most of the information gathered by Dr. Watson is useful only when working with a Microsoft technical professional to diagnose an application error. Data captured by Dr. Watson is stored in the DRWTSN32.LOG file. Dr. Watson can also be used to create a binary crash dump file of the memory where the failing application operates.

Dr. Watson launches itself automatically whenever an application error occurs. However, to configure Dr. Watson, you can launch it by executing DRWTSN32 at the command prompt or in the Run dialog box. Dr. Watson's configuration options are fairly obvious; the only two that might cause some confusion are Dump Symbol Table and Dump All Thread Contexts, which are discussed in the following:

➤ **Dump Symbol Table** Adds the corresponding symbol data to the dump file, greatly increasing its size.

➤ **Dump All Thread Contexts** Forces a dump file to be created for all active threads, not just those owned by the failed application.

BOOT.INI Switches

To improve the bootup's troubleshooting capabilities, you can use one of the following switches after each OS line in the BOOT.INI file (remember those have the ARC name followed by the displayable name in quotes):

➤ **/BASEVIDEO** Boots using the standard VGA video driver.

➤ **/BAUDRATE=**n Sets the debugging communication baud rate when using the Kernel Debugger. The defaults are 9,600 for a modem and 19,200 for a null modem cable.

➤ **/CRASHDEBUG** Loads the debugger into memory, where it remains inactive unless a Kernel error occurs.

➤ **/DEBUG** Loads the debugger into memory to be activated by a host debugger connected to the computer.

➤ **/DEBUGPORT=** com$x$ Sets the debugging COM port.

➤ **/MAXMEM:n** Sets the maximum amount of RAM Windows NT can use.

➤ **/NODEBUG** Indicates that no debugging information is being used.

➤ **/NOSERIALMICE=[COM*x* | COM*x,y,z*...]** Disables serial mouse detection of the specified COM port(s).

➤ **/SOS** Specifies to display each driver name when it is loaded.

VGA Mode

If you set your video driver to something that prevents a readable display, you can select VGA Mode from the boot menu to boot using the standard VGA driver. Then, you can modify the display drivers to correct the problem.

NTDETECT Debugged

If NTDETECT fails to detect the proper hardware, it might be corrupted or damaged, or your hardware might not be functioning properly. A debugged or checked version of NTDETECT is stored on the CD-ROM in the Support\Debug\I386 directory. First, rename NTDETECT.COM to NTDETECT.BAK; then copy the file named NTDETECT.CHK to the system partition and rename it NTDETECT.COM. Now, you can reboot. This version of NTDETECT gives a verbose display of all detection activities to help you isolate the problem. NTDETECT.COM has the attributes of Hidden, System, and Read-Only set. You need to deselect these attributes before renaming the file and then reset them after the renaming process. Once you've solved the hardware detection problem, return the original NTDETECT from NTDETECT.BAK or the ERD.

ESDI Hard Drives

Some ESDI hard drives are not supported by Windows NT. ESDI hard drives are pre-IDE-type storage devices that have the capability of being low-level formatted with various sector values per track. Due to special formatting geometry and drive controllers, Windows NT may be capable of accessing cylinders beyond 1,024. If Windows NT has direct access to the cylinders above 1,024, only Windows NT (and not DOS) can access these areas. If the controller performs a transparent translation for these cylinders, both Windows NT and DOS can access above 1,024 cylinder areas.

Determining whether Windows NT can even use an ESDI disk cannot be done until an installation is attempted. If Windows NT fails to install properly on an ESDI disk, a "Fatal System Error:0x0000006b" message will be displayed after NTLDR starts. When this occurs, you can deduce that Windows NT does not support the ESDI drive.

Now that we've wrapped up many troubleshooting loose ends, let's look at some advanced troubleshooting issues.

Creating A Boot Floppy

A boot floppy can be used to boot your system in the event of a boot failure with your system partition. That boot floppy should contain the following files:

➤ BOOT.INI

➤ NTLDR

➤ NTDETECT.COM

➤ NTBOOTDD.SYS Only if you are using a SCSI controller with BIOS translation disabled (or missing)

➤ BOOTSECT.DOS Only if you need to boot into MS-DOS or another operating system present on your computer

You may need to edit the BOOT.INI file to match parameters and the location of boot and system partitions.

Advanced Troubleshooting

In addition to the tools and utilities listed earlier in this chapter, there are two more troubleshooting mechanisms that require a professional support engineer to interpret them. These mechanisms—blue screen and memory dump—are listed here only for your general understanding.

Blue Screen

No matter what "they" tell you, Windows NT has general protection faults (GPFs), but they aren't called that. When a GPF occurs under Windows NT, the "blue screen of death" appears. This is a test display of the STOP message error. Lots of details are included on this screen, such as the location of the error, the type of error, and whether a memory dump is created. Unfortunately, most of the data will appear in hexadecimal or a strange acronym shorthand you won't be able to read.

Memory Dump

A memory dump is the act of writing the entire contents of memory to a file when a STOP error occurs. The contents of this file can be inspected to determine the cause of the failure. A machine with 2 GB of memory can generate up to a 2 GB dump file. Memory dumps are configured on the Startup/Shutdown tab of the System applet. The options are:

➤ Write An Event To The System Log

➤ Send An Administrative Alert

➤ Write A Dump File

➤ Automatically Reboot

The default location and name of the memory dump file is Winnt\ MEMORY.DMP. The DUMPEXAM.EXE utility can be used to view the contents of a memory dump file. However, most of the contents will require a Microsoft technical professional to interpret them.

Practice Questions

Question 1

Which of the following can be corrected by the repair process using the three installation disks and a recent Emergency Repair Disk? [Check all correct answers]

- ❏ a. Boot sector corruption
- ❏ b. Unable to locate Master Boot Record
- ❏ c. NTLDR not found
- ❏ d. Corrupt NTOSKRNL

Answers a, c, and d are correct. The ERD repair process can often correct boot sector problems, replace the NTLDR, and repair the NTOSKRNL. Answer b is incorrect. The MBR cannot be repaired with the ERD or the installation floppies—that requires a DOS setup disk.

Question 2

Your Windows NT Workstation experiences a STOP error due to a runaway process from a custom application developed in-house. Where can information about this error be found once the machine has been rebooted?

- ○ a. Kernel Debugger
- ○ b. Performance Monitor
- ○ c. Event Viewer
- ○ d. Windows NT Diagnostics

Answer c is correct. The Event Viewer can be used to view the System log where all STOP errors are recorded. The Kernel Debugger is a troubleshooting tool found on Windows NT Server, not Windows NT Workstation. Also, it can view STOP error information only when specifically configured and installed on two connected machines. Therefore, answer a is incorrect. The Performance Monitor and Windows NT Diagnostics cannot record any information about a STOP error. Therefore, answers b and d are incorrect.

Question 3

> Which two parameter switches are present by default on the VGA
> Mode selection ARC name line in the BOOT.INI file? [Check all
> correct answers]
>
> ❏ a. **/NODEBUG**
>
> ❏ b. **/BASEVIDEO**
>
> ❏ c. **/NOSERIALMICE**
>
> ❏ d. **/SOS**
>
> ❏ e. **/VGAVIDEO**

Answers b and d are correct. The parameters **/BASEVIDEO** and **/SOS** are
present on the VGA Mode line by default. The parameters **/NODEBUG**
and **/NOSERIALMICE** are not present on the VGA Mode line by default. Therefore, answers a and c are incorrect. The parameter **/VGAVIDEO**
is not a valid parameter. Therefore, answer e is incorrect.

Question 4

> The **SYSTEM** Registry key contains errors. You do not have a
> recent ERD, but you do have a copy of the **SYSTEM** key itself on
> floppy. Which of the following programs should you use to
> restore the **SYSTEM** key from the floppy?
>
> ○ a. Disk Administrator
>
> ○ b. The System applet
>
> ○ c. User Manager
>
> ○ d. The three Windows NT setup disks

Answer a is correct. The Disk Administrator is the correct utility to use to
restore the **SYSTEM** key if you have a stored copy. The System applet and
User Manager do not offer Registry restoration options. Therefore, answers b and c are incorrect. Because no ERD is available, the setup disks
cannot be used.

Question 5

> Your Windows NT Workstation has recently been experiencing numerous STOP errors. In order to help pinpoint the problem, where should you configure Windows NT so that a memory dump will occur before the system reboots?
>
> ○ a. The Network applet's properties
>
> ○ b. The recovery option in Dr. Watson
>
> ○ c. The Tracking tab of the Task Manager
>
> ○ d. On the Startup/Shutdown tab of the System applet

Answer d is correct. The Startup/Shutdown tab of the System applet is the location of the memory dump options for Windows NT. The Network applet does not offer memory dump configuration options. Therefore, answer a is incorrect. Dr. Watson is used to perform memory dumps on application faults, not for Windows NT's system itself. Therefore, answer b is incorrect. The Task Manager does not have a Tracking tab nor does it offer memory dump options. Therefore, answer c is incorrect.

Question 6

> After installing a new SCSI driver, you discover that Windows NT will not successfully boot. No other changes have been made to the system. What is the easiest way to return the system to a state where it will boot properly?
>
> ○ a. Use the repair process with the ERD
>
> ○ b. Use the Last Known Good Configuration
>
> ○ c. Configure a memory dump
>
> ○ d. Boot to DOS and run the setup utility to change the installed drivers

Answer b is correct. The LKGC is the fastest way to return to a bootable configuration, especially because only a single change was made to the system. The ERD repair process will restore the system so that it can boot; however, this requires a recent ERD and all three installation disks. In addition, this process can take at least 30 minutes. Therefore, answer a is incorrect. A memory dump will not only be useless to resolving this problem, it cannot even be configured due to the inability to boot. Therefore, answer c is incorrect. There is no DOS setup utility in Windows NT; that utility was available only for Windows 3.x. Therefore, answer d is incorrect.

Question 7

> During the boot process, you receive the following error message:
>
> "Windows NT could not start because the following file is missing or corrupt: \winnt\system32\ntoskrnl.exe. Please reinstall a copy of the above file."
>
> What are the possible explanations for this error? [Check all correct answers]
>
> ❏ a. NTOSKRNL.EXE is missing
> ❏ b. BOOT.INI points to the wrong partition
> ❏ c. NTOSKRNL.EXE is corrupt
> ❏ d. BOOT.INI file is missing

Answers a, b, and c are correct. When the boot process cannot find NTOSKRNL.EXE, it does not indicate if the problem is with the file itself, its location, or the pointers to it. Therefore, answers a and c are correct. If the BOOT.INI file was actually missing, a different error would appear stating such. Therefore, answer b is correct. Without the BOOT.INI pointer, there's no mechanism to seek the NTOSKRNL.EXE file, so that error message would not appear. Therefore, answer d is incorrect.

Question 8

> Which of the files on the ERD lists the files installed during setup and the checksums of each of these files?
>
> ○ a. INSTALLED.DAT
> ○ b. CONFIG.NT
> ○ c. DEFAULT._
> ○ d. SOFTWARE._
> ○ e. SETUP.LOG

Trick! question

Answer e is correct. The file SETUP.LOG is the only file on the ERD that lists the files installed during setup and their corresponding checksums. The file INSTALLED.DAT is not present on an ERD. Therefore, answer a is incorrect. The files CONFIG.NT, DEFAULT._, and SOFTWARE._ are all on an ERD, but they do not contain installed file and checksum information. Therefore, answers b, c, and d are incorrect. To get this right, you must not only know which files are present on the ERD, but also which ones provide checksum information.

Question 9

Your Windows NT Workstation experiences yet another STOP error. Fortunately, you enabled the memory dump option through the System applet. What utility can you use to view the contents of the DMP file?

○ a. Event Viewer

○ b. Debug Inspector

○ c. DUMPEXAM.EXE

○ d. Windows NT Diagnostics

Answer c is correct. Only DUMPEXAM.EXE can be used to view the contents of DMP files. The Event Viewer and Windows NT Diagnostics cannot be used to view the contents of a memory dump file. Therefore, answers a and d are incorrect. The Debug Inspector does not exist. Therefore, answer b is incorrect.

Question 10

Which of the following are valid ways to make full or partial backups of the Registry? [Check all correct answers]

❑ a. Create an ERD using the **rdisk /s** command

❑ b. Use Windows NT Backup

❑ c. Copy all the contents of the \Winnt\System32\Config directory

❑ d. Use the Disk Administrator

❑ e. Use REGEDT32

Answers a, b, c, d, and e are all correct. All these methods are valid ways to create full or partial backups of the Windows NT Registry. However, note that the files stored in \Winnt\System32\Config are only as current as the last reboot or the execution of **rdisk /s**.

Need To Know More?

Perkins, Charles, Matthew Strebe, and James Chellis: *MCSE: NT Workstation Study Guide, 2nd Edition*. Sybex Network Press, San Francisco, CA, 1998. ISBN 0-7821-2223-X. Chapter 17 has extensive coverage of NT troubleshooting techniques.

Tittel, Ed, Christa Anderson, and David Johnson: *NT Workstation 4 Exam Prep*. Coriolis, Scottsdale, AZ, 1998. ISBN: 1-57610-238-6. Chapter 16 includes comprehensive coverage for most Windows NT Troubleshooting needs.

Searching the TechNet CD (or its online version through **www.microsoft.com**) and the *Windows NT Workstation Resource Kit* CD using the keyword "troubleshooting" will result in numerous hits on relevant materials. However, for more focused searching, use keywords associated with the topic in question, such as "boot," "installation," "printing," "Emergency Repair Disk," or "Registry."

Sample Test #1

In this chapter, we provide pointers to help you develop a successful test-taking strategy, including how to choose proper answers, how to decode ambiguity, how to work within the Microsoft testing framework, how to decide what you need to memorize, and how to prepare for the test. At the end of the chapter, we include 60 questions on subject matter pertinent to Microsoft Exam 70-073: "Implementing and Supporting Microsoft Windows NT Workstation 4.0." In Chapter 21, you will find another complete sample test as well, followed by another answer key. In addition, we provide you with some practice scenario questions in the Scenarios section following Chapter 22.

Also, remember that you can take adaptive practice exams on Windows NT Workstation 4.0 online at **www.coriolis.com/cip/core4rev/** to help you prepare even more. Good luck!

Questions, Questions, Questions

There should be no doubt in your mind that you are facing a test full of specific and pointed questions. Currently, the Windows NT Workstation 4.0 test may be either fixed-length, short form, adaptive, or a combination of short-form and adaptive. The software should tell you which type the test is as you begin the exam. See Chapter 1 for more information on the various exam types.

No matter which type of test you take, for this exam, questions belong to one of five basic types:

➤ Multiple-choice with a single answer

➤ Multiple-choice with multiple answers

➤ Multipart with a single answer

➤ Multipart with multiple answers

➤ Pick one or more spots on a graphic

Always take the time to read a question at least twice before selecting an answer, and always look for an Exhibit button as you examine each question. Exhibits include graphics information related to a question. An exhibit is usually a screen capture of program output or GUI information that you must examine to analyze the question's contents and formulate an answer. Thus, the Exhibit button brings up graphics and charts used to help explain a question, provide additional data, or illustrate page layout or program behavior.

Not every question has only one answer; many questions require multiple answers. Therefore, it's important to read each question carefully, to determine how many answers are necessary or possible, and to look for additional hints or instructions when selecting answers. Such instructions often occur in brackets, immediately following the question itself (as they do for all multiple-choice, multiple-answer questions).

Picking Proper Answers

Obviously, the only way to pass any exam is to select enough of the right answers to obtain a passing score. However, Microsoft's exams are not standardized like the SAT and GRE exams; they are far more diabolical and convoluted. In some cases, questions are strangely worded, and deciphering them can be a real challenge. In those cases, you may need to rely on answer-elimination skills. Almost always, at least one answer out of the possible choices for a question can be eliminated immediately because it matches one of these conditions:

➤ The answer does not apply to the situation.

➤ The answer describes a nonexistent issue, an invalid option, or an imaginary state.

➤ The answer may be eliminated because of the question itself.

After you eliminate all answers that are obviously wrong, you can apply your retained knowledge to eliminate further answers. Look for items that sound correct but refer to actions, commands, or features that are not present or not available in the situation that the question describes.

If you're still faced with a blind guess among two or more potentially correct answers, reread the question. Try to picture how each of the possible remaining answers would alter the situation. Be especially sensitive to terminology; sometimes, the choice of words ("remove" instead of "disable") can make the difference between a right answer and a wrong one.

Only when you've exhausted your ability to eliminate answers, but remain unclear about which of the remaining possibilities is correct should you guess at an answer. An unanswered question offers you no points, but guessing gives you at least some chance of getting a question right; just don't be too hasty when making a blind guess.

If you're taking a fixed-length test, you can wait until the last round of reviewing marked questions (just as you're about to run out of time, or out of unanswered questions) before you start making guesses. If you're taking an adaptive test, you'll have to guess to move on to the next question if you can't figure out an answer some other way. Either way, guessing should be your technique of last resort!

Decoding Ambiguity

Microsoft exams have a reputation for including questions that can be difficult to interpret, confusing, or ambiguous. In our experience with numerous exams, we consider this reputation to be completely justified. The Microsoft exams are tough, and deliberately made that way.

The only way to beat Microsoft at its own game is to be prepared. You'll discover that many exam questions test your knowledge of things that are not directly related to the issue raised by a question. This means that the answers you must choose from, even incorrect ones, are just as much a part of the skill assessment as the question itself. If you don't know something about most aspects of Windows NT Workstation 4.0, you may not be able to eliminate obviously wrong answers because they relate to a different area of Windows NT Workstation than the one that's addressed by the question at hand. In other words, the more you know about the software, the easier it will be for you to tell right from wrong.

Questions often give away their answers, but you have to be Sherlock Holmes to see the clues. Often, subtle hints appear in the question text in such a way that they seem almost irrelevant to the situation. You must realize that each question is a test unto itself and that you need to inspect and successfully navigate each question to pass the exam. Look for small clues, such as the mention of times, group permissions and names, and configuration settings. Little things like these can point at the right answer if properly understood; if missed, they can leave you facing a blind guess.

Another common difficulty with certification exams is vocabulary. Microsoft has an uncanny knack for naming some utilities and features entirely obviously in some cases, and completely inanely in other instances. Be sure to brush up on the key terms presented at the beginning of each chapter. You may also want to read through the Glossary at the end of this book the day before you take the test.

Working Within The Framework

The test questions appear in random order, and many elements or issues that receive mention in one question may also crop up in other questions. It's not uncommon to find that an incorrect answer to one question is the correct answer to another question, or vice-versa. Take the time to read every answer to each question, even if you recognize the correct answer to a question immediately. That extra reading may spark a memory, or remind you about a Windows NT Workstation feature or function, that helps you on another question elsewhere in the exam.

If you're taking a fixed-length test, you can revisit any question as many times as you like. If you're uncertain of the answer to a question, check the box that's provided to mark it for easy return later on. You should also mark questions you think may offer information that you can use to answer other questions. On fixed-length tests, we usually mark somewhere between 25 and 50 percent of the questions on exams we've taken. The testing software is designed to let you mark every question if you choose; use this framework to your advantage. Everything you will want to see again should be marked; the testing software can then help you return to marked questions quickly and easily.

For fixed-length tests, we strongly recommend that you first read through the entire test quickly, before getting caught up in answering individual questions. This will help to jog your memory as you review the potential answers and can help identify questions that you want to mark for easy access to their contents. It will also let you identify and mark the really tricky questions for easy return as well. The key is to make a quick pass over the territory to begin with, so that you know what you're up against; and then to survey that territory more thoroughly on a second pass, when you can begin to answer all questions systematically and consistently.

If you're taking an adaptive test, and you see something in a question or one of the answers that jogs your memory on a topic, or that you feel you should record if the topic appears in another question, write it down on your piece of paper. Just because you can't go back to a question in an adaptive test doesn't mean you can't take notes on what you see early in the test, in hopes that it might help you later in the test.

For adaptive tests, don't be afraid to take notes on what you see in various questions. Sometimes, what you record from one question, especially if it's not as familiar as it should be or reminds you of the name or use of some utility or interface details, can help you on other questions later on.

Deciding What To Memorize

The amount of memorization you must undertake for an exam depends on how well you remember what you've read, and how well you know the software by heart. If you are a visual thinker, and you can see the drop-down menus and dialog boxes in your head, you won't need to memorize as much as someone who's less visually oriented. The tests will stretch your recollection of commands and functions of Windows NT Workstation.

At a minimum, you'll want to memorize the following kinds of information:

➤ The various types of utilities and settings needed to handle unattended installations of Windows NT Workstation

➤ How to install, configure, and manage Windows NT Workstation networking protocols and functions

➤ Managing 16-bit DOS and Windows applications within the Windows NT Workstation environment

➤ Understand how Windows NT boots, what files are involved, and how to troubleshoot Windows NT boot problems

If you work your way through this book while sitting at a machine with Windows NT Workstation 4.0 installed, and try to manipulate this environment's features and functions as they're discussed throughout, you should have little or no difficulty mastering this material. Also, don't forget that The Cram Sheet at the front of the book is designed to capture the material that is most important to memorize; use this to guide your studies as well.

Preparing For The Test

The best way to prepare for the test—after you've studied—is to take at least one practice exam. We've included one here in this chapter for that reason, and another in Chapter 21; the test questions are located in the pages that follow (and unlike the preceding chapters in this book, the answers don't follow the questions immediately; you'll have to flip to Chapters 20 and 22 to review the answers separately).

Give yourself 90 minutes to take the exam, keep yourself on the honor system, and don't look at earlier text in the book or jump ahead to the answer key. When your time is up, or you've finished the questions, you can check your work in Chapter 20 (or 22). Pay special attention to the explanations for the incorrect answers; these can also help to reinforce your knowledge of the material. Knowing how to recognize correct answers is good, but understanding why incorrect answers are wrong can be equally valuable.

Taking The Test

Relax. Once you're sitting in front of the testing computer, there's nothing more you can do to increase your knowledge or preparation. Take a deep breath, stretch, and start reading that first question.

There's no need to rush, either. You have plenty of time to complete each question and to return to those questions that you skip or mark for return (if you are taking a fixed-length test). If you read a question twice and remain clueless, you can mark it if you're taking a fixed-length test; if you're taking an adaptive test, you'll have to guess and move on. Both easy and difficult questions are intermixed throughout the test in random order. If you're taking a fixed-length test, don't cheat yourself by spending too much time on a hard question early on in the test, thereby depriving yourself of the time you need to answer the questions at the end of the test. If you're taking an adaptive test, don't spend more than five minutes on any single question—if it takes you that long to get nowhere, it's time to guess and move on.

On a fixed-length test, you can read through the entire test, and before returning to marked questions for a second visit, figure out how much time you've got per question. As you answer each question, remove its mark. Continue to review the remaining marked questions until you run out of time, or you complete the test.

On an adaptive test, set a maximum time limit for questions, and watch your time on long or complex questions. If you hit your limit, it's time to guess and move on. Don't deprive yourself of the opportunity to see more questions by taking too long to puzzle over questions, unless you think you can figure out the answer. Otherwise, you're limiting your opportunities to pass.

That's it for pointers. Here are some questions for you to practice on!

Sample Test #1

Question 1

Using the Task Manager, what are the possible priority settings you can make for an active process? [Check all correct answers]

❑ a. Low

❑ b. Realtime

❑ c. System

❑ d. Normal

❑ e. Pause

❑ f. High

Question 2

Windows NT fails to boot after you have modified the Registry. What is the quickest and simplest way to get the machine to boot?

○ a. Start the computer from the Windows NT boot disks and restore the Registry from a backup.

○ b. Start the computer from the Windows NT boot disks and select the Emergency Repair option.

○ c. Start the computer from the Emergency Repair Disk and follow the prompts.

○ d. Choose the Last Known Good Configuration option when it appears during bootup.

Question 3

A new application is installed onto your Windows NT Workstation. You attempt to use this new application, but it conflicts with your existing word processor. The conflict causes both programs to terminate prematurely. Which audit event type should be tracked to obtain information about the conflict and to determine which programs are affected?

○ a. File And Object Access

○ b. Security Policy Changes

○ c. Restart, Shutdown, And System

○ d. Process Tracking

○ e. Application Activity

Question 4

A normal user, who is a member of the Users group, is able to set what priority levels for processes? [Check all correct answers]

❑ a. Realtime (24)

❑ b. High (13)

❑ c. Normal (8)

❑ d. Low (4)

❑ e. System (31)

Question 5

At XYZ Corp., a handful of NetWare 3.11 clients remain in use. These machines need access to files on a newly installed Windows NT subnet. To support such access without changes to existing clients, which of the following services and/or protocols must be available on Windows NT? [Check all correct answers]

❑ a. Gateway Service For NetWare (GSNW)

❑ b. Client Service For NetWare (CSNW)

❑ c. File And Print Services For NetWare (FPNW)

❑ d. The NWLink protocol

Question 6

One of the new interns used your computer over the weekend. She left a note stating that she attempted to install a new application but it didn't work, so she deleted all the files she thought belonged to the new software. She left the machine powered off, so you try to start it up. During the boot process, you receive the following error message.

"Windows NT could not start because the following file is missing or corrupt:

\winnt\system32\ntoskrnl.exe.

Please reinstall a copy of the file."

What are possible explanations for this error? [Check all correct answers]

❑ a. NTOSKRNL.EXE is missing.

❑ b. BOOT.INI points to the wrong partition.

❑ c. NTOSKRNL.EXE is corrupt.

❑ d. BOOT.INI is missing.

Question 7

You want to improve the performance of name resolution over a RAS connection. If static name resolution is used, what is the proper location of the HOSTS and LMHOSTS files to optimize lookup time?

○ a. Both HOSTS and LMHOSTS should be stored on the RAS clients.

○ b. HOSTS should be stored on the RAS server, and LMHOSTS should be stored on the RAS clients.

○ c. Both HOSTS and LMHOSTS should be stored on the RAS server.

○ d. HOSTS should be stored on the RAS clients, and LMHOSTS should be stored on the RAS server.

Question 8

Where do the configuration options reside that can save a memory dump file in the event of a STOP error?

○ a. The Network applet

○ b. The recovery option in Dr. Watson

○ c. The Tracking tab of the Task Manager

○ d. On the Startup/Shutdown tab of the System applet

Question 9

After installing a new application, the instructions state that you must manually modify the PATH statement so that the software will function properly. How can this be accomplished?

○ a. Edit the PATH.BAT file

○ b. Modify the PATH variable on the Environment tab of the System applet

○ c. Edit the CONFIG.NT file

○ d. Edit the PATH value in the Registry located in the \HKEY_LOCAL_MACHINE\CurrentControlSet\System\ key

Question 10

Threaded execution is employed by which Windows NT Workstation subsystems? [Check all correct answers]

❑ a. Win32

❑ b. WOW/Win16

❑ c. VDM/DOS

❑ d. POSIX

❑ e. OS/2

Question 11

> Your Windows NT Workstation computer has two hard drives—
> one for Windows NT system files and a second for your data files.
> You recently added more RAM to the machine to bring it up to
> 128 MB. What changes should be made to your pagefile?
>
> ○ a. No change to the pagefile size is recommended, but it
> should be placed on the data drive.
>
> ○ b. The pagefile should be increased to 140 MB and placed
> on the data drive.
>
> ○ c. The pagefile should be increased by 12 MB.
>
> ○ d. The pagefile should be increased to 140 MB.

Question 12

> You need to set up two new Web sites to be hosted by a single
> installation of Peer Web Services. Each Web site will require its
> own directory, a unique URL, and a unique IP address. What should
> you do to implement this configuration? [Check all correct an-
> swers]
>
> ❑ a. Install RIP For IP on the PWS system.
>
> ❑ b. Assign each of the IP addresses to be used to the NIC in
> the PWS system and then associate each IP address with
> the appropriate Web directory.
>
> ❑ c. Set up the DHCP Relay Agent.
>
> ❑ d. Configure DNS so it contains the FQDN for each site and
> correlates that name to its IP address.
>
> ❑ e. Configure WINS by adding the NetBIOS names and IP
> addresses of the sites to the static list of sites.

Question 13

If your network has only a single printer, how can you configure the system so your executives' print jobs will print before other users' documents?

○ a. Create a separate logical printer, assign rights to the Executive group, and set the printer priority to 1.

○ b. Create a separate logical printer, assign rights to the Executive group, and set the printer priority to 99.

○ c. Create a separate logical printer for the Executive group and configure the printer to start printing immediately.

○ d. Create a separate logical printer for the Executive group and configure the printer to print directly to the physical print device.

Question 14

A Windows NT PC is configured with two 2.2 GB EIDE hard drives, with both drives attached to a controller built into the motherboard. Each disk contains a single primary partition; the Windows NT system files reside on Disk 1, and the boot files reside on Disk 2. Which of the following ARC names correctly identifies the boot partition that appears in the BOOT.INI file?

○ a. multi(0)disk(0)rdisk(0)partition(1)

○ b. multi(0)disk(1)rdisk(0)partition(1)

○ c. multi(0)disk(0)rdisk(0)partition(0)

○ d. multi(1)disk(0)rdisk(0)partition(0)

○ e. multi(0)disk(0)rdisk(1)partition(1)

Question 15

On a network that contains multiple versions of NetWare, some clients are configured for NetWare 2.2, whereas others are configured for NetWare 4.11. Among other protocols, NWLink is used on this network. NetWare 2.2 clients use an 802.3 raw frame type, whereas NetWare 4.11 clients use the 802.2 frame type. What kinds of information must be supplied in the NWLink IPX/SPX Properties dialog box to allow the same Windows NT Workstation to recognize both flavors of NetWare clients on this network?

○ a. Select Auto Frame Type Detection and add the clients' IPX network numbers and frame types to the frame type configuration list.

○ b. Select Manual Frame Type Detection and add the network numbers and frame types for both 2.2 and 4.11 clients to the frame type configuration list.

○ c. Select only Auto Frame Type Detection; the rest is automatic.

○ d. Select Manual Frame Type Detection and add the 2.2 clients' network numbers and frame types to the frame type configuration list.

Question 16

Several users complain that after repeated tries, their documents never print. You open the print queue for the suspect printer. There you see all the print jobs, but you're unable to delete them. What is the next step in resolving this problem?

○ a. Verify that the pause spool option is not checked on the print server.

○ b. Delete the stalled printer from the print server, create a new printer, and tell your users to resend their jobs to the new printer.

○ c. Delete all files from the spool folder on the print server and tell your users to resend them.

○ d. Stop the spooler service and then restart it.

Question 17

One feature of Windows NT is its capability to hide or isolate complicated, behind-the-scenes activity from users and applications. What Windows NT component is responsible for the operating system's redirection and network processes?

○ a. NetBIOS Extended User Interface (NetBEUI)

○ b. Multiple Universal Naming Convention Provider (MUP)

○ c. InterProcess Communications (IPC)

○ d. Internetwork Packet Exchange/Sequenced Packet Exchange (IPX/SPX)

Question 18

User MaryJane is a member of the Accounting, Managers, and Print Operators groups. For a share named Marketing, these groups have the following share permissions:

• Accounting: Change

• Managers: Read

• Print Operators: Full Control

In addition, MaryJane's NTFS permissions for the Marketing directory and its contents are Read. What is MaryJane able to do with files from the Marketing directory when she accesses them through the share?

○ a. Nothing, she has no access.

○ b. Read and Execute.

○ c. Read, Write, Execute, and Delete.

○ d. Read, Write, Execute, Delete, Change Permissions, and Take Ownership.

Question 19

Using the Disk Administrator, you've just created a new partition from free space on a SCSI hard drive. The new drive appears in the Disk Administrator display. What should you do next in the process to create new storage space?

○ a. Assign a drive letter

○ b. Select Configuration|Save

○ c. Format

○ d. Commit Changes Now

Question 20

Which of the following components belong to the Windows NT Kernel? [Check all correct answers]

❏ a. HAL

❏ b. Executive Services

❏ c. Security Reference Monitor

❏ d. Logon process

❏ e. I/O Manager

❏ f. User applications

Question 21

A user's job description has changed. She no longer uses one single computer, but moves around the organization as her project requires. What applet in Control Panel can help this user maintain her profile no matter where she logs on?

○ a. System

○ b. Network

○ c. Regional Settings

○ d. User Manager

Question 22

What files should be placed on a boot disk to boot Windows NT? Assume the drive controller is SCSI and does not support BIOS translation. [Check all correct answers]

❑ a. NTDETECT.COM

❑ b. BOOT.INI

❑ c. NTLDR

❑ d. WINA20.386

❑ e. NTBOOTDD.SYS

Question 23

An LMHOSTS file contains what type of information?

○ a. A static list of NetBIOS names mapped to IP addresses

○ b. A dynamic list of NetBIOS names mapped to IP addresses

○ c. A static list of FQDNs mapped to IP addresses

○ d. A dynamic list of FQDNs mapped to IP addresses

Question 24

Why would a user want to connect to a remote printer share rather than create a new printer on his or her Windows NT Workstation?

○ a. More options for scheduling accessibility

○ b. Local spooling of print jobs

○ c. The print driver does not have to be manually installed

○ d. Local print queues

Question 25

DHCP is used for what purpose?

○ a. To maintain a dynamic relationship database between IP addresses and NetBIOS names

○ b. To route IP packets across routers to other subnets

○ c. To assign IP addresses to clients

○ d. To resolve FQDNs into IP addresses

Question 26

Sixteen-bit Windows on 32-bit Windows (WOW) is not a stand-alone subsystem. What other two Windows NT subsystems support the WOW environment? [Check all correct answers]

❏ a. Win32

❏ b. VDM

❏ c. POSIX

❏ d. OS/2

Question 27

What steps might be required to install a new SCSI-based tape device? [Check all correct answers]

❏ a. Reboot

❏ b. Install SCSI controller drivers through the SCSI Adapters applet

❏ c. Use the Add New Hardware applet

❏ d. Detect the tape device through the Tape Devices applet

Question 28

What activities can a user sitting at a Windows NT Workstation computer attached to a network perform if the PDC fails? (Assume that a BDC is present on the network.) [Check all correct answers]

❑ a. Log on locally to the Workstation

❑ b. Maintain a current active session on the network

❑ c. Change his or her password

❑ d. Log on to the network

Question 29

You need to create user accounts for 12 new employees. All will have the same level of user access and permissions as the existing Bob Smith account. You decide to make copies of Bob Smith's user account to create these accounts for the new users. What pieces of information are reset or left blank when you copy a user account? Assume the User Cannot Change Password checkbox is selected on the original account. [Check all correct answers]

❑ a. User Must Change Password At Next Logon

❑ b. Username

❑ c. Account Disabled

❑ d. Password Never Expires

❑ e. Profile Settings

❑ f. Password

❑ g. Group Memberships

Question 30

> Your dial-up connection to the office network is not functioning as it should. Where can you find information related to RAS problems to aid in troubleshooting? [Check all correct answers]
>
> ❏ a. Event Viewer
>
> ❏ b. DEVICE.LOG
>
> ❏ c. Dr. Watson
>
> ❏ d. MODEMLOG.TXT
>
> ❏ e. Windows NT Diagnostics

Question 31

> Which of the following ARC names indicates the third partition of the fourth SCSI drive on the second controller that has its BIOS disabled?
>
> ○ a. multi(1)disk(3)rdisk(0)partition(3)
>
> ○ b. multi(1)disk(0)rdisk(3)partition(3)
>
> ○ c. scsi(1)disk(3)rdisk(0)partition(3)
>
> ○ d. scsi(1)disk(3)rdisk(0)partition(4)

Question 32

> Everything within the Windows NT environment is an object. Which of the following are object attributes? [Check all correct answers]
>
> ❏ a. Data
>
> ❏ b ACL
>
> ❏ c. Services
>
> ❏ d. Name

Question 33

IPC (InterProcess Communications) provides Windows NT with fast, efficient communication channels among its own components. Which of the following are supported IPC elements? [Check all correct answers]

❑ a. NetBIOS

❑ b. MPR

❑ c. NetDDE

❑ d. Windows Sockets

❑ e. RPC

Question 34

By booting from the three boot/setup floppies for Windows NT Workstation, selecting R at the menu for Repair, and supplying a recent Emergency Repair Disk—which of the following problems can be corrected? [Check all correct answers]

❑ a. Boot sector corruption

❑ b. Unable to locate Master Boot Record

❑ c. NTLDR not found

❑ d. Corrupt NTOSKRNL

Question 35

Windows NT Workstation can participate as a member of a workgroup. Which of the following are characteristics of workgroups? [Check all correct answers]

❑ a. No central control

❑ b. Share-level security

❑ c. Requires a PDC

❑ d. All user accounts must be created on each member

❑ e. Recommended for more than 10 users/computers

. . . .

Question 36

Your Windows NT Workstation fails to restart and you assume it's because your boot sector is corrupted and needs to be restored. What are two of the ways to restore it?

○ a. Boot with MS-DOS and run WINNT, or Boot from the Windows NT installation disk and use the Emergency Repair Disk.

○ b. Boot with an NTFS Boot Disk and use the sys command, or Boot from the Windows NT installation disk and choose to reinstall.

○ c. Boot with MS-DOS and run WINNT32, or boot from the Windows NT installation disk and use the Emergency Repair Disk.

○ d. Boot with MS-DOS and run REGEDIT, or boot from the Windows NT installation disk and use the Emergency Repair Disk.

Question 37

The standard permissions for directories and files are quite similar. Which of the following is not a standard file and directory permission?

○ a. Read

○ b. List

○ c. Create Directory

○ d. Change

○ e. Add

Question 38

It is your responsibility to install Windows NT Workstation on 50 new, identical computers located in the tech support wing of your building. Which tools, files, and/ or utilities might you use to automate and deploy this process? [Check all correct answers]

❑ a. Setup Manager

❑ b. UNATTEND.TXT

❑ c. Uniqueness Database File

❑ d. WINNT.EXE or WINNT32.EXE

Question 39

Your organization has several salespeople who travel from city to city every week. They want to connect to the office LAN to keep tabs on quotas, prices, and stock levels. Therefore, they want to connect to the LAN as if they were in their own offices. However, they can only gain access by establishing a PPP connection using RAS. What Windows NT networking activities are supported over such a connection? [Check all correct answers]

❑ a. Printer share access

❑ b. Named pipes

❑ c. WinSOCK API applications over TCP/IP

❑ d. InterProcess Communications (IPC)

❑ e. User logon authentication

Question 40

You need to install help desk systems hosted by Windows NT Workstation onto 35 newly purchased, identical machines. The help desk system has six installation routines, a database add-on, two patches, and a service update. You want to use SYSDIFF to create a special installation data file so that each computer will be installed with Windows NT and the complicated help desk application with a single command line of WINNT.EXE. What SYSDIFF command should you use to establish this scenario?

○ a. sysdiff /dump difference_file dump_file

○ b. sysdiff /apply /m [/log:log_file] difference_file

○ c. sysdiff /inf /m [/u] difference_file oem_root

○ d. sysdiff /snap [/log:log_file] snapshot_file

Question 41

Windows NT Workstation, when the TCP/IP protocol is installed, has several TCP/IP tools and utilities. Which of the following can report on your connection to a remote system? [Check all correct answers]

❑ a. IPCONFIG

❑ b. TRACERT

❑ c. FINGER

❑ d. PING

❑ e. Telnet

Question 42

You open the BOOT.INI file to edit it. Which two parameter switches are present on the VGA Mode selection? [Check two answers]

❑ a. /NODEBUG

❑ b. /BASEVIDEO

❑ c. /NOSERIALMICE

❑ d /SOS

❑ e. /VGAVIDEO

Question 43

The Windows NT Workstation architecture provides support for which types of applications? [Check all correct answers]

- ❑ a. POSIX
- ❑ b. Win16
- ❑ c. DOS
- ❑ d. Mac OS
- ❑ e. Win32
- ❑ f. OS/2 1.1 (character mode)
- ❑ g. Solaris

Question 44

With CSNW installed on a Windows NT Workstation, which of the following NetWare command-line utilities does Microsoft support?

- ○ a. SLIST
- ○ b. LOGOUT
- ○ c. SYSCON
- ○ d. CAPTURE
- ○ e. ATTACH

Question 45

On your Windows NT Workstation computer, you establish a direct access file transfer area for users on your network. The range of clients that require access to this area include PCs running DOS, Windows 3.1x, Windows 95, and Windows NT, as well as Macintoshes, and Unix machines. You create a 50 MB partition on your Windows NT Workstation. You do not want to impose any access restrictions on the volume, but instead leave policing of the area up to its users. What file system is recommended for such use by Microsoft?

- ○ a. FAT
- ○ b. NTFS
- ○ c. HPFS

Question 46

Your organization requires callback security on all RAS connections made into the office LAN. However, you have an important technician who travels across the country regularly who must periodically establish a connection. How can you configure her account so that she is able to gain access while also supporting your organization's security?

○ a. Set the callback security to No Call Back for her account only.

○ b. Enable callback security with Set By Caller selected.

○ c. Set the callback security to Preset To with her home phone number.

○ d. Set the callback security to Roaming and give her the page number to configure the callback number remotely.

○ e. Turn on the callback Caller ID capture.

Question 47

You map a drive to a newly created network share using the following command:

```
Net use H: \\devel3\documents
```

A user deposits a file for you in the document share named RESULTS.TXT. What additional setting must be made to grant you access to the RESULTS.TXT file?

○ a. Set the Read permission on the Documents folder to your user account

○ b. Your user account must be added to the Everyone group

○ c. None, Full Control to all users is the default on all new shares

○ d. A new group must be created and your account added as a member

Question 48

You recently purchased a UPS to protect your computer from power failures and spikes. You have taken the precaution of adding the /NOSERIALMICE parameter to your BOOT.INI file. After charging the UPS and attaching it to the correct serial port, you boot your Windows NT Workstation computer. You test your configuration by unplugging the UPS from the wall. After five minutes, the UPS battery is drained, cutting off power to your computer. Windows NT did not shut down gracefully, even though you heard repeated beeps from the UPS. What is the best explanation for this behavior?

- ○ a. The UPS drivers were not installed through the Devices applet.
- ○ b. The voltages were reversed in the UPS applet.
- ○ c. Windows NT is not compatible with UPS devices.
- ○ d. The UPS variables were not defined in the System applet on the Environment tab.

Question 49

You suspect that some member of the Marketing group is accessing a directory that he should be prevented from reaching. You aren't sure who it is, but you do know which directory is involved. What feature of Windows NT will let you track who gains access to this directory?

- ○ a. NTFS file activity logging
- ○ b. Event auditing
- ○ c. Event Viewer
- ○ d. Account lockout

Question 50

You've obtained an HP network interface print device and plan to use your Windows NT Workstation computer as the print server for this new device. However, you are unable to locate any option to install a port for this printer. Why?

○ a. PostScript printing is enabled on the print device and must be disabled.

○ b. You didn't install the print driver on the print server.

○ c. The print processor is corrupt and must be fixed.

○ d. The DLC protocol is not installed on the print server.

Question 51

Your Windows NT Workstation computer is on an isolated TCP/IP network with no routing and no external connections. After assigning an IP address to this machine, what additional parameter must be specified to enable proper communication?

○ a. The subnet mask

○ b. The default gateway

○ c. The DHCP server IP address

○ d. The WINS server IP address

Question 52

You want to upgrade from Windows NT Workstation 3.51 to 4. Your main data directory, H:, is an HPFS volume. After Windows NT 4 is installed, you can use the CONVERT.EXE utility to convert H: from HPFS to NTFS.

○ a. True

○ b. False

Question 53

The binding order for protocols can significantly affect performance between a client and server. Where should this binding order be modified to improve network communications?

○ a. On the domain controllers only

○ b. On the workstations only

○ c. On the servers only

○ d. On both the workstations and servers (including the domain controllers)

Question 54

Your Windows NT Workstation computer is configured to create a memory dump file each time a STOP error occurs. What utility can you use to view the contents of the DMP file?

○ a. Event Viewer

○ b. Debug Inspector

○ c. DUMPEXAM.EXE

○ d. Windows NT Diagnostics

Question 55

You need to change permission settings for several NTFS directories in the wake of a security breach. Which of the following choices represent valid ways to perform this task? [Check all correct answers]

❑ a. The CACLS command utility

❑ b. Moving the directories to a new partition

❑ c. The Share properties tab

❑ d. Taking ownership

❑ e. The Permissions button on the Security properties tab

Chapter 19

Question 56

Which of the following commands are required to configure Windows NT so it performs a scheduled backup every Monday, Wednesday, and Friday at 11:00 P.M.? [Check all correct answers]

❑ a. ntbackup backup 23:00 /every:M,W,F MYBACKUP.CMD

❑ b. ntbackup backup c: /B /L "c:\backup.log"

❑ c. schedule ntbackup 11:00 c: /B

❑ d. AT 23:00 /every:M,W,F MYBACKUP.CMD

❑ e. AT 23:00 /every:M,W,F ntbackup backup c: /B /L
      "c:\backup.log"

Question 57

What happens to the permission and long file names when you copy a file from an NTFS folder to a folder on a FAT partition on a Windows NT Workstation system?

○ a. Permissions and file names are retained.

○ b. Permissions of target partition are inherited and long file names are retained.

○ c. Permissions are lost, long file names are retained.

○ d. Permissions and long file names are lost.

Question 58

You're installing Windows NT on 12 identical computers. You've already created the necessary install scripts. After the following commands are issued from a computer booted with Network Installation Startup Disk:

```
net use x: \\corpnet\ver4.0
cd x:
```

Which command should be used to install Windows NT on the third system?

○ a. winnt32 / u:corpclnt12.txt /udf:3, corp-ids.txt

○ b. winnt /ox /udf:3, corp-ids.txt

○ c. winnt /u:corpclnt12.txt /udf:3, corp-ids.txt

○ d. winnt32 /o

○ e. winnt /s:corpclnt12.txt

Question 59

which application would you use to send print jobs to a Unix-based print device?

○ a. LPR

○ b. Spooler

○ c. Print Manager

○ d. Windows Explorer

Question 60

You have an MS-DOS application that uses a TSR to manage a COM port. How do you set it up to run on Windows NT Workstation?

○ a. Edit the Registry.

○ b. Create/edit Autoexec.nt.

○ c. Edit the environment path.

○ d. Create/edit the Win.ini file.

Answer Key #1

1.	a, b, d, f	21.	a	41.	b, d
2.	d	22.	a, b, c, e	42.	b, d
3.	d	23.	a	43.	a, b, c, e, f
4.	b, c, d	24.	c	44.	c
5.	c, d	25.	c	45.	a
6.	a, b, c	26.	a, b	46.	b
7.	a	27.	a, b, d	47.	c
8.	d	28.	a, b, d	48.	b
9.	b	29.	a, b, c, f	49.	b
10.	a, b, c, d, e	30.	a, b, d	50.	d
11.	b	31.	c	51.	a
12.	b, d, e	32.	a, b, d	52.	b
13.	b	33.	a, c, d, e	53.	b
14.	a	34.	a, c, d	54.	c
15.	b	35.	a, b, d	55.	a, b, e
16.	d	36.	a	56.	b, d
17.	b	37.	c	57.	c
18.	b	38.	a, b, c, d	58.	c
19.	d	39.	a, b, c, d, e	59.	a
20.	a, b, c, e	40.	c	60.	b

Here are the answers to the questions presented in the sample test in Chapter 19, Sample Test #1.

Question 1

Answers a, b, d, and f are correct. Low, High, Normal, and Realtime are the possible priority settings. There are no System or Pause priority settings. Therefore, answers c and e are incorrect.

Question 2

Answer d is correct. The easiest approach to this kind of problem—be it caused by untoward edits to the Registry or installation of drivers or new system components—is to choose the Last Known Good Configuration option during bootup. Answers a and b may produce the same results eventually, but they're nowhere near as easy (and perhaps not as up-to-date as the Last Known Good Configuration). Answer c is flat wrong, because you can't boot from the ERD.

Question 3

Answer d is correct. Process Tracking tracks threads and processes, including applications. File And Object Access is for tracking NTFS objects such as files and printers. Therefore, answer a is incorrect. Security Policy Changes tracks modifications to security and policies. Therefore, answer b is incorrect. Restart, Shutdown, And System tracks system restarts. Therefore, answer c is incorrect. Application Activity is not a valid selection. Therefore, answer e is incorrect.

Question 4

Answers b, c, and d are correct. As a non-administrator, any user can set priority to High, Normal, or Low. Only administrators can set process priority to Realtime. Therefore, answer a is incorrect. Only the system itself can launch processes with the highest level of priority—namely, System. Therefore, answer e is incorrect.

Question 5

Answers c and d are correct. File And Print Services For NetWare make a Windows NT Server look like a NetWare server to NetWare network clients, so it's what provides file access—this means that answer c must be checked. But native NetWare 3.x clients need IPX/SPX to access real

NetWare servers, or Windows NT Servers running FPNW; because NWLink is Microsoft's implementation of IPX/SPX, answer d must be checked as well. GSNW provides mediated access to NetWare services for Microsoft Network clients, so it's not required—meaning answer a is incorrect. Likewise, CSNW makes it possible for Windows NT Workstations and servers to obtain direct access to a NetWare server. Therefore, answer b is incorrect.

Question 6

Answers a, b, and c are correct. Any of these explanations can result in the given error message. When the boot process cannot find NTOSKRNL.EXE, it does not indicate if the problem is with the file itself, its location, or the pointers to it. If the BOOT.INI file is actually missing, a different error would appear stating such. Without the BOOT.INI pointer, there is no mechanism to seek the NTOSKRNL.EXE file so that error message would not appear. Therefore, answer d is incorrect.

Question 7

Answer a is correct. The fastest lookup time occurs when both HOSTS and LMHOSTS files are stored on the local hard drive of each RAS client, because no WAN traffic need occur to resolve a resource location. All others answers are incorrect because they require storing these files somewhere other than on the client, which increases the lookup time.

Question 8

Answer d is correct. The Startup/Shutdown tab of the System applet is where memory dump options for Windows NT appear. The Network applet does not offer memory dump configuration options. Therefore, answer a is incorrect. Dr. Watson is used to perform memory dumps for application faults, not for the Windows NT system itself. Therefore, answer b is incorrect. The Task Manager does not have a Tracking tab, nor does it offer memory dump options. Therefore, answer c is incorrect.

Question 9

Answer b is correct. The Environment tab of the System applet is the proper place to modify the PATH variable. There is no such thing as a PATH.BAT file. Therefore, answer a is incorrect. The CONFIG.NT file does not contain path information. Therefore, answer c is incorrect. The Registry key listed for a PATH value is fictitious. Therefore, answer d is incorrect.

Question 10

Answers a, b, c, d, and e are correct. All of the subsystems within Windows NT are executed through threads. Even though a VDM, and subsequently WOW, uses only a single thread, all of these subsystems use threaded execution nevertheless.

Question 11

Answer b is correct. The pagefile should be 140 MB and placed on a different drive than where the system files reside (if possible). Microsoft recommends a pagefile be set equal in size to the amount of physical RAM on a system, plus 12 MB. Therefore, answer a is incorrect. The pagefile should be the size of physical RAM plus 12 MB. Therefore, answer c is incorrect. The pagefile should be 140 MB and placed on a drive other than the one where the system files reside. Therefore, answer d is incorrect.

Question 12

Answers b, d, and e are all correct. Assigning the additional IP addresses to the server's NIC is an important step. Therefore, answer b is correct. Because this site is within a private network, you will need both DNS and WINS to support name resolution. Therefore, answers d and e are both correct. RIP For IP should not be used in this situation; also, you do not know if there is more than one NIC in the machine. Therefore, answer a is incorrect. The DHCP Relay Agent does not apply to this situation. Therefore, answer c is incorrect. The trick to this question is to realize that even though Windows NT Workstation does not host DNS or WINS servers, a workstation machine can be the subject of a reference in a DNS or WINS server database.

Question 13

Answer b is correct. The highest priority is 99. It is possible to set priorities among groups of documents by creating different logical printers for a single physical print device and then setting different priorities for each logical printer. To set printer priority, select the Scheduling tab in Printer Properties. The lowest priority is 1. Therefore, answer a is incorrect. There is no "start printing immediately" option. Therefore, answer c is incorrect. Any Windows NT printer automatically prints to the print device. Therefore, answer d is incorrect.

Question 14

Answer a is correct. Because each of the partitions mentioned in this question is the one and only on its drive, it must be **partition(1)**. The partition that appears in BOOT.INI is the boot partition, which contains the Windows NT system files. This means that the correct answer is the ARC name for Disk 1, where the Windows NT system files reside. The options for the first element in an ARC name are either **scsi** or **multi**, but **scsi** applies only to a genuine SCSI drive whose onboard BIOS has been disabled. Because **multi(*)** appears at the start of all five choices, all of them are correct to that point. The number that follows **multi** within the parentheses is the ordinal number of the disk controller to which the drive (or drives) is attached. Ordinal numbers start with 0; because there is only one controller mentioned, that immediately rules out answer d, because it alludes to a second controller (as denoted by **multi(1)**) to which neither drive in the question is attached. The **disk(*)** element in an ARC name designates the SCSI bus number for a SCSI drive with its BIOS disabled, and it is always zero for a non-SCSI disk. This eliminates answer b. The **rdisk(*)** element in an ARC name indicates the SCSI logical unit number (LUN) or selects the drive that contains the operating system. The **rdisk(*)** element is always set to zero when an ARC name starts with **scsi**—because this one starts with **multi**, it indicates the position in the order in which drives are attached to the controller. Furthermore, the question indicates that the Windows NT system files are on the first disk, and boot files on the second disk. Because **rdisk** numbers begin with zero, this means that the Windows NT system files (the boot partition) live on the drive named **multi(0)disk(0)rdisk(0)partition(1)** and that the boot files (the system partition) live on the drive named **multi(0)disk(0)rdisk(1)partition(1)**. One small trick to ARC names is that although **scsi**, **multi**, **disk**, and **rdisk** all number ordinally, starting with 0, partition numbers start with 1. Therefore, any valid ARC name will never have zero as a value for **partition(*)**.

Question 15

Answer b is correct. The secret to answering this question is to understand how automatic frame type detection works in Windows NT. As long as only a single frame type is used on the network, automatic detection works fine. But because this situation uses several frame types, Manual Frame Type Detection must be selected during the configuration process. This eliminates answers a and c from consideration. Answer d is incorrect because Manual Frame Type Detection requires entry of all frame types and network numbers in use. Only answer b covers all these requirements.

Question 16

Answer d is correct. This scenario is a quintessential example of a stalled print spooler. To fix the problem, select Services in Control Panel, stop the spooler service, and then restart it. There is no pause spool option. Therefore, answer a is incorrect. There's no need to re-create the printer from scratch. Therefore, answer b is also incorrect. You should never have to involve users in the problem-solving process (other than to gather information from them). Therefore, answer c is also incorrect.

Question 17

Answer b is correct. Multiple Universal Naming Convention Provider (MUP) hides multiple redirectors behind a single interface. NetBEUI is a protocol used by Windows NT, but it's not the unified redirector interface. Therefore, answer a is incorrect. IPC is not a redirector. Therefore, answer c is incorrect. IPX/SPX is the Novell protocol that Microsoft re-created as NWLink; it is not a redirector. Therefore, answer d is incorrect.

Question 18

Answer b is correct. The less permissive of Read and Full Control is Read, so Mary Jane's effective permission to Marketing is Read. Read access includes both Read and Execute. To calculate share and NTFS permissions combined, take the most permissive of each kind and then the least permissive of the remaining share and NTFS permissions. If No Access appears anywhere, the resulting permission will always be No Access. Of the three share permissions that pertain to Marketing by virtue of Mary Jane's group memberships, Full Control is the most permissive, so that becomes her share permission. The NTFS permission is Read.

Question 19

Answer d is correct. You must use the Commit Changes Now command to save the partition creation changes as the next step, then proceed to format the partition, and finally, assign it a drive letter. It is not possible to assign a drive letter to a partition unless it is formatted. Therefore, answer a is incorrect. The Configuration|Save command stores the current configuration status as stored in the Registry to an Emergency Repair Disk, but this is not a step in creating a usable volume. Therefore, answer b is incorrect. Formatting a partition to create a volume is a required step, but this cannot be performed until the partition creation changes are committed. Therefore, answer c is also incorrect.

Question 20

Answers a, b, c, and e are correct. The Kernel is host to the HAL, the Executive Services, the Security Reference Monitor, and the I/O Manager. The Logon process and User applications exist in User mode. Therefore, answers d and f are incorrect.

Question 21

Answer a is correct. The User Profile tab located in the System applet is where roaming profiles are established. The Network applet is not involved in the creation of user profiles. Therefore, answer b is incorrect. The Regional Settings applet makes changes that are stored in a user profile, but roaming profiles are not managed through this tool. Therefore, answer c is incorrect. The User Manager is not a Control Panel applet. Also, it is only able to establish the path of a profile; it is not used to create profiles. Therefore, answer d is incorrect.

Question 22

Answers a, b, c, and e are correct. NTDETECT.COM is required on the boot floppy. Therefore, answer a is correct. BOOT.INI is required on the boot floppy. Therefore, answer b is also correct. NTLDR is required on the boot floppy. Therefore, answer c is also correct. NTBOOTDD.SYS is the driver for SCSI translation required for non-BIOS controllers. Therefore, answer e is also correct. WINA20.386 is a Windows 3.x device driver that is not needed on the boot floppy. Therefore, answer d is incorrect.

Question 23

Answer a is correct. LMHOSTS is a predecessor to WINS and is a static list of NetBIOS names mapped to IP addresses. A dynamic list of NetBIOS names mapped to IP addresses is WINS. Therefore, answer b is incorrect. The HOSTS file is a static list of FQDNs mapped to IP addresses. Therefore, answer c is incorrect. The DNS database, in essence, represents a dynamic list of FQDNs mapped to IP addresses. Therefore, answer d is incorrect.

Question 24

Answer c is correct. Print drivers do not need to be installed locally on each Windows NT Workstation that connects to a network share printer. There are no additional scheduling options in either case. Therefore, answer a is incorrect. There is no local spooling of print jobs for network connection over printers; a logical printer is simply a redirector to the real print server where all spooling takes place. Therefore, answer b is incorrect. The logical printer used to connect to a print share will display a print queue, but it is the entire print queue for the printer as seen by the print server that is displayed. There is no individual print queue for each local machine; however, only those print jobs owned by the workstation user can be manipulated by that user. Therefore, answer d is incorrect.

Question 25

Answer c is correct. The service that assigns IP addresses to clients is DHCP. The service that maintains a dynamic relationship database between IP addresses and NetBIOS names is WINS. Therefore, answer a is incorrect. The service that routes IP packets is RIP For IP. Therefore, answer b is incorrect. The service that resolves FQDNs to IP addresses is DNS. Therefore, answer d is incorrect.

Question 26

Answers a and b are correct. The WOW subsystem is launched within a VDM that is itself launched within Win32. POSIX and OS/2 are not associated with WOW in any way. Therefore, answers c an d are incorrect.

Question 27

Answers a, b, and d are correct. Rebooting, the SCSI Adapters applet, and the Tape Devices applet are all required elements when installing a new SCSI-based tape device. There is no Add New Hardware applet in Windows NT. Therefore, answer c is incorrect.

Question 28

Answers a, b, and d are correct. Without a PDC, you can still log on locally, maintain current network access, and log on to the network (through BDC authentication). You cannot change your password because a BDC cannot modify the SAM database. Therefore, answer c is incorrect.

Question 29

Answers a, b, c, and f are correct. The items that are reset or left blank when a user account is copied are User Must Change Password At Next Logon, Username, Account Disabled, and Password. Password Never Expires, Profile Settings, and Group Membership options remain as set in the original account. Therefore, answers d, e, and g are incorrect.

Question 30

Answers a, b, and d are correct. The Event Viewer, DEVICE.LOG, and MODEMLOG.TXT can be useful troubleshooting tools for RAS problems. Dr. Watson doesn't track RAS events; it focuses on applications. Therefore, answer c is incorrect. Windows NT Diagnostics provides no useful RAS-related information. Therefore, answer e is incorrect.

Question 31

Answer c is correct. Answer c indicates the third partition on the fourth drive on a non-BIOS SCSI controller. Answers a and b begin with **multi**, which indicates a BIOS-enabled controller. Therefore, answers a and b are both incorrect. Answer d indicates the fourth partition. Therefore, answer d is incorrect.

Question 32

Answers a, b, and d are correct. The data in an object is an attribute. Therefore, answer a is correct. The ACL of an object is an attribute. Therefore, answer b is correct. The name of an object is an attribute. Therefore, answer d is correct. The services for an object are not attributes. Therefore, answer c is incorrect.

Question 33

Answers a, c, d, and e are correct. The programming interface elements of IPC are NetBIOS, NetDDE, Windows Sockets, and RPC. MPR is a redirector, not an IPC element. Therefore, answer b is incorrect.

Question 34

Answers a, c, and d are correct. The ERD repair process can often correct boot sector problems, replace NTLDR, and repair NTOSKRNL. Neither ERD nor installation floppies can repair the MBR—that requires a DOS setup disk. Therefore, answer b is incorrect.

Question 35

Answers a, b, and d are correct. Workgroups have no central control and use share-level security; also, user accounts must be created on each member. Workgroups do not require a PDC and are recommended for 10 or fewer users/computers. Therefore, answers c and e are incorrect.

Question 36

Answer a is correct. If your boot sector is corrupt, it needs to be restored/repaired. By booting with MS-DOS and running WINNT, you'll be able to reinstall Windows NT, which would correct the problem. A better solution, however, is to boot up the machine using the original Windows NT installation disk. When prompted, insert the Emergency Repair Disk. There's no such thing as an NTFS Boot Disk. Therefore, answer b is incorrect. WINNT32 is used to upgrade from Windows NT 3.51 to 4.0; it cannot be run from MS-DOS. Therefore, answer c is incorrect. REGEDIT is a utility used to read and edit the Registry files and has nothing to do with your boot sector. Therefore, answer d is incorrect.

Question 37

Answer c is correct. Create Directory is not a permission. Read and Change are both directory and file permissions. Therefore, answers a and d are incorrect. List and Add are directory permissions. Therefore, answers b and e are incorrect.

Question 38

Answers a, b, c, and d are all correct. All of these items can be or are involved in an automated or customized installation of Windows NT.

Question 39

Answers a, b, c, d, and e are correct. Because a RAS-connected client is no different than a direct-connected client (other than in its speed of data transfer), all standard network activities still occur over the WAN link.

Question 40

Answer c is correct. The command **sysdiff /inf /m [/u] difference_file oem_root** enables Windows NT and custom applications to be installed automatically with a single command. Answer a creates a contents list of a difference file; answer b applies a difference file to an installation of Windows NT; and answer d creates an initial snapshot of Windows NT. Therefore, answers a, b, and d are all incorrect.

Question 41

Answers b and d are correct. The TRACERT utility displays the route taken by packets to the remote system. Therefore, answer b is correct. PING indicates whether or not a remote system is currently online. Therefore, answer d is correct. The IPCONFIG utility is only useful for identifying local TCP/IP configurations. Therefore, answer a is incorrect. The FINGER utility is used to obtain user information, but it offers no connection diagnostics. Therefore, answer c is incorrect. The Telnet utility is used to establish a terminal emulation session with a remote system, but it offers no connection diagnostics. Therefore, answer e is incorrect.

Question 42

Answers b and d are correct. The parameters **/BASEVIDEO** and **/SOS** are present on the VGA Mode line by default. The parameters **/NODEBUG** and **/NOSERIALMICE** are not present on the VGA Mode line by default. Therefore, answers a and c are incorrect. The parameter **/VGAVIDEO** is not a valid parameter. Therefore, answer e is incorrect.

Question 43

Answers a, b, c, e, and f are correct. Windows NT provides application support for Win32, Win16, DOS, POSIX, and OS/2 1.1 (character mode). Windows NT does not support Mac OS or Solaris applications. Therefore, answers d and g are incorrect.

Question 44

Answer c is correct. The only command-line utility on this list that works inside Windows NT is SYSCON. All the other utilities are not supported by Windows NT, but their functions can be performed using Windows NT's NET command equivalents. Therefore, answers a, b, d, and e are incorrect.

Question 45

Answer a is correct. Windows NT FAT is the proper file system to use, because it works well with small volumes, imposes no security restrictions, is backwards compatible with FAT, and is supported by Windows NT. NTFS isn't suitable because of the need for broad cross-platform access and the partition's size. Therefore, answer b is incorrect. HPFS is not supported in Windows NT 4. Therefore, answer c is incorrect.

Question 46

Answer b is correct. Setting the Set By Caller option allows her to input a callback number each time she connects. Setting the No Call Back option violates the organization's security policy. Therefore, answer a is incorrect. Setting the Preset To number does not allow her to access the network because she's never in the same place. Therefore, answer c is incorrect. There is no Roaming callback setting. Therefore, answer d is incorrect. Windows NT has no Caller ID capture setting, but this service can be obtained from third-party software. Therefore, because this service is not required for this situation, answer e is also incorrect.

Question 47

Answer c is correct. No action is required because your account belongs to the domain's Everyone group with Full Control to new shares, by default. Assigning specific permissions for the object for your user account is unnecessary. Because your account belongs, by default, to the Everyone group, and new shares offer Full Control to this group, answer a is incorrect. Your user account automatically becomes a member of the Everyone group when it's created. Therefore, answer b is incorrect. A new group is not required to gain access to the new share. Therefore, answer d is incorrect.

Question 48

Answer b is correct. If the voltages that define communications from a UPS are reversed, the computer will fail to understand its signals. The Devices applet is not used to install drivers; also, a UPS requires no additional drivers to operate. Therefore, answer a is incorrect. Windows NT is UPS compatible. Therefore, answer c is incorrect. There are no UPS variables to be defined through the System applet. Therefore, answer d is incorrect.

Question 49

Answer b is correct. Event auditing tracks activity around any object within Windows NT. NTFS file activity logging is a fault tolerance feature used to ensure the integrity of stored data; it cannot be used to track access. Therefore, answer a is incorrect. The Event Viewer is used to review the logs created by the auditing system, but it is not what does the actual tracking. Therefore, answer c is incorrect. Account lockout is the feature used to prevent compromised accounts from being used. Therefore, answer d is incorrect.

Question 50

Answer d is correct. For Windows NT to support HP network interface print devices, you must install DLC (Data Link Control) or the LPR (line printer remote) protocol. You can't install a printer driver if Windows NT cannot recognize the print device. PostScript printing has nothing to do with print device installation. Therefore, answer a is incorrect. You can't install a driver if Windows NT can't recognize a print device. Therefore, answer b is incorrect. The print processor is not involved in printer installation. Therefore, answer c is also incorrect.

Question 51

Answer a is correct. When installing TCP/IP on a nonrouted network, the IP address and subnet mask parameters must be specified. If a default gateway is not specified, the machine can only communicate with other machines within its subnet. Because this is not mandatory on a nonrouted network, answer b is incorrect. DHCP and WINS are not mandatory for IP networks of any kind. Therefore, answers c and d are incorrect, as well.

Question 52

Answer b is correct. Because Windows NT 4 no longer supports HPFS, you'll have to obtain the ACLCONV.EXE utility from Microsoft to convert an HPFS partition into NTFS. The Windows NT 4 utility CONVERT.EXE can only transform FAT partitions into NTFS. Because Windows NT 3.51's convert utility works with HPFS, it might be even better to convert HPFS to NTFS before installing the upgrade to Windows NT 4.

Question 53

Answer b is correct. Because Windows NT Servers use the protocol sent to them by workstations, the binding order need only change on the workstations. Network speed is affected by the binding order on the workstations, but not on servers. Therefore, answers a, c, and d are all incorrect.

Question 54

Answer c is correct. Only DUMPEXAM.EXE can be used to view the contents of DMP files. The Event Viewer and Windows NT Diagnostics are not able to view the contents of a memory dump file. Therefore, answers a and d are incorrect. There is no Debug Inspector. Therefore, answer b is incorrect.

Question 55

Answers a, b, and e are correct. The CACLS command-line utility can be used to change ACLs or permissions for files and folders. Therefore, answer a is correct. Moving a file or directory to a new partition causes that object to take on the settings of its new container, thus its permissions are changed. Therefore, answer b is correct. The Permissions button on the Security properties tab is the easiest method for changing NTFS permissions. Therefore, answer e is correct (and preferred). The Share properties tab can only change permissions for a share, not NTFS permissions for files or directories. Therefore, answer c is incorrect. Taking ownership gives users the ability to change permissions, but the act of taking ownership alters no permissions. Therefore, answer d is incorrect.

Question 56

Answers b and d are correct. The command (**ntbackup backup c: /B /L "c:\backup.log"**) should be saved in a text file named MYBACKUP.CMD. The command (**AT 23:00 /every:M,W,F MYBACKUP.CMD**) is then issued from a command prompt. The command in selection a is not a valid NTBACKUP command line construction. Therefore, answer a is incorrect. Schedule is not a valid command. Therefore, answer c is incorrect. The command in selection d is not a valid command construction. Therefore, answer e is incorrect.

Question 57

Answer c is correct. Both the FAT and NTFS file systems support long file names. Only NTFS supports file-level permissions. Therefore, answers a, b, and d are incorrect.

Question 58

Answer c is correct. The command in selection c starts the automated install with the answer file and uniqueness database. WINNT32 cannot be launched from DOS. Therefore, answer a is incorrect. The command in selection b is invalid. It combines the /OX parameter to build setup floppies without installing with a uniqueness database. The former should be used alone whereas the latter requires an answer file. Therefore, answer b is incorrect. The command in selection d just builds setup floppies. Therefore, answer d is incorrect. The command in selection e is invalid; the /s parameter defines a new source directory, not the location of the answer file. Therefore, answer e is incorrect.

Question 59

Answer a is correct. LPR is the command to send print jobs to LPD print devices (i.e., Unix printers). Spooler is not an application, but a component of the Windows NT print system. Therefore, answer b is incorrect. The Print Manager is not used to send print jobs to a Unix printer. Plus, the Print Manager is a term from Windows NT 3.51; the printer interface is now called the Printers folder or the printer queue. The Printers folder or the printer queue serves the functions the Print Manager handled. Therefore, answer c is incorrect. Windows Explorer is not used to send print jobs to Unix printers. Therefore, answer d is incorrect.

Question 60

Answer b is correct. To create custom startup files for an MS-DOS program, you will need to create or edit the Autoexec.nt file located in the %systemroot%\system32 folder. The required results cannot be achieved by editing the Registry. Therefore, answer a is incorrect. The environment path is equivalent to a path statement in the MS-DOS autoexec.bat file. Therefore, answer c is incorrect. Win.ini is a Windows 3.1 file and not applicable to Windows NT. Therefore, answer d is incorrect.

Sample Test #2

See Chapter 19 for Sample Test #1 and pointers to help you develop a successful test-taking strategy, including how to choose proper answers, how to decode ambiguity, how to work within the Microsoft testing framework, how to decide what you need to memorize, and how to prepare for the test. In this chapter, we include another test on subject matter pertinent to Microsoft Exam 70-073: "Implementing and Supporting Microsoft Windows NT Workstation 4.0 Exam." After this chapter, you'll find the answer key to this test.

Also, remember that you can take adaptive practice exams on Windows NT Workstation 4 online at **www.coriolis.com/cip/core4rev/** to help you prepare even more. Good luck!

Question 1

What is the command for starting an application minimized with a high priority?

- ○ a. Start app.exe /min /max
- ○ b. Start /min app.exe /high
- ○ c. Start /min /high app.exe
- ○ d. Start /min high app.exe

Question 2

Why are TSRs not launched from the AUTOEXEC.NT and CONFIG.NT files?

- ○ a. Windows NT does not support TSRs.
- ○ b. TSRs are always launched by the application requiring them.
- ○ c. Multiple copies of the TSRs would be launched.
- ○ d. WIN.INI is used to launch TSRs.

Question 3

Which protocol should be at the top of the binding order under Windows NT Workstation?

- ○ a. The fastest one
- ○ b. The one with the least amount of overhead
- ○ c. Only transport protocols should be bound to the top of the binding order
- ○ d. The one most frequently used

Question 4

How can you ensure that you perform a complete backup of your system including the Registry? [Check all correct answers]

❑ a. Use Windows NT's native backup utility.

❑ b. Back up the root directory.

❑ c. Choose the Backup Local Registry option in Windows NT's backup utility.

❑ d. Make sure you are logged on as a Backup Operator.

Question 5

Your organization's domain consists of one Primary Domain Controller, three Backup Domain Controllers, and one member server. You have created a system policy on the Primary Domain Controller but many of the users complain that they are still getting their old settings. Why is this happening?

○ a. You haven't enabled system policies with the Server application.

○ b. You haven't assigned the policy to the groups.

○ c. You haven't replicated the policies to the BDCs.

○ d. You haven't enabled the system option under User Manager.

Question 6

Which of the following are actions or functions that can be performed during the ERD repair process? [Check all correct answers]

❑ a. Inspect Registry Files

❑ b. Inspect Startup Environment

❑ c. Verify Windows NT System Files

❑ d. Inspect Boot Sector

❑ e. Repair Master Boot Record

Question 7

Your company uses frame relay to make a permanent connection to the Internet. Your Windows NT Workstation is also a member of your company's local domain. You want to do everything you can to make sure hackers can't access your system. You have disabled your Server service and removed the binding on other unnecessary services. What else should you do to help secure your system?

○ a. Disable the Workstation service.

○ b. Set your IP address to 127.0.0.1 to enable local loopback.

○ c. Zero out your subnet mask.

○ d. Disable IP forwarding.

Question 8

Your Windows NT Workstation fails to restart and you assume it is because your boot sector has gotten corrupted and needs to be restored. What are two ways to do this?

○ a. Boot with MS-DOS and run Winnt, or boot from the Windows NT installation disk and use the Emergency Repair Disk.

○ b. Boot with an NTFS boot disk and use the **sys** command, or boot from the Windows NT installation disk and choose to reinstall.

○ c. Boot with MS-DOS and run Winnt32, or boot from the Windows NT installation disk and use the Emergency Repair Disk.

○ d. Boot with MS-DOS and run regedit, or boot from the Windows NT installation disk and use the Emergency Repair Disk.

Question 9

You are using Performance Monitor to monitor several hard drives on your Windows NT Workstation. However, the readings on the counters are always zero. Why?

○ a. You didn't use the **diskperf** command to start the counters.

○ b. You didn't use the **diskperf -y** command to enable the counters.

○ c. You need to go into Disk Administrator and enable monitoring.

○ d. You need to go into User Manager and enable auditing for your disk devices.

Question 10

The Guest account has which type of profile by default?

○ a. Local only

○ b. Roaming

○ c. Local mandatory

○ d. Roaming mandatory

Question 11

You have three part-time workers who all share the same Windows NT Workstation. They all want to keep their own desktop settings. How many user accounts would you need for them to manage their own settings and log in and out of the system?

○ a. Three user accounts

○ b. One user account

○ c. Three user accounts on the Primary Domain Controller

○ d. Six user accounts: three on the Primary Domain Controller and three on the local workstation

Question 12

You want to install Windows NT Workstation over your network. How do you do it?

- ○ a. Connect to a shared folder on the network and run winnt32.

- ○ b. Format the active partition to NTFS and boot to it with an MS-DOS boot disk. Make sure it contains the network drivers. Connect to a share and run winnt.exe.

- ○ c. It can't be done. Windows NT Workstation must be installed from local media. It does not support network installations.

- ○ d. Share the folder on the network drive, making sure it contains the install files. Connect to that share and run winnt.exe.

Question 13

Which files are found on a RISC system's system partition? [Check all correct answers]

- ❑ a. NTDETECT.COM

- ❑ b. OSLOADER.EXE

- ❑ c. NTLDR

- ❑ d. HAL.DLL

- ❑ e. BOOT.INI

Question 14

Which of the following must you configure under TCP/IP if you want your Windows NT Workstation to connect to a different subnet?

- ○ a. A remote IP address

- ○ b. A remote IP scope

- ○ c. A default gateway

- ○ d. A WINS server address

Question 15

Which of the following is not true about using DHCP?

○ a. It can assign a client a dedicated IP address.

○ b. It can assign a client's IP address dynamically.

○ c. It can assign a client's subnet mask.

○ d. It can assign a host's computer name.

Question 16

If you're making a connection to a Unix server at an ISP instead of a Windows NT Server hosting RAS from your Windows NT Workstation dial-up client, which setting must you typically change in the phonebook entry from its default or current setting?

○ a. Dial-Up server type

○ b. Whether to open a terminal window after dialing

○ c. Authentication and encryption policy

○ d. Disable software compression

○ e. X.25

Question 17

Billy is a member of the ACCOUNTING, FINANCE, and MARKETING groups. He needs to access a file in the \PAYEES folder and he has full rights to it. The groups have the following rights: ACCOUNTING has Read and Execute, FINANCE has Read and Execute, and MARKETING has No Access. What is Billy able to do with documents in the PAYEES folder?

○ a. Read

○ b. Nothing

○ c. Read, Copy

○ d. Read, Copy, and Move

Question 18

You have a Windows NT Workstation acting as a print server for about 20 Windows NT clients. You need to upgrade the drivers for the print device with the least amount of effort. What's the best way to do it?

○ a. Upgrade the driver on the print server.

○ b. Share the new print drivers and allow all users access to them.

○ c. Create a new printer with the new print drivers.

○ d. Install a new compatible print device.

Question 19

What must be installed on your Windows NT Workstation to change the password for a NetWare user account?

○ a. File And Print Services For NetWare

○ b. GSNW

○ c. CSNW

○ d. TCP/IP

Question 20

Which of the following is not a true statement about the paging file?

○ a. The paging file can be split across multiple drives.

○ b. The paging file must be at least 2 MB on the boot partition if STOP error information is dumped to a file.

○ c. The paging file must have access set to a minimum of Everyone (R).

○ d. The paging file can be placed on a HPFS volume.

Question 21

Your boss's Windows NT Workstation is running slow. You want to speed up access to the files and hard disks. How do you do it?

○ a. Create a volume set.

○ b. Create a second page file on the same partition.

○ c. Create a new page file and erase the old one.

○ d. Implement a stripe set.

Question 22

You are concerned about security on your Windows NT Workstation when it is left unattended for more than 20 minutes. What can you do about it?

○ a. Enable a screen saver with password protection.

○ b. Create a system policy that will log the workstation off the domain after 20 minutes of inactivity.

○ c. Implement the suspend feature in that workstation's BIOS and set its timeout to 20 minutes.

○ d. Edit the Registry and set the HKEY_LOCAL_MACHINE/ ADMINISTRATION/TIME_OUT to TIME_OUT = 20.

Question 23

What causes all Win 16 applications to fail when one of them fails?

○ a. Their 16-bit code

○ b. Thunking

○ c. Shared memory space

○ d. 8.3 file name support

○ e. A single message queue

Question 24

> You need to make sure that your Windows NT Workstation can communicate with your organization's IBM mainframe. What protocol must you install?
>
> ○ a. TCP/IP
>
> ○ b. SNMP
>
> ○ c. DLC
>
> ○ d. NWLink

Question 25

> What type of installation is used when installing Windows NT Workstation on a RISC-based system?
>
> ○ a. Local CD-ROM
>
> ○ b. Shared network
>
> ○ c. Floppy disk
>
> ○ d. Remote CD-ROM

Question 26

> You are setting up Dial-Up Networking to connect to a local Internet Service Provider. What IP address do you need to use on your system?
>
> ○ a. The IP address of the PPP server you're dialing into.
>
> ○ b. You'll use the IP address that is dynamically assigned to you from the ISP's PPP server.
>
> ○ c. The IP address of the ISP's primary router.
>
> ○ d. The ISP's default gateway address.

Question 27

You want to test Windows NT Workstation 4.0. The only computer you have is a Windows NT 3.51 Server used for production. How can you install Windows NT Workstation with the least effort and still not compromise the functionality of the Windows NT 3.51 Server?

O a. Create an extended partition on the server and install Windows NT Workstation on it.

O b. Install a second hard drive into the server and install Windows NT Workstation on it.

O c. Install Windows NT Workstation on a different directory.

O d. Create a volume set on the server and install Windows NT Workstation on the newly created volume.

Question 28

You want to upgrade your Windows 95 users to Windows NT Workstation 4.0. They all want to keep their desktop settings and applications the same. How would you do this?

O a. Install into a different directory using winnt.exe. Then, reinstall all applications and reconfigure user environment. Then, remove Windows 95.

O b. Install into a different directory and import the Windows 95 Registry. Then, delete Windows 95.

O c. Boot into Windows 95 and run winnt32.exe. Install into different directory and run the upgrade.exe utility.

O d. Perform a typical installation of Windows NT Workstation using winnt.exe. You will be prompted to upgrade and migrate user settings. Choose Yes.

Question 29

How can you change the boot delay time for Windows NT Workstation? [Check all correct answers]

❑ a. Edit the boot.sys file.

❑ b. Edit the boot.ini file.

❑ c. Use the Startup/Shutdown tab of the System applet.

❑ d. Change the boot time setting in the Services applet.

Question 30

You want to make sure part-time employees using several of your Windows NT Workstations can't shut down the machines from the login dialog box. How do you disable the Shutdown button in the login dialog box?

○ a. Change the Registry value of ShutdownWithoutLogon from 1 to 0.

○ b. Change the Registry value of ShowLogonShutdown from 1 to 0.

○ c. Use the System applet in the Control Panel to change the logout setting from Yes to No.

○ d. It can't be done.

Question 31

Where are the two places you can go to view information about memory utilization? [Check all correct answers]

❑ a. Task Manager

❑ b. System applet

❑ c. Performance Monitor

❑ d. Event Log

Question 32

You are dual-booting Windows NT Workstation and MS-DOS. You have decided to remove Windows NT. Which of the following steps do you need to take? [Check all correct answers]

❑ a. Boot from an MS-DOS boot disk.

❑ b. Transfer the system files.

❑ c. Start up Windows NT Workstation, go to the System applet in the Control Panel, and choose Uninstall from the File menu.

❑ d. Delete the Windows NT files.

Question 33

On which of the following installation methods will an error result if your 4 GB hard drive is initially partitioned with a single 50 MB MS-DOS partition? [Check all correct answers]

❑ a. A network installation

❑ b. Installing using the three setup floppies

❑ c. Executing "winnt /b" from the CD

Question 34

Which built-in groups can create and share a folder under Windows NT Workstation? [Check all correct answers]

❑ a. Administrators

❑ b. Power Users

❑ c. Backup Operators

❑ d. Users

Question 35

You want to consolidate the free space on several drives into one logical drive. Performance is not an issue, but you want to be able to increase the logical drive's size at a later time should you decide to add another drive. Which disk method would you use?

○ a. Volume set

○ b. Stripe set with parity

○ c. Disk duplexing

○ d. Stripe set

Question 36

You have been assigned to set up the RAS connections at your company's branch office. It has two ISDN lines with two B channels each and an ISDN router. The computer is running Windows NT Workstation 4.0 with Service Pack 3. How do you configure the RAS connections to allow for maximum bandwidth?

O a. Create two phonebook entries and enable Multilink PPP.

O b. Create one phonebook entry and assign a phone number for each of the four B channels.

O c. Create two phonebook entries and enter the primary B channel's identification number into each entry.

O d. Create one phonebook entry. Assign each ISDN D channel's identification number to the entry.

Question 37

John has a notebook computer with a PC card slot. When he's at the office, he uses a 10BaseT Ethernet card to attach to the company LAN; when he's at home, he uses a modem card to enable Dial-Up Networking. He wants Windows NT Workstation to disable the network card and enable the modem when he's away from the office. How does he do it?

O a. He must make sure that the NIC is plugged in when he attaches to the company LAN. Windows NT takes care of the rest.

O b. He goes to the Services applet in the Control Panel and makes sure that the Plug and Play service is set to Automatic. He creates two hardware profiles: one with the network card for the office and the second with the modem for when he's at home.

O c. He starts the Plug and Play service with the modem plugged in and selects Save Changes To Registry; he then stops the service and repeats the process with the network card plugged in.

O d. He creates two hardware profiles: one with the network card for the office and the second with the modem for when he's at home.

Question 38

You install a new print device on your Windows NT Workstation.
You need to make sure that all the Windows 95, Windows NT 4.0,
and Windows NT 3.51 clients can print to it. Where would you set
up the printer and its drivers?

○ a. Install the drivers on each client.

○ b. It can't be done. You have to set the printer up as either a
Windows 95, Windows NT 4, or Windows NT 3.51 logical
printer.

○ c. You need to set up TCP/IP on the host and assign the
printer an IP address, making it a network printer.

○ d. Install drivers for each operating system on the print
server computer.

Question 39

What happens to accounts and passwords when you do a restore/
fix using the Emergency Repair Disk?

○ a. All accounts are reset to the Last Known Good Configuration.

○ b. All accounts are restored as they were when you created
the Emergency Repair Disk.

○ c. All accounts are restored to their default settings.

○ d. All accounts are restored to the original state they were in
after you initially installed Windows NT.

Question 40

Your boss wants to be able to see the security log on your Windows NT Workstation. How can you make sure he has access to it?

○ a. Include him in the local administrator group.

○ b. Replicate your security log to the server and assign the
EVERYONE group Read permissions to it.

○ c. Create a global Admin group on your workstation and
make your boss a member of it.

○ d. Add your local administrator account to the GLOBAL
administrator group and make your boss a member of
that group.

Question 41

You have 100 identical computers on your network. You want to replicate the installation of all applications on all machines. How are you going to do it?

○ a. Run sysdiff /snap INSTALL applications and Run sysdiff / diff INSTALL on other machines.

○ b. Create one UDF and one Unattend.txt and use them to replicate all installations.

○ c. Create a template machine and then copy its Registry and application directory to the server. Then, run setup from each workstation.

○ d. It can't be done. You'll have to install the software directly onto each workstation.

Question 42

Which permission level is able to alter the access permissions on an object?

○ a. Read

○ b. Change

○ c. Delete

○ d. Full Control

○ e. No Access

Question 43

Windows NT supports three major networking protocols: TCP/IP, NWLink (IPX/SPX), and NetBEUI. Which of these three protocols works for RAS dial-out, but not for RAS dial-in?

○ a. NetBEUI, because it can't be routed.

○ b. NWLink, because Windows NT does not include a SAP agent.

○ c. None of the listed protocols are limited to one direction; all three protocols work both ways with RAS.

○ d. TCP/IP, unless an external IP router is available.

○ e. NetBEUI and NWLink.

Question 44

You are installing Windows NT and get the following error: "Non-Critical Error. The external library procedure, CopySingleFile, reported the following error: Unable to do the specified file copy operation." What is causing the error?

○ a. The Hardware Abstraction Layer can't find your hard disk.

○ b. You are trying to install an unsupported driver.

○ c. An unsupported CD-ROM or network drive is being used.

○ d. Your installation CD is bad and you'll have to order replacement media.

Question 45

You want to print to a TCP/IP printer on your LOCAL domain. Which of the following must be true? [Check all correct answers]

❑ a. You must specify the IP address.

❑ b. The DLC protocol needs to be installed.

❑ c. You must specify the printer's name.

❑ d. You must provide the HPMON Driver with support for network printers.

Question 46

Which of the following must you define when joining a routed environment? [Check all correct answers]

❑ a. IP address

❑ b. DNS address

❑ c. Subnet mask

❑ d. Default gateway

Question 47

Your sales director has given his two weeks' notice. What is the best way (according to Microsoft) to give the new director all the same rights and permissions on that Windows NT Workstation?

○ a. Use the current director's account as a template and create the new account based on it.

○ b. Copy the current director's account, rename it, and then disable the existing one.

○ c. Rename the current director's local account and change the password.

○ d. Give the new director the user name and password for the existing account.

Question 48

What is the best order in which to install the following operating systems to ensure proper automatic configuration as a multi-boot system?

○ a. Windows NT, Windows 95, MS-DOS

○ b. MS-DOS, Windows NT, Windows 95

○ c. Windows 95, Windows NT, MS-DOS

○ d. MS-DOS, Windows 95, Windows NT

○ e. Windows NT, MS-DOS, Windows 95

Question 49

You need to install Windows NT Workstation on 250 machines. They all have exactly the same applications. Which files will you need to automate the installation routine?

○ a. Unattend.txt, UDF, boot.ini

○ b. Config.nt, Sysdiff.exe, Unattend.txt, UDF

○ c. Unattend.txt, Sysdiff.exe, UDF

○ d. Unattend.txt, Sysdiff.exe, UDF, Win.ini

Question 50

You move a file from your NTFS C:\ drive to your NTFS D:\ drive, which has just been formatted for use (no other changes have been made). The permission on the original file is No Access for the Users group. After the move across partitions, what will be the effective permissions of the Users group on that file?

○ a. Read

○ b. Read, Execute

○ c. No Access

○ d. Full Control

Question 51

Your company employs numerous independent consultants who operate throughout the United States. They regularly dial in to the central Windows NT Server-based LAN to upload new orders and download the latest product descriptions. Each user purchased his or her own equipment and operating system. In this situation, what is the highest level of native Windows NT security you can implement and still allow your users to connect via RAS?

○ a. Allow Any Authentication Including Clear Text

○ b. Microsoft Encrypted Authentication

○ c. PGP Encryption

○ d. Require Encrypted Authentication

Question 52

You are using CSNW to print to a print device attached to a NetWare server. You want to be notified when the print jobs are done. How is this possible?

○ a. Use Printcon on the NetWare Server and enable the Notify Client option.

○ b. Use the Printer option under Windows NT to enable the Print Notification option.

○ c. In CSNW, enable the Notify When Printed option.

○ d. Just make sure you have the Alert Service running on Windows NT. You'll automatically be notified when a print job completes.

Question 53

Which of the following conditions must exist if a complete memory dump file is to be created in the event of a STOP error? [Check all correct answers]

❑ a. An IDE hard drive must be present.

❑ b. Dr. Watson must be disabled.

❑ c. A 2 MB paging file must exist on the system partition.

❑ d. An administrator must be logged on.

❑ e. Enough free space must exist on the system partition to store the contents of memory.

Question 54

You have a computer that can dual-boot between MS-DOS and Windows NT Workstation. However, every time you start the machine, it automatically boots into Windows NT and doesn't give you an option of choosing MS-DOS. What is the most likely problem?

○ a. Your boot.ini file is missing.

○ b. The timeout value in the boot.ini file is set to 0.

○ c. You don't have the ntosloader file installed on your workstation.

○ d. You haven't enabled the multiboot option under the System applet in the Control Panel.

Question 55

Your Windows NT Workstation has just encountered a major error and has received stop errors. Where would you look for more information about the stop errors?

○ a. Stop log

○ b. Dr. Watson's error log

○ c. Memory dump log

○ d. Event Viewer

Question 56

Following a successful Windows NT Workstation installation, you notice that the built-in Windows NTBACKUP utility was installed automatically. Yet when you try to use your tape drive, it won't work. Select the best explanation for this phenomenon from the following list:

○ a. You must install CSNW before NTBACKUP will work.

○ b. Before you can run NTBACKUP, you must restart the machine.

○ c. RAS must be running before NTBACKUP will work.

○ d. Although NTBACKUP installed as a default system component, you must still install drivers for the tape drive you'll be using.

Question 57

While installing Windows NT on an older computer, Windows NT fails to recognize the third SCSI drive during the hardware detection phase. Which of the following recommendations might help to resolve this problem? [Check all correct answers]

❏ a. Abort the installation and start over. It should recognize the drive on your second try.

❏ b. Complete the install program, and then provide driver and configuration information in the SCSI applet in Control Panel immediately thereafter.

❏ c. Remove the hard disk that wasn't recognized, and replace it with a drive that appears on the Hardware Compatibility List.

❏ d. Press the S key during the hard disk detection phase to force the install program to search for SCSI devices during installation.

❏ e. Complete the install program, run the System Applet, and then provide configuration information for the Add Drive entry on the Hardware Profiles tab.

Question 58

Which of the following conditions will prevent Windows NT Workstation from being installed onto a Windows 95 system?

○ a. Logical block addressing EIDE addressing scheme

○ b. Compressed boot drive

○ c. An HPFS formatted drive in the extended partition

○ d. 150 MB of free space on the boot drive

Question 59

On Windows NT Workstation, Disk Administrator can be used to create which disk configurations? [Check all correct answers]

❑ a. Volume sets

❑ b. Stripe sets

❑ c. Duplexed drives

❑ d. Stripe sets with parity

Question 60

Following a reconfiguration of a Windows NT Workstation, a reboot provokes the following error message:

```
I/O Error accessing boot sector file:
multi(0)disk(0)rdisk(0)partition(2):bootsect.dos
```

Of the following options, which represents the quickest way to fix this problem?

○ a. Hit the space bar during bootup, and start from the Last Known Good Configuration.

○ b. Boot the computer from the ERD and follow the prompts.

○ c. Start the computer from the Windows NT Boot disks, and initiate the ERD repair process.

○ d. Start the computer from the Windows NT Boot disks, and copy BOOTSECT.DOS from another machine.

Answer Key #2

1. c	21. d	41. a
2. c	22. a	42. d
3. d	23. c	43. c
4. a, c	24. c	44. c
5. c	25. a	45. a, c
6. a, b, c, d	26. b	46. a, c, d
7. d	27. c	47. c
8. a	28. a	48. d
9. b	29. b, c	49. c
10. c	30. a	50. d
11. a	31. a, c	51. a
12. d	32. a, b, d	52. c
13. b, d	33. a, c	53. c, e
14. c	34. a, b	54. b
15. d	35. a	55. d
16. c	36. b	56. d
17. b	37. d	57. b, c, d
18. a	38. d	58. b
19. c	39. b	59. a, b
20. d	40. a	60. c

Question 1

Answer c is correct. The correct parameters for the start command are: start ["title"] [/dpath] [/i] [/min] [/max] [/separate] [/low] [/normal] [/high] [/realtime] [/wait] [/b] [filename] [parameters]. In this case, only answer c contains the correct syntax. Answers a, b, and d are incorrect.

Question 2

Answer c is correct. Each time a DOS application is launched, the AUTOEXEC.NT and CONFIG.NT files will be used again and again. Windows NT does support or at least allow TSRs. Therefore, answer a is incorrect. TSRs are typically required before an application can properly launch. Therefore, answer b is incorrect. WIN.INI is not used by Windows NT, especially not with DOS applications; it exists for backward compatibility for Windows 3.1 and Windows 95 applications. Therefore, answer d is incorrect.

Question 3

Answer d is correct. The protocol most frequently used is the one that should be placed at the top of the binding order so it will be accessed before the others. The speed and overhead of a protocol is generally not considered a factor in its use and deployment, making answers a and b incorrect. Just because a protocol is considered a transport protocol makes no difference in its place in the binding order. Therefore, answer c is also incorrect.

Question 4

Answers a and c are correct. To make sure that the local Registry on your Windows NT Workstation is backed up, you'll need to use the backup utility that is located in the Start|Programs|Administrative Tools menu. Once you have picked the files you want backed up and a tape drive to use, you will be given the opportunity to name and configure the backup before it executes. Make sure that you check the box labeled Backup Local Registry. Answer b is incorrect because backing up the root directory does not ensure that the Registry is backed up. Answer d is incorrect because you do not have to be a Backup Operator to perform backups that include the Registry. Server Operators and Administrators can perform this action as well.

Question 5

Answer c is correct because system policies need to be replicated to all the Backup Domain Controllers so they can propagate through the system. System policies are administered through the User Manager. Therefore, answer a is incorrect. Only some of the users are experiencing problems, as opposed to a specific group, making answer b incorrect. There is no system option in User Manager as specified in answer d, so it also is incorrect.

Question 6

Answers a, b, c, and d are correct. Inspect Registry Files, Inspect Startup Environment, Verify Windows NT System Files, and Inspect Boot Sector are the four repair functions offered by the ERD repair process. Repair Master Boot Record is not a function of the ERD repair process. Therefore, answer e is incorrect.

Question 7

Answer d is correct. To minimize the risk of a hacker using your workstation as an access point to your company's domain, you should disable IP forwarding. IP forwarding, as the name implies, allows for the forwarding of IP packets. The Workstation Service provides network connections and communications, so it cannot be disabled and shouldn't be removed, making answer a incorrect. Answer b is incorrect because the IP address of 127.0.0.1 is not a valid address. It is used to PING your local adapter to ensure that the TCP/IP protocol is installed correctly. Using all zeros in your subnet mask would result in an incorrect subnet mask. Therefore, answer c is incorrect.

Question 8

Answer a is correct. If your boot sector is corrupt, it needs to be restored/repaired. By booting with MSDOS and running Winnt you'll be able to reinstall Windows NT, which would correct the problem. A better solution, however, is to boot up the machine using the original Windows NT installation disk. When prompted, insert the Emergency Repair Disk. Answer b is only half right because there is no such thing as an NTFS boot disk. Answer c is incorrect because Winnt32 is used to upgrade from Windows NT 3.51 to 4.0. Regedit is a utility used to read and edit the Registry files and has nothing to do with your boot sector, making answer d incorrect also.

Question 9

Answer b is correct. Windows NT's Performance Monitor allows you to monitor and report on a wide variety of system functions. Diskperf is a utility that can be used to monitor hard drives. To turn Diskperf on, at the command prompt type diskperf -y. To turn it off, type diskperf -n. Answer a is incorrect because it does not include the switch "-y". Answers c and d are incorrect because they do not mention the Diskperf utility.

Question 10

Answer c is correct The Guest account has a local mandatory profile. Therefore, answers a, b, and d are incorrect.

Question 11

Answer a is correct. One of the components of a user account is a user profile. A user profile is a collection of, among other things, desktop settings and preferences. For each of the three part-time workers to have their own settings, they each need individual user accounts. Answer b is incorrect because the sharing of one user account would mean they all have the same settings. Answers c and d are incorrect because there is no need for the account to be located on a server; they only need to reside locally.

Question 12

Answer d is correct. To install Windows NT, you must have access to the installation files. In the case of a network installation, you'll need access to the files. This is accomplished by accessing the shared folder on the network drive that contains the files. You will also have to start the installation by running the Winnt executable. Answer a makes no mention of the folder containing the installation files and Winnt32 is used to upgrade an existing Windows NT installation. Therefore, answer a is incorrect. It is not required that a partition be formatted with NTFS before you install Windows NT Workstation. Therefore, answer b is incorrect. There is also no need to use local media as opposed to networking. Therefore, answer c is incorrect.

Question 13

Answers b and d are correct. A RISC system's system partition hosts OSLOADER.EXE and HAL.DLL files. Intel system's system partition hosts NTDETECT.COM, NTLDR, and BOOT.INI. Therefore, answers a, c, and e are incorrect.

Question 14

Answer c is correct. You must define a default gateway if you want your Windows NT Workstation to connect to a different subnet. In most cases, your default gateway will generally be a router or a multihomed Windows NT Server. Answer a is incorrect because there is no place under the TCP/IP utility to store various remote IP addresses. Answer b is incorrect because an IP scope is a range of IP addresses you configure if and when you want to set up a DHCP server, which automatically assigns IP addresses to hosts that ask for them. Answer d is incorrect because a WINS server is not required to access another subnet.

Question 15

Answer d is correct. DHCP cannot assign a host's computer name to a client. Answer d is therefore false. DHCP can issue a "reservation for an IP address that always delivers the same IP address to a specific MAC address. Thus, DHCP can indeed assign a dedicated IP address to a client. DHCP is used to assign IP addressing information dynamically to any host that requests it. Most often, a range of addresses is available to the DHCP server for it to assign the various IP addresses dynamically. It can assign an IP address and subnet mask. Therefore, answers a, b, and c are true statements, making them incorrect.

Question 16

Answer c is correct. The default authentication and encryption policy is to accept only encrypted authentication. Most ISPs do not use encrypted authentication, so this must be switched to accept clear text before connecting to a Unix server. Both Unix and Windows NT are included under the default PPP selection. Therefore, answer a is incorrect. A terminal window is not enabled by default and is not typically required by either Unix or Windows NT dial-up systems. Therefore, answer b is incorrect. Software compression is typically not an issue; it's enabled by default. Therefore, answer d is incorrect. X.25 settings should not need to change if that is the communication technology used to connect to both system types. Therefore, answer e is incorrect.

Question 17

Answer b is correct. With regard to access permissions at the group level, always remember that the most restrictive permission always wins. In the case of the No Access permission, it always supercedes any other permissions that have been granted, regardless of the group that grants them. In this case, because Billy is a member of the Marketing group, which has No Access to the Payees folder, he will be unable to read, copy, or move any files. That makes answers a, c, and d incorrect.

Question 18

Answer a is correct. To upgrade the drivers for the print device, you need to upgrade the drivers on the print server. You don't need to update the driver on Windows NT client machines. It is not necessary for your Windows NT clients to upgrade drivers. Therefore, answer b is incorrect. Answer c would work, but is more effort than required and the question asked for the least amount of effort, so it is incorrect. Answer d involves actually adding/installing a new printer, which is also more effort than is necessary, and is therefore incorrect.

Question 19

Answer c is correct. CSNW (Client Service For NetWare) enables Windows NT Workstation to make direct connections to file and printer resources on NetWare servers that are running NetWare 2.x or later. It also allows you access to other services such as changing passwords. Answer a is incorrect because File And Print Services For NetWare is a Windows NT Server component that enables a computer running Windows NT Server to provide file and print services directly to NetWare-compatible client computers. GSNW (Gateway Services For NetWare) is a Windows NT Server service that cannot be installed on Windows NT Workstation. Therefore, answer b is incorrect. TCP/IP is a protocol that has no relation to the ability to change passwords for NetWare user accounts. Therefore, answer d is incorrect.

Question 20

Answer d is correct. HPFS volumes are not accessible by Windows NT in any way; therefore, they cannot host a paging file. Answers a, b, and c are all true. Therefore, answers a, b, and c are incorrect.

Question 21

Answer d is correct. With stripe sets, the data is written across multiple drives in sequence, allowing for quicker read/write performance, which in turn speeds up access to files and hard disks. A volume set allows you to take two or more free spaces and combine them into one volume. It does not, however, speed up performance. Therefore, answer a is incorrect. You cannot create multiple page files on a single partition. Therefore, answer b is incorrect. Answer c is incorrect because creating a new page file would have no effect on performance.

Question 22

Answer a is correct. The quickest way to enable security on a workstation you know will be left unattended is to enable a screen saver with a password. Answer b is incorrect because logging off the domain will not prevent access to the local machine, only access to the rest of the network. The suspend feature in a machine's BIOS is a power-saving feature used to spin down the hard drive and place the machine in sleep mode. It does not affect security. Therefore, answer c is also incorrect. Answer d refers to a nonexistent Registry entry, so it is also incorrect.

Question 23

Answer c is correct. Win 16 applications fail together because of their shared memory space. 16-bit code, thunking, 8.3 filename support, and a single message queue are not the causes of the "all fail if one fails" problem. Therefore, answers a, b, d, and e are incorrect.

Question 24

Answer c is correct. DLC (Data Link Control) is the protocol that is primarily used to access IBM mainframes. TCP/IP is actually a suite of protocols designed for internetworking. It does not provide mainframe connectivity. Therefore, answer a is incorrect. SNMP (Simple Network Management Protocol) is a network management protocol installed with TCP/IP. It is used on TCP/IP and IPX networks. It does not provide for mainframe connectivity. Therefore, answer b is incorrect. Answer d is incorrect because NWLink is Windows NT's IPX/SPX-compatible protocol and deals with NetWare connectivity.

Question 25

Answer a is correct. To install Windows NT Workstation on a RISC-based system, you must use a local CD-ROM. Answers b, c, and d are not possible, and are therefore incorrect.

Question 26

Answer b is correct. Dial-Up Networking allows Windows NT to use a modem to dial up and connect with remote networks. When connecting to an Internet Service Provider, you will be dynamically assigned an IP address from that ISP's server. All IP addresses across a given system must be unique so you cannot have the same IP address as the server you're connecting to. Therefore, answers a, c, and d are incorrect.

Question 27

Answer c is correct. Installing Windows NT Workstation on a different directory will ensure that it doesn't interfere with the functionality of the existing Windows NT 3.51 production server. Creating an extended partition on the server and installing Windows NT Workstation onto it will work. However, it is more work than is needed. Therefore, answer a is incorrect. Likewise, installing a second hard drive is not needed. Therefore, answer b is incorrect. Creating a volume set and installing Windows NT Workstation onto it would corrupt the Windows NT 3.51 installation. Therefore, answer d is incorrect.

Question 28

Answer a is correct. Currently there is no direct migration utility for moving users from a Windows 95 environment to Windows NT Workstation. To upgrade a Windows 95 machine to Windows NT you would have to perform the following steps. First, use winnt.exe to install Windows NT Workstation into the default \Winnt directory. Second, reinstall all the applications that were being used under Windows 95. Third, reconfigure all of your users' desktop and environmental settings. Finally, you would delete the old Windows 95 directory. Only answer a includes all these steps. Therefore, answers b, c, and d are incorrect.

Question 29

Answers b and c are correct. There are two ways to change the boot delay time of Windows NT Workstation. The first is to edit the boot.ini file. Open the file and change the line "timeout=x"; replace the "x" with a number equal to the number of seconds you prefer. The second way is to use the Startup/Shut Down tab of the System applet in the Control Panel. Answer a is incorrect because boot.sys is not a valid file. Answer d is incorrect because there are no settings for controlling the boot time in the Services applet.

Question 30

Answer a is correct. To disable the Shutdown button on the login dialog box, perform the following steps. First, open the Registry with the regedit.exe utility. Second, go to the HKEY_LOCAL_MACHINE\SOFTWARE\ MICROSOFT\WINDOWS NT\CURRENTVERSION\Winlogon key. Third, double-click on ShutdownWithoutLogon option and change its value from 1 to 0. Answer b is incorrect because it refers to an incorrect Registry setting. Answer c is incorrect because the System applet cannot be used to change the functionality of the login dialog box. Answer d is also incorrect because this is one of many custom modifications that can be done to Windows NT by editing the Registry.

Question 31

Answers a and c are correct. The Task Manager and Performance Monitor allow you to view information about memory utilization. Neither the System applet nor Event Log has information about memory utilization. Therefore, answers b and d are incorrect.

Question 32

Answers a, b, and d are all correct. The quickest way to remove an installation of Windows NT Workstation on an Intel-compatible machine is to first boot off an MS-DOS disk, transfer the system files, and delete the Windows NT files. Once you are at the A: prompt, you'll need to transfer the system files by typing sys c:. That will transfer the MS-DOS system files to the root directory of the C drive. At this point, all you have to do is delete the Windows NT files. Answer c is incorrect because there is no uninstall option for the operating system.

Question 33

Answers a and c are correct. A network installation and a floppyless installation both require a 120 MB pre-partitioned space to store the temporary files. The floppy initialized installation creates the destination partition and formats it before the temporary files are transferred. Therefore, answer b is incorrect.

Question 34

Answers a and b are correct. To share a folder in Windows NT Workstation, you need to be a member of either the Administrators or Power Users groups. Neither the Backup Operators nor Users groups have specific rights create shares. Therefore, answers c and d are incorrect.

Question 35

Answer a is correct. You can add additional free space to a volume set at any time. Answers b, c, and d are incorrect because they cannot be extended.

Question 36

Answer b is correct. The best option is to create one phonebook entry and assign a phone number for each of the four B channels. It is unnecessary to create multiple phonebook entries. Therefore, answer a is incorrect. Each B channel of an ISDN line will have its own phone and identification numbers. You would need to create a phonebook entry and assign each of the B channels' phone numbers to it. Answer c is incorrect for the same reason as answer a. Answer d is incorrect because an ISDN's D channel is reserved for additional channel information and does not have a phone or identification number attached to it.

Question 37

Answer d is correct because it makes John create two hardware profiles. John needs to configure separate hardware profiles for home and work. Windows NT will not automatically take care of this. Therefore, answer a is incorrect. Answers b and c are incorrect because Windows NT does not have true Plug and Play services.

Question 38

Answer d is correct. All you need to do is install all the different drivers on the print server computer to which the print device is physically attached. There is no need to install the various print drivers on each of the client machines. Therefore, answer a is incorrect. You can have multiple print drivers installed and working on a single host machine. Therefore, answer b is incorrect. There is also no need to have a network print device with an IP addressee in order to run multiple print drivers, making answer c incorrect.

Question 39

Answer b is correct. When you make an Emergency Repair Disk, it captures a snapshot of your Registry and system settings. It uses this snapshot to return your system to that state. That also means that any changes you have made since the last update/creation of your Emergency Repair Disk will be lost. That's why it's a good idea to make sure your ERD is always current. The Last Known Good Configuration is offered as an option when you first boot a Windows NT Workstation. It will start the computer using the settings that were working the last time you booted, hence its name. Therefore, answer a is incorrect. The purpose of an Emergency Repair Disk is to have something other than default settings. Therefore, answer c is incorrect. Answer d is also incorrect because settings are returned to the state in the ERD.

Question 40

Answer a is correct. Anyone who is a member of your local administrators group will have permissions to view the security log using Event Viewer. There is no need for any replication. Therefore, answer b is incorrect. Answer c is incorrect because there are no global groups on Windows NT Workstation. They apply to Windows NT Server. For that reason, answer d is also incorrect.

Question 41

Answer a is correct. The key to this question is the use of the sysdiff utility. To replicate the installation of all the application, you'll need to first run sysdiff and take a snapshot of the system. Once you have installed all your applications, you need to update that snapshot with all the differences by using the /diff switch. Answer a meets all these requirements. Answer b is incorrect because it does not capture the installed application information. You can't directly copy Registry information and achieve the results needed. Therefore, answer c is also incorrect. Answer d, of course, is incorrect because it can be done.

Question 42

Answer d is correct. Only Full Control can alter the access permissions on an object. Therefore, answers a, b, c, and e are incorrect.

Question 43

Answer c is correct. All three protocols work for dial-in and dial-out with RAS. Therefore, answers a, b, d, and e are incorrect.

Question 44

Answer c is correct. This error occurs when an unsupported CD-ROM or a network drive is being used. The HAL (Hardware Abstraction Layer) is not involved, per se, in file copies. Therefore, answer a is incorrect. Windows NT's installation program would allow you to copy an unsupported driver but it may not be able to utilize it. Therefore, answer b is incorrect. Answer d would certainly cause you problems and cause installation errors, but it would not generate this specific error. Therefore, answer d is incorrect.

Question 45

Answers a and c are correct. Answer a is correct because you do need to have the IP address of the printer you are trying to print/install. Answer c is correct because, in addition to an IP address, you'll also need the printer's name. Answer b is incorrect; the DLC protocol is primarily used to communicate with IBM mainframes and is not used for network printing with TCP/IP. Answer d refers to an HP print monitor, which does not need to be installed. Therefore, answer d is incorrect.

Question 46

Answers a, c, and d are correct. In a routed environment, you must define the IP address of the default gateway/router, a unique IP address, and the subnet mask for the subnet to which your machine belongs. There is no innate need to provide the IP address of a DNS server when setting up a client in a routed environment. Therefore, answer b is incorrect.

Question 47

Answer c is correct. The best way to ensure that the new sales director has the same access and permissions is to remove the existing account and change the password. This is the official Microsoft party line and at odds with some security experts' recommendations. None of the other answers offer the best solution according to Microsoft. Therefore, answers a, c, and d are incorrect.

Question 48

Answer d is correct. The order of MS-DOS, Windows 95, Windows NT will properly configure the boot menus of both Windows NT and Windows 95. Therefore, answers a, b, c, and e are incorrect.

Question 49

Answer c is correct because it supplies the right combination of files needed to automate the installation of the Windows NT Workstations. Answers a, b, and c are incorrect. They do not supply the needed files or contain files that aren't required or even used during setup.

Question 50

Answer d is correct. If a file is moved from folder to folder on the same partition, it retains its permissions. However, the act of moving it to another partition resets all permissions. In this case, the permission changes from No Access to Full Control because that is the state of permissions on a newly formatted partition. Therefore, answers a, b, and c are incorrect.

Question 51

Answer a is correct. With nonstandardized configurations, implementing any encryption security other than Allow Any Authentication Including Clear Text results in some clients being restricted from accessing the network via RAS. Microsoft Encrypted Authentication and Require Encrypted Authentication are encryption security schemes that require special configuration or operating systems. Therefore, answers b and d are incorrect. PGP Encryption is not a native option of Windows NT. Therefore, answer c is incorrect.

Question 52

Answer c is correct. You can change the print notification of a print job attached to a NetWare server through the Client Service For NetWare. Answer a is incorrect; Printcon is a print utility that is native to NetWare and cannot be used for this purpose. Answers b and d are also incorrect because they do not allow for notification of when a print job is done.

Question 53

Answers c and e are correct. A minimum of 2 MB paging file and enough free space to store the memory dump file must exist on the system partition. An IDE hard drive is not required to record a memory dump file. Therefore, answer a is incorrect. Dr. Watson is not involved in the memory dump process for STOP errors. Therefore, answer b is incorrect. The administrator does not need to be logged in for the system to record a memory dump file. Therefore, answer d is incorrect.

Question 54

Answer b is correct. The most likely reason you are not given time to choose an operating system is because the timeout value is set to 0 in your boot.ini file. To fix it, you have to open the file and edit the line "Timeout=0", replacing the 0 with the number of seconds you'd like to have. Answers a and c are incorrect because if your boot.ini file was missing, Windows NT would not load. Answer d is also incorrect because you don't enable multiboot with the System applet.

Question 55

Answer d is correct. Any STOP error information can be viewed with the Event Viewer. Answer a is incorrect because it refers to a fictitious entity. Answers b and c are incorrect because stop error information is not written to the Dr. Watson Log or the Memory dump.

Question 56

Answer d is correct. The missing ingredients are the drivers; because Windows NT does not support Plug and Play, it has no way of knowing what drivers will be needed—that's why you have to install them (usually in the Tape Drives applet in Control Panel) before NTBACKUP can work. NetWare and backup have no necessary relationship; this answer is completely irrelevant. Therefore, answer a is incorrect. Even if you restart your machine, without drivers for the tape drive, NTBACKUP can't work. Therefore, answer b is incorrect. RAS and backup have no necessary relationship; this answer is completely irrelevant. Therefore, answer c is incorrect.

Question 57

Answers b, c, and d are correct. The solution in selection b might work, provided you have access to Windows NT drivers for the device that don't appear on the installation media. The solution in selection c will always work, provided that Windows NT can recognize the drive (the HCL you're using may be newer than the one that informs the install program on the CD-ROM). The solution in selection d will often work, because it forces Windows NT to detect additional SCSI hardware is all that's required to get it to recognize multiple drives on a system. If Windows NT doesn't recognize a device on a first try at installation, it probably won't recognize it on a second try, either. Therefore, answer a is incorrect. There is no Add Drive entry on the Hardware Profiles tab in the System applet. Therefore, answer e is incorrect.

Question 58

Answer b is correct. Windows NT cannot be installed onto a system with a compressed boot drive. Windows NT supports LBA EIDE addressing. Therefore, answer a is incorrect. The HPFS volume in the extended partition will not be accessible from Windows NT, but it does not prevent

Windows NT from being installed. Therefore, answer c is incorrect. Windows NT requires only about 120 MB of free space to be installed. Thus, 150 MB can easily accommodate the installation. Therefore, answer d is incorrect.

Question 59

Answers a and b are correct. Windows NT Workstation's Disk Administrator can create volume and stripe sets. Only Windows NT Server supports the creation of the fault tolerant drive configurations of duplexed drives and stripe sets with parity. Therefore, answers c and d are incorrect.

Question 60

Answer c is correct. The ERD repair process can be used to repair or replace damaged startup files, including BOOTSECT.DOS. BOOTSECT.DOS describes disk partition information for multi-boot machines that include DOS or Windows 95 among their boot OSs. Because the machine won't boot all the way when this problem occurs, the Last Known Good Configuration option never appears. Therefore, answer a is incorrect. The ERD is not bootable, so this approach is doomed from the start. Therefore, answer b is incorrect. Booting the system with the setup disks will not offer a prompt or mechanism for copying files to the system, thus you will be unable perform this action. Booting with a DOS floppy, then copying the file over, would be possible, but that's not what was prescribed in this selection. Therefore, answer d is incorrect.

Scenarios

Scenario 1

Suppose the following situation exists:

You must select and deploy an operating system.

Required result:

- Ensure the operating system supports two CPUs.

Optional desired results:

- Offer file-level security.
- Offer file-storage encryption.

Proposed solution:

- Deploy Windows NT Workstation.

Which results does the proposed solution produce?

- ○ a. The proposed solution produces the required result and produces both of the optional desired results.

- ○ b. The proposed solution produces the required result and produces only one of the optional desired results.

- ○ c. The proposed solution produces the required result but does not produce any of the optional desired results.

- ○ d. The proposed solution does not produce the required result.

The correct answer is b. The proposed solution of deploying Windows NT Workstation will provide support for two CPUs and file-level security, but it does not support native file-system encryption. Therefore, the proposed solution fulfills the required result and only one of the optional desired results.

Scenario 2

Suppose the following situation exists:

You need to install Windows NT Workstation onto a computer that will act as a standalone system. The computer has the following components and features:

- **CPU** Intel Pentium 133

- **Memory** 32 MB

- **Drive Space** 2 GB free

- **Video** VGA

- **CD-ROM** None

- **Network** NIC present and connected to existing Microsoft network

- **OS** MS-DOS 6.22

Required result:

- Install Windows NT Workstation as a standalone system.

Optional desired results:

- Allow the ability to install additional components after installation is complete.

- Require the least amount of work to complete the installation.

Proposed solution:

- Create a "Microsoft Network Client for MS-DOS" boot disk on a Windows NT Server system via the Network Client Administrator.

- Boot the destination computer with the boot disk.

- Create and format a 1 GB partition on the destination computer. Create a directory named "NTW-CD" in this partition.

- Copy the entire contents of the Windows NT Workstation CD from a network share of a CD-ROM to the NTW-CD directory.

(continued)

Scenario 2 (continued)

> - Initiate the installation routine by launching "c:\ntw-cd\winnt /b".
>
> - During the installation, deselect the Wired To The Network option.
>
> Which results does the proposed solution produce?
>
> ○ a. The proposed solution produces the required result and produces both of the optional desired results.
>
> ○ b. The proposed solution produces the required result and produces only one of the optional desired results.
>
> ○ c. The proposed solution produces the required result but does not produce any of the optional desired results.
>
> ○ d. The proposed solution does not produce the required result.

The correct answer is a. The proposed solution provides a means to install Windows NT Workstation onto a system that does not have a local CD-ROM. By copying the entire CD to the local drive, components can be installed later from the local copy. This is the method that requires the least amount of work to perform the installation, assuming a CD-ROM device is not added to the configuration. By deselecting the Wired To The Network option during setup, the networking components are not installed and Windows NT Workstation will be configured as a standalone system. Therefore, the proposed solution fulfills the required result and both optional desired results.

Scenario 3

> Suppose the following situation exists:
>
> Your installation of Windows NT Workstation is functioning poorly. You suspect a few files have been damaged by a virus that has since been located and removed.
>
> Required result:
>
> - Return the system to normal operation.
>
> Optional desired results:
>
> - Retain Registry and application configuration.
>
> - Retain the current SID.

(continued)

Scenario 3 (continued)

Proposed Solution:

- Perform an upgrade installation of Windows NT Workstation.

Which results does the proposed solution produce?

○ a. The proposed solution produces the required result and produces both of the optional desired results.

○ b. The proposed solution produces the required result and produces only one of the optional desired results.

○ c. The proposed solution produces the required result but does not produce any of the optional desired results.

○ d. The proposed solution does not produce the required result.

The correct answer is a. The proposed solution of an upgrade installation will most likely return the system to a functioning state while retaining Registry and application configuration and the original SID. Therefore, the proposed solution fulfills the required result and both the optional desired results.

Scenario 4

Suppose the following situation exists:

A multiboot computer currently hosts Windows 95 and DOS. You want to add Windows NT Workstation to this system.

Required result:

- Create a multiboot configuration with DOS, Windows 95, and Windows NT Workstation.

Optional desired results:

- Retain the current Windows 95 configuration.

- Support file-level security under Windows NT Workstation.

Proposed solution:

- Using DOS FDISK, create a new partition of at least 1 GB.

- Format the new partition with FAT.

- Launch the installation process from the CD using the WINNT32 /b command from DOS or the Run command from Windows 95.

(continued)

Scenario 4 (continued)

> • During installation, use the new partition as the boot
> partition for Windows NT Workstation, and select to
> convert it to NTFS.
>
> Which results does the proposed solution produce?
>
> ○ a. The proposed solution produces the required result and
> produces both of the optional desired results.
>
> ○ b. The proposed solution produces the required result and
> produces only one of the optional desired results.
>
> ○ c. The proposed solution produces the required result but
> does not produce any of the optional desired results.
>
> ○ d. The proposed solution does not produce the required
> result.

The correct answer is d. The proposed solution fails to install Windows
NT Workstation, because the WINNT32 command is a 32-bit command
that does not function under DOS or Windows 95. Under these two operating systems, the WINNT command must be used. Therefore, the proposed solution fails to fulfill the required result.

Scenario 5

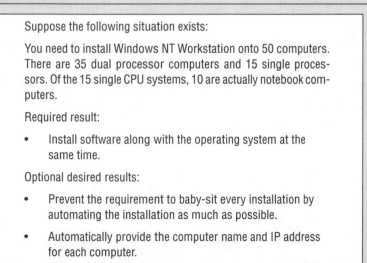

> Suppose the following situation exists:
>
> You need to install Windows NT Workstation onto 50 computers.
> There are 35 dual processor computers and 15 single proces-
> sors. Of the 15 single CPU systems, 10 are actually notebook com-
> puters.
>
> Required result:
>
> • Install software along with the operating system at the
> same time.
>
> Optional desired results:
>
> • Prevent the requirement to baby-sit every installation by
> automating the installation as much as possible.
>
> • Automatically provide the computer name and IP address
> for each computer.

(continued)

Scenario 5 (continued)

Proposed solution:

- Install Windows NT Workstation onto one of the dual processor computers.

- Create a SYSDIFF snapshot of the system.

- Perform all necessary software installations and system configurations.

- Create a SYSDIFF difference file of the system.

- Create an UNATTEND.TXT file and a UDF for the installation of the remaining systems.

- Using SYSDIFF snapshot, difference file, UNATTEND.TXT, and UDF files, launch the installation on each system.

Which results does the proposed solution produce?

○   a.   The proposed solution produces the required result and produces both of the optional desired results.

○   b.   The proposed solution produces the required result and produces only one of the optional desired results.

○   c.   The proposed solution produces the required result but does not produce any of the optional desired results.

○   d.   The proposed solution does not produce the required result.

The correct answer is b. The proposed solution of using SYSDIFF and the automated installation mechanisms is correct, but because there are three types of systems, three different sets of automation scripts are needed. The described process will install software along with the OS and will be able to provide the computer name and IP address, but it will not fully automate the process because only the 35 dual CPU systems will be automated. The other 15 systems will require additional work. Therefore, the proposed solution fulfills the required result but only one of the optional desired results.

Scenario 6

Suppose the following situation exists:

You need to install Windows NT Workstation onto 50 computers. There are 35 dual processor computers and 15 single processors. Of the 15 single CPU systems, 10 are actually notebook computers.

Required result:

- Install software along with the operating system at the same time.

Optional desired results:

- Prevent the requirement to baby-sit every installation by automating the installation as much as possible.

- Automatically provide the computer name and IP address for each computer.

Proposed solution:

- Create one or more UNATTEND.TXT files and a UDF for the installation of the remaining systems.

- Using SYSDIFF snapshot, difference file, UNATTEND.TXT, and UDF files, launch the installation on each system.

Which results does the proposed solution produce?

- ○ a. The proposed solution produces the required result and produces both of the optional desired results.

- ○ b. The proposed solution produces the required result and produces only one of the optional desired results.

- ○ c. The proposed solution produces the required result but does not produce any of the optional desired results.

- ○ d. The proposed solution does not produce the required result.

The correct answer is d. The proposed solution is an automated solution that would result in the installation of Windows NT Workstation, but it does not address the issue of software installation along with the main OS, which requires the use of the SYSDIFF tool. Therefore, the proposed solution does not fulfill the required result.

Scenario 7

Suppose the following situation exists:

Several users need to be granted access to several shared folders. They also need to be able to perform a handful of other important tasks. The shares have already had the Full Control for Everyone permission removed.

Required result:

*   Grant users the ability to access the shared folders with Change permissions.

Optional desired results:

*   Grant users the ability to shut down their Windows NT Workstation computer.

*   Grant users the ability to Change the system time.

Proposed solution:

*   Create a new group called "ShareAccess". Set permissions on the shares for this new group to Change.

Which results does the proposed solution produce?

○   a. The proposed solution produces the required result and produces both of the optional desired results.

○   b. The proposed solution produces the required result and produces only one of the optional desired results.

○   c. The proposed solution produces the required result but does not produce any of the optional desired results.

○   d. The proposed solution does not produce the required result.

The correct answer is b. The proposed solution of creating a new group and granting that group access to the shared folders allows you to specify the users' access to those shares. In addition, all users are members of the Users group by default, so they have the Shutdown Local System user right. However, only Power Users have the Change System Time user right by default. Normal users are not members of the Power Users group by default. Because no mention of altering the user rights settings or other group memberships is included in the solution, the ability to change the system time is not granted. Therefore, the proposed solution fulfills the required result and only one of the optional desired results.

Scenario 8

Suppose the following situation exists:

You've just installed Windows NT Workstation onto a computer. No changes whatsoever have been made to the defaults.

Required result:

*   Enable access to temporary users.

Optional desired results:

*   Allow access to all resources offered to the Everyone group.

*   Do not save changes to the environment when the temporary user logs out.

Proposed solution:

*   Do nothing.

Which results does the proposed solution produce?

❍   a. The proposed solution produces the required result and produces both of the optional desired results.

❍   b. The proposed solution produces the required result and produces only one of the optional desired results.

❍   c. The proposed solution produces the required result but does not produce any of the optional desired results.

❍   d. The proposed solution does not produce the required result.

The correct answer is a. The proposed solution is sufficient, because the Guest account on Windows NT Workstation systems is enabled by default. It can be used to gain access to the system, because its username is Guest and it has a blank password by default. Also, the Guest account is a member of the Everyone group, and it uses a mandatory profile. Therefore, the proposed solution fulfills the required result and both optional desired results.

Scenario 9

Suppose the following situation exists:

You've recently attached a printer to your Windows NT Workstation client. You want to offer access to the printer to the network but still retain some control over its use.

Required result:

- Grant print access to network users in general.

Optional desired results:

- Retain administrative or management privileges over the printer.

- Grant several local users access to the printer.

Proposed solution:

- Using User Manager, create a local group named "NUPrint". Make the Domain Users group a member of NUPrint.

- Grant NUPrint print access to the printer.

- Grant your user account Full Control access to the printer.

- Using User Manager, add the local user accounts to the Domain Users group.

Which results does the proposed solution produce?

○ a. The proposed solution produces the required result and produces both of the optional desired results.

○ b. The proposed solution produces the required result and produces only one of the optional desired results.

○ c. The proposed solution produces the required result but does not produce any of the optional desired results.

○ d. The proposed solution does not produce the required result.

The correct answer is b. The proposed solution grants access to network users and retains administrative control of the printer for your user account. However, you're unable to manage the membership of global groups from User Manager. Therefore, the proposed solution fulfills the required result and only one of the optional desired results. An optimal solution for this scenario would include adding the local user accounts to the NUPrint local group.

Scenario 10

Suppose the following situation exists:

You want to add a Windows NT Workstation client to a NetWare network.

Required result:

- Ensure access to NetWare resources from the Windows NT Workstation client.

Optional desired results:

- Provide the ability to change your NetWare network user account's password from your client.

- Limit the protocols on your system to one.

Proposed solution:

- Deploy File and Print Services for NetWare.

Which results does the proposed solution produce?

- ○   a.   The proposed solution produces the required result and produces both of the optional desired results.

- ○   b.   The proposed solution produces the required result and produces only one of the optional desired results.

- ○   c.   The proposed solution produces the required result but does not produce any of the optional desired results.

- ○   d.   The proposed solution does not produce the required result.

The correct answer is d. The proposed solution of deploying FPNW will not grant the Windows NT Workstation client access to NetWare resources. Therefore, the proposed solution does not fulfill the required result. An optimal solution for this scenario would involve using Client Services For NetWare. This would grant access to many NetWare command-line tools, including SETPASS, which is used to change the account password. In addition, the system can be configured to use only NWLink.

Scenario 11

Suppose the following situation exists:

You've been assigned the responsibility of configuring the security of an organization's standalone Windows NT Workstation systems. You'll need to configure the same settings on all three computers. Each computer has six unique users, each with his or her own user account.

Required result:

- Ensure complex passwords are used.

Optional desired results:

- Ensure passwords are not reused for at least a year.

- Suspend a user account if three sequential logons fail for that user account.

Proposed solution:

- Configure the Account policy so passwords expire in 45 days, with a minimum age of 30 days; require at least 9 characters in the password; and maintain a history of 14 passwords.

- Enable account lockout by setting the Lockout After value to 3, Count Reset to 30 minutes, and Duration to Forever.

Which results does the proposed solution produce?

- ○   a. The proposed solution produces the required result and produces both of the optional desired results.

- ○   b. The proposed solution produces the required result and produces only one of the optional desired results.

- ○   c. The proposed solution produces the required result but does not produce any of the optional desired results.

- ○   d. The proposed solution does not produce the required result.

The correct answer is a. The proposed solution requires a lengthy password (nine characters or more), which is as complex as the account policy built into Windows NT can enforce. The proposed solution also prevents passwords from being reused until 14 password changes have occurred. With a minimum age of 30 days this prevents passwords from being reused within a year. In addition, the account lockout will lock out all user accounts after 3 sequential failed logons occur within 30 minutes. Therefore, the proposed solution fulfills the required result and both optional desired results.

Scenario 12

Suppose the following situation exists:

A user complains that her custom desktop settings do no follow her around the network. Each time she logs into a new Windows NT Workstation client, she gets the default desktop layout.

Required result:

- Configure a profile to follow this user around the network.

Optional desired results:

- Allow the user to configure her own profile.

- Prevent other users from altering her profile.

Proposed solution:

- From one of the client systems where the user has logged in previously, copy the local profile to a network share.

- Change the configuration setting of the profile from Local to Roaming on the Profiles tab of the System applet.

- Change the settings on the network stored location of the profile to Administrators: Full Control, and grant Change access to that user.

Which results does the proposed solution produce?

- ○ a. The proposed solution produces the required result and produces both of the optional desired results.

- ○ b. The proposed solution produces the required result and produces only one of the optional desired results.

- ○ c. The proposed solution produces the required result but does not produce any of the optional desired results.

- ○ d. The proposed solution does not produce the required result.

The correct answer is a. The proposed solution creates a roaming profile that will follow the user to any Windows NT Workstation client on the network, which will allow her to customize her desktop environment and prevent other users from accessing anything within her profile storage area on the network share. Therefore, the proposed solution fulfills the required result and both of the optional desired results.

Scenario 13

Suppose the following situation exists:

You need to impose fault tolerance on your Windows NT Workstation client. You've just installed a second SCSI drive controller and connected four new hard drives to it.

Required result:

- Create a fault-tolerant drive configuration.

Optional desired results:

- Enable file access auditing.

- Place no restrictions on the number of files in the root directory.

Proposed solution:

- Create a disk stripe set with parity using the four new hard drives. Format the set with NTFS.

- Enable auditing for File and Object access, and enable auditing on various file objects by selecting the service and user/group(s) to monitor.

Which results does the proposed solution produce?

○ a. The proposed solution produces the required result and produces both of the optional desired results.

○ b. The proposed solution produces the required result and produces only one of the optional desired results.

○ c. The proposed solution produces the required result but does not produce any of the optional desired results.

○ d. The proposed solution does not produce the required result.

The correct answer is d. The proposed solution of deploying a disk stripe set with parity on a Windows NT Workstation system is not possible because it's not supported by Windows NT Workstation. Only Windows NT Server offers fault tolerance drive configuration support. Therefore, the proposed solution does not fulfill the required result. An optimal solution for this scenario would include creating individual volumes (not multidrive or multipartition volumes) on the new drives and an automated backup, which is as fault tolerant as possible on a Windows NT Workstation.

Scenario 14

Suppose the following situation exists:

Your computer is a multiboot system hosting DOS, Windows 98, and Windows NT Workstation.

Required result:

- Allow data to be accessible from all three operating systems.

Optional desired results:

- Retain long file name capabilities.

- Support file sizes up to 1.3 GB.

Proposed solution:

- Format a partition with FAT to serve as the data drive.

Which results does the proposed solution produce?

- ○ a. The proposed solution produces the required result and produces both of the optional desired results.

- ○ b. The proposed solution produces the required result and produces only one of the optional desired results.

- ○ c. The proposed solution produces the required result but does not produce any of the optional desired results.

- ○ d. The proposed solution does not produce the required result.

The correct answer is a. The proposed solution offers a mechanism by which data can be shared between the three operating systems on the computer, namely FAT. FAT supports or at least retains long file names. Care will need to be taken when using DOS or Windows 3.1 applications, which only support 8.3 file names. Depending on which operating system is used to format the data partition, file sizes of 2 GB (DOS/Windows 9x) or 4 GB (Windows NT) are possible, thus 1.3 GB is easily handled. Therefore, the proposed solution fulfills the required result and both optional desired results.

Scenario 15

Suppose the following situation exists:

You need to add a Windows NT Workstation client to an existing network. The network uses NetWare 3.11 and NetWare 4 servers.

Required result:

- Enable communications with all members of the network.

Optional desired results:

- Grant access to resources hosted on the Windows NT Workstation client with the network.

- Enable network management from the new client.

Proposed solution:

- Install NWLink. Set the frame type to manual and define all the frame types used on the network.

- Install and configure CSNW.

Which results does the proposed solution produce?

- ○ a. The proposed solution produces the required result and produces both of the optional desired results.

- ○ b. The proposed solution produces the required result and produces only one of the optional desired results.

- ○ c. The proposed solution produces the required result but does not produce any of the optional desired results.

- ○ d. The proposed solution does not produce the required result.

The correct answer is c. The proposed solution allows the Windows NT Workstation client to communicate with all members of the network, but it does not grant NetWare clients access to Windows NT Workstation hosted resources, nor does it offer network management control from the Windows NT Workstation client. Therefore, the proposed solution only fulfills the required result.

Scenario 16

Suppose the following situation exists:

Security is the most important feature of your company's network. You've been granted permission to configure your Windows NT Workstation client to accept inbound connections, which allows you to dial-in from home and gain access not only to your desktop resources, but also the entire LAN's resources.

Required result:

- Enforce security on the telecommuter link.

Optional desired results:

- Distinguish between local and remote access.

- Log all attempts to connect over the RAS link.

Proposed solution:

- Install Remote Access Services.

- Configure auditing for Logon and Logoff.

- Ask the network administrator to create a duplicate user account for you to use when connecting over the RAS link. Grant only the second account dial-up access. Set the Callback option to a predefined number.

- Audit all File and Object Access for the dial-up enabled user accounts.

- Configure the RAS server to use Microsoft Encrypted Authentication and to encrypt all data.

Which results does the proposed solution produce?

- ○ a. The proposed solution produces the required result and produces both of the optional desired results.

- ○ b. The proposed solution produces the required result and produces only one of the optional desired results.

- ○ c. The proposed solution produces the required result but does not produce any of the optional desired results.

- ○ d. The proposed solution does not produce the required result.

The correct answer is a. The proposed solution allows you to connect to your Windows NT Workstation network client over a secured connection that employs predefined callback and MS-CHAP authentication and data encryption. The solution also provides for auditing of connection attempts. Therefore, the proposed solution fulfills the required result and both optional desired results.

Scenario 17

Suppose the following situation exists:

You've been given a notebook computer with Windows NT Workstation installed to be used as your LAN client and mobile workstation. The notebook is equipped with a modem and a NIC. The modem is built into the motherboard of the notebook, and the NIC is a PC card. The company policy expressly forbids any LAN client from have a working modem while connected to the LAN.

Required result:

- Comply with the company's security policy.

Optional desired results:

- Automate the compliance with the security policy.

- Allow modem access when not connected to the LAN.

Proposed solution:

- Create two hardware profiles. Name one Office LAN and the other Mobile Computing.

- Disable the modem in the Office LAN profile.

- Disable the NIC in the Mobile Computing profile.

- Remove the NIC and leave it attached to the network media cable at your cubicle desk whenever you leave the office.

Which results does the proposed solution produce?

- ○ a. The proposed solution produces the required result and produces both of the optional desired results.

- ○ b. The proposed solution produces the required result and produces only one of the optional desired results.

- ○ c. The proposed solution produces the required result but does not produce any of the optional desired results.

- ○ d. The proposed solution does not produce the required result.

The correct answer is a. The proposed solution complies with the security policy by disabling the modem when the computer is connected to the network. By removing the NIC when not at the office, you will automate the detection process and allow the operating system to select the hardware profile based on the presence or absence of the NIC. The second hardware profile will not be encumbered by the NIC drivers, but will allow full use of the modem. Therefore, the proposed solution fulfills the required result and both optional desired results.

Scenario 18

Suppose the following situation exists:

Your Windows NT Server network allows remote Windows NT Workstation clients to dial-in. Your primary network is a routed network that is not quite complex enough to justify a DNS server but it does change often. When RAS clients request resource access, response is very slow. You've determined this response latency is not due to the RAS link bandwidth.

Required result:

- Improve resource access responsiveness.

Optional desired results:

- Fully automate the RAS improvement solution.

- Keep administration to a minimum.

Proposed solution:

- Create a HOSTS file.

- Once a month, copy the updated HOSTS file to each of the remote clients. You can accomplish this by mapping to a hidden share on each of the clients while they are connected to the LAN.

Which results does the proposed solution produce?

- ○ a. The proposed solution produces the required result and produces both of the optional desired results.

- ○ b. The proposed solution produces the required result and produces only one of the optional desired results.

- ○ c. The proposed solution produces the required result but does not produce any of the optional desired results.

- ○ d. The proposed solution does not produce the required result.

The correct answer is c. The proposed solution of placing a HOSTS file on each of the remote clients will improve resource access responsiveness by reducing resolution traffic over the RAS link. However, the solution is not automated and requires significant administration overhead to maintain. Therefore, the proposed solution only fulfills the required result. An optimal solution for this scenario would be to create a logon script that copies the HOSTS file to the remote client each time the client connects to the network. This would automate the distribution process and significantly reduce the administration responsibilities to just maintaining the central copy of the HOSTS file.

Scenario 19

Suppose the following situation exists:

At the XYZ Corporation, the Research department produces 100+ page documents on a regular basis, yet they have all kinds of shorter documents they need to print during working hours. You've been asked to configure their print services so shorter jobs will not be impeded by the longer book-length printouts. The Research group is the only group that should have access to their printer.

Required result:

• Set up print services so book-length jobs print only during non-work hours, from 11:00 P.M. through 5:00 A.M..

Optional desired results:

• Configure short jobs to print immediately.

• Block users who do not work in Research from using the Research group's printers.

Proposed solution:

• Create two logical printers for the network printer.

• Set up the first logical printer for short print jobs and permit the printer to operate only between the hours of 5:00 A.M. and 11:00 P.M..

• Set up the second logical printer for long print jobs.

• Check permissions on the logical printers to make sure only members of the Research group have print access.

• Instruct users to print short print jobs to the first printer and book-length print jobs to the second printer.

Which results does the proposed solution produce?

○ a. The proposed solution produces the required result and produces both of the optional desired results.

○ b. The proposed solution produces the required result and produces only one of the optional desired results.

○ c. The proposed solution produces the required result but does not produce any of the optional desired results.

○ d. The proposed solution does not produce the required result.

The correct answer is d. The proposed solution does not restrict the printing of long documents to non-working hours. Instead, it only limits the printing of short documents to working hours. Therefore, the proposed solution does not fulfill the required result. An optimal solution for this scenario would require the second logical printer to be configured to restrict printing to non-working hours.

Scenario 20

Suppose the following situation exists:

A Windows 95 system hosts a CD-ROM drive that functions perfectly under Windows 95 but is incompatible with Windows NT. This computer is attached to the network. It will be used as a test platform for new Windows NT Workstation software before being deployed on production Windows NT Workstation systems.

Required result:

- Install Windows NT Workstation onto the system.

Optional desired results:

- Configure the system to dual boot between Windows 95 and Windows NT Workstation.

- Provide a method or mechanism for installing CD-ROM applications onto Windows NT Workstation after installation is complete.

Proposed solution:

- Boot to Windows 95.

- Launch WINNT /B from the \i386 directory on the Windows NT Workstation CD.

- Select to perform an upgrade installation of Windows NT Workstation, and then accept the defaults.

Which results does the proposed solution produce?

- ○ a. The proposed solution produces the required result and produces both of the optional desired results.

- ○ b. The proposed solution produces the required result and produces only one of the optional desired results.

- ○ c. The proposed solution produces the required result but does not produce any of the optional desired results.

- ○ d. The proposed solution does not produce the required result.

The correct answer is c. The proposed solution installs Windows NT Workstation, but it doesn't create a dual-boot system with Windows 95. The prescribed actions will overwrite the existing OS and replace it with Windows

NT Workstation. This will also prevent CD-based software from being installed, because the CD-ROM drive is not compatible with Windows NT. Therefore, the proposed solution meets the required result but neither of the optional desired results.

Scenario 21

Suppose the following situation exists:

You're configuring a Windows NT Server to support several types of applications.

Required result:

- Enable native support for OS/2 and POSIX files.

Optional desired results:

- Allow for file-level compression.

- Allow long file names.

Proposed solution:

- Format all drives with FAT.

Which results does the proposed solution produce?

○ a. The proposed solution produces the required result and produces both of the optional desired results.

○ b. The proposed solution produces the required result and produces only one of the optional desired results.

○ c. The proposed solution produces the required result but does not produce any of the optional desired results.

○ d. The proposed solution does not produce the required result.

The correct answer is d. The proposed solution of using FAT does not support OS/2 or POSIX files. Both OS/2 and POSIX require an NTFS partition to provide full support for their special file system requirements. Therefore, the proposed solution does not fulfill the required result.

Scenario 22

Suppose the following situation exists:

Bob is a new user on the domain. He's working in the Sales group but has been assigned to a project from Research. The Research project involves data from both the Development department and the Accounting department. Group permissions on the related data shares are:

- Sales Share:
    - **Sales Group** Change
    - **Research Group** Read
    - **Development Group** Change
    - **Accounting Group** Change
- Research Share:
    - **Sales Group** None Defined
    - **Research Group** Change
    - **Development Group** None Defined
    - **Accounting Group** Read
- Development Share:
    - **Sales Group** No Access
    - **Research Group** None Defined
    - **Development Group** Change
    - **Accounting Group** Read
- Accounting Share:
    - **Sales Group** No Access
    - **Research Group** None Defined
    - **Development Group** Read
    - **Accounting Group** Change

Required result:

- Grant Bob the ability to access all data required for this job and project.

Optional desired results:

- Retain existing group permissions on file/folder/share objects.

(continued)

Scenarios

Scenario 22 (continued)

> - Prevent non-Accounting division workers from changing Accounting data.
>
> Proposed solution:
>
> - Make Bob a member of the Research, Development, and Sales groups.
>
> Which results does the proposed solution produce?
>
> ○ a. The proposed solution produces the required result and produces both of the optional desired results.
>
> ○ b. The proposed solution produces the required result and produces only one of the optional desired results.
>
> ○ c. The proposed solution produces the required result but does not produce any of the optional desired results.
>
> ○ d. The proposed solution does not produce the required result.

The correct answer is d. The proposed solution fails to grant Bob the minimal access requirements to accomplish his required tasks. The Sales group has No Access on both the Development and Account shares. Therefore, the proposed solution does not fulfill the required result.

Scenario 23

Suppose the following situation exists:

You've just purchased a new 36 GB EIDE drive to use as a data storage device. Your computer currently has two EIDE 8 GB drives installed; the first hosts both the system and boot partitions for Windows NT Workstation, and the second is being used as a data drive. You also have a SCSI drive controller that hosts three 4 GB drives that are almost completely full. Your office has several additional 4 GB SCSI drives that are currently unused in the storage closet.

Required result:

- Migrate the data from the second 8 GB EIDE drive to the new 36 GB EIDE drive.

Optional desired results:

- Retain the folder structure and all long file names.

- Retain all file-level permission and audit settings.

Proposed solution:

- Install two more 4 GB SCSI drives onto your existing SCSI chain.

- Create a volume set of 8 GB out of these two new drives.

- Format the new volume set with FAT.

- Copy the data from the second 8 GB EIDE drive to the new volume set using Windows Explorer.

- Replace the second 8 GB EIDE drive with the new 36 GB EIDE drive.

- Format the new 36 GB EIDE drive with NTFS.

- Using Windows Explorer again, copy the data from the volume set to the 36 GB EIDE drive.

- Destroy the partitions on the two added SCSI drives, and then return them to the storage closet.

Which results does the proposed solution produce?

- ○ a. The proposed solution produces the required result and produces both of the optional desired results.

- ○ b. The proposed solution produces the required result and produces only one of the optional desired results.

- ○ c. The proposed solution produces the required result but does not produce any of the optional desired results.

- ○ d. The proposed solution does not produce the required result.

The correct answer is b. The proposed solution migrates the data and retains the folder structure and long file names, but it does not retain the file-level permission and audit settings. Therefore, the proposed solution fulfills the required result but only one of the optional desired results. An optimal solution for this scenario would require the volume set to be formatted with NTFS instead of FAT. Another alternative would be to create a backup of the data and then restore it from backup to the new device.

Scenario 24

Suppose the following situation exists:

Your organization functions 24 hours a day using three 8-hour shifts. Until now, all employees worked from a central office. However, several dozen employees have been selected to begin telecommuting.

Your system is able to support roughly only 1/3 of the total workforce without suffering from severe performance degradations. All workers are assigned a specific shift. Workers do not change shifts. However, some telecommuters will work additional hours at the end of their shifts to complete tasks or get ahead on work. In-house workers are unable to work the extra hours because there are only enough workstations for each shift. Each in-house worker must leave the workstation at the end of his or her shift to allow the next shift to log on and begin work.

All in-house users log onto the network with a common shift user account; therefore, there are three shift accounts. All telecommuting users log into the network with a unique user account, and callback security is employed with a predefined number. All users identify themselves to the application where they perform most of their daily work.

Required result:

- Prevent telecommuters from establishing new sessions outside of their normal working hours.

Optional desired results:

- Allow workers to work beyond their assigned shifts.

- Retain existing passwords and settings on user accounts used by telecommuters.

(continued)

Scenario 24 (continued)

Proposed solution:

- Create three template accounts; name them 8to4, 4to12, and 12to8; and assign them logon hours of 8:00 A.M. through 4:00 P.M., 4:00 P.M. through 12:00 A.M., 12:00 A.M. through 8:00 P.M., respectively.

- Using the template accounts, create new user accounts for the telecommuters according to their assigned shift hours.

- Configure the Accounts Policy so the Forcibly Disconnect Remote Users When Logon Hours Expire checkbox is not selected.

Which results does the proposed solution produce?

- ○ a. The proposed solution produces the required result and produces both of the optional desired results.

- ○ b. The proposed solution produces the required result and produces only one of the optional desired results.

- ○ c. The proposed solution produces the required result but does not produce any of the optional desired results.

- ○ d. The proposed solution does not produce the required result.

The correct answer is b. The proposed solution prevents telecommuters from initiating new connections after their logon hours and it allows them to continue working beyond their logon hours if they're already connected. The solution does not allow telecommuters to retain the passwords and settings used previously, because new accounts are created to comply with the need for callback security. Therefore, the proposed solution fulfills the required result and only one of the optional desired results.

Scenario 25

Suppose the following situation exists:

Your Windows NT Workstation is a client on a heterogeneous network. Several network protocols are in use. You notice that accessing Internet resources (your most common activity), occurs at a significantly slower pace than any other network resource accessing action.

Required result:

- Improve access speeds to your most common activities.

Optional desired results:

- Retain the ability to communicate with the heterogeneous network.
- Prevent external probing of your NetBIOS resources.

Proposed solution:

- Inspect the binding order of all protocols installed on the system.
- Change the binding order so TCP/IP is highest on the list, and then arrange the remaining protocols in descending order of most used to least used.

Which results does the proposed solution produce?

- ○ a. The proposed solution produces the required result and produces both of the optional desired results.
- ○ b. The proposed solution produces the required result and produces only one of the optional desired results.
- ○ c. The proposed solution produces the required result but does not produce any of the optional desired results.
- ○ d. The proposed solution does not produce the required result.

The correct answer is b. The proposed solution of altering the binding order is the most likely process to gain access improvements when multiple protocols are in use. The prescribed solution does not remove any protocols, so full communication with the network is retained. The prescribed solution does not mention anything about altering NetBIOS traffic to prevent external probing. Therefore, the proposed solution fulfills the required result and only one of the optional desired results.

Scenario 26

Suppose the following situation exists:

A new printer is added to your network. Your Windows NT Workstation client is the print server for the new printer. You must provide print access to users. You must also allow all managers to print documents in priority to normal users.

Required result:

- Grant all users the ability to print to the new printer.

Optional desired results:

- Enable managers to print documents in priority to all users.

- Reduce the amount of time a user must wait to continue work after submitting a print job.

Proposed solution:

- Create a logical printer, set it to a priority of 1, and grant the Domain Users group print access to this logical printer.

- Create another logical printer, set it to a priority of 99, and grant the Managers group print access to this logical printer.

- Set both logical printers to spool printed documents and begin printing only after the entire print job is spooled.

Which results does the proposed solution produce?

- ○ a. The proposed solution produces the required result and produces both of the optional desired results.

- ○ b. The proposed solution produces the required result and produces only one of the optional desired results.

- ○ c. The proposed solution produces the required result but does not produce any of the optional desired results.

- ○ d. The proposed solution does not produce the required result.

The correct answer is a. The proposed solution grants access to all users, grants managers priority access, and returns application control to the user as quickly as possible. Therefore, the proposed solution fulfills the required result and both optional desired results.

Scenario 27

Suppose the following situation exists:

You install a new Windows NT Workstation client and are concerned about security of sensitive data and performance for users who access it from the network. The client is equipped with 256 MB RAM and two Adaptec 2940 SCSI controllers with three 2 GB SCSI drives on each controller.

Required result:

* Maximize access and operating system performance.

Optional desired results:

* Provide the ability to set object-level security to sensitive data files.

* Provide for recovery in case of failure.

Proposed solution:

* Create a stripe set using five drives.

* Convert or format all volumes to NTFS.

* Move the paging file to the stripe set.

Which results does the proposed solution produce?

○ a. The proposed solution produces the required result and produces both of the optional desired results.

○ b. The proposed solution produces the required result and produces only one of the optional desired results.

○ c. The proposed solution produces the required result but does not produce any of the optional desired results.

○ d. The proposed solution does not produce the required result.

The correct answer is b. The proposed solution improves performance and allows for object-level security, but it does not provide for recovery in the case of failure. Therefore, the proposed solution fulfills the required result and only one of the optional desired results. An optimal solution would be to configure the drives as five individual volumes instead of a stripe set and employ an automated backup solution.

Scenario 28

Suppose the following situation exists:

Your Windows NT Workstation system has a drive failure of the system partition. The system partition was the only partition on a 100 MB IDE hard drive. Your boot partition is on a SCSI drive.

Required result:

• Return the system to a functional state.

Optional desired results:

• Retain the system's existing SID.

• Keep system's downtime to a minimum.

Proposed solution:

• Remove the failed drive.

• Install a new SCSI drive onto the SCSI chain.

• Format a partition on the new SCSI drive with FAT and mark it active.

• Using your recently created ERD, launch the ERD repair process using the three setup floppies.

Which results does the proposed solution produce?

○ a. The proposed solution produces the required result and produces both of the optional desired results.

○ b. The proposed solution produces the required result and produces only one of the optional desired results.

○ c. The proposed solution produces the required result but does not produce any of the optional desired results.

○ d. The proposed solution does not produce the required result.

The correct answer is a. The proposed solution of using the ERD repair process to restore a system partition to a new drive should return the system to a functioning state. This also retains the existing SID, because the OS is not reinstalled and it's probably the fastest, permanent solution possible. Therefore, the proposed solution fulfills the required result and both optional desired results.

Online
Resources

Here's a collection of online resources that might help you to prepare for your Microsoft certification exam. Many of these Web sites include sample questions, study materials, and study tips for Windows NT Workstation 4 and other exams.

➤ **http://209.207.167.177** is the BrainDump Heaven site, on which you can find peer discussions on topics and issues.

➤ **http://home.nycap.rr.com/blaineman/mcselinks.html** is a personal page that contains links to MCSE-related sites.

➤ **http://imedoff.virtualave.net/mcse.htm** is a personal page that contains links to MCSE-related sites.

➤ **http://leuthard.ch/mcse/** is the Checkpoint MCSE site, on which you can find free practice tests and links to MCSE-related sites.

➤ **http://stsware.com/microsts.htm** is the Self Test Software site that has practice tests for sale.

➤ **www.america.net/~dhack/mcse** is a personal MCSE page that contains links to newsgroups and other resources.

➤ **www.axxa.com/certcorner/default.asp** is the Axxa Corporation page that contains a collection of study materials, reference sites, and MCSE information.

➤ www.certificationinsider.com is The Coriolis Group's Certification Insider Press site, on which you can find information about Exam Cram/Exam Prep books and other certification products, as well as free online sample tests.

➤ www.certificationshack.com is the Certification Shack site, on which you can find general MCSE information.

➤ www.certify.com is the Cyber Pass site. You can order MCSE practice tests from this site.

➤ www.commandcentral.com is the CommandCentral site, on which you can find free practice tests.

➤ www.computingcentral.msn.com/topics/windowsnt/chat.asp is the MSN, Computing Central, Windows NT chat forum where you can ask questions of peers and experts.

➤ www.cramsession.com is the CramSession site, on which you can find study guides, free practice questions via email and online, and general certification information.

➤ www.cyber-1.com/mcse is an MCSE study group site.

➤ www.geocities.com/~mcse_mct is a personal page that contains MCSE information and resource links.

➤ www.goodground.com/index.htm is the GoodGround site, on which you can find links and free online sample tests.

➤ www.hardcoremcse.com is the HardcoreMCSE site, which contains study aids and links, and sells practice exams.

➤ www.inquiry.com is the Inquiry.com site, on which you can find general technology information.

➤ www.internexis.com/mcp is an MCSE chat and study site.

➤ www.learnquick.com is LearnQuick's site, which offers accelerated MCSE training and tons of MCSE resources.

➤ www.matisse.net/files/glossary.html contains a glossary of Internet terms that can be very helpful.

➤ www.mattscasa.com/netindex.htm is a personal site that contains free practice tests.

➤ www.mcpmag.com is the Microsoft Certified Professional online magazine.

➤ www.mcseinfo.com is the MCSEInfo.com site that includes study tips, review information, and links to MCSE-related sites.

➤ www.mcsetutor.com is the MCSETutor.com site that offers test discussions, book reviews, and links to free online tests.

➤ www.network-info.com/Links/links.html is the Network-Info.com site, on which you can find links to MCSE-related sites.

➤ www.ptek.com/links.asp is a personal page that contains many MCSE/MCP-related links.

➤ www.rad.com/networks/netterms.htm is RAD University's general networking information and reference page. It's not MCSE specific.

➤ www.saluki.com/mcp is the MCP Online site that contains questions and topical discussions. This site is the host of an MCSE mailing list.

➤ www.tekmetrics.com/cert is the e-certifications site that contains information about non-Microsoft certifications.

➤ www.testfree.com is the TestFree site that offers free practice tests.

Glossary

· ·

access token—The collection of security settings generated at user login that tells Windows NT which resources a user can access as well as the extent of that access.

account policy—A file that establishes security settings, including how passwords on a domain or a workstation are used.

ACL (access control list)—The attribute list for all system objects. It defines which users and groups have what level of access to each object.

ACLCONV.EXE—A Microsoft conversion utility that converts HPFS volumes (from LAN Manager, LAN Server, or Windows NT 3.51 or earlier NT versions) to an NTFS equivalent.

administrative alert—An alert generated by Windows NT Workstation Performance Monitor when it detects a problem in the Windows NT system environment.

administrative tools—A group of tools and utilities provided by Windows NT that control the management and configuration of components such as user rights, system security, and disk drives.

administrator account—A default account created by Windows NT that has full access and full control over the entire system.

ANSI (American National Standards Institute)—The U.S. representative on the International Standardization Organization (ISO), a worldwide standards-making body. ANSI creates and publishes standards for networking, communications, and programming languages.

API (application programming interface)—A set of interface subroutines that define the methods for programs to access external services.

AppleTalk—Apple Computer's networking protocols and software used for network communication with Macintosh computers.

Application log—This utility documents events noted by the Windows NT system and user applications. It also records their warnings and error messages. The Application log is located in the Event Viewer.

ARCNet (Attached Resource Computer Network)—An inexpensive and flexible network architecture created by Datapoint Corporation in 1977. It uses the token-passing channel access method.

ARP (Address Resolution Protocol)—A protocol in the TCP/IP suite used to associate logical addresses to physical addresses.

ASCII (American Standard Code for Information Interchange)—A way of coding that translates letters, numbers, and symbols into digital form.

AT.EXE—A utility used on a batch file with the NTBACKUP link that schedules the batch file to run at a specific time. AT.EXE schedules commands to be run by the scheduling service in Windows NT.

AUTOEXEC.BAT—A DOS batch file that is launched when a computer is started or booted.

Backup Browser—Computers on a Windows NT network that maintain a duplicate list of the network's resources and act in a similar way within the Browser Service as BDCs act for domain control.

Backup Operators—A built-in group in Windows NT that has the permission to log on to a domain and back up a particular server or workstation.

basevideo—A command-line parameter switch used on the BOOT.INI file. It forces Windows NT to boot using 16-color VGA video at 640×480. This setting appears by default on the ARC name line identified by "[VGA mode]".

BDC (Backup Domain Controller)—A backup server that protects the integrity and availability of the SAM database. BDCs are not able to make any changes or modifications, but they can use the database to authenticate users.

BIOS (Basic Input/Output System)—A system that houses the buffers used to transfer information from a program to the hardware devices receiving the information.

BOOT.INI—One of the files placed on the system partition that contains the location of the system files for each OS installed on the machine. The locations are listed using ARC names.

BOOTSECT.DOS—The file containing DOS boot sector data, which appears in the system partition only on a multiboot machine that numbers DOS, Windows, Windows 95, Windows 98, or some other near DOS-equivalent among the list of boot options in BOOT.INI.

bottleneck—The effect of trying to force too much information through a system with inadequate bandwidth, causing the system to slow significantly.

Browser Service—A Windows NT utility that maintains a list of network resources within a domain, and provides lists of these domains, servers, and resource objects to any Explorer-type interface that requests it (e.g., browse lists).

cache—A specified area of high-speed memory used to contain data that is going to be or recently has been accessed.

CACLS command—A command used to display or modify the ACL.

CDFS (Compact Disk File System)—A special read-only file system supported by Windows 95, Windows 98, and Windows NT 3.51 and higher. CDFS permits easy access to CDs within these operating systems.

client/server subsystem—A Win32 subsystem that handles support for 32-bit Windows applications (Win32 applications). Also called the CSR.

computer name—The name of a computer on a LAN that is specific to an individual workstation or server.

Control Panel—In Windows, this is the area where you modify system settings, such as fonts, screen color, SCSI hardware, and printers, among others.

CONVERT.EXE—A utility in Windows NT that converts FAT volumes to NTFS equivalents.

CPU (central processing unit)—The "brains" of your computer. This is the area where all functions are performed.

dependency failures—When one or more dependent services fail due to the absence of a foundational service, hardware, or driver.

DHCP (Dynamic Host Configuration Protocol)—A service that enables the assignment of dynamic TCP/IP network addresses, based on a specified pool of available addresses.

DHCP Relay Agent—Intercepts the DHCP broadcasts, then transmits the broadcasts directly to the DHCP server.

Disk Administrator—An administration application in the Administrative Tools group that lets an administrator create and delete stripe sets and various disk partitions, change the assignment of drive letters, and display facts about a partition's size and setup.

disk controller—A piece of hardware that controls how data is written and retrieved from the computer's disk drive.

disk duplexing—A fault tolerance method used by Windows NT that uses a duplicate physical and logical drive on a separate hard disk where the drive is connected to the system via a separate controller. If the original drive or controller fails, the system continues to operate using the duplexed drive.

disk partition—A portion of a hard disk that acts like a physically separate unit.

disk striping—A fault tolerance method used by Windows NT that stores data across multiple physical storage devices.

DLC (Data Link Control)—A protocol used to interoperate with IBM mainframes and provide connectivity to network-attached print devices.

DLL (dynamic link libraries)—Small executable program routines or device drivers stored in separate files and loaded by the OS when called upon by a process or hardware device.

DMB (Domain Master Browser)—In Windows NT networks, a browser that communicates resource lists across subnets within the same domain.

DMP file—A memory dump file with the extension .DMP.

DNS (Domain Name Service)—A system used to resolve fully qualified domain names into IP addresses.

domain—A group of computers and peripheral devices that share a common security database.

domain controllers—A computer that authenticates domain logons as well as manages the Security Accounts Manager (SAM) database.

DOS (Disk Operating System)—The most common of all PC operating systems.

DUN (Dial-Up Networking)—A utility found in the RAS Phone book|Programs|Accessories folder of the Start menu that controls the dial-out capabilities of RAS.

election packet—The electronic communication used by a browser (Master, Backup, or Potential) to initiate a new selection of a Master Browser when the current Master Browser is no longer accessible or when a new machine goes online.

encryption—A method of coding data in which a person has to have a decoding key to decipher the information.

ERD (Emergency Repair Disk)—A miniature first aid kit for Windows NT. This single floppy contains all the files needed to repair system partition and many boot partition related problems.

ESDI (Enhanced Small Device Interface)—A pre-IDE type storage device that is low-level formatted with various values of sector per track.

Ethernet—The most widely used type of LAN, originally developed by Xerox.

exabytes—One billion gigabytes.

Exam Preparation Guides—Guides that provide information specific to Microsoft Certified Professional exams to help students prepare for the exam.

Exam Study Guide—Short for *Microsoft Certified Professional Program Exam Study Guide*, it contains information about the Microsoft Certified Professional exams.

FAT (File Allocation Table)—A table originally used by the DOS file system to keep information about the properties, location, and size of files being stored on a disk.

fault tolerance—The ability of a computer to work continuously, even when there is a system failure.

firewall—A barrier between two networks made of software and/or hardware that permits only authorized communication to pass.

firmware—A type of software that becomes part of the hardware function after it has been saved into a Programmable Read-Only Memory chip (PROM).

FQDN (fully qualified domain name)—The complete site name of an Internet computer system.

FTP (File Transfer Protocol)—A protocol that transfers files to and from a local hard drive to an FTP server located elsewhere on another TCP/IP-based network (such as the Internet).

GDI (Graphics Device Interface)—Provides network applications with a system for presenting graphical information. The GDI works as a translator between an application's print request and a device driver interface (DDI) so a job is rendered accurately.

Gopher—An Internet service that provides text-only information, most suited to large documents with little or no formatting or images.

GSNW (Gateway Service For NetWare)—A service that enables Windows NT Servers to map a drive to a NetWare server and provides access to NetWare server resources for Windows NT Workstations (via a gateway).

GUI (graphical user interface)—A computer interface that uses graphics, windows, and a trackball or mouse as the method of interaction with the computer.

HAL (Hardware Abstraction Layer)—In the Windows NT operating system, it creates a bridge between the Windows NT operating system and a computer's CPU.

hard drive—Permanent storage area for data. It is also called the hard disk.

hardware—The physical components of a computer system.

HCL (Hardware Compatibility List)—A list that comes with Windows NT Server that tells you what hardware is compatible with the software. The most updated versions of this list can be found on the Microsoft Web site or on the TechNet CD.

HOSTS file—A static list of FQDNs mapped to IP addresses.

HPFS (High Performance File System)—The first PC-compatible file system that supported LFNs. Like FAT, HPFS maintains a directory structure, but it adds automatic sorting of the directory and includes support for special attributes to better accommodate multiple naming conventions and file-level security. HPFS is no longer supported in Windows NT 4.

HTTP (Hypertext Transfer Protocol)—This is the World Wide Web protocol that allows for the transfer of HTML documents over the Internet or intranets that respond to actions, like a user clicking on hypertext links.

IDE (Integrated Device Electronics)—A type of storage device interface where the electronics required to operate the drive are stored on the drive itself, thus eliminating the need for a separate controller card.

IIS (Internet Information Server)—A Web Server software by Microsoft. It is included and implemented with Windows NT Server.

instructor-led course—Usually held in a classroom setting, a course led by an instructor.

Internet—The collection of TCP/IP-based networks around the world.

intranet—An internal private network that uses the same protocols and standards as the Internet.

I/O Manager—The module in the Executive Services that oversees all input and output. It acts like a proxy by intercepting an application's requests and directing commands to the appropriate hardware drivers.

IP address—Four sets of numbers separated by decimal points that represent the numeric address of a computer attached to a TCP/IP network, such as the Internet.

IPC (InterProcess Communications)—Within an operating system, it is the exchange of data between applications.

IPX (Internetwork Packet Exchange)—A network and Transport layer protocol developed by Novell, most commonly associated with NetWare networks.

IPX/SPX (Internetwork Packet Exchange/Sequenced Packet Exchange)—The name of Novell's NetWare protocol that was reinvented by Microsoft and implemented in Windows NT under the name "NWLink". This protocol is fully compatible with Novell's version and, in many cases, is a better implementation than the original.

ISDN (Integrated Services Digital Network)—A dedicated form of digital communication that has a bandwidth of 128 Kbps.

job function expert—A person who knows just about everything about a particular job function and the software products/technologies related to that job. Typically, a job function expert is performing the job, has recently performed the job, or is training people to perform the job.

Kernel—The essential part of an operating system that provides basic services.

LAN (local area network)—A network confined to a single building or geographic area and comprised of servers, workstations, peripheral devices, a network operating system, and a communications link.

Last Known Good Configuration—A recording made by Windows NT of all the Registry settings that existed the last time a user successfully logged in to a server.

leased lines—Communications connections that are provided to consumers by third-party communications carriers for a fee.

LFN (long files names)—File names of up to 256 characters.

LMHOSTS—The predecessor to WINS, it is a static list of NetBIOS names mapped to IP addresses.

local procedure call facility—The module in the Executive Services manager that maintains communications user applications and environmental subsystems.

lockout—In Windows NT security, it is a feature used to prevent compromised accounts from being used.

logical partitions—The segments created when a physical hard drive is divided. Each segment can be used independently of the others, including belonging to separate volumes and hosting different file systems. Most logical partitions have a drive letter assigned to them and can be referred to by an ARC name.

logical printers—The software component used by Windows NT to direct print jobs from applications to a print server. A physical printer can be serviced by numerous logical printers.

logoff—The process by which a user quits using a computer system.

logon—The process by which a user gains access or signs onto a computer system.

logon scripts—Files that consist of a set of network commands that must be carried out in a particular order.

LPD (Line Printer Daemon)—Originally a Unix component, it receives documents from LPR clients and sends them to a printer. An LPD is essentially a print server.

LPR (Line Printer Remote)—A command-line utility provided by Windows NT used for directing and monitoring print jobs aimed for Unix host printers.

Master Browser—A tool used to maintain the main list of all available resources within a domain (including links to external domains).

MB—The abbreviation for megabyte, 1,024 kilobytes.

MBR (Master Boot Record)—A BIOS bootstrap routine used by low-level, hardware-based system code stored in Read-Only Memory (ROM) to initiate the boot sequence on a PC.

MCI (multiple-choice item)—An item within a series of items that is the answer to a question (single-response MCI) or one of the answers to a question (multiple-response MCI).

MCP (Microsoft Certified Professional)—An individual who has taken and passed a series of certification exams, thereby earning one or more of the following certifications: Microsoft Certified Trainer, Microsoft Certified Solution Developer, Microsoft Certified Systems Engineer, or Microsoft Certified Product Specialist.

MCPS (Microsoft Certified Product Specialist)—An individual who has passed at least one of the Microsoft operating system exams.

MCSD (Microsoft Certified Solution Developer)—An individual who has taken and passed a series of certification exams, thereby classified as qualified to create and develop business solutions using the Microsoft development tools, technologies, and platforms.

MCSE (Microsoft Certified Systems Engineer)—An individual who has taken and passed a series of certification exams, thereby classified as an expert on Windows NT and the Microsoft BackOffice integrated family of server software. This individual can also plan, implement, maintain, and support information systems associated with these products.

MCT (Microsoft Certified Trainer)—An individual who has taken and passed a series of certification exams, thereby qualified by Microsoft to instruct Microsoft Education courses at sites authorized by Microsoft.

Microsoft certification exam—A test created by Microsoft to verify the mastery of a software product, technology, or computing topic.

Microsoft Certified Professional Certification Update—A newsletter for Microsoft Certified Professional candidates and Microsoft Certified Professionals.

Microsoft official curriculum—Microsoft education courses that support the certification exam process and are created by the Microsoft product groups.

Microsoft Roadmap To Education And Certification—An application based on Microsoft Windows that takes you through the process of determining your certification goals and planning how you can achieve them.

Microsoft Sales Fax Service—A service provided by Microsoft where you can obtain Exam Preparation Guides, fact sheets, and additional information about the Microsoft Certified Professional program.

Microsoft Solution Provider—An organization not directly related to Microsoft that provides integration, consulting, technical support, and other services related to Microsoft products.

Microsoft TechNet (Technical Information Network)—A service provided by Microsoft that provides helpful information via a monthly CD-ROM disk. TechNet is the primary source of technical information for people who support and/or educate end users, create automated solutions, or administer networks and/or databases.

MOLI (Microsoft Online Institute)—An organization that offers training materials, online forums, user groups, and online classes.

motherboard—A term that refers to the main circuit board in a computer system.

MPR (Multi-Protocol Router)—A device that converts various email formats.

MRI (multiple-rating item)—An item that gives you a task and a proposed solution. Every time a task is given, an alternate solution is provided, and the candidate must choose the answer that gives the best results produced by one solution.

MSDN (Microsoft Developer Network)—The official source for Software Development Kits (SDKs), Device Driver Kits (DDKs), operating systems, and programming information associated with creating applications for Microsoft Windows and Windows NT.

Multilink PPP—The combining of the bandwidth of multiple physical links, which increases the total bandwidth that can be used for a RAS connection.

NDA (nondisclosure agreement)—A legal agreement that binds two parties to maintain secrecy regarding the subject of the agreement. This is an instrument commonly used by Microsoft to keep its partners and vendors quiet about software until it's commercially released.

NetBEUI (NetBIOS Extended User Interface)—A simple Network layer transport protocol that was developed to support NetBIOS networks.

NetBIOS (Network Basic Input/Output System)—Originally developed by IBM in the 1980s, it provides the underlying communication mechanism for some basic Windows NT functions, such as browsing and interprocess communications between network servers.

Netstat—A utility that displays TCP/IP status and statistics.

NetWare—A popular network operating system from Novell.

Network Dynamic Data Exchange (NetDDE)—An API developed by Microsoft that supports DDE applications over a network.

Network Monitor—A tool used for investigating network-related problems.

Network Neighborhood—Within Explorer or My Computer, this is the area in which you access other computers on the network.

NFS (Network Filing System)—A popular distributed file system on Unix networks.

NIC (network interface card)—An adapter card used to connect a computer to a network.

NMA (Network Monitor Agent)—A network service tool that gathers counter readings from network related objects.

NOS (network operating system)—A specialized collection of software that gives a computer the ability to communicate over a network and to take advantage of a broad range of networking services. Windows NT is a network operating system available in Workstation and Server versions; Windows 95, Windows 98, and Windows For Workgroups also include built-in network client and peer-to-peer capabilities.

NT (Network Termination)—Part of the network connection device in an ISDN network.

NTBACKUP.EXE—A backup utility that is shipped with Windows NT.

NTDETECT.COM—A hardware recognition program that collects a list of currently installed components and returns the information to NTLDR.

NTFS (New Technology File System)—The powerful, secure file system that's a mainstay of the Windows NT operating system.

NTLDR file—The executable program launched by the boot files that load the Windows NT Kernel. The name is a shortened version of "NT Loader."

null modem cable—An RS-232 cable used to enable two computers within close proximity to communicate without a modem.

NWLink—Microsoft's "clean room" implementation of Novell's IPX/SPX protocol suite for NetWare networks.

Object Manager—The module in the Executive Services that controls activities related to objects, such as use, naming, removing, tracking, and security of objects.

OS (operating system)—A software program that controls the operations of a computer system.

OSLOADER.EXE—The OS loader program for RISC computers. This program provides all of the services and information provided by NTDETECT.COM, BOOTSECT.DOS, NTDETECT.COM, and NTLDR on PCs. It resides wherever the nonvolatile RAM location data indicates.

OSR2—The only current Microsoft operating system that supports FAT32.

page faults—A counter that should be measured when you suspect there is not enough memory in the system.

pagefile—The file used by the Virtual Memory Manager to temporarily store segments or pages of memory to hard disk.

partition—A portion of a hard disk that acts as a separate, bootable logical drive (primary partition) or as a collection of unbootable logical drives (extended partitions).

password—A word used by an individual to gain access to a particular system or application.

PDC (Primary Domain Controller)—The central storage and management server for the SAM database.

Performance Monitor—A graphical application that lets you set, graph, log, and report alerts. It is also referred to as PerfMon.

peripheral devices—Hardware device, such as keyboard, mouse, and so on, connected to a computer.

Phonebook entry—A collection of settings used by RAS to establish a connection with a remote dial-up server. A Phonebook entry contains details such as phone number, name, password, protocol settings, and encryption type.

POSIX—An operating system type that complies with the IEEE Std 1003.1 standard. Windows NT supports only POSIX.1.

POST (Power-On Self-Test)—The set of internal diagnostic and status-checking routines a PC and its peripheral devices go through each time the computer is powered on.

power users—A user group found on Windows NT Workstation. Also, a user who is well versed in the operation and modification of a computing system—someone who pushes an operating system to its limits.

PPP (Point-to-Point Protocol)—An industry standard protocol used to establish network-protocol-supporting links over POTS lines using modems.

PPTP (Point-to-Point Tunneling Protocol)—Enables "tunneling" of IPX, NetBEUI, and TCP/IP inside PPP packets in such a way as to establish a secure link between a client and server over the Internet.

printer—Typically refers to the logical printer (software component) within the Windows NT environment as opposed to the physical printing device.

Process manager—The module in the Executive Services that manages process activities, such as creation, deletion, and tracking.

protocols—In networking, this is a set of rules that define how information is transmitted over a network.

PWS (Peer Web Services)—Windows NT Workstation's equivalent of Windows NT Server's Internet Information Server.

RAS (Remote Access Service)—A Windows NT service that provides remote network communication for remote clients over telecommunication lines. RAS connections are different from standard, direct-network connections only in relation to speed.

Registry—The hierarchical database that serves as a repository for hardware, software, and OS configuration information.

REXEC—The TCP/IP connectivity command that executes commands on a remote system running the rexec service.

RIP (Routing Information Protocol)—A router protocol that enables communication between routers on a network to facilitate the exchange of routing tables.

RISC (Reduced Instruction Set Computer)—A set of processor instructions that speed up processing by using simple computer instructions. Also, a type of computer platform.

RPC (Remote Procedure Calls)—A network interprocess communications mechanism.

SAM (Security Accounts Manager)—The security database of Windows NT that maintains a record of all users, groups, and permissions within a domain. The SAM is stored on the PDC and duplicated on the BDCs.

SCSI (Small Computer System Interface)—A standard interface defined by ANSI that provides high-speed connections to devices such as hard drives, scanners, and printers.

security—A manner of protecting data by restricting access to authorized users.

Security reference monitor—The module in the Executive Services that handles logon procedures, user authentication, access validation, and the security subsystem in the User mode.

Server Manager—The Windows NT Server administration utility where computer accounts are managed.

Server Operators—The built-in group whose members can manage domain servers.

SID (Security ID)—A code assigned to users, groups, and computers by Windows NT to identify them. Even when the name of an object changes, Windows NT recognizes the object by its SID. Every SID is unique.

SLIP (Serial Line Internet Protocol)—An older industry standard for RAS communication links. SLIP is included with Windows NT only for establishing connections with Unix systems that do not support the newer PPP standard.

SMS (Systems Management Server)—A Microsoft product used for high-end management and administration of an enterprise-level network.

SMTP (Simple Mail Transfer Protocol)—An Internet protocol used to distribute email from one mail server to another over a TCP/IP network.

SNA (Systems Network Architecture)—A communications interface used to establish a link with IBM mainframes and AS/400 hosts.

SNMP (Simple Network Management Protocol)—A protocol used to monitor remote hosts over a TCP/IP network.

spooler—A software component of the print system that stores print jobs on a hard drive while they wait in the print queue.

SQL Server—A Microsoft product that supports a network-enabled relational database system.

stripe set—A hard disk construct where segments of data are written in sequence across multiple drives.

subnet—A portion or segment of a TCP/IP network.

tape drives—Devices used for backing up data that employs metal film cassettes for storage.

TAPI (Telephony Application Programming Interface)—An interface and API that defines how applications can interact with data/fax/voice devices and calls.

TCP/IP (Transmission Control Protocol/Internet Protocol)—The most widely used protocol in networking today because it is the most flexible of the transport protocols and is able to span wide areas.

Telnet—A terminal emulation utility used to interact with remote computers.

UDF (uniqueness database file)—A script file used in conjunction with the UNATTEND.TXT file to specify different computer specific details without having to create a unique UNATTEND.TXT for each machine.

UDP (User Datagram Protocol)—A TCP/IP component that transmits data through a connectionless service but does not guarantee the delivery or sequencing of sent packets.

UNC (Universal Naming Convention)—A standardized naming method for NetBIOS networks (and Microsoft networks in particular) taking the form of *servername**sharename*.

Unix—An interactive, time-sharing, operating system developed in 1969 by a hacker to play games. This system developed into the most widely used industrial-strength computer in the world and ultimately supported the birth of the Internet.

UPS (uninterruptible power supply)—A semi-intelligent, rechargeable battery system that protects a computer from power failures and fluctuations.

user account—The collection of information, such as name, password, group memberships, access privileges, and user rights, stored by Windows NT about a specific network user. User accounts are managed through the User Manager utility.

user name—The human-friendly name of a user account. The user name is one of two items of data used to log on to Windows NT. Windows NT does not recognize an account by the user name, but rather by the SID.

user profiles—The collection of desktop and environmental settings that define the work area of a local computer.

user rights—Settings that define the ability of a user to access a computer or a domain.

users group—This is another term for "group."

VDM (Virtual DOS Machine)—A Win32 application that creates an operational environment for DOS applications.

VFAT (Virtual File Allocation Table)—This file system is currently supported by Windows 95, Windows NT 3.51, and Windows NT 4. VFAT provides 32-bit Protected Mode access for file manipulation.

VGA (Video Graphics Array)—A PC display standard of 640×480 pixels, 16 colors, and a 4:3 aspect ratio.

Virtual Memory Manager (VMM)—The executive service within Windows NT's Kernel that manages physical and virtual (swap or pagefile) memory.

VPN (virtual private networks)—A WAN, provided by a common communications carrier, that works like a private network; however, the backbone of the network is shared with all of the customers in a public network.

WAN (wide area network)—A network that spans geographically distant segments. Often, the distance of two miles or more is used to define a WAN; however, Microsoft equates any RAS connection as establishing a WAN.

Web server—A computer connected to the Internet or an intranet that stores Web documents and displays them upon request.

Windows NT Diagnostics—Windows NT's GUI rendition of MSD (Microsoft Diagnostics). Windows NT Diagnostics provides detailed system configuration information from the Windows NT Registry.

Windows Sockets—An API that provides a standard for application interaction with transport protocols, such as TCP/IP over PPP.

WinLogon utility—A utility that displays the logon dialog box and sends the inputted data to the security manager.

WINMSD (Windows NT Diagnostics)—A Windows NT utility that gives you a shallow insight into the current configuration of the Windows NT software and the hardware it is operating on.

WINS (Windows Internet Name Service)—A Windows network service used to resolve NetBIOS names to IP addresses.

workgroups—A collection of networked computers that participate in a peer-to-peer relationship.

WOW (Windows On Windows)—The DOS application that supports Windows 16-bit applications WOW executes within a VDM, which itself runs as a Win32 process.

Write permissions—This setting grants the ability to create or modify files and directories.

WWW (World Wide Web)—An information-distribution system hosted on TCP/IP networks. The Web supports text, graphics, and multimedia. The IIS component of NT is a Web server (which can distribute Web documents).

Index

Workstations, **435–436**
  Directory Replication Service, 228
  domains and, 224
  local accounts, 133
  logging on to, 225, **230, 233**
  workgroups and, 222, **369**
  workstation accounts, 225, **230, 233**
  WOW, 301–302, **306, 307, 366**
Workstation service redirector, 168

WOW (Windows-on-Windows), 301–302, **306, 307, 366**
WOWEXEC.EXE, 302
WWW (World Wide Web), 179, 189

X

X (Execute permission), 120, **363**

Look for All of the Exam Cram Brand Certification Study Systems

ALL NEW! Exam Cram Personal Trainer Systems

The Exam Cram Personal Trainer systems are an exciting new category in certification training products. These CD-ROM based systems offer extensive capabilities at a moderate price and are the first certification-specific testing product to completely link learning with testing.

This Exam Cram Study Guide turned interactive course lets you customize the way you learn.

Each system includes:
- A Personalized Practice Test engine with multiple test methods,
- A database of nearly 300 questions linked directly to the subject matter within the Exam Cram on which that question is based.

Exam Cram Audio Review Systems

Written and read by certification instructors, each set contains four cassettes jam-packed with the certification exam information you must have. Designed to be used on their own or as a complement to our Exam Cram Study Guides, Flash Cards, and Practice Tests.

Each system includes:
- Study preparation tips with an essential last-minute review for the exam
- Hours of lessons highlighting key terms and techniques
- A comprehensive overview of all exam objectives
- 45 minutes of review questions complete with answers and explanations

Exam Cram Flash Cards

These pocket-sized study tools are 100% focused on exams. Key questions appear on side one of each card and in-depth answers on side two. Each card features either a cross-reference to the appropriate Exam Cram Study Guide chapter or to another valuable resource. Comes with a CD-ROM featuring electronic versions of the flash cards and a complete practice exam.

Exam Cram Practice Tests

Our readers told us that extra practice exams were vital to certification success, so we created the perfect companion book for certification study material.

Each book contains:
- Several practice exams
- Electronic versions of practice exams on the accompanying CD-ROM presented in an interactive format enabling practice in an environment similar to that of the actual exam
- Each practice question is followed by the corresponding answer (why the right answers are right and the wrong answers are wrong)
- References to the Exam Cram Study Guide chapter or other resource for that topic

The Coriolis Exam Cram Personal Trainer
An exciting new category in certification training products

The Exam Cram Personal trainer is the first certification-specific testing product that completely links learning with testing to:

- **Increase your comprehension**
- **Decrease the time it takes you to learn**

No system blends learning content with test questions as effectively as the Exam Cram Personal Trainer.

Only the Exam Cram Personal Trainer offers this much power at this price.

Its unique Personalized Test Engine provides a real-time test environment and an authentic representation of what you will encounter during your actual certification exams.

Much More Than Just Another CBT!

Most current CBT learning systems offer simple review questions at the end of a chapter with an overall test at the end of the course, with no links back to the lessons. But Exam Cram Personal Trainer takes learning to a higher level.

Its four main components are:

- The complete text of an Exam Cram study guide in an HTML format,
- A Personalized Practice Test Engine with multiple test methods

Adaptive:	25-35 questions
Fixed-length:	Four unique exams on critical areas
Random:	Each randomly generated test is unique
Test All:	Drawn from the complete database of questions
Topic:	Organized by Exam Cram chapters
Review:	Questions with answers are presented

Scenario-based questions: Just like the real thing

- A database of nearly 300 questions linked directly to an Exam Cram chapter
- Over two hours of Exam Cram Audio Review

Plus, additional features include:

- **Hint:** Not sure of your answer? Click Hint and the software goes to the text that covers that topic.
- **Lesson:** Still not enough detail? Click Lesson and the software goes to the beginning of the chapter.
- **Update feature:** Need even more questions? Click Update to download more questions from the Coriolis Web site.
- **Notes:** Create your own memory joggers.
- **Graphic analysis:** How did you do? View your score, the required score to pass, and other information.
- **Personalized Cram Sheet:** Print unique study information just for you.

MCSE Networking Essentials Exam Cram Personal Trainer
ISBN:1-57610-644-6

MCSE NT Server 4 Exam Cram Personal Trainer
ISBN: 1-57610-645-4

MCSE NT Server 4 in the Enterprise Exam Cram Personal Trainer
ISBN: 1-57610-646-2

MCSE NT Workstation 4 Exam Cram Personal Trainer
ISBN:1-57610-647-0

A+ Exam Cram Personal Trainer
ISBN: 1-57610-658-6

$70.99 U.S. • $119.99 Canada

Available: March 2000

CORIOLIS™
Certification Insider Press

**The Smartest Way to Get Certified
Just Got Smarter**™